RULE OF LAW ON THE INTERNATIONAL AGENDA

RULE OF LAW ON THE INTERNATIONAL AGENDA

International support to legal and judicial reform in international administration, transition and development co-operation

PER BERGLING

intersentia
Antwerpen – Oxford

Distribution for the UK:
Hart Publishing
Salter's Boat Yard
Folly Bridge
Abingdon Road
Oxford OX1 4LB
UK
Tel: + 44 1865 24 55 33
Fax: + 44 1865 79 48 82

Distribution for North America:
Gaunt Inc.
Gaunt Building
3011 Gulf Drive
Holmes Beach
Florida 34217-2199
USA
Tel: + 1 941 778 5211
Fax: + 1 941 778 5252

Distribution for Switzerland and Germany:
Schulthess Verlag
Zwingliplatz 2
CH-8022 Zürich
Switzerland
Tel: + 41 1 251 93 36
Fax: + 41 1 261 63 94

Distribution for other countries:
Intersentia Publishers
Groenstraat 31
BE-2640 Mortsel
Belgium
Tel: + 32 3 680 15 50
Fax: + 32 3 658 71 21

Rule of Law on the International Agenda
Per Bergling

ISBN-10: 90-5095-581-9
ISBN-13: 978-50-5095-581-2
D/2006/7849/41
NUR 828

For Maria

TABLE OF CONTENTS

ACKNOWLEDGEMENTS

My research has been facilitated by the generosity of many individuals and institutions. Thus I have incurred many debts in writing this book, and I want to thank all those organisations, colleagues and friends who have helped me in one way or another.

I am particularly grateful to the Swedish International Development Cooperation Agency (Sida), particularly its Department for Research Cooperation (Sarec), for making a substantial grant available for research and travel.

Academic colleagues who have been especially helpful in reflecting on ideas, reading drafts, providing suggestions and highlighting important aspects of the topic generally include Anders Fogelklou, Pär Hallström, Erik Häggqvist, Clark Lombardi, William Neilson, Erik Persson, Anita Ramasastry, Claes Sandgren, Per Sevastik, Veronica Taylor, and many others.

Much of the final drafting was completed during my time as Garvey, Schubert and Barer Visiting Professor of Asian Law with the Asian Law Center of the University of Washington Law School. My warm thanks go to the law firm Garvey, Schubert and Barer for their generous endowment and to Professor Veronica Taylor for inviting me to the Center.

I am also very grateful to my students in the courses "Crisis Management and International Law" and "Rule of Law and International Organisations" at Umeå University; "Rule of Law" at Stockholm University; "Southeast Asian Law" and "Law Reform in Transition Economies" at the University of Washington. Your generosity with reflections and suggestions has made this a better book.

Finally, many thanks to Jenny Ederlöf for always being ready to help with research, editing and constructive critique.

ACRONYMS AND INITIALS

ABA-CEELI	American Bar Association – Central European and Eurasian Law Initiative Initiative
ADB	Asian Development Bank
AFTA	ASEAN Free Trade Area
APEC	Asia-Pacific Economic Cooperation
ASEAN	Association of Southeast Asian Nations
AU	African Union
AusAid	Australian Agency for International Development
BiH	Bosnia and Herzegovina
BTA	US – Vietnam Bilateral Trade Agreement
CIDA	Canadian International Development Agency
CIS	Commonwealth of Independent States
CIJL	Centre for the Independence of Judges and Lawyers (UN/ICJ)
CoE	Council of Europe
DAC	Development Co-operation Directorate (OECD)
DANIDA	Danish Agency for Development Assistance
DFID	Department for International Development (UK)
ECHR	European Convention on Human Rights
EU	European Union
FRY	Federal Republic of Yugoslavia
GNP	Gross National Product
GTZ	Gesellschaft für Technische Zusammenarbeit (Germany)
HJPC	High Judicial and Prosecutorial Council (BiH)
IBA	International Bar Association
ICC	International Criminal Court
ICCPR	International Covenant on Civil and Political Rights
ICESCR	International Covenant on Economic, Social and Cultural Rights
ICG	International Crisis Group
ICTY	International Criminal Tribunal for the Former Yugoslavia

ICTR	International Criminal Tribunal for Rwanda
IFI	International Financial Institution
IJC	Independent Judicial Commission (BiH)
IMF	International Monetary Fund
INTERFET	International Force for East Timor (UN)
IPTF	International Police Task Force (UN/Bosnia and Herzegovina)
JIAS	Joint Interim Administrative Structure (Kosovo)
JICA	Japan International Cooperation Agency
JSR	Justice Sector Reform
JSSR	Justice and Security Sector Reform
LFA	Logical Framework Approach
MFN	Most Favoured Nation
NATO	North Atlantic Treaty Organization
NEPAD	New Partnership for Africa's Development
NGO	Non-governmental Organization
NIC	Newly Industrialised Country
OECD	Organisation for Economic Co-operation and Development
OHR	Office of the High Representative (Bosnia and Herzegovina)
OSCE	Organization for Security and Cooperation in Europe
PISG	Provisional Institutions of Self-Government (Kosovo)
PVO	Public Voluntary Organization
SADC	Southern African Development Community
SCU	Serious Crimes Unit (East Timor/Timor-Leste)
Sida	Swedish International Development Co-operation Agency
SOE	State Owned Enterprise
SPSC	Special Panels for Serious Crimes (East Timor/Timor-Leste)
SRSG	Special Representative of the Secretary General (UN)
STAR	Support for Trade Acceleration in Vietnam (USAID)
SWAP	Sector-Wide Approaches (Programs)
UN	United Nations
UNAMA	United Nations Assistance Mission in Afghanistan
UNBCPR	United Nations Bureau for Crisis Prevention and Recovery
UNBPIJ	United Nations Basic Principles on the Independence of the Judiciary
UNBPRL	United Nations Basic Principles on the Role of Lawyers
UNCITRAL	United Nations Commission on International Trade Law

UNDP	United Nations Development Program
UNHCHR	United Nations High Commissioner for Human Rights
UNMIBH	United Nations Mission in Bosnia and Herzegovina
UNMIK	United Nations Mission in Kosovo
UNMISET	United Nations Mission of Support in East Timor
UNOTIL	United Nations Office in Timor-Leste
UNSC	United Nations Security Council
UNTAC	United Nations Transitional Authority in Cambodia
USAID	United States Agency for International Development
USIP	United States Institute for Peace
WB	World Bank
WTO	World Trade Organization

1. INTRODUCTION

Legal and judicial reform, or "rule of law promotion", is now a top priority among international organizations, national governments and development agencies.[1] This is evidenced, *inter alia*, by the number of new technical assistance projects directed at reforming aspects of law and justice in developing and transition countries, the presence of "human rights" and "rule of law" among the official strategic goals of most assistance providers, and the establishment of new units and divisions within aid agencies to deal exclusively with the topic.[2] The discrete projects address a wide range of issues, from comprehensive constitutional amendments to access to justice initiatives at the grass root level. Conservative estimates are that approximately USD 3 billion has been allocated to various such activities in the past decade only.[3]

A number of factors have contributed to the rapid elevation of legal and judicial reform on the international agenda. First and foremost is the believed instrumental role of laws and judicial institutions (as part of "good governance") in promoting economic growth and otherwise eradicating poverty in developing countries (including helping them respond to the dynamics of "economic globalisation").[4] Another factor is the recognition that the dramatic political and economic transformations in the general direction of democracy and market economy of the 1980s and 1990s in Eastern Europe and the former Soviet Union necessitate fundamental reforms of the legal framework and the supporting institutional infrastructure in these countries. Yet another impetus is the growing acceptance of a universal concept of human rights and the ensuing perceived need among international organisations to assist in transforming this concept into reality. For similar reasons, international organisations pursue various

1 The concept of the rule of law as it is used in current efforts at supporting development and state building is analysed in Chapter 2.3 below. In essence, the rule of law is believed to prevail where the government itself is bound by the law, every person in society is treated equally under the law, the human dignity of each individual is recognized and protected by law, and justice is accessible to all. See *e.g.* Legal and Judicial Reform: Strategic Directions 2003.

2 The International Bar Association's International Rule of Law Directory, available at http://www.roldirectory.org/, provides an overview of some of the organisations and programs currently promoting activities in this area.

3 McInerney 2004 p. 4.

4 Issues of "governance" (defined by the World Bank in 1989 as the "manner in which power is exercised in the management of a country's economic and social resources for development", and subsequently slightly modified in meaning in later WB documents), including the rule of law, are core in "second generation" or "post-Washington consensus" reforms packages promoted by the international financial institutions.

strategies to introduce a degree of law and order in politically volatile and post-war environments as part of "security sector reform", which, in turn, is part of greater efforts at "state building". A well functioning legal and judicial system is thus regarded both as an end in itself and as a means to facilitate and leverage the achievement of other development objectives.

The means to reach these ends are many and vary between countries and actors depending on local conditions, political agenda, resources available, etc. Some broad generic areas of support nevertheless frequently reappear, among them reforming constitutions and basic laws to provide for specific political and economic goals; promoting judicial independence; facilitating legal and judicial training; reforming court administration and case management; establishing bar associations and professional organisations; fighting corruption; and providing for access to justice. It is not the case that all assistance providers aspire to do everything. Rather, the typical donor confines the scope of his engagement to a few distinct components in the list above, hoping that the host government, perhaps in alliance with other donors, will be able to address the rest. Further, it is rarely or never the donor agency that actually implements an activity. The administration and implementation of interventions, whether multi-year or *ad hoc*, are typically contracted to consultancy firms, university departments, law firms, NGOs, and similar bodies.

Like in other areas of development co-operation, the assistance providers and their consultants confess to the idea that strong domestic "demand", "lead" and "ownership" in the reform process ensure efficiency and sustainable results. It rarely happens that an assistance provider dictates or even suggests what is needed. Rather, the support is most often provided at the invitation of a host government that agrees, or has realised the utility of pretending to agree, that there is some kind of positive relationship between good laws, effective judicial agencies, and some aspect of development.[5] For example, developing countries may ask donors to help them introduce "modern" market-oriented laws in order to attract and regulate foreign and domestic investment; transition countries may ask for assistance in elaborating the legal and regulatory structures needed for integration into international and regional bodies such as the WTO or the EU; and governments of post-crisis states may seek international assistance in rebuilding shattered judicial structures and other essentials of law and order. Assistance providers may thus argue that there is confluence of interests between donor goals and recipient preferences, providing sufficient legitimacy to their

[5] There are of course examples of situations where assistance providers have encouraged recipient governments to ask for specific support, made support conditional on specific reforms, or even imposed specific norms and institutions by virtue of a UN Security Council mandate, as will be discussed in Chapter 4.4 and 5.3 below.

involvement. In any case, the pressure to mimic international and regional norms and rules is both externally imposed and internally generated.

Although there is unprecedented activity in this area of international co-operation, the nexus between law and various aspects of development remains problematic and little understood. Behind the rule of law consensus are still different and potentially contradictory, visions and approaches.[6] At a more technical level, lawyers and legal scholars continue to struggle to understand if and how different legal concepts can be meaningfully "borrowed", as well as the complex processes by which societies absorb or reject norms associated with international law. Development specialists have also noted that there seem to be apparent limitations as to what can be achieved by means of technical assistance in reforming laws and legal agencies.

This book attempts to (i) present the major political, economic and moral imperatives guiding and limiting current international efforts at supporting legal and judicial reforms in developing, transition and post-crisis environments; (ii) provide an overview of the main donor strategies and methods for supporting and implementing such reform projects; and (iii) explain some of the strengths and weaknesses of the same strategies and methods.[7]

In the chapter "*Theoretical Framework*", the basic concepts and imperatives underpinning recent attempts at supporting legal and judicial reforms are discussed. Special emphasis is paid to the so-called "governance" doctrine, the meaning of the rule of law in the development and state building debate, and the impact of international law and human rights norms on assistance programs. The chapter also discusses what factors that are thought to determine the conditions for success or failure in "transplanting", "borrowing" and "diffusing" laws and institutions.

The next chapter, "*Typical Problems and Remedies*", provides a short and schematic overview of some characteristic features of law and judicial organisation in states struggling with the challenges of development, transition, and post-crisis recovery, and explains how international organisations and other assistance providers make policy and organise themselves to effectively respond to the needs of the respective problem situations.

---

6 Carothers 1998 pp. 96-98; McInerney 2004 p. 5; Trubek 2003 p. 2.

7 It should be noted that the terminology in this field is not entirely settled. The meaning of many terms of both legal and development language varies between countries and legal cultures. States and interest groups may also try to create a terminology or give individual terms a meaning or content which suit their specific agenda. Consequently, the meaning of frequently used terms is often disputed, changing with the development of international law and politics, or wholly or partially overlapping with other concepts and definitions.

The discussion is taken a step further in the following chapter, "*Technical Assistance Approaches*", where a number of authentic policies and programs developed for addressing the needs of developing and transition societies are presented and analysed. The chapter begins with a presentation of the current debate on issues of speed and sequencing, and then moves on to discuss the increasing use of structured assessments for determining that the problems discussed really exist and that the proposed remedies will actually help to resolve them. The ensuing presentation of specific reform topics and methods follows the conventional reform sequence, *i.e.* constituency building, constitutional and legal reforms, institution building, and access creation. The spectrum of activities thus discussed includes, *inter alia*, support to legislative reforms; strengthening legal and judicial agencies; promoting judicial independence; training of judges, prosecutors and court personnel; empowering defence counsels and restructuring bar associations; and improving access to justice through legal counselling, advocacy and aid.

The chapter "*International Administration Approaches*" discusses the specific problems associated with international and UN efforts at restoring law and order and rebuilding the justice sector in countries and territories haunted by war or gross violations of human rights. Such efforts at "post-conflict justice" have two separate but interlinked components, namely providing for retributive justice with respect to crimes that occurred during the course of the conflict and helping to build something new and supposedly better for the future.[8] Some commentators make a distinction between the retributive and reconstructive aspect, but it is rarely a matter of reconstructing exactly those structures that once proved unable of preventing the collapse, or even caused it. The discussion in this book focuses on the forward-looking aspect of the effort, and particularly on the prospects and limitations of imposing a certain vision of a good state by virtue of a Security Council mandate under Chapter VII of the UN Charter.

The final chapter, "*Conclusions*", presents cross-cutting reflections on past and present attempts at supporting legal and judicial reforms in developing, transition and post-crisis environments, and provides some recommendations for the future. It argues that the best results are achieved when interventions are: (i) a response to a genuine domestic demand for assistance as expressed by the legitimate representatives of the people, (ii) based on careful assessment (evidence-based), (iii) comprehensive in scope, and (iv) realistic in ambition. There is also a discussion on how the seemingly

8 Often the retributive and restorative aspects seem to have received more attention by the international community that rebuilding and enhancing collapsed or weakened justice systems, perhaps because of the higher moral and justice imperatives associated with the former aspect and the costs and difficulties associated with the latter. See Bassiouni 2002 pp. XV and XVIII; Kritz 2002 pp. 84-85.

conflicting imperatives of expediency (quick and cost effective international engagements) and sustainability (creating legitimate local institutions) can be reconciled. The book is concluded with some reflections on ways to improve the conditions for inter-agency communication and co-ordination, thus helping to ensure that scarce resources are not wasted on duplication or the pursuit of conflicting agenda.

The selection of countries and initiatives discussed deserves a comment. Rather than trying to cover everything technical assistance providers do in the developing world, the ambition has been to identify and discuss a limited number of projects that illustrate typical as well as particularly successful or innovate approaches to legal and judicial reform. With regard to rule of law initiatives in post-crisis environments, the presentation essentially follows the chronology of the interventions of the last two decades (Cambodia, Bosnia and Herzegovina, Kosovo, and Afghanistan) but stops short of systematically addressing the most recent and on-going interventions in Africa (Liberia, the Democratic Republic of Congo).

A short selection of international and regional instruments with particular relevance for the promotion of legal and justice sector reforms is annexed to this book. Although far from exhaustive, it allows the reader to quickly access some of the most frequently invoked normative instruments guiding and limiting international efforts in this area.

2. THEORETICAL FRAMEWORK

2.1 ACTORS, PERSPECTIVES AND SUPPORT MODALITIES

A great number of actors provide support to legal and judicial reforms in developing, transition and post-crisis countries. These agencies also frequently change their policies and methods. It is consequently not possible to precisely account for their identities and the orientation of their work. This chapter instead provides an overview of the different *kinds* of actors, and a schematic presentation of what characterises their main support modalities.

The terms "donor" and "assistance provider" as they are used in this presentation refer to the entire community of agencies engaged in promoting and facilitating legal and judicial reform programs, comprising *inter alia* the bilateral assistance agencies (Sida, USAID, DFID, GTZ and others); the multilateral development banks (among them the World Bank and the Asian Development Bank); the United Nations (principally the UNDP but occasionally other specialized agencies); and various international and national foundations. The assistance providers operate through both grants and loans. The UN and most bilateral agencies rely mainly on grants-based approaches, not least because of the flexibility they have in placing the grants: if a national government does not seem like a suitable recipient, they can work with local or international NGOs, professional associations, etc. The development banks provide almost all of their support in the form of loans, which means that they have to work predominantly with national governments.[9]

Although the term "development project" is often used, not all grants and loans are "projectized", *i.e.* explicitly programmed to a series of inputs and outputs linked to some larger objective. For example, the structural or sector adjustment loans offered by the development banks often specify goals, but not the means by which they should be achieved. The trend seems to be that the development banks and some other donors are moving away from projectized activities towards various forms of result-oriented frameworks and sector support modalities, presumably because of the lower costs of design, implementation and reporting associated with such modalities. In these cases, it is typically the recipient (a government through a ministry or some *ad hoc*

9 Hammergren 2003 p. 292.

government body) that manages the funds and executes the program. The donor supervision is based on occasional visits, the recipient's progress reports, financial accounting, and tracking conditionality.[10]

That the responsibility for implementing the project is often contracted to a consultancy firm, university, institute, non-governmental organisation, or some other body, means that the donor is detached from the day-to-day work in the field and that operative decisions are worked out directly between the beneficiary and the implementing body. Increasingly, assistance providers also contract the responsibility for initial assessments, project identification and formulation, monitoring, evaluation, and other policy-oriented functions to various service providers. In some cases, these service providers are even functionally integrated into the organisation of the donors, with all the political and legal sensitivities that entails.

The field for big contracts with the multilateral agencies and development banks tends to be dominated by a few consultancy firms with a global or regional presence. A number of smaller firms, NGOs, universities, and research institutes successfully bid for mid- and small-size contracts, and frequently appear as subcontractors to the large firms. Bilateral donor agencies may also "contract" other state agencies in their respective countries to lead the implementation of technical assistance activities. Some such agencies may even have separate and specialised technical assistance divisions or programs for such work. For example, the Swedish Parliament, National Police Board, and Enforcement Service, are frequently instructed to enter into various forms of cooperative arrangements with "twin" agencies in developing and transition countries. US government support to law enforcement and prosecutorial reform is similarly frequently provided by two U.S. Department of Justice offices: the International Criminal Investigative Training Assistance Program and the Overseas Prosecutorial Development Assistance and Training Program. The implementing agency often relies on resident consultants and advisers to work closely with sector organizations in the recipient country over longer periods of time. In addition to their specific assignments, these advisers are expected to provide general suggestions, help detect problems or areas for attention, and recommend modifications in program design ("accompaniment").[11]

Interestingly, the variations in donor agenda and formal justifications for their work do not produce corresponding variations in what they actually do. Rather, differences in how programs are organized and conducted are for the most part a function of the agencies' general operating rules, organization, resources and other mundane factors.

---

10 Hammergren 2003 pp. 292-293.

11 Hammergren 2003 p. 296.

Linn Hammergren's interpretation is that donors find virtue in necessity: The reason that the World Bank works "long distance" while USAID, DFID, and GTZ use in-country managers and advisers is not that these agencies have decided after careful assessment that this would be the best way to conduct the projects. It is simply the way they implement all programs.[12] Allowing for the evident differences in the size of programs and projects, there is thus considerable similarity in the kind of activities being sponsored (study tours, expert advise to law makers, topical training, conferences, resident advisors, acquisition of information technology, production of information materials, etc.). That some large donors are moving into what they call comprehensive, integrated, or "holistic" programs, means little more than the pursuit of multiple objectives by combining an equal or greater number of conventional project components. Hammergren also notes that the strategic linkages among the goals, components, and activities in such comprehensive programs are often weak.[13]

The formulation of new and more innovative policies for the future is made difficult by the problems inherent in assessing the "impact" or "results" of rule of law programs. For example, while donors may argue that documented and significant declines in human rights abuses (extrajudicial killings, police brutality, etc.) in some countries should be attributed to their interventions targeting these problems, such changes could also be attributed to the end of periods of political unrest, external diplomatic pressure, civil society activity, or some other factor. Other quantitative and qualitative changes in the legal and judicial universe (reductions in the percentage of prisoners awaiting trial, "better" criminal investigation, etc.) may be difficult to document because of unreliable statistics, crude measurement systems, and manipulation of data.

Another factor that complicates impact assessment and policy development is the reduced role of the state and its agencies in guiding and limiting processes of cross-border legal change. Already in the 1960s and 1970s did political and legal scholars begin to realise that a comprehensive understanding of these processes required expanding the focus from relations between monolithic spheres (states, governments) to comprise a wide range of relations across borders by a multitude of actors and entities above, below, besides and within states, *e. g.* international and supranational organisations, non-governmental organizations, transnational corporations, and "parts" of states such as legislatures, courts and regulatory agencies.[14] That sub-state entities, NGOs, corporations, etc. form coalitions and networks with twin institutions in other countries struggling with similar problems allows for a more dynamic exchange of ideas and create pressure for global or regional concepts of law and judicial

12 Hammergren 2003 p. 307.
13 Hammergren 2003 p. 306.
14 Slaughter 2002.

organisation. In particular, these transnational networks offer opportunities for the internalisation in key occupational groups ("rule of law communities") of "metanorms" such as judicial independence, regulatory transparency and public participation.[15] These networks may also influence the making and implementing of international and national law in a wide range of areas, from grand principles human rights to details of judicial organisation.[16] On the private side, multinational corporations (national companies with foreign subsidiaries) are similarly giving way to transnational corporations (corporations with diffuse national belonging and specialised facilities all over the world, producing for a global market). In this pursuit, they are assisted by international consultancy and law firms. These corporations and their advisors generate their own norms and push for favourable or at least uniform and recognizable legal and judicial standards.[17]

2.2 CONCEPTS AND CRITIQUES

Among the many paradigms underpinning current development agenda, the arguably most influential and definitely most debated is the "governance" or "good governance" doctrine. This doctrine has its roots in a group of theories referred to as the "Washington Consensus", which, in turn, suggests that economic development and poverty reduction are most likely to result from policies that promote private entrepreneurship by reducing the role of the state, breaking up the dominance of rent-seeking political elites, and encouraging foreign investment. However, the many attempts to apply the doctrine in its purest form have generated results much different from those envisaged.[18] In many instances, the opportunities provided by economic liberalisation have been captured by pre-existing political elites. It seems that the juxtaposition of enhanced private power and a weakened state often put in jeopardy the property rights and potential economic opportunities of less powerful individuals and groups. This experience has led policy makers to conclude that reform prescription should not stop at shrinking the state and liberalizing the economy, but also comprise initiatives to strengthen and open up the institutions that protect and enforce these new freedoms.[19]

---

15 Slaughter 2002 pp. 18-19.

16 Sikkink 2002 pp. 38-40; Slaughter 2002 p. 16.

17 Dezalay & Garth 1996; 2001; 2002a; 2002b.

18 Some critical commentators argue that the reorganisation of aid mechanisms inherent in such programs has actually contributed to system collapse in countries such as Somalia and Zaire. See Kjaer 2004 p. 174 for analysis and references.

19 See for example Legal and Judicial Reform: Strategic Directions 2003 pp. 11-15.

A refined "post-Washington Consensus" definition of the doctrine accordingly came to prescribe that there should be support for establishing or consolidating certain critical aspects of governance, among them judicial autonomy. The World Bank and other influential assistance providers soon started to talk specifically of "the rule of law" as a necessary component of any sustainable economic growth policy. In recent years, the doctrine has been reinterpreted again to include also some substantive dimensions of the rule of law, such as the core of human rights and protection of vulnerable groups.[20] The current definition of governance thus emphasises both the constructive role of the state in creating and maintaining certain laws and judicial institutions, and in making sure that the nature of those laws and institutions is such that the benefits of economic liberalisation and growth come to the benefit of the population at large.[21]

There are some areas where the governance doctrine remains ambivalent or even internally inconsistent. For example, while it maintains that it is imperative to strengthen and insulate the economic sphere (governed by private law) *vis-à-vis* the political sphere (governed by administrative regulation), governance programs are increasingly concerned with "regulatory reforms", *i.e.* helping states develop and regularise the procedures for agency rule-making and adjudication of disputes. Governance programs thus end up providing support to regulatory agencies in order to achieve the goal of deregulation. Critical commentators point out that massive governmental rearmament and intervention seem to be required to end massive governmental intervention.[22] Another area is alternative dispute resolution. While the governance doctrine identifies the formal judicial institutions (the courts) as the preferred administrators of law in general and private law in particular, governance programs simultaneously seek to circumvent unreliable, overburdened and incompetent courts by supporting the development of alternative mediation and arbitration structures. Recipient countries and bodies within them may for example be supported in developing arbitration laws, procedures, and model arbitration clauses. A benevolent interpretation would be that such policies are reflective of the ambition to privilege private over public legal ordering, or to "privatize" the private law.

Critics have questioned how an organization like the World Bank could suddenly move away from its traditional reconstructive mandate and engage in something as "intrusive" as reforming governments, rewriting laws, and fighting political

[20] Brietzke 2002 p. 111; Jayasuriya 2002 pp. 24-26; Rittich 2004 pp. 1-3; and Legal and Judicial Reform: Strategic Directions 2003 p. 15.

[21] See www.worldbank.org/wbi/governance/. For commentary, see Kjaer 2004 p. 173; Rittich 2004 p 3.

[22] Brietzke 2002 p. 111.

corruption.[23] The reason is to be found in the circumstance that the World Bank is not an international organisation or treaty body in the traditional sense, rather first and foremost a bank, and as such principally accountable to its shareholders. If there is majority among these (USA, Germany and Japan being the biggest) for a change in policy, and the new policy is not obviously contrary to the Articles of Agreement governing its operations, then there is no formal reason why the Bank should be prevented from implementing it. In this specific case, the Bank was also pressed by the UN and a number of other frustrated donors to take steps in that direction.[24] The philosophical underpinnings of the Bank's new stance on issues of law and justice are sometimes referred to as the "Shihata doctrine", named after the World Bank's former Chief Counsellor Ibrahim Shihata.[25]

The governance paradigm is implicitly underpinned by a specific economic theory of law, namely an essentially Weberian theory of legal-formal rationality in the rise of capitalism, as developed by the Chicago School of Law and Economics and the New Institutional Economics. The more recent incarnations of the Chicago School argues that the primary function of private law in capitalist societies should be the achievement of economic efficiency. The law should accordingly be structured (by legislators and judges) in such a way that it facilitates fast and reliable market transactions to mutual advantage. The Chicago School also claims that it is possible to distinguish good private law (which promotes these goals) from improper regulation (which impairs economic efficiency). The New Institutional Economics School develops the theory about the efficiency-promoting functions of the law a step further and merges it with an analysis of the history and comparative viability of "institutions" (understood as formalised and established sets of rules for human interaction, modes of government, etc.). The advocates of this school accordingly argue that there are specific legal institutions that have demonstrated their viability and effectiveness over time (with the minimization of transaction costs being the most important criteria of effectiveness).[26] Examples of such institutions include enforceable contracts and the limited liability company (two constructions developed to limit the financial risks involved in anonymous and large-scale transactions). Inherent in the theory on the comparative effectiveness of certain legal institutions is also the implicit assumption that such laws and legal agencies, if replicated in new environments, would be conducive to equally beneficial outcomes.

---

23 According to the Articles of Agreement of the World Bank, Art. IV, section 10, the Bank should not work on issues that have a bearing on the political regime of creditor countries.

24 Kjaer 2004 p. 179.

25 Shihata 1991 pp. 53-97.

26 North 1981 and 1990.

While there have always been groups of lawyers and economists that have doubted the relevance of such theories for current efforts at restructuring underperforming economies, a new kind of criticism is levied by commentators who think that the subtle aspects of these theories are ignored or flattened when translated to serve the purpose of prescribing legal reform recommendations. Scott Newton, at a recent conference at Cornell University, criticised the way the Chicago School's complex concept of law as the efficiency-attuned guarantor of pricing has been reduced to a sort of vulgarized Weberianism in the Shihata doctrine. Newton also pointed out that the ideas of New Institutional Economics of the competitively selected legal institution have been similarly transformed into the business management concept of "best practice" (a term that denotes a proven successful approach to a recurrent business challenge), essentially suggesting that there should be optimal off-the-shelf laws for all aspects of economic life.

Another criticised aspect of the governance doctrine is the use of "conditionalities", *i.e.* the stipulation of specific reforms that client countries have to implement in order to be eligible for policy-oriented support. The most famous and debated case may be the conditions attached to the IMF's financial rescue packages for Thailand, Indonesia and South Korea in 1997-1999 in the wake of the Asian financial crisis, where these governments had to itemize in so called Letters of Intent which specific legal and judicial reforms they would undertake in return for support.[27] Among the specific laws such introduced and revised were laws on bankruptcy and other instruments the lenders perceived as necessary in a transparent and effective market economy. Throughout the entire governance era, the international financial institutions have defended such intrusive and fast-track approaches with arguments that the urgency of the situation and the technical and "apolitical" character of the issues addressed made the copying international or foreign models justified and feasible.

As of recent, it seems that the World Bank and the International Monetary Fund have become more cautious in conditioning support on the creation of certain kinds of legislation. Behind this change in policy is recognition that such arrangements are difficult to monitor, provoke massive political controversy, and that their success depend on the existence of a supporting institutional framework beyond the reach of any donor policy. Perhaps the next step is the transformation of good governance from an end state that is believed to be possible to induce from the outside to a criterion against which to decide who qualifies for assistance.[28]

---

27 Neilson 1999.

28 Kjaer 2004 p. 175.

Although development language and agenda are regularly reinterpreted and restated, the current emphasis on law and judicial organisation among the major assistance providers seems unlikely to be transitory. Rather, the current policies of these organisations suggest that not just "economic" law, but good law in general, has been accepted both as ends in themselves and as critical means to other ends.[29] The World Bank now includes criminal law and justice within its programs on grounds that high levels of crime are not just a disincentive to investment but also disproportionately affect the poor, women and other vulnerable groups, and prevent these groups from meaningfully participate in economic, social and political activities conducive to economic growth.[30] The efforts spent on establishing conceptual and practical links between already existing legal and judicial reform programs and more recent high-level instruments such as the Millennium Development Goals (MDGs) is yet another indication that these organisations will continue to work in this area for a long time to come.[31] At the same time, when influential donors and financial institutions concede the importance of law in the broad sense in reform prescriptions, they also assert their right to decide on a much wider range of political matters in recipient states and open up for using support modalities to influence the manner in which domestic social and distributive objectives are to be conceptualized, prioritized and implemented.[32]

2.3 RULE OF LAW AS MEANS AND END

A common feature of current and recent support strategies, whether addressing the needs of adjustment in the wake of transition, the dynamics of globalisation, membership of international and regional bodies, or state-building in the wake of war, is the emphasis on the rule of law. Frequently, the rule of law is also regarded as something tangible and definable, and something that will be easy to put into place once the right technical assistance instruments have been found and enough political muscle mobilized.

29 Rittich 2004 pp. 4-5.

30 Legal and Judicial Reform: Strategic Directions, 2003, pp. 33-34.

31 In September 2000 the member states of the United Nations unanimously adopted the Millennium Declaration. The most important part of the roadmap for implementing the Declaration is the eight Millennium Development Goals, namely to eradicate extreme poverty and hunger; achieve universal primary education; promote gender equality and empower women; reduce child mortality; improve maternal health; combat HIV/AIDS, malaria and other diseases; ensure environmental sustainability; and develop global partnership for development.

32 Rittich 2004 pp. 4, 6 and 12.

However, the concept is inherently vague and complicated, and legal scholars have wrestled for centuries with defining what it means.[33] The doctrine of the rule of law as elaborated by A. V. Dicey in nineteenth century England was to a large extent a reflection of a disdain among the leading legal English academics of the time for Continental-European models of government, and the doctrine consequently came to emphasize the role of the common law courts as the primary producers and administrators of law. It also emphasised that even legitimate power could be dangerous and needed to be controlled by a system of checks and balances.[34] The continental concept of the *Rechtsstaat*, meanwhile, emphasized the role of the state, rested on positivist grounds and was equally concerned with legality in public administration.[35] Still today, in the age of international law and routine cross-border legal co-operation, common law and civil law lawyers seem insufficiently aware of the differences in historical origin and meaning. Even greater becomes the confusion when disparate and often insufficiently articulated concepts of the rule of law intersect and need to be reconciled with recipient country preferences about the role of law in government and society. That the rule of law means different things to different people, and serves a variety of political agenda ranging from libertarianism to statist socialism, cast the idea of a "rule of law consensus" in serious doubt.[36]

The rule of law can similarly malfunction or collapse at different levels. Rama Mani identifies three "states of disrepair" in the rule of law in crisis and post crisis environments, but the suggested typology seems to be applicable also in developmental and transitional settings. Where the rule of law is *illegitimate but functional*, it remains operational at some level. There is a written law, certain core institutions continue to function and there is a judiciary and trials are held. In minimalist terms, human rights may be violated by laws that discriminate against certain groups of the population, while the state claims to uphold the law procedurally. In other words, the rule of law in this scenario has become a tool of state repression. Zimbabwe may serve as an example. The rule of law is *corrupt and dysfunctional* when it the judiciary has lost or is losing its independence and impartiality, and is easily manipulated by the executive, the military or other influential groups. Justice is here seen as serving the elite only and being denied to the ordinary population. In this scenario, the appearance of the rule of law continues to exist, but loses most of its defining characteristics. Bosnia and Herzegovina typify this state of the rule of law. The rule of law is *devastated*

33 Carothers 1998; Clarke, D. 1999; Ehrenreich 2003; Jayasuriya 1999; Kennedy 2003; McInerney 2004; Orth 1998; Peerenboom 2004; and Trubek 2003.

34 Orth 1998 pp. 75-76.

35 See Clarke D. 1999 p. 31; Orth 1998 pp 72-76; and Fogelklou 1997(b) pp. 35-36.

36 Orth 1998 pp. 76-79; Peerenboom 2004 p. 1; and Trubek 2003 p. 11.

and non-functional when the entire formal legal apparatus collapses and disintegrates. Sierra Leone and Liberia exemplify this scenario.[37]

In order to explain the relevance of such observations regarding the nature of the rule of law to current attempts to bolster the concept in developing and transition countries, Randall Peerenboom suggests that the rule of law is divided into two general types, "thin" and "thick", which, in turn, are understood to be conducive to different political goals and purposes. The thin conception, which essentially aims at preventing a "Hobbesian" war of all against all by ensuring law and order, limiting arbitrariness and providing for a degree of predictability in social and economic affairs, stresses the formal or instrumental aspects of the rule of law, *i.e.* those features that any legal system allegedly must possess to function effectively as a system of laws, regardless of whether the legal system is part of a democratic or authoritarian, secular or theocratic, society. The constitutive elements of the thin conception thus include, in addition to restraints on state actors, rules determining which actors that make laws, procedures for making laws, and mechanisms for making laws public and readily accessible. The laws must also be generally applicable, clear, consistent, relatively stable, and enforced in a fair and effective way. Moreover, the laws must be reasonably acceptable to the majority of the population (or at least the key groups affected). Peerenboom and many others point out that not even the thinnest concept is in any way apolitical or independent of a particular political, economic and social context. Rather, any legal system that meets the standards of a thin rule of law is inevitably embedded in a particular set of political and cultural values, whether liberal democratic, statist socialist, soft authoritarian, etc. This is evidenced, if not by other things, when the regime confesses to its own thin definition and simultaneously refutes alternative thick or substantive definitions. The thick or substantive conception, meanwhile, includes all the elements of a thin conception, but then also specifically enumerates elements of law and justice that are believed to be conducive to the realisation of a certain political vision or morality, whether liberal democracy, free-market capitalism, "Asian developmental state" or specific conceptions of human rights.[38] All versions of the rule of law should accordingly be understood as interlinked with, and dependent on, a greater political, economic and social surround.[39]

The practical implication is that before the rule of law can be meaningfully used as a development concept, or effectively promoted from the outside, it must be put in a policy framework.[40] After considerable hesitation and procrastination, the major

37 Mani 2002.

38 Peerenboom 2004 pp. 3-5.

39 Clarke D. 1999 p. 28; Ehrenreich 2003 p. 2285.

40 Orth 1998 pp. 78-79.

organisations are now taking steps in this direction. The World Bank says that the ambition is to supplant autocratic and state-centred systems with a rule of law that operates objectively, is accessible, reasonably efficient, transparent, predictable, enforceable, and protects human rights and legitimate state interests, etc.[41] The UN Secretary General's strategic report "The Rule of Law and Transitional Justice in Conflict and Post-Conflict Societies" similarly seeks to adopt a common language and a set of priorities for rule of law programs undertaken by UN agencies. Most significant is that the report enunciates a definition of the rule of law that integrates procedural, institutional and substantive principles: "*[The rule of law] ...refers to a principle of governance in which all persons, institutions and entities, public and private, including the State itself, are accountable to laws that are publicly promulgated, equally enforced and independently adjudicated and which are consistent with international human rights norms and standards. It requires, as well, measures to ensure adherence to principles of supremacy of law, equality before the law, fairness in the application of law, separation of powers, participation in decision-making, legal certainty, avoidance of arbitrariness and procedural and legal transparency.*"[42]

However, most individual project documents are still either silent on how the rule of law should be understood, or provide essentially procedural definitions.[43] The reasons for avoiding specificity are practical as well as political.[44] The practical consideration is based on the recognition that law is a central process used by competing political and economic agents in recipient countries to structure state power, and that the success of a reform project is highly dependent on the way the initiative is greeted by these agents. For example, party and government officials accustomed to convenient concepts such as "interest of state" and "socio-cultural interests" might find the idea of introducing individual rights (as inherent in the "thick" definition of the rule of law) threatening and therefore resist its implementation, while an initiative that does not aim to radically alter the fundamental premises on which the system rests would be easier both to understand and accept, and thus to implement.[45] A vaguely defined

41 Dietrich 2000 pp. 4-5.

42 Report of the United Nations Secretary General on the Rule of Law and Transitional Justice in Conflict and Post-Conflict Societies 2004. UNSG Report S/2004/616 p. 4.

43 Ehrenreich 2003 pp. 2283-2284. On the difficulties of transforming high-level rule of law policies into operative principles in UN peace-keeping operations, see Hurwitz and Studdard 2004 pp. 2-3.

44 Kennedy 2003 p. 17; McInerney 2004 p. 13. Tolonen (1996 p. 128) points out that many of the goals of "transformation" and "transition", such as market economy, political democracy and rule of law, have received their content in a bipolar world where they expressed the self-identity of the rich Western nations against the opposites, the socialist countries. Now that this bipolarity is vanishing with the tides of history, the goals are becoming accepted as slogans, while their real content is becoming more vague.

45 "Thin" rule of law reforms are not immune to bureaucratic resistance either. Gillespie (2004 p. 164) points out that Vietnamese official have shown great ingenuity in blocking regulatory transparency by introducing new controls by stealth, etc., essentially in order to maintain their prerogatives and

or procedural rule of law is also attractive because is allows assistance providers to avoid getting directly involved in the many sensitive distributive questions (about status, wealth, power, etc.) that inevitably arise when changes to legal and judicial structures are contemplated. It is also believed to provide entry into societies and processes that would otherwise be closed to international cooperation because of irreconcilable differences in political agenda between assistance providers and recipients.

The greatest problem with a vague, formalistic or definition is that the rule of law risks become conceptually overburdened and unstable when it is invoked for too many and potentially opposed reasons.[46] Too much latitude in meaning may even be directly at odds with the greater aspirational goals of the support. For example, is the rule of law considered important to empower and protect vulnerable groups, promote business, or merely to bring subordinates into line?[47] Independent observers of development work point out that the main effect of the IFI-policy to promote a "sectorial" rule of law for the economic area may be the strengthening and consolidation of already authoritarian regimes, without furthering any balancing political liberalisation or providing corresponding protection of the political rights of the individual.[48] The are also conspicuous legal-technical difficulties in emphasising transparency, judicial independence, and other traditional traits of rule of law in the economic area, while having a more ambivalent policy with regard to the more politically sensitive areas of civil, criminal and administrative law. There are reasons to concur with those who argue that the legal and administrative "paradigm", *i.e.* the core of shared understandings, theories and methodologies, must be essentially the same in all sectors to provide the system with the basic characteristics of a consistent and sustainable legal order.[49] Observers of processes of economic transition are similarly warning that support to narrowly defined or sectoral rule of law reforms may be counter-productive in environments where the economic system still contains elements of central planning and *dirigisme* and vest far-reaching discretionary power in the hands of administrative authorities. There are also justified doubts whether rule

privileged position intact. On issues of how reform programs can weaken or empower various key groups in "palace wars", see Dezalay and Garth 2002a pp. 246-250.

46 Peerenboom 2004 p. 7.

47 Clarke D. 1999 p. 34; Trubek 2003 pp. 14-15.

48 See for example Jayasuria 1999; Clarke D. 1999; and Peerenboom 2004.

49 On the concept of "legal paradigms", see Van Hoecke and Warrington 1998 pp. 514-515. According to Mattei's theory of "legal families" (1997 pp. 5, 16, 23 and 27), consisting of rule of professional law, rule of political law, and rule of traditional law, a sudden move in some sector of the legal system, *e. g.* from rule of political law to rule of professional law, is likely to create enormous tensions in the internal "taxonomy" or "grammar" of the system, and perhaps even create need for an entirely new ground of legitimacy of the law. Note that the subject of discussion here is not the related but different issue of whether there can be a "dual state" (Fraenkel 1941), for example a capitalist economy within the hard shell of an authoritarian regime.

by law and similar policies can ever be strong and comprehensive enough penetrate rooted and protected conditions of patronage, nepotism and corruption (see Chapter 4.6.5).

That the rule of law is controversial and insufficiently theorized does not mean that the concept lacks utility. Rather, it has inherent qualities as a political declaration because its core elements, however defined, are minimum requirements of any decent society.[50] Assistance providers should therefore spend more effort on analysing its normative foundations, legal and institutional implications, and most effective technical assistance vehicles. Empowered with this knowledge, it will be easier to assess country-specific needs, set up realistic goals, formulate strategic and comprehensive programs, maintain focus in implementation, and determine success and failure.[51]

2.4 INTERNATIONAL NORMS AND PRACTICES

While many legal and judicial reform programs seek to promote, directly or indirectly, goals that are ultimately political or ideological in nature, success in implementation often paradoxically depends on the ability of the donors to play down or obscure the element of ideological confrontation and instead couch the specific activities in politically neutral or otherwise mutually acceptable terms. Formalistic definitions of the rule of law have already been mentioned as means to this end. Another is to argue for compliance with binding norms and practices that transcend domestic law and politics, notably international law.[52] This approach to legal change may also be described as an attempt at "socializing" individual states to comply with a commonly accepted set of norms. Among the most important tools in this process are conveying knowledge about what is desirable and what is not, the emulation of "heroes" and positive examples, praise for conformity, critique for deviation, etc.[53] Obviously, socialization in this sense is not always a benign process, but can involve sensitive interactions and choices. Besides governments and international organisations, various non-state actors such as professional groups and NGOs are also pursuing such agenda *inter alia*, by bringing new ideas and issues into policy debates, serving as sources of information and testimony, monitoring compliance, and documenting rule-breaking behaviour. The relative effectiveness of non-state actors in this area is largely

---

50 Peerenboom 2004 pp. 9, 13 and 34-35.

51 John Orth (1998 pp. 79-81) argues that a workable policy framework needs be clear as to what institutions that need to be created; resolute on the issue of local political commitment; realistic with regard to the goals; and patient (the accumulation of appropriate constitutional norms, professional cultures, and personal characteristics for the rule of law in Europe took long time, and there is little reason to expect that the process should be much faster in other places).

52 See *e. g.* Corell 2004 p. 341; Sikkink 2002 p. 38; and Teitel 2000 pp. 20-21.

53 Sikkink 2002 pp. 49-50.

attributable to the fact that the sanctions for breaking an international or universal norm, unlike a law, are essentially social and related to exposure, *i.e.* resonate well with the informal and issue-oriented nature of NGO work.[54]

The explosive post-WWII growth in international and human rights law, notably UN treaties such as the International Covenant on Civil and Political Rights and accompanying implementing legislation, provides an important source of normative support to those arguing that there are universally accepted concepts of good law and judicial organisation.[55] But it is important to remember that international law is also a constraint to what the UN and other assistance providers can do. For example, the UN Secretary General confesses to the principle that "*The normative foundation for our work in advancing the rule of law is the Charter of the United Nations itself, together with the four pillars of the modern international legal system: international human rights law; international humanitarian law; international criminal law; and international refugee law. This includes the wealth of United Nations human rights and criminal justice standards developed in the last half-century. These represent universally applicable standards adopted under the auspices of the United Nations and must therefore serve as the normative basis for all United Nations activities in support of justice and the rule of law.*"[56] On the issue of how these norms relate to local notions of law and justice, the Secretary General argues that "*United Nations norms and standards have been developed and adopted by countries across the globe and have been accommodated by the full range of legal systems of member states, whether based in common law, civil law, Islamic law, or other legal traditions. As such, these norms and standards bring a legitimacy that cannot be said to attach to exported national models, which, all too often, reflect more the individual interests or experience of donors and assistance providers than they do the best interests or legal development needs of host countries.*"[57]

Concepts of international law and human rights are also bolstered in "second generation" or "Post-Washington Consensus" governance doctrines. Kerry Rittich suggests that behind this elevation is recognition that they contribute directly to good economic outcomes and that they constitute official "ends" in themselves. But Rittich underlines that the significance of the inclusion of human rights norms extends much longer than this and surfaces in many more ways. Sophisticated domestic political actors may for example seek to frame national debates over labour standards, education, health care and many more social matters, as matters of human rights and issues that attract international attention. At the same time, Rittich notes that the

---

54 Sikkink 2002 pp. 38-40.

55 Clarke D. 1999 p. 33.

56 Report of the United Nations Secretary General on the Rule of Law and Transitional Justice in Conflict and Post-Conflict Societies 2004. UNSG Report S/2004/616 p. 5.

57 Ibid.

references to human rights within the policies of the IFIs rarely share the perspectives of the activist community and topical human rights institutions. In the typical case, they are rather references to a limited domain of core civil and political rights. There is also resistance to the idea of rights-based development on grounds that this idea involves recognizing a virtually unlimited range of rights to which people should be entitled, and that these entitlements should ultimately determine the assistance agenda.[58]

The potential of human rights arguments as political "levers" becomes apparent when considering that most developing and transition countries are already members of various international and regional bodies, notably the United Nations, and thus formally bound to adhere to the rules and principles of these organizations. These states may also be parties to specific international and regional instruments with significance for the rule of law, human rights and judicial organisation, such as the International Covenant on Civil and Political Rights and its optional protocols. For example, as a member of the United Nations and a party to the ICCPR, a state must respect that everyone is entitled to a "*fair and public hearing by a competent, independent and impartial tribunal established by law*".[59] It is consequently an explicit obligation for the member state to ensure for this goal by providing and maintaining high standards for the manner in which judges are appointed, promoted and dismissed, safeguarding their tenure, and guaranteeing the actual independence of the judiciary from the executive and legislative branches. The First Optional Protocol similarly allows individual petition; the Second Optional Protocol aims at abolishing the death penalty; and the Convention against Torture and Other Cruel, Inhuman or Degrading Treatment or Punishment forbids member states and their agents to perform such acts, etc.

However, these conventions and other similar instruments provide little direct guidance as to how the respective norms should be made operative in the domestic sphere. This is problematic because it is the details of domestic implementation that the conditions for success and failure in technical assistance are often determined. To get to the level of detail required, assistance providers must often look to international or regional instruments that are not formally binding. In some cases, the only source of guidance may be instruments developed by civil society actors (for example the International Bar Association and other NGOs). Among the most important non-binding international and regional instruments are the United Nations Basic Principles on the Independence of the Judiciary (UNBPIJ); the Council of Europe Recommendation on the Independence, Efficiency, and Role of Judges; and the Council of Europe's

58 Rittich 2004 p. 17.
59 ICCPR art. 14(1).

European Charter on the Statute for Judges.[60] The UNBPIJ provide that each member state should organize and administer justice in accordance with the Universal Declaration of Human Rights, the ICCPR and the ICESCR, and enumerate a number of specific principles by which member states should seek to guarantee the independence of their judiciaries. Besides various political guarantees for impartiality and fairness, these principles also include that each member state must ensure and provide the judiciary with adequate resources for it to properly perform its functions.

The 1990 United Nations Basic Principles on the Role of Lawyers (UNBPRL) similarly stipulate that member states shall organize and administer justice in accordance with the Universal Declaration of Human Rights, the ICCPR and the ICESCR, and specifically mention a number of principles for ensuring the proper role of lawyers in the administration of justice. Most significant among these are perhaps the guarantees of access to lawyer and legal services, meaning that the government shall ensure that efficient procedures and responsive mechanisms for effective and equal access to lawyers are provided to all persons without discrimination of any kind. There are also guarantees for the functioning of lawyers, essentially obliging the state to ensure that lawyers are able to perform all their professional functions without intimidation, hindrance, harassment or improper interference; able to travel and to consult with their clients freely; and that lawyers are not prosecuted or threatened with prosecution or administrative, economic or other sanctions for any action taken in accordance with recognized professional duties, standards and ethics.[61] If the security of lawyers is threatened as a result of their carrying out their functions, then the authorities shall provide adequate safeguard for them.[62] There are also provisions on the freedom of expression and association of lawyers, stating that lawyers are entitled to freedom of expression, belief, association and assembly. In particular, lawyers have the right to participate in public discussions of matters concerning the law, the administration of justice and the promotion and protection of human rights.[63]

The United Nations, and particularly the United Nations Development Program (UNDP), works in various ways to strengthen the respect for the principles spelled out in these international instruments. A priority in recent years have been aspects of access justice, with the goal being that everyone, especially the poor, women and other disadvantaged groups, should be able to seek and obtain justice under national laws that conform to international human rights standards and national constitutional

[60] For the large group of developing countries in Asia and Africa that were formerly British colonies, there are also various Commonwealth bodies and instruments aiming at safeguarding and promoting judicial independence, rule of law and human rights, notable among them the Harare Commonwealth Declaration of 1991 and the Latimer House Guidelines of 1998.

[61] UNBPRL art. 16.

[62] Art. 17.

[63] Art. 23.

norms. Most activities have targeted capacity bottlenecks and other problems in the judiciary and prosecution, but UNDP has also sought to promote alternative fora and mechanisms.

International and regional norms and principles similarly influence the course of legal change through the prestige and prospect of aid that come with membership of topical organisations. Prospects of WTO membership in particular have spurred local interest in departing on far-reaching reform policies, particularly as regards the rules and procedures for trade.[64] Under the WTO framework, members (currently about 150 states) must accept a comprehensive body of rules and standards for trade-related issues known as the "single undertaking". Member states are also bound to accept new rules and disciplines developed by the organisation, and to submit to its mechanisms for the settlement of international trade disputes. The definition of trade should here be understood as rather wide, comprising almost all aspects of administrative and judicial decision-making with implications for the way business is conducted. Another example is membership of the Council of Europe. Once admitted, member states are formally obliged to adhere to the European Convention on Human Rights (ECHR), the European Social Charter, the Convention for Prevention of Torture and Inhuman or Degrading Treatment, the Framework Convention for the Protection of National Minorities, and other binding instruments, and to accept decisions of the various control and redress mechanisms, including the European Court of Human Rights. The Council has also promoted a set of widely accepted standards by which the justice sector in member and candidate countries can be assessed and on which new structures can be based.[65] Membership of the European Union is similarly conditioned on legal and judicial adjustments to accommodate for the *aquis communitaire.*

---

64 See Ajanant 1996; Footer 2003; McGivern 1996; Potter 1996; and Wong 1996.

65 Among these instruments can be mentioned: Resolution (76) 5 on legal aid in civil, commercial and administrative matters; Resolution (78) 8 on legal aid and advice; Recommendation No R (81) 7 on measures access to justice; Recommendation No R (84) 5 on the principle of civil procedure designed to improve the functioning of justice; Recommendation No R (86) 12 concerning measures to prevent and reduce the excessive workload in the courts; Recommendation No R (87) 18 concerning the simplification of criminal justice; Recommendation No R (93) 1 on effective access to the law and to justice for the very poor; Recommendation No R (94) 12 on the independence, efficiency and role of judges; Recommendation No R (95) 5 concerning the introduction and improvement of the functioning of appeal systems and procedures in civil and commercial cases; Recommendation No R (95) 12 on the management of criminal justice; Recommendation No R (2000) 19 on the role of public prosecution in the criminal justice system; Recommendation No R (2000) 21 on the freedom of exercise of the profession of lawyer; Recommendation No R (2001) 2 concerning the design and re-design of court systems and legal information systems in a cost-effective manner; Recommendation No R (2001) 3 on the delivery of court and other legal services to the citizen through the use of new technologies; Recommendation No R (2001) 9 on alternatives to litigation between administrative authorities and private parties; Recommendation No R (2003) 14 on the interoperability of information systems in the justice sector; Recommendation No R (2003) 16 on the execution of administrative and judicial decisions in the field of administrative law; and Recommendation No R (2003) 17 on enforcement.

Legal and judicial reform processes can also be incited by bilateral (trade) agreements of various kinds. For example, the US – Vietnam Bilateral Trade Agreement (which reflect many internationally recognized rules and procedures under the WTO and other international conventions that govern global trade and investment relations) requires far-reaching reforms of the Vietnamese legal and judicial framework to provide for transparency, dispute settlement, intellectual property protection, market access for services, etc. The principal incentive for Vietnam to implement this reform package was being granted Most Favoured Nation (MFN) status, and thereby get to benefit from reduced U.S. tariffs on its exports (on average a reduction from around 40 per cent to 3-4 per cent).

While presenting a strong reform incentive, membership of such bodies and the ensuing need to provide for the highest standards or "best practices" of rule of law and human rights also puts great burdens on already stretched national administrations.[66] In Vietnam and Laos, membership of the Association of Southeast Asian Nations (ASEAN), and the resulting explicit and implicit obligation to adhere to its common goals and principles, have necessitated the allocation of much resources to the ASEAN desks of the ministries concerned, often at the expense of other important tasks. The process of accommodation has also been ideologically painful: these nominally socialist states have needed to embrace ASEAN political principles that until very recently symbolized virtually everything they considered despicable and dangerous.[67] On a more mundane level, issues such as language and negotiation skills have posed great difficulties. It is estimated that there are over 200 ASEAN officials and ministerial meetings annually, in which the working language is English. Thousands of Vietnamese civil servants therefore need to take advanced training programs in law, English, ASEAN diplomatic relations, and economic terminology.

International and regional organisations that understand the risks of setting up too ambitious or internally conflicting reform agenda often offer technical assistance and other forms of support to make the harmonisation of rules and other accession

---

66 Footer 2003 pp. 109 and 113.

67 ASEAN came into being with the signing of the Bangkok Declaration in August 1967, primarily then as an anticommunist containment pact. Since then, the organization has developed into the world's fourth largest trading group, ranking behind the United States, the European Union, and Japan. At their Singapore Summit of 27-28 January 1992, the ASEAN leaders had adopted a legal framework to promote economic co-operation in the region. The system is visualised in three documents. The Singapore Declaration summarises agreements in a variety of fields, *i.a.* communications and education, and outlines a broad-based programme for economic integration that is adaptable enough to encompass the needs of the ASEAN nations on different development levels. The Framework Agreement on Enhancing ASEAN Economic Cooperation establishes the ASEAN Free Trade Area (AFTA), which is implemented primarily through the provisions of the third document, the Agreement on the Common Effective Preferential Tariff Scheme. Le Thu Son 1996; Neilson 1998.

requirement easier to accomplish and otherwise lighten the burden on the national administrations and judiciaries. Since long, there are such support modalities to facilitate entry into the WTO, but ambitious programs have also been developed for helping with accession to the European Union, the Council of Europe, and various other bodies and treaties.

2.5 SOVEREIGN STATES AND THE FORCES OF GLOBALIZATION

Whether obligated by international law or not, nation-states are pressured to undertake technical adjustments of laws and practices to catch up and compete in a globalized world. While most assistance providers embrace theories of "legal convergence" and happily offer to assist in the internationalization of law, "cultural-essentialist" critics in the developed and developing world argue that laws will always be inseparable from the greater geographic, political and cultural context and that the "Western" pursuit of reforms in this sphere is a function of a desire for global hegemony through the universalisation of Western values. This criticism is particularly loud and common with regard to improvements in the human rights situation. In the "Asian values" polemic, a group of East Asian authoritative regimes (comprising *i.a.* the disparate group of Singapore, China, Vietnam, Malaysia, and Indonesia) argued that "Western" and "Asian" notions of culture and social organisation are simply incompatible, and that the former seeks to destroy or at least disorient the latter.[68]

The critics of ideas of global concepts of law and human rights are also quick to underline the limited participation and say of developing states in the fora where important policy decisions are made (for example in the various WTO rounds), and that as a consequence thereof, the development agenda comprises many issues that not long ago would have been considered beyond the reach of any international financial institution or donor agency. For example, while "policy-based lending" was originally confined to providing the conditions for economic growth by isolating a set of narrowly defined economic issues from the wider zone of "corrupting" politics, the "Post-Washington Consensus" has brought with it a full-fledged "good governance" agenda that places a much wider range of new legal and institutional issues within the donors' reach.[69]

---

68 As this debate has contained an element of confrontation with important political allies and trading partners, the arguments have almost always been presented in universal and abstract terms. Ghai 1994 p. 5.

69 Footer 2003 pp. 109, 112-113; Rittich 2004 p. 18.

Paradoxically, in defending what they say is uniquely theirs, authoritarian regimes often rely on a traditional and distinctively "Western" sovereignty doctrine, essentially suggesting that issues of law and human rights in the broad sense is exclusively a concern of the nation state and no concern of others. Little have they taken notice or accepted that the doctrine of sovereignty is subjected to constant reinterpretation and that the concept has always been carefully tied to, and qualified by, corresponding limits on state power. The sovereignty principle is associated with dependence on a wider legitimating universal or international political culture, and the local law is much more "isomorphic" and dependent on outside factors than hard-line sovereignty advocates may suggest. Elizabeth Heger Boyle and John Meyer point out that states and governments maintain their domestic and international legitimacy through responsiveness to the interests of influential groups of citizens (notable among them the legal profession) and through compliance with universal principles of law and politics.[70] Heinz Klug provides examples from South Africa, where the drafters of the post-apartheid constitution abandoned many of the core principles of the ANC political rhetoric of the liberation struggle (for example with regard to property) in favour of concepts of law and justice that that could be legitimized with references to internationally accepted principles of law and justice.[71]

Another frequently encountered cultural-essentialist argument is that the relative (or evolutionist) nature of rights should make it impossible to insist on an absolute or literal definition and interpretation of any rights doctrine. Challenged by international interlocutors on the issue of lack of respect or commitment to human rights, authoritarian regimes may consequently assert that the existence, prioritisation and implementation of a specific right must always determined by the political, economic and cultural conditions of the day. They may accordingly consider civil and political rights neither meaningful nor feasible in conditions of poverty. The right to free speech, for example, could therefore be sacrificed for the more pressing need to provide food and shelter. Similar considerations explain the strong support from many development countries for the 1986 Declaration on the Right to Development, which ties the realisation of human rights in developing countries to international economic aid.

Although much of the initial enthusiasm for "the right to development" seems to have disappeared, the ill-defined and controversial Declaration continues to give rise to confusion and consternation in the North-South dialogue, and particularly among the organisations supposed to transform the rhetoric into reality. The prevailing view seems to be that the "right of development" as articulated in the Declaration does not

---

70 Heger Boyle & Meyer 2002 pp. 71-76.
71 Klug 2002 pp. 281-295.

have the quality of other human rights (which typically inhere in individuals or groups and are possible to enforce against the state), but rather should be understood as a statement of an aspiration. Yash Ghai critically points out that while there are sections of the Declaration that may be used to advance the more traditional cause of human rights, the gist of it actually seeks to establish a reason for the failure to realise human rights in certain political systems, and that the Declaration accepts some serious encroachments on the principle and practice of self-determination while simultaneously affirming the problematic assertion that the primary responsibility for human rights is vested in states as part of their sovereignty. In other words, the essence of the construction is that the rich countries must provide economic assistance to the poor countries, but must not question their human rights situation.[72]

While the relativist opponents of the universalist argument have most often taken the Western discourse as a point of departure, and thus implicitly accepted large segments of it, some regimes in East Asia have gone as far as to suggest that the cultural matrix within which relations between individuals and the state are embedded in their countries are so fundamentally different (placing society over self, emphasising traditional family values, etc.) that any point of departure in Western concepts is pointless and misleading. However, these regimes have not spent much effort on empirically substantiating the existence of this alternative matrix, or on explaining why a *status quo* should be accepted. Human rights advocates also find the issue of representation problematic: Those who claim to speak for "the people" when arguing against "Western" concepts of human rights and in favour of "Asian" alternatives frequently lack a democratic mandate to do so. More often than not, they rather represent a privileged elite, geographically and materially remote from the people, and chiefly concerned with remaining in power.

Just like progressive groups can be empowered by overseas support, reactionary, religious and nationalist groups preying on the fear for the new and unknown may find a *raison d'etre* in resisting such support.[73] Assistance providers must be aware of the extent to which domestic political competition affects the conditions for receiving and rejecting foreign and international concepts of law. Dezalay and Garth suggest that the process can be characterised as a palace war in which various state and non-state actors fight for power and influence by pursuing international strategies. In this sense, international strategies should be understood as domestic strategies first.[74]

72 Ghai 1994 pp. 5-6.

73 Heydebrand 2001 p. 122. Harding (2001 p. 202) thinks that the "globalisation-law" debate has resulted in a renewed emphasis on culture and society as guides to the analysis and understanding of law, and points to another paradox: The Asian cliché "new state: old society" has given way to "old state: new society", and that law as envisaged by commercial actors, civil society, and ordinary people, now grates against the official law.

74 Dezalay and Garth 2001 pp. 249-250.

2.6 TRANSPLANTING, BORROWING AND DIFFUSING FOREIGN CONCEPTS

The "aid factor" strongly influences how constrained local leaderships seek to explain and justify their policies on law and justice, both internally towards its own population and externality *vis-à-vis* the donor community. The officially presented rhetoric may even be constructed with the explicit purpose of maximising the amounts of aid by providing assistance providers with exactly the kind of justifications they want to hear.[75] At the same time, there is much evidence to suggest that "transplanted", "received" or "borrowed" laws only coincidentally induce the same behaviour in a new environment, because inevitably people and institutions choose how to behave not only in response to the law, but also to a surround of other social, economic, physical and subjective factors arising from history, custom, geography, technology, etc.[76]

In this sense, current international attempts at supporting justice sector reforms could stand to face the same fate as the Law and Development Movement of the 1950s 1960s.[77] This movement, which was inspired and led by a relatively small group of Western (essentially US) lawyers working in development agencies, foundations and universities, sought to create interest in law and legal reforms as a development tool. A popular idea was that the legal cultures of the developing world were predominantly "formalistic", meaning that rules were developed, interpreted and applied without careful attention to policy goals. The reasons for this formalism, in turn, were believed to be that formalist law teachers taught law as an abstract system to be applied without concern for policy relevance or impact, that formalist legislatures copied foreign models or followed abstract principles instead of shaping rules for instrumental ends, and that formalist judges applied rules in a rigid and mechanical fashion rather than accepted that adjudication inevitably contains an element of discretion and must be related to policy goals. David Trubek writes that "*[i]f formalism was the source of bad laws, weak enforcement, and ineffective or counterproductive lawyering, then the most important thing to do was to create a new, more instrumental legal culture.*"[78] The ensuing projects thus typically focused on removing what was perceived to be "lags"

75 For a general discussion, see Seidman and Seidman 1994 pp. 57-59.

76 The doctrine on this issue is vast. Corne (1997); Gillespie (1996); Greenberg (1980); Potter (1994); Waelde & Gunderson (1994); and Watson (1974) provide numerous examples from Brazil, Chile, China, the republics of the former Soviet Union; Ethiopia, Mexico, New Zealand, Scotland, Turkey and other countries.

77 The definition of the field of "Law and Development" has always been relatively flexible and not rigidly limited by any particular accepted theory. It has often been referred to as the specialised area of academic study concerned with the relationship between the legal systems and various aspects of "development", *i.e.* social, economic and political changes taking place in developing countries. For an overview of the debate, *see* Tamanaha 1995 and Trubek 2003.

78 Trubek 2003 p. 4.

or "barriers" to development by means of drafting and transplanting new "instrumental" laws, reorganising legal and judicial agencies, and reforming legal education.

Many of these initial attempts to link law with aspects of economic development were directly or indirectly inspired by the works by Max Weber, notably "*Economy and Society*", where Weber attempts to identify and explain systematically the role of the modern legal system in the emergence of Western capitalism. Weber's analysis goes beyond the observation that far-reaching legal reforms were undertaken simultaneously with the political and economic transformations that led to the emergence of the industrialised system and the nation-state, and suggests that these changes were mutually causative. The essence of Weber's argument is that the more "rational" a legal system is, the more conducive it is to the emergence of a capitalist and industrialised system. A rational system is here understood to be characterised by consciously (instrumentally) devised laws, autonomous and consistent application of the law, etc. Its opposites, the religious and charismatic systems, will not be conducive to such transitions because the norms are here typically derived from sources that are sacred or "politically correct", and thus immutable.[79]

It should come as no surprise that most of the pioneering efforts of the Law and Development Movement failed to create anything near the results envisaged. Instead there were countless examples of projects that never worked or even made problems worse.[80] This apparent failure led to much criticism of the theoretical foundations of the Movement as well as the way specific projects had been implemented. Particular criticism was levied against the assumption that it would be possible to meaningfully transplant legal concepts from one environment to another despite profound differences in the "context", *i.e.* in history, politics, economy, and "culture".[81] A notion of a "Law of Non-Transferability of Law" emerged, essentially suggesting that copying models from other countries would never lead to the envisaged results unless exactly the same patterns of individual and institutional behaviour that characterised the model country were simultaneously induced.[82]

Changes in the *Zeitgeist* also contributed to the Movement's fall from fame. The Law and Development Movement had originally been conceived in a time (the early 1960s)

---

79 On Weber's role for the Law and Development debate, see Trubek 1972 pp. 11-16 and Dalberg-Larsen 1984 pp. 60-65.

80 See Carty 1992 p. xiii; Franck 1972 pp. 788-789; and Greenberg 1980 pp. 130-133.

81 David Trubek and Marc Galanter, once among the promoters of the Law and Development movement, published in 1974 the article "Scholars in Self-Estrangement" which drew attention to some of the serious flaws of the enterprise.

82 See Seidman and Seidman 1994 pp. 44–47.

when liberal notions of internationalism were cherished,[83] but when the first experiences were made public and debated, the development paradigm had dramatically changed to reflect a new set of political ideas inspired by socialism. Many critics thus focused on what they perceived to be problematic features of the political economy dimension of the Law and Development Movement and applied to the Movement the ideas of structuralism and dependency theory. The core of this critique was that it was wrong and misleading to focus on the structures (political, legal and economic) of developing states in isolation. The subject of study should rather be the unfair power relationship between the industrialised and exploitative "North" and the impoverished and exploited "South". Inherent in this critique was also that Law and Development projects represented a new and disguised form of imperialism.

The hasty start and refutation of the Law and Development Movement left behind a knowledge lacuna. Nobody knew with certainty why these early efforts had failed: because of political ambivalence, differences in culture, technical difficulties, or because certain other crucial factors had been misinterpreted or overlooked ? It did not take long before some scholars of legal sociology, comparative law and political science began to examine the underpinnings of the Movement and seek more refined theories to explain the relationship between law and development.[84] Such theories, it was hoped, would both explain and justify the optimistic early projects and chart the way for future more informed efforts. However, instead of providing a justification for what had been done and map a way ahead, the re-examination once again underlined the serious flaws in the original approach (particularly the crude notion that local or traditional structures always hinder development and that "Western" legal paraphernalia automatically speed up development), and did not offer any robust alternatives to orient future action.

Should then current efforts at promoting legal and judicial reforms in transition and developing countries be regarded as a mere continuation of the Law and Development Movement or as something new and different? It has already been mentioned (Chapter 1) that the current emphasis on the rule of law is essentially a reaction to a set of new political imperatives, prominent among them poverty eradication, post-socialist transition, and reconstruction of failed states. Another difference is that the projects are now much bigger, more ambitious in their goals, and comprehensive than was the case in the Law and Development era. Further, the assumption is no longer that the

---

83 The Law and Development Movement emerged in a period in which international economic policy and the Bretton Woods institutions were supportive of state-led initiatives in partially closed economies, often described as the era of "embedded liberalism". In this sense, embedded liberalism was an international regime that operated to facilitate domestic politics of a certain kind. The ideal condition of this regime was a balance between openness, democracy and economic fairness.

84 See Trubek 2003 p. 2.

mechanisms of legal change are led or controlled solely by states or actors "internal" to the formal legal system such as lawmakers, government lawyers and others. Rather, donors recognize that pressures for legal change come also from actors above, besides and under states such as international organisations, NGOs, professions, and other epistemic communities.[85]

At the same time, the ways by which the assistance providers seek to implement their policies are essentially the same (study tours, help in drafting legal instruments, topical training, etc.). The current donor view on the conditions for transplanting, diffusing or borrowing of legal and judicial also remains optimistic and is in many ways similar to Alan Watson's argument (1974, 1977, 1985a, 1985b, 1991) that the way law grows can in great part can be explained by the transplantation of legal rules between legal systems, or by the elaboration of existing ideas within systems as to apply them by analogy to new circumstances. It flows from this notion that "mirror theories" of law and social change (that law always reflects the political, economic or social needs of society in a consistent way) remain incompatible with development policy. In fact, for a development agency to accept such theories and simultaneously try to induce change by means of transplantation would be impossible almost by definition. Yet another parallel is to be found in the analysis of which "local" factors that may make the introduction of new laws and institutions difficult. The discussion once again focuses on what is described as irrational aspects of local "culture" or "legal culture", although there is somewhat greater awareness among assistance providers and commentators that the concept of culture is difficult to define and should not be understood as altogether disabling.[86]

Besides culture, it is difficult to say what other factors that present-day assistance providers consider most influential in determining the prospects of success and failure. One issue is of course how success and failure should be defined. It can be noted that policy and project documents rarely provide normative descriptions against which the degree of success of a specific initiative can be determined.[87] Most such documents similarly avoid using tainted terms like "transplanting", and consequently leave little guidance as to whether the new rules or institutions are expected to achieve essentially the same results in their society of adoption as in their society of origin. In this sense,

85 Cotterrell 2001 pp. 86-87; Slaughter 2002 pp. 18-19.

86 Lindsey (2002 pp. 1-2 and 5-6) argues that in the world of international legal cooperation, "culture" is still a kind of grab-bag of everything the assistance providers do not know or are unable to find out about the host country or subject matter, *inter alia* local ideas and theories about law, the practical operation of the local legal system and political issues impinging on it. Lindsay points out that such definitions risk making the concept protean, evasive and virtually impossible to meaningfully grasp and use.

87 Nelken 2001 pp. 38 and 46.

assistance providers seem to embrace the idea that a legal rule never is, rather always becomes, and may thus well develop in ways that do not parallel developments in its original society.[88] This does not mean that international organisations and donor agencies confine their ambitions to introduce "laws of the books". Rather, the emphasis on "impact assessment" shows that there is a strong expectation that certain real-world results will come about as result of the assistance provided. Assistance providers also spend much effort on justifying cases of deviance from the expected in terms that resonate well with the ulterior political rationale of the intervention.

The orientation of the support says something about where the assistance providers consider the prospects for success in transplanting, exporting or otherwise diffusing laws and institutions the greatest, and on what factors they base their considerations. It appears that initially, older comparative law doctrines on differences with regard to the prospects of successful reception and implementation between different substantive areas of law, exerted considerable influence on donor policy. These doctrines often suggested that among the least likely to travel well should be family law, land law and other strongly religiously or historically anchored or otherwise "affective" areas of law. More likely to travel well would be the areas of law that are more loosely connected with the past and "instrumental", such as the law of commerce.[89] Current donor practice, just like modern comparative law, provide a more mixed picture. While ideas that instrumental areas of law are easier to address linger, an increasing number of projects aim at reforming some rather affective aspect of society, for example gender inequalities, and seek to do so by changing traditional or religious norms.

With regard to the prospects of combining elements of different legal families or cultures in the same system, notably common law and civil law concepts, assistance providers host a notion that this need not be as problematic as often assumed. Rather, there is a pragmatic view that the real issue is substance rather than form, and awareness of the dangers of succumbing to the kind of conservatism and parochial

---

88 Mattei 1997 p. 14.

89 See for example Levy 1950 p. 244. Cotterrell (2001 p. 82) argues that that the prospects of success or failure are related to which form of law or "community" that the specific transplanted or borrowed concept has a bearing on. He derives from Max Weber's four pure types of social action (traditional, affective, purpose rational and value rational) four types of pure communities (instrumental, traditional, community of beliefs, and affective community) and argues that while the prospects of successfully introducing foreign or international concepts are often good with regard to matters that address instrumental communities, the prospects are much slimmer with regard to affective ditto. Other researchers have made different observations. For example, Andrew Harding (2001 p. 213) notes with regard to the retention and survival of transplanted laws in Southeast Asia (essentially laws imposed by colonial administrations) that "the more public law is, the more it has diverged from Western law; but the more private or commercial law is, the less it has diverged."

interests that divert attention from core reform objectives.[90] This optimistic notion resonates well with modern comparative law theories suggesting that there are more similarities than differences between countries at the "deep structure of law" (types of arguments, patterns of justification, etc.) and that these similarities, in turn, work to produce laws and decisions at the surface level of similar content.[91] Donors and hosts are similarly aware of the global trend, also comprising developed and advanced jurisdictions (Quebec, Louisiana, South Africa, and the small systems of the Seychelles and Vanuatu, etc.) of borrowing and successfully combining elements of both traditions. When problem have actually occurred in combining civil law and common law concepts in reform projects, they have often been attributable to simple misunderstandings, language errors, ignorant or insensitive experts, etc., rather than some kind of structural incompatibility.[92]

90 Fogelklou 2000 p. 103; Rose 1998 p. 105; and Waelde & Gunderson 1994 pp. 372–373.

91 Touri 1997. Fogelklou (2000 pp. 119-120) points out that the exception seems to be situations where there is a vacuum in the deep structure, leading to pathological cases where there is abuse of power, hidden behind the syllogism of legal application.

92 Bogdan 1997 p. 78.

3. TYPICAL PROBLEMS AND REMEDIES

3.1 STYLISED PROBLEMS AND REMEDIES

To facilitate a structured discussion in the following chapters (4-6) on typical problems and remedies, this chapter provides a very schematic overview of some common problem situations and suggests how the international community typically responds to each of them. The broad problem categories used are *Authoritarian Rule and Democratisation*; *Poverty and Development*; *Socialism and Transition*, and *State Failure and State Building*.[93]

3.2 AUTHORITARIAN RULE AND DEMOCRATISATION

In systems of dictatorship and other forms of authoritative government, the law and the justice sector typically reflect the political imperative of maintaining effective control of society and suppressing any potential opposition. Another characteristic feature is that the police and security apparatus is politically stronger than the judiciary. The political strategy to control and incapacitate the judiciary seems often to have equally serious effects on civil society, particularly organisations concerned with justice and human rights-related issues. Free media and academia are generally being similarly targeted, which renders the remaining space for independent analysis and debate very limited. Ugo Mattei describes such systems as characterised by the "rule of political law".[94] Many countries qualify for membership of this group, for example Zimbabwe and Myanmar.[95]

---

93 Many of the concepts from "development language" applied here are inherently vague and value-charged, *e.g.* development, transition and state building, and others can be criticised for being ethnocentric, *e.g.* good governance, but they are used for want of better terms.

94 Mattei 1997 p. 31.

95 In Zimbabwe, Robert Mugabe's ZANU-PF has been able to continue to rule the country without a popular mandate to do so because of a political strategy to incapacitate and control balancing and potentially oppositional forces in society, including the judicial branch of the state. The Constitutional amendments of 1987 created the position of the Executive President and vested with President Mugabe near absolute powers in critical political and constitutional processes, including a right to dissolve the Parliament without having to justify his decision. As of recent, the Supreme Court has been expanded and "packed" with judges loyal to Mugabe. On the structural plane, Mugabe has promoted a series of new Presidential decrees and hastily written legislative amendments

Assistance providers are increasingly restrictive in providing support to state bodies in such countries, much because such support risks legitimising and otherwise making these regimes stronger. Assistance providers instead seek to support the building of opinion for political change and nourish reformers for the future. In order to be effective in this work, a concerted regional and international political strategy is often needed, comprising combinations of critical political and human rights dialogue, and support to agents of change outside the realms of the state such as human rights-oriented NGOs, professional groups and associations, etc. (Chapter 4.4). Donors may also engage with such groups and other progressive constituencies in planning for the orderly introduction of something better once the regime has come to an end. Recent history (South Africa, Namibia, Argentina, etc.) has demonstrated that after long periods of authoritarian rule, there are enormous expectations on far-reaching constitutional, legal and judicial reforms. At the same time, the capacity of the new regime to formulate and implement any policy is likely to be limited. The provision of such support is discussed in Chapters 4.5-4.8.

3.3 POVERTY AND DEVELOPMENT

In the disparate group of "developing countries" (some of which may also display the characteristic features of authoritarian rule) the general scarcity of human and material resources constrains the state in formulating sensible laws, as well as the administration and judiciary in transforming them into reality. The lawmakers may be poorly educated and trained, the judiciary underpaid and lacking motivation, the physical infrastructure inadequate, the management tools and support functions underdeveloped, etc.

Another problem in the formulation of sensible policies and laws in the developing world is historical discontinuity and disorientation. Many developing countries were colonized at some point in history, and consequently experienced hasty imposition of "Western" or colonial legal and judicial concepts lacking the necessary political and social foundations. After achieving independence, many countries experienced an equally abrupt introduction of "revolutionary" laws and institutions. Angola, Uganda, Zambia and Cambodia all display these characteristic features. A variety of contemporary social and cultural factors may further undercut the potency of law a reform tool, for example strong emphasis on family, ethnicity, religion, etc. Widespread corruption is yet another factor reducing the relevance of law and making reforms difficult. That many influential people enjoy substantial income from the system in the form of fees

---

overhauling a range of security, access to information, media, and electoral laws under a "Fast Track" procedure.

and bribes explains why there is often lack of domestic incentive to deal seriously with the problem.

In the group of development countries impressed with various forms of socialism and communism, the aforementioned problems of colonialism, poverty and corruption are intertwined with the specific problems of transition to create an almost overwhelmingly complex situation.[96] Particularly great are the difficulties where a nostalgic and reactionary leadership still regards human rights and the rule of law as fictions veiling the true class character of the law and suspects the development community of being hostile agents in disguise. Sometimes the principles of socialism and communism are also being reinterpreted in the light "traditional" or "national" values (*i.e.* elements of authoritarian Confucianism), resulting in a politically convenient amalgam of Soviet-inspired socialism and allegedly domestic yet authoritarian concepts of law and social organisation. For example, political preferences may be considered under the pretext of group solidarity or some other culturally sanctioned paradigm in mediation and judicial procedures.[97]

The most common international strategies for addressing legal and institutional problems in this category of countries are discussed in Chapters 4.1-4.8, comprising a range of technical assistance tools and sector support.

3.4 POST-COMMUNIST TRANSITION

Virtually all the formerly "socialist" states of Central and Eastern Europe, including Russia and many of its former "client states" in the developing world, are engaged in a fundamental transition from various forms of Party rule and command economy to systems based on democratic principles and market economy. This transition of the political and economic universe drastically impacts on the legal and judicial landscape, both as regards the content of the law and the ways the law is administered.

While the claim regarding law under the Marxist-Leninist ideology was that the societal *Grundnorm*, *i.e.* the class struggle, should impregnate the substance of legal instruments and assign to legal agents certain political responsibilities,[98] the new norm as manifested in the current constitutions is essentially some definition of "the rule of law" or rather the continental-European concept of the *Rechtsstaat*.

---

96 See generally Costea 1990.

97 Corne 1997 pp. 25-28.

98 Costea 1990 p. 276.

Despite some common features, the processes of legal transition follow different paths and render different results in these states depending on their unique political, cultural and economic features. For example, the conditions for retaining or reviving elements of a previous order, and thus maintaining a degree of legal continuity, have been much better in those countries where there is a preceding history of democratic government and rule of law (*e. g.* Poland and Estonia), than in those countries that were autocratic even before the introduction of communism (*e. g.* Russia and Kyrgyzstan).

While many formerly socialist countries have been relatively successful in quickly creating a new legal framework for various aspects of political and economic life, the transformation of the law into reality has been more difficult and time-consuming. There are political as well as legal-technical reasons. Karlo Tuori's model for the analysis of national legal orders, consisting of three "levels of law", is helpful in explaining some of the philosophical difficulties: The "surface level" of law consists of individual statutes, court decisions and similar material. The "mid-level" consists of general principles, patterns of legal reasoning, etc., as applied by various categories of legal professionals. The "deep structure" of law, finally, is a kind of *a priori* or *episteme* for each epoch in history and changes very slowly. While changes at the surface level of law (adoption of new laws, etc.) can be undertaken relatively quickly, the resulting changes at the deeper levels are likely to be slow and incremental. The fundamental principles and patterns of thought of the deeper levels also have latent and profound influence on policy formulation and decision making at the higher levels.[99]

Some problems in implementing the new laws may also be explained by vested interests in the *status quo*. Many influential people still have an interest in maintaining a refined version of the *nomenklatura* system that allows them to control the bastions of power and wealth. While it is wrong to blame the reform process *per se* for the growth of corruption and rent-seeking, there are cases where the liberalisation of the economy has provided additional incentive to resist further reforms as these groups now control access to benefits of much greater value.

The international response strategies are discussed in Chapter 4.5–4.7, typically comprising various structural, institutional, access creation, and anti-corruption initiatives. There may also be specific support modalities to help these countries become members of various international and regional organisations with human rights and the rule of law on the agenda (Chapters 2.1 and 2.4).

---

99 Tuori 1997 pp. 432-442. For an application of Tuori's model on East European countries, especially the Russian Federation, see Fogelklou 2000 pp. 98-99.

3.5 STATE FAILURE AND STATE BUILDING

The world has witnessed a number of states and territories slipping into chaos or collapsing as a result of war, perpetuated rebellions, gross violations of human rights, and other eruptions of systematic violence. Among recent examples can be mentioned Cambodia, Somalia, Bosnia and Herzegovina, Kosovo, East Timor and Afghanistan. There are indications that the institutions of law and justice are often systematically targeted for, and particularly vulnerable to, destruction in such situations. Court buildings may be burned down, judges and prosecutors killed or forced to flee, etc. There may alternatively be attempts by rivalling groups to turn law and justice into tools of repression under their control. Other interest groups, comprising disparate elements such as crime syndicates, religious fundamentalists, and terror groups, may also benefit from paralysed or manipulated legal and judicial system.

Having noted the threat to peace, security and human rights that such conditions pose, the international community has deemed it to be an international concern to re-establish basic conditions of law and order in these countries and territories. The typical response strategies are discussed in Chapter 5, comprising the related by often separately constructed efforts at retributive and reconstructive justice as parts of "transitional justice".[100] The prime mover in the reconstructive effort is often a UN mission ("International Territorial Administration") mandated by the Security Council under Chapter VII of the UN Charter to "take any measures necessary" to attain the goals of the respective empowering instrument. Parallel to the work of the International Territorial Administrations, a number of bilateral agencies and civil society actors promote legal and judicial reform projects in these countries and territories with a range of conventional technical assistance tools.

[100] Bassiouni 2002 p. XV; Kritz 2002 pp. 84-85.

4. TECHNICAL ASSISTANCE APPROACHES

4.1 INTRODUCTION

The spectrum of possible international responses to problems in the legal and judicial systems of host countries is enormous, ranging from ambitious sector reform programs at one extreme to small-scale civil society initiatives at the other. There is no pretence in this chapter to discuss them all. The ambition is rather to describe a small selection of "typical" or "representative" technical assistance initiatives, as they have visualised in the real-world of development co-operation.

The chapter begins with a discussion on the policy-related issues of sequencing, speed, and initial assessment. The ensuing presentation of specific reform initiatives is structured into sub-chapters dealing with political opinion, legal reform, institution building, and access creation, respectively. It should be stressed from the outset that it is impossible to say that a specific problem situation is, or should always bc, addressed in a specific way. Rather, country-specific and unique problems call for contextual and carefully tailored solutions. Neither is it certain that that the response strategies actually pursued are exclusively or even primarily determined by the real-world problems at hand. Rather, subjective and agency-internal factors such as internal policies and directives, management preferences, habits, etc. exert considerable influence over what assistance providers do and how they justify their decisions.

4.2 SPEED AND SEQUENCE

One of the most frequently debated aspects of legal and judicial reform processes in developing and transition countries is the appropriate speed and sequencing of various reform initiatives, and consequently when and in which form international organisations and development agencies should offer their assistance. The uniqueness of conditions, the interdependence of law and other political and social factors, and the latent interplay between choice and circumstance, are just some of the factors conditioning such decisions and strategies.[101]

---

101 For a general discussion, see Gray C. W. 1997 p. 15; Seidman and Seidman 1994 pp. 42-43.

In practice, legal and judicial reform sequences have often looked something like the figure below.[102]

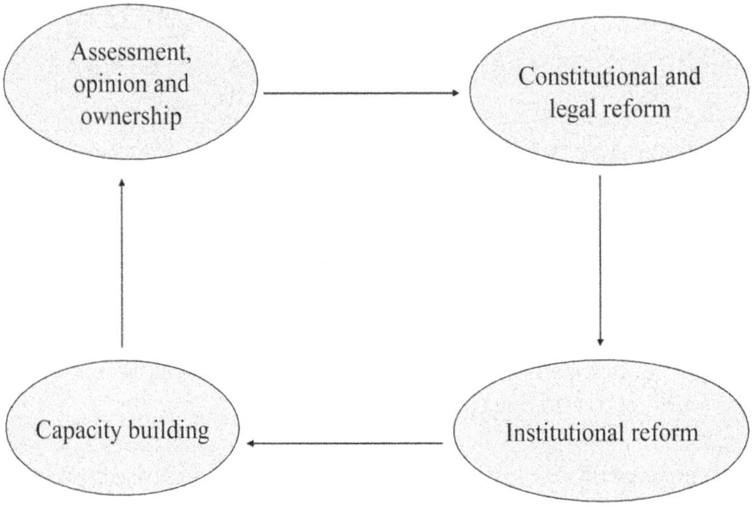

According to this stylised and simplified model, a support initiative begins with ensuring that there is sufficient political support for embarking on a reform policy (or launching a specific project) among key local stakeholders. Ideally, this stage also comprises assessing that the problems discussed really exist and that the proposed remedies will actually help to solve them. The next step is to promote and facilitate legal and constitutional reforms. This phase is followed by efforts to help the legal and judicial institutions (police, prosecution, courts) effectively transform the language of the law into reality. The final phase consists of ensuring that the users of the system (whether businessmen, the general public, certain vulnerable groups, etc.) are aware of the reforms and have easy access to the judicial system. From a donor perspective, this means that if the leadership of a recipient country is judged to be insufficiently committed to the greater goals of legal and judicial reform (rule of law, human rights, etc. as outlined in Chapters 2.2.–2.4.), or to the goals and modalities of a specific support initiative, then the appropriate policy would be to either refrain from providing support or to direct the support to building such commitment.

This model has sustained increasing criticism in recent years, not least on grounds that it seems to be constructed for an archetypical post-communism transition context, rather than the inherently more complex setting in which most current efforts at

102 See *e.g.* Blair and Hansen 1994 pp. 10-15; Legal and Judicial Reform: Strategic Directions 2003 pp. 55-57.

supporting legal and judicial reforms in developing countries are undertaken. Critics have also pointed out that it reflects a false sense of urgency and crisis, while there is rarely a legal vacuum or completely dysfunctional institutions. There are indications that the rigor of the model is breaking up. Although many projects still rests on the assumption that the black letter law is some sort of conceptual and practical *a priori* that needs to be in place before other reforms can be undertaken, legislative drafting assistance no longer occupies quite the prominent position it used to have, and many projects are conceived to focus primarily or exclusively on reforming institutions, building capacity, or creating access.

The degree of domestic progress in reforming the system is yet another factor influencing what assistance is sought and provided. With regard to post-socialist transitions, Anders Fogelklou suggests that it is possible to discern four general stages or phases, namely liberalisation, activisation, consolidation and implementation.[103] During the liberalisation phase in Central and Eastern Europe, which roughly covered the years of 1989-1991, the main issue at hand was the abolishing of the main structural obstacles to political and economic reform and liberalisation. In the activisation phase, which roughly covered the period 1991 to 1996, the main task was to create a large number of new legal and constitutional instruments. In the consolidation phase, beginning in the mid 1990s and still not completed, domestic lawmakers and foreign advisors have worked on making the new laws more coherent and consistent, for example by enacting comprehensive codes covering various subject areas. Closer co-operation and eventually membership of international and regional organisations (European Union, Council of Europe, etc.) have also been typical traits of this phase. The implementation phase, finally, may be described as latent but most pronounced and resource-demanding in the later stages of the reform process.[104]

The World Bank's Legal and Judicial Reform Project in Cambodia, launched in 2001, is an example of a project displaying many characteristic elements of the conventional legal and judicial reform model. It merits discussion also because it was probably the first to include all steps of the reform sequence within the framework of one single project. Yet another interesting aspect of the project is that it was designed not only to address domestic needs, but also to remedy some apparent problems at the side of the donor community, notably lack of coordination between the assistance providers and a common oversight function. One may add that the Bank's role of supreme donor co-ordinator was largely self-assumed.[105]

---

103 Fogelklou 2000 p. 97

104 Id. pp. 97-98.

105 At the project website, the Bank writes: "*The Bank's deep involvement in the social and economic development of Cambodia, coupled with the wealth of experience that it has acquired in legal and judicial reform matters, makes it uniquely suited to contribute to legal and judicial reform in Cambodia. Both*

Before the project was launched, the Government of Cambodia appointed a team of consultants to undertake a comprehensive diagnostic study of the legal and judicial framework and to recommend what reform priorities that should be included in the project. The findings of this study were presented, discussed and confirmed in a workshop in april 2000. After the workshop, a draft legislative reform program was prepared, which set out the elements of a proposed legislative reform agenda and gave details of the purpose and objectives of each proposed piece of legislation. A steering committee, made up of representatives from the executive, judicial and legislative branches, as well as the civil society and the fledgling bar association, was also established to review further the recommendations of the consultants and to develop a legal and judicial reform strategy. The draft strategy paper was widely disseminated and subsequently discussed with what was considered to be the most important stakeholders, among them donors, public officials, and civil society representatives. The final version provided a comprehensive strategy for developing a comprehensive program of legal and judicial training, strengthening the judiciary, improving the lawmaking process and establishing a legislative reform program.

The ensuing project came to focus on what was perceived to be the most important underpinnings of a legal and judicial system based upon the rule of law. Among the six components of the project, component 1, "Legislative Reform and Institutional Strengthening", essentially aimed to support the executive branch to improve the quality, efficiency, consistency, transparency and effectiveness of the laws and regulations, and to streamline the lawmaking process. It consisted of three principal activities: (a) development of a legislative reform program of priority legislation essential to the creation of a credible legal and judicial framework; (b) establishment of a mechanism to coordinate legislative reform process across principal government units and institutions charged with responsibility for legislative reform; (c) development of the capacity of agencies and institutions responsible for legislative reform to consider, initiate, review and adopt legislation.

Component 2, "Judicial Strengthening", offered a program of support to help develop the institutional capacity of the system. This component focused on (a) creating a legal framework governing appointments and promotions and exercise of discipline in the judiciary; (b) providing a legal framework governing court organization and administration of justice; (c) laying down terms and conditions of employment of judges; (d) improving the work environment; and (e) providing for alternative dispute resolution mechanisms.

---

in the development of the legal and judicial reform agenda, and in the context of the preparation of the strategy paper, the Bank continues, as it has done in the past, to take a lead role, maintaining close donor coordination and promoting the SWAP or partnership approach as developed in the CAS."

Component 3, "Legal Training", sought to establish training programs and to support exchange and co-operation programs with partner institutions. The goal of component 4, "Legal Information and Public Access" was to improve the quality of and access to legal information for government officials, judges, legal education institutions, legal scholars, practicing attorneys, businessmen and society as a whole. Component 5, "Law and Justice Facilitation Fund", was created to ensure private sector participation in the legal and judicial reform process through the establishment of a facilitation fund with the means to provide resources on a matching grant basis for the realisation of private initiatives consistent with the greater project objectives. Component 6, "Project Management and Implementation", was designed to provide technical advisory services, equipment, and training to the project management. The total budget for this 5-years project amounted to USD 5.5 million.

There are some equally generalising models or schools for illustrating the issue of speed. Often these schools are thought to differ with respect to the total number of disadvantages they generate. Vastly simplified, a "gradualist" school advocates a policy of gradual or "phased" legal and constitutional reform through slow deregulation and regulation, while a "radical" school argues in favour of a very fast all-out reform, "shock therapy" or "big bang." It is argued that rapid and comprehensive constitutional and legal amendments make it harder for those with vested interests in the *status quo* to slow down or stop the reform process. The advocates of speed further emphasise that the gaps and inconsistencies in the legal and institutional framework that may ensue from a slow or hesitant transition may cause uncertainty regarding the commitment to and motives behind the reform policy and threaten the survival of the whole process. An approach where new and old laws and institutional arrangements conflict and overlap in also believed to create fertile ground for corruption. The gradualists, on the other hand, typically argue that most attempts to realise major legal transitions in a single leap and create supporting institutions from scratch have failed. One suggested reason is that when radically changing a legal and institutional framework, there logically comes a point at which the old system has been dismantled but the new order has yet to be consolidated. At this point the there are so much uncertainty and confusion, and the institutional capacity so severely stretched, that the entire state machinery risks to collapse.

It may be argued that the difficulties in determining whether a particular reform experience belongs to one school or another, and in determining whether this belonging has contributed to its success or failure (see Chapter 4.3.), render the debate on speed and sequencing essentially academic. For example, with regard to Vietnam, a relatively small number of big bang theorists would maintain that the application of shock therapy following the Eastern European model of transition successfully thrusted Vietnam into the market economy.[106] However, a larger number of commentators would describe the process as gradual. The World Bank, for example, notes that Vietnam (together with China) has combined structural and institutional elements of planning and market, thus feeling for the stepping-stones to cross the river before attaining its own typical form of "socialist-oriented market economy".[107] Among the members of the latter group, it is also a common view that much of Vietnam's and China's success in the economic sphere is attributable to the fact that remaining political controls, *i.e.* the continued authority of the Party and its elaborate control apparatus, have fulfilled a co-ordinating function and limited disruptions to production and trade during the phased build-up of market institutions. The advocates of fast all-out reforms, on the other hand, would argue that the gradual policy has not been without costs, including accelerating corruption and growing regional disparities, and most significantly, the forgone benefits that would have accrued from a faster integration into world trade.

4.3 MATCHING MEANS AND ENDS

4.3.1 EVIDENCE AND BEST PRACTICE

Although numerous strategic documents emanating out of assistance agencies stress that any new project should be grounded in thorough assessment that the problems discussed really exist and the proposed remedies will help to solve them, there is significant difference between rhetoric and reality. In the real world, the element of strategic thinking and prior analysis is often merely symbolical or absent. There seems to be a perception among assistance providers that the "urgency" and "uniqueness" of each situation, in combination with the perceived "straightforwardness" of the contemplated intervention, make serious pre-intervention assessment unnecessary or even impossible. Thus crude postulates about law and its relationship to development tend to resurface every time the international community is confronted with a new type of institutional crisis. The *ad hoc* approach to policy formulation and project evaluation, where each agency essentially follows its own templates, also prevents systematic accumulation of knowledge. Those few project planners who actually seek information about what works and what doesn't have consequently little means to know whether a specific approach was successful because of wisdom, *Fingerspitzengefühl*, or coincidence, or whether it failed because of political ambiva-

106 Gillespie (1999 p. 120) notes that this is also the favoured interpretation among Vietnamese policy makers, essentially because it reinforces government mythology about a strong state, capable of engineering economic development.

107 From Plan to Market 1996 pp. 23–25.

lence, technical difficulties, or because certain crucial factors were misinterpreted or overlooked.

The recent establishment of the Millennium Development Goals and the ensuing political need to systematically link interventions to certain development targets (*e.g.* rule of law to poverty eradication) generate strong pressure to apply evidence-based and result-oriented approaches to project formulation.[108] Particularly high expectations are placed on so called "impact evaluations" to provide concrete and statistically relevant data on whether particular projects have been conducive to the respective development goals and should stand as models for future interventions. There is recognition that the influence of legal and judicial systems, and thus support to reforms thereof, extend far beyond the courtroom and the litigants to comprise an range of social issues impacting on how people decide to behave in different situations. The World Bank uses the following example to demonstrate the linkage between legal systems, support to legal and judicial reforms, and the three separate Millennium Development Goals of poverty reduction, empowerment of women, and increased investment in education: If a woman sees that the law or the court will not protect her right to own property or to keep earned income, she may rationally decline to make costly investments in her own education, or the education of her daughters. This woman's decision not to invest her own human capital will take place even though she never enters any courtroom. The conclusion is accordingly that the most significant effects of reforms that change the way courts work are not be found among the few cases actually adjudicated, but in the thousands or millions of individual decisions determined by subjective expectations about what litigation entails.[109]

The World Bank's approach to classifying projects for the purpose of impact measurement divides legal and judicial reform activities into three broad categories: legal reform, supply-side judicial reform, and demand side judicial reform. The logic of the Bank is that legal reform, which has a main focus on the law-making process and substantive law reform, should be best measured by their direct and indirect effects on production and investment. For example, property law reforms that enhance security of tenure should be expected to increase incentives to invest in property improvements as well as to establish collateral that can be used access capital, both of which would in turn result in increased investment, land productivity, and output. By the same token, enhancement of anti-discrimination laws should be expected to reduce the exclusion of persons from economic activities and thus, reduce poverty in affected groups while increasing productivity in affected sectors.[110]

---

108 See *e. g.* Legal and Judicial Reform: Strategic Directions 2003 p. 16.

109 Id. pp. 17-18.

110 Id. p. 18.

With regard to judicial reforms, the World Bank notes that they tend to have both a demand and supply side. Supply-side reforms are those that address issues such as judicial independence, transparency, anti-corruption, judicial training, judicial administration, etc. These types of activities would be expected to largely impact on the expectations and incentives of the public by changing the "transaction costs" involved in various forms of behaviour, whether economic, criminal, etc. For example, the expected "costs" of committing a crime could be calculated as the probability of being apprehended times the probability of being prosecuted times the probability of being convicted times the economic equivalent of the penalty (if convicted), times the probability that the sentence will be enforced. Effective supply-side such reforms would be expected to increase one or more of these probabilities, thus raising the cost of the crime to the presumptive perpetrator. Such reforms should be expected to affect the judiciary's own costs as well, as greater operational efficiency will enable it to reduce operating costs, increase effectiveness, prioritise urgent matters, and thus maximize deterrence. The Bank points out that there are two optimization problems that arise: maximizing deterrence with given resources, and finding the level of total resources necessary so that the marginal cost of deterrence equals the marginal cost of the crime. Judicial reform projects should generally be expected to direct resources to the aspects of the system where they have the highest marginal productivity. Demand-side judicial reforms typically involve access to justice issues, which can be further broken down into the costs of access and availability of legal information and public education. In essence, what is required is that decision-makers in all sectors (including ordinary citizens) understand the role of the judicial system in protecting rights and resolving conflicts, respect the process and its outcomes, and expect that these fair and effective services would be readily available in the event of need. According to the Bank, the impact of access to justice reforms would then be expected to visualise in increased willingness and ability of the public to use the system to resolve disputes, and in enhancement of the direct effects of substantive law reforms and supply-side improvements in the judicial process.[111]

4.3.2 GRAND ASSESSMENTS AND ASSESSMENT DESIGN

As mentioned, donor agencies and international organisations are beginning to realise the political and technical importance of having better analytical foundations for their efforts.[112] The World Bank devotes a significant part of its "Strategic Directions"

111 Id. pp. 18-20.

112 See for example the ADB-commissioned report "The Role of Law and Legal Institutions in Asian Economic Development 1960–1995" (Pistor & Wellons 1998), which tests competing theories about law and its relation to economic development against the experience of six Asian economies between 1960 and 1995; and the World Bank document "An Analysis of the Causes of Corruption in the

document to the issue and writes: "*Recognizing that legal and judicial reform is complex and of a long-term nature, following a disciplined and programmatic approach is critical. A necessary first step is to assess and diagnose the legal and judicial system. Such an assessment and diagnosis not only provides baseline knowledge of the country's laws and legal systems and institutions, but just as valuable provides for a constructive dialogue with stakeholders in that country for their input and buy-in.*"[113] The Bank and other assistance providers similarly confess to the importance of considering in assessments and similar documents not only the unique legal, political, and economic conditions of the specific country, but also the degree of international attention attributed to the country and problems at hand; whether the assistance community has been able to unity around common policies and approaches; and the short and long-term effects of current and contemplated donor activities.[114]

A number of instruments have been developed to make the assessment of legal and judicial systems easier, among them the World Bank-sponsored "Worldwide Legal and Judicial Indicators" and "Legal and Judicial Sector Assessment Manual", and the American Bar Association – Central and Eastern European Law Initiative-sponsored "Judicial Reform Index". There is also a range of instruments developed for helping in assessing subject-specific issues. For example, information on the level of corruption in a given country can be found in indexes developed by Transparency International, and information on human rights compliance and "freedom" in the Observer Human Rights Index and Freedom House Freedom in the World Rankings.

The most influential and frequently used among the general indexes, the Worldwide Legal and Judicial Indicators, was developed to make the definition of clear purposes and goals for international support to legal and judicial reform easier by providing a structured set of baseline data, impact indicators, performance indicators, etc.[115] Project planners can thus find qualitative and quantitative information regarding a specific legal and judicial system, including information on the judicial career; the justice sector budget; personnel and salaries; and legal education system, in one database. The database also allows cross-country comparisons of specific indicators. The ABA-CEELI Index similarly provides a tool (searchable on-line) to diagnose

---

Judiciary" (Buscaglia & Dakolias 1999), which empirically examines the principal causes for corruption in the judiciary in a number of Latin American countries.

113 Legal and Judicial Reform: Strategic Directions 2003 p. 25.

114 *Ibid.*

115 Available at www.worldbank.org/ljr. The World Bank hopes to encourage "*interested organizations to design, plan and implement legal and judicial modernization processes based on benchmarking techniques and best practices indicators" [. . .] "the academic world and related institutions to carry out research projects in the area of legal and judicial reform" [. . .]* and "*civil society organizations and NGOs to take a more active interest in the importance of legal and judicial reform and, especially, the rule of law.*" The World Bank at http://www4.worldbank.org/legal/database/Justice/default.htm.

systems, assess specific needs and propose solutions. A special quality with the CEELI Index is that it evaluates the judiciary on the basis of 30 factors derived from specific international agreements on judicial independence and accountability.

Most assistance providers recognize that the mere study of "the law" or "available written materials" on a given topic or jurisdiction is not enough. It may be true that the opening of many formerly closed countries to the outside world, and the simultaneous emergence of the Internet as a tool of information and exchange, have remedied some of the problems as regards the quantity of data about formerly closed systems, but the quality of the information remains more than varied. Considerable caution must still be exercised in reading and interpreting the official materials that exist on legal and judicial issues in developing and transition countries, particularly where there is still a one-party monopoly and limited transparency. It is only too common that official inquiries and statistics are manipulated to sway the opinions of the regime. Even where there are democratic government and genuine ambitions to reform the system, official statistics may be unreliable because adequate means for collection and analysis of input data are absent or because figures have been juggled to promote other goals, for example encouraging investment or meeting membership requirements of international organisations. Donald Clarke points out that this problem does not exist solely as a dichotomy between the written and the oral or "empirical", but also within the field of written sources, where researchers are often inclined to ask questions that can be answered with references to indexed sources or databases, instead of penetrating massive volumes of unstructured information, such as several years of newspaper articles, etc. Clarke uses as a metaphor the drunk who looks for his lost keys under the streetlamp because there is light there.[116]

The contextual nature of legal and judicial reform rather calls for methodologies that go beyond describing or establishing the "truth" about a given legal and judicial circumstance to analyse the "significance" of various legal phenomena and how they relate to a greater social, political and economic surround. Too often, what foreign researchers and development planners think carries significance is merely a reflection of their pre-existing ("internal") knowledge about the subject matter (*i.a.* contract law if the topic of discussion happens to be of a transactional nature) and may not be very important in the eyes of the actual beneficiaries of the contemplated reforms.[117] Thomas McInerney similarly argues that one of the principal reasons why legal reform

---

116 See Clarke, D. C. 1996 p. 205 and 2004 p. 181.

117 Clarke D. C. (1996: 206-207) points out that people never investigate a subject in which they have no interest and since by hypothesis the interest precedes the investigation, it is clear that the interest must stem form something other than (extrinsic to) the object of investigation.

projects have so often failed is that it has been cognitively impossible for a donors or small group of analysts to determine *ex ante* appropriate legal solutions for a given problem or country.[118]

The way the system actually works, including matters such as competing norms, inter-institutional relationships, individual agency organisation, and capacity issues, should therefore be discussed with a wide range of people, comprising judges, prosecutors, lawyers in public and private service, law enforcement staff, and others with first-hand knowledge. Even in politically "difficult" countries, sensitive issues such as political and ideological controversies within the system are often possible to probe in interviews if there is good *rapport* and a strict promise of anonymity. Besides enhancing the precision of reform initiatives, such collective and inclusive efforts help to build political opinion among key stakeholders for the ensuing reform recommendations, as will be discussed in Chapter 4.4. Yet, such discussions will only provide a fragmented picture, as provided by a selective legal and social elite. Polls and other forms of broad-based field surveys may therefore be conducted to contrast the official view of problems and remedies with the perceptions and reactions of those who are supposed to benefit from the legal reforms, whether the general public or a more narrowly defined target group (private businesses, women, children, etc.). Thanks to their inherent flexibility, qualitative interview techniques can often be helpful in revealing in-depth information regarding the motivations, attitudes, etc. of the respondents *vis-à-vis* the law and legal institutions.[119]

At the same time, development planners and researchers need to be aware that errors caused by bad input data are commonplace in qualitative studies. A particular problem in ensuring general and representative data is that reliable and up-to-date central registries of people and firms and other basic conditions for selecting representative respondents are often lacking. Interviewer and respondent bias is another potential problem.[120] For example, respondents whom are suspicious of the motives for the study or suspect the interviewers of having a hidden agenda may provide a too rosy picture of the state of affairs. Questions on the role of the state could similarly spur respondents who are disappointed with the government or judiciary to exaggerate the problems.[121] The literature on fieldwork methods in developing countries suggests an array of tested tools and techniques to be used to minimise the risks and effects of bias, among them detailed explanation of the purpose of an interview and careful wording

118 McInerney 2004 pp. 9-11.

119 On social survey techniques in developing countries generally, see *e. g.* Bourque & Fielder 1995; Bulmer 1983a-c; Jones 1983; Mikkelsen 1995; Peil 1983; and Ward 1983.

120 Bulmer 1983c pp. 209-213; Jones 1983 *in extenso*; and Mitchell 1983 p. 235.

121 Wuelker (1983 pp. 164–165) discusses the effects of authoritarian government and other political factors on empirical social research in developing countries.

of questions to clearly establish the image of the interviewer, reduce erroneous or tacit assumptions and breach the courtesy barrier.

Issues of language in general, and the translation of questions and terms in particular, raise a particular set of problems. The most obvious problem, *i.e.* the rendering of questions asked in for example English in the same words when asked in Chinese, Bahasa Indonesian, or Swahili (lexical equivalence), can sometimes be dealt with by "back translation" and similar methods.[122] However, such methods may lull the analyst into believing that equivalence has been achieved when it has not, because words, as language terms, always depend on the context in which they are used. More important than perfect lexical equivalence is to ensure a reasonable degree of conceptual equivalence, *i.e.* equivalence in meaning or simply talking about the same thing.[123] The concepts used, whether these are theoretical constructions such as "rights", or terms with a more direct empirical reference like "payment," must transfer without losing their core meaning from one language to another, and back again. A good measure of knowledge of the local culture in the broad sense, enhanced further by the active participation of unbiased local lawyers and experts in the articulation of questions and analysis of answers, help to ensure a reasonable degree of such equivalence and otherwise contribute to better data.

There are no strict formulae for the analysis of data originating from interviews and discussions. Rather, social scientists have noted that the procedures for analysing qualitative data are often a form of "craftsmanship".[124] In the course of gathering data, new ideas may also emerge about analysis and interpretation. Although such initial impressions can sometimes distort additional data collection, it seems that such overlapping of collection and analysis often help to improve the quality of both the data collected and the analysis. As the main interest is often on issues or topics, the analysis may begin with a description of variations in the description of the interview topics and proceed to seek patterns and links. Various methods of triangulation, *i.e.* crosschecking with official sources and literature, can be used to detect any possible lapses and inconsistencies.

It should be mentioned that very ambitious assessments may create exaggerated expectations about the ensuing projects. Further, participation in comprehensive and inclusive assessments puts a great burden on already constrained local agencies. One need also call to mind that no research product, however structured, will ever produce

122 The material, *e.g.* a questionnaire, is translated from one language to another, and then translated independently, by another translator, back into the original language. The results are then compared to identify and correct semantic errors in the translation.

123 Bogdan 1993 pp. 52-55; Bulmer 1983a p. 12; and Bulmer and Warwick 1983 pp. 152–153.

124 *See e.g.* Mikkelsen 1995 pp. 114–116.

a final and unchallengeable understanding of the issue. Assistance providers and local stakeholders operating with scarce resources and pressured by time may therefore be content with an assessment that brings to the table a small selection of alternative perspectives and possible ways ahead, some of them presumably new.

Below a few selected real-world initiatives to map legal and judicial sectors are presented, chosen among many because they display important differences in goals, approaches and presentation.[125] The first, "An Introduction to the Vietnamese Legal System", may be described as a joint donor-host initiative. The second, "UNMIBH Judicial System Assessment Program" is an assessment of a post-war judiciary commissioned by the United Nations Security Council. The third, "Comprehensive Legal System Needs Assessment for Vietnam" is a multi-agency initiative inspired by similar efforts in neighbouring countries.

4.3.3 "AN INTRODUCTION TO THE VIETNAMESE LEGAL SYSTEM"

In the wake of the economic reform program called *doi moi*, Vietnam approached Sweden in 1991 with a proposal for assistance in the development of a "legal framework" to consolidate the achievements made in the economic area and move the country towards a greater degree of rule of law. An agreement to this end was signed between the Swedish International Development Authority (SIDA), the Ministry of Justice in Hanoi and the designated consultant, the Department of Law at Umeå University, in 1992. Under the framework of the ensuing project "Strengthening the Rule of Law in Vietnam", various forms of drafting assistance, topical training, and hard-ware such as computers and books, were offered to the Ministry of Justice and other Vietnamese legal agencies in need of support.

However, it soon became apparent that a systematic approach to capacity building necessitated some kind of agreed analysis and road map of problems and remedies. There was also concern in SIDA that that the demand-driven approach, while being instrumental in ensuring local commitment, also made it difficult for the Swedish government to ensure that important rule of law or human rights dimensions of the cooperation were given due consideration. SIDA and the Department of Law therefore

125 There are many other examples of comprehensive and careful assessments meriting discussion, for example World Bank and UNDP-sponsored initiatives in a range of Central American, African and Southeast Asian Countries. See for example the 2005 "*Baseline Study Report for the comprehensive justice system program in Ethiopia*", formally commissioned by the Ethiopian Ministry for capacity Building and implemented with the assistance of the Center for International Legal Cooperation at Leiden University.

proposed to the Ministry of Justice that the parties to the cooperation should join forces to produce a joint analysis of problems and their potential remedies. After lengthy discussions (including high level political consultations in Vietnam), the Ministry of Justice accepted the idea. A joint team of researchers from the Department of Law, the Ministry of Justice, and the Office of the Vietnamese Government could then commence with the task.

While the effort was initially described as a "sector analysis" and expected by some to include the conventional elements of such instruments (inventories of problems, strategic plans, action plans, etc.), it soon became apparent that there were neither political acceptance nor skills on the Vietnamese side for such an approach. Politics and law were still essentially united in theory and practice, and the Vietnamese members of the team (who were civil servants and presumably Party members) felt uncomfortable describing and analysing many important aspects of their own system, particularly matters pertaining to human rights and the role of the Communist Party in legal and judicial affairs. The team therefore decided to produce a general description of the basic features of the Vietnamese legal and judicial universe.

The absence of reliable statistics and other baseline data on the legal system, court organisation, the legal profession, etc., made it necessary for the team to spend much time and energy on collecting such information by means of interviews with representatives of various Vietnamese political, legal and judicial bodies, professional associations, and international and regional organisations. After an analytical and writing phase that stretched over more than a year, the work was concluded with the publishing in Vietnam and Sweden of a short book, "*An Introduction to the Vietnamese Legal System*", consisting of eight topical chapters describing the processes of law-making, main areas substantive law, civil and criminal procedure, legal education, international co-operation, etc., and an appendix with a number of important Vietnamese laws and administrative instruments in English translation.

4.3.4 "UNITED NATIONS JUDICIAL SYSTEM ASSESSMENT PROGRAM"

The United Nations Judicial System Assessment Program (JSAP) in the new state of Bosnia and Herzegovina (BiH) was essentially an international attempt at analysing systematic problems in a judicial system fragmented along ethnic and political lines. It was launched by UN Security Council resolution, became operational in late 1998 (three years after the end of the war that had cost about 250,000 lives), and was formally mandated to monitor and assess the court system in BiH as part of an overall programme of legal reform under the co-ordination of the highest international executive authority "in theatre", the High Representative.[126]

The original impetus for establishing this body came from security considerations, namely that progress with internationally promoted police reforms in BiH needed to be followed with similar efforts to reform the clogged and biased court system. After some initial confusion as to whether JSAP was going to monitor and assess the work of the judiciary more generally or focus high profile cases specifically, JSAP decided to devote most of its attention to assessing the general "quality of justice" in BiH as compared to international standards of justice, particularly the European Convention on Human Rights. JSAP adopted a conceptual framework for assessing the judicial system in three main aspects: (1) technical, covering legislation and other legal norms and standards; (2) institutional, relating to the capacity of the system in terms of physical resources, personnel, etc.; and (3) political, *i.e.* the political framework and factors determining the operation and level of independence of the judicial agencies and their staff.

Establishing a presence on the ground in post-war BiH was complicated for a variety of political and physical reasons, but recruiting staff proved easier than expected. When the UN advertised internationally for people with suitable professional background and practical experience of work in transition countries, there were around 600-1,000 applications for less than 20 international positions. Many local lawyers were also attracted by the chance of finding a comparatively high-paid job in an international organisation. In order to allow JSAP to draw on the knowledge and resources of the UN presence in BiH, it was decided to organise the mission in teams and to deploy one team in each of the seven existing "UN Regions" of BiH. Each team came to consist of two international Judicial System Officers, one National (Bosnian) Professional Officer (normally a lawyer with a background in the judiciary or prosecution service), and two language assistants.

The teams worked under the guidance of the JSAP Headquarter in Sarajevo, which consisted of an international Head of Programme (initially a Swedish judge, later a Norwegian judge), three international experts, one national expert, two language assistants, and an international administrative assistant. Besides guiding the work of the teams, the HQ had an important function to liaise with other international agencies and Bosnian authorities, and to make sure that the goals and priorities of the program were consistent with the overall goals and principles for the international support to the judicial reform effort as elaborated by the Office of the High Representative.

126 Established by UN Security Council Resolution 1184 (1998).

Much initial effort was spent on collecting relevant data from courts and prosecution offices on staffing, material resources, budgeting, caseload, professional qualifications, etc., and on compiling these data into a computerised data-base. Once this work had been completed, the teams could shift attention to their core task of performing in-depth topical studies of matters of special importance for the independency and effectiveness of the judiciary. The results of these studies were compiled by the HQ and published in a number of topical reports made available to the Office of the High Representative, the UN Special Representative, and others concerned with human rights and rule of law issues in BiH.[127]

While JSAP was well equipped to supervise and assess, it had neither the mandate nor the resources to make sure that its recommendations were actually implemented. The implicit, and in many respects naive, idea was that local agencies would be persuaded to accept the conclusions and recommendations emanating out of JSAP by means of persistent political dialogue. The "build-in" problems in this construction rendered JSAP much less effective than anticipated. In an attempt at reviving and energizing the judicial reform process, the High Representative established the Independent Judicial Commission for Bosnia and Herzegovina (IJC) in 2000, and tasked it to take the lead in both assessing the system and implementing reforms.[128]

4.3.5 "COMPREHENSIVE LEGAL SYSTEM NEEDS ASSESSMENT FOR VIETNAM"

The impetus for the Comprehensive Legal System Needs Assessment for Vietnam (LNA) came from a conclusion in the Vietnamese leadership that important national development goals would not be possible to achieve without a facilitating and

127 *Inter alia* Serving the Public: The Delivery of Justice in BiH (Nov. 2000); The Independence of the Judiciary in BiH (Nov. 2000); Prosecuting Corruption – A Study of the Weakness of the Criminal System in BiH (Nov. 2000); On Arrest Warrants, Amnesty and Trials in Absentia (Dec. 1999). All reports were made available at the UNMIBH website, www.unmibh.org.

128 This decision was made in accordance with the directives of the Peace Implementation Steering Board in Lisbon in May 2000 and was endorsed by UNMiBH, OSCE and the CoE. The IJC was also given an important role in providing opinions and advice in judicial reform and rule of law issued directly to the Federation and Republika Srpska ministries of justice, members of the judiciary, court administrators and members of the international community. The Director of the IJC could recommend to the High Representative the use of his powers as elaborated in the December 1997 Bonn Peace Implementation Council Declaration, *e.g.* regarding the need to impose legislation or to remove officials, including judges. Other than those circumstances, the Director could decide upon actions to be taken on the basis of powers authorized by the High Representative.

consolidating legal framework.[129] The successful establishment of such a framework, in turn, was believed to require a strategic approach to legal and judicial reform and a method to allow prioritisation and allocation of scarce resources to the most important reform objectives. In coming to this conclusion, the Vietnamese government was also inspired by similar efforts in other developing and transition countries, among them Indonesia and Mongolia, and attracted by the support that international organisations, notably the World Bank and the UNDP, had provided for their implementation.[130] A group of assistance provides (comprising among others the World Bank, ADB, UNDP, Sida, DANIDA, JICA, and AusAid) did prove willing to provide money, equipment and advise to the Vietnamese ditto. Most of the financial contributions to the LNA were designated for empirical research, workshops and conferences, in-country travel, secretarial support, communications, translation, interpretation, document production, and coordinating functions.

Virtually all significant Vietnamese agencies concerned with legal and judicial issues participated in the LNA, *inter alia* the Ministry of Justice, Supreme People's Court, Supreme People's Procuracy, Office of the National Assembly, Office of the Government, Internal Affairs Commission of the Central Committee of the Communist Party, and the Ministry of Planning and Investment. At the request of the Government, the Ministry of Justice was designated as coordinator of the whole effort. Most of the work was carried out by four subject-area teams: Framework of laws and international instruments; Legal and judicial institutions; Legal education and training; and Legal information and dissemination. Each team consisted of 12 to 15 designated experts from the participating agencies. A fifth team was responsible for merging the subject area reports into one comprehensive report and action plan. The subject area teams also included auxiliary experts from legal education, training and research institutions.[131] One or more international specialists with previous experience of Vietnam were also seconded to each team by the sponsoring donor agencies. The role of these international experts was not to "lead" or "drive" the work of the teams, rather

129 The national development goals are (1) building a state ruled by law as mandated by the 1992 constitution; (2) increasing democracy; (3) changing the economic system from central planning to a socialist-oriented market economy under state management; (4) integrating Vietnam into the regional and international economies; and (5) making Vietnam a modern industrialized state by the year 2020.

130 The first of these World Bank-sponsored assessments was completed in Ecuador in 1994, and involved reviewing different aspects of the administration of justice. As a result of the priorities identified, the ensuing Ecuador Judicial Reform Project came to include a broader range of components than previous World Bank legal and judicial reform projects.

131 *Inter alia* the Central Institute for Economic Management, Hanoi Law University, the Institute of State and Law, the Institute of Legal Research, and the Legal Professional Training School of the Ministry of Justice.

to provide insights and find materials that were not readily accessible to the Vietnamese team members.[132]

The five teams were overseen by, and received further instructions from, an *ad hoc* Inter-Agency Steering Committee (IASC) consisting of eight minister- or vice-minister level representatives of the key state agencies in the legal field. A Vice-Minister of Justice performed the day-to-day supervision of the progress of the LNA. A Secretariat for the IASC was formed within the Ministry of Justice (Department of International Law and Co-operation) to facilitate the practical work of the teams, *i.a.* by assisting in scheduling and holding meetings and workshops; preparing notes and minutes of team meetings; making regular reports to the Committee on team and other LNA activities; preparing for larger-scale external workshops; compiling a regular newsletter on LNA activities and news; and assisting the Committee and individual teams to establish and maintain contact with international donors and international experts.

The work proceeded basically as follows: The LNA was kicked off with a 2-day Launching Workshop in March 2001, with the participation of some 40 persons representing relevant Vietnamese agencies, donor organizations, and international experts. Besides signaling high-level and broad-based support for the LNA, the workshop served to introduce to the participants the specific objectives, activities, and proposed main outputs of the exercise. This meant that it was clear from the beginning that the LNA should be understood as a rather instrumental enterprise, aimed at making sure that resources devoted to future reforms would support specific priority goals rather than "justice" or "rule of law" generally. Another workshop to the same end was held in June 2001, in which particular attention was paid to consolidating a common and better understanding among the participants of the implications of the socio-economic strategy of Vietnam for 2001–2010 on long-term legal sector development on the one hand, and of the instrumental role of the legal system in achieving these broad goals on the other.

The teams could then proceed to develop and agree on a consistent procedure and methodology for analyzing the aforementioned main areas of the legal and judicial system. The next step was fact-finding. The teams began with making an inventory of existing analyses, reports and statistics (international analyses were provided by embassies and international organizations represented in Vietnam) and summarizing their main findings. The work proceeded with gathering and compiling additional and in-depth "empirical" information where needed by means of polls and interviews.

132 The General and Team-specific ToR spelled out that the teams should own and drive the processes of fact-finding, policy analysis, and drafting, while the role of the foreign experts should be advisory and catalytic.

After having completed the phase of fact-finding, the teams started to identify perceived problems and gaps, as well as any notable successes, in the functioning of each area of the system. They also sought to analyse the underlying causes, including linkages to official social and economic policies in Vietnam, for example whether economic policies were incompatible with legal structures. The final analytical step was to find and present effective solutions for the identified problems. The problems and reform recommendations were compiled into thematic reports and merged by the high-level fifth team into a comprehensive synthesis report, setting out: a statement of the major needs for Vietnam's legal system development in light of relevant priority social and economic policy goals; a proposed comprehensive strategy for Vietnam's legal system development to 2010; a proposed action plan to carry out the strategy; and a proposed framework for international support to the implementation of the action plan. Draft versions of the thematic and overall reports were circulated for comment among state and local agencies, mass organizations, individual citizens, etc.

An international conference was held in november 2001 to allow the teams to meet with donor agencies and other international stakeholders and discuss both the draft report and the LNA process more generally. This conference resulted in a new draft report, reflecting selected comments of the participants. Then, in February 2002, yet another revised draft of the Overall LNA Report was reviewed again by Vietnamese agencies and international experts in a series of small-scale workshops focusing on the priorities set out in the Action Plan and the institutional arrangements for implementation of the plan, particularly the proposed framework for cooperation and coordination with international donors. After this, Team 5 proceeded to prepare the 9th and final draft, taking into account most pertinent comments of Vietnamese stakeholders, international donors, and participating international experts. At the same time, the Inter-Agency Steering Committee held an intensive series of meetings on this Report with all major state agencies. A third international conference, in which the official version of the final draft was presented, was held in april 2002. The focus of the discussion was again the forward-looking parts of the report, *i.e.* the implementation of the Action Plan and the mechanisms for cooperation and coordination with international donors. After the conference, the teams (mainly Team 5) and the Secretariat could begin in earnest the work to identify the specific needs for external assistance to Vietnam's legal system development and to develop a framework for the administration of such assistance.

While the LNA would not have been possible without the strong backing of the Party, its involvement in the LNA also signaled that there were explicit and implicit restrictions as to what the teams could find and propose. Although a great number of Vietnamese agencies were encouraged to participate, the chances for political and bureaucratic "outsiders" to influence the agenda or substance were also slim. It was further symptomatic that almost all the proposed "implementers" of the action plan items were state or public agencies, or bodies affiliated to the Party. The political taboos were particularly palpable where the discussion touched upon issues of democracy and human rights. In most cases, the teams simply avoided these topics, or tried to confine the discussion to a non-committal minimum. When it was deemed necessary to open for some debate (because of foreign pressure, credibility considerations, etc.) the teams were careful to avoid clear definitions and categorical statements. There were also many examples of "newspeak", *i.e.* giving concepts that already have a more or less commonly accepted definition a new and uniquely "Vietnamese" meaning (*e.g.* human rights becoming "legitimate and democratic human rights" and rule of law becoming "Socialist Rule of Law State").

It could have been feared that the long tradition of fighting bureaucratic "turf battles" in Vietnam would have made the work in the inter-agency teams difficult or even impossible. While there were some such tendencies, the LNA leadership was rather successful in maintaining a façade of relative unity *vis-à-vis* the donor community and other observers. Even in the synthesis of the various thematic reports, where policy and priority decisions had to be made in the face of interest advocacy, little leaked out of Team 5 or any of the participating agencies to indicate that painful battles were won or lost. On the other hand, there was a fairly consistent view, both domestically and in the donor community, that the resulting Strategy and Action Plan basically prioritized everything and omitted nothing. Further, these documents were regarded to lack sufficient detail to be operative. For example, it was not enough to say that a National Legal Information Center and a National Legal Database should be established, rather it needed to be spelled out which consecutive steps that should be taken, and by whom, to accomplish this goal.

Although the LNA was launched as a domestic analytical enterprise without donor commitment to the ensuing reform recommendations, the "aid factor" clearly influenced how the teams described problems and suggested remedies. This was only to be expected as the donor community (notably the World Bank and the UNDP) at an early point in the assessment phase opened up for a parallel discussion about how to link overseas development assistance to specific reform priorities. Obviously, the teams took notice of this and sought to position themselves to get the most out of the opportunities it provided. The perceived need to compete for overseas resources also made the participating agencies suspicious of how the Ministry of Justice would act as co-ordinating agency and made some of them believe that the Ministry would seek to channel the bulk of the foreign support to its own pet projects.

It came a point when this side-show had to be transferred to a public forum. A special workshop with representatives for the subject area teams, Team 5, and the donor agencies and their consultants, was organized to this end. It soon became apparent that the participants came there with rather different expectations and mandates. While the Vietnamese participants seemed to be there under the false assumption that it would be a straightforward matter of matching specific priority items in the LNA Action Plan and the subsequently elaborated Legal System Development Strategy with willing donors, the donors representatives were neither willing nor prepared to enter into such discussions, not least because this would mean anticipating and overruling their own agency-internal processes for strategy development, planning and programming. The apparent mismatch of expectations and mandates, and the resulting recognition among the participants that the allocation of resources would not be a straightforward matter, cooled off much of the initial enthusiasm for the LNA project. After this debacle, the UNDP assumed lead responsibility for harboring the initiative and keeping it alive within the donor community, while the LNA leadership continued to push for domestic high-level endorsement for the Action Plan and Strategy.

4.3.6 LOGICAL FRAMEWORK APPROACH: PROSPECTS AND LIMITS

One of the most popular tools among assistance providers for matching problems and remedies is the Logical Framework Approach (LFA). The LFA, as described with small variations in numerous handbooks,[133] should essentially be understood as a tool or process that can help donors and hosts analyse the existing situation during project preparation; establish a logical hierarchy of means by which objectives will be reached; identify the potential risks to achieving the objectives; and establish how outputs and outcomes might best be monitored and evaluated. The origins of this tool can be traced back to private sector management theory, such as the "management by objectives" approach that became popular in the 1960s. LFA has since been adopted as the principal planning tool by a large number of assistance providers, among them the AusAID, USAID, DFID, CIDA, Sida, GTZ, OECD/DAC, and EU.

One of the reasons why LFA seems particularly attractive to policy-makers and project planners concerned with legal and justice sector reform may be its inherent emphasis on project planning and management as "team tasks", meaning that many different state- and non-state stakeholders should be given opportunity to provide input to the LFA process and the ensuing projects. At the same time, most advocates of LFA do recognise that LFA is not a tool that all stakeholders necessarily need to understand or use. While "logical" in concept, it is clear that its effective application poses many challenges, even to experienced users.

133 The description of the LFA process is essentially based on the AusAID LFA Manual, available at http://www.ausaid.gov.au/ausguide/ausguidelines/1-4.cfm.

The LFA cycle consists of four main analytical elements or phases, namely problem analysis; stakeholder analysis; objectives analysis; identification of risks; and selection of preferred implementation strategy. Although this terminology suggests a linear set of prescribed steps, the use of the LFA in development work rests on the assumption that effective development planning should be approached as an iterative process. For example, while stakeholder analysis is presented in LFA guidelines as coming after problem analysis, in practise, stakeholder analysis is supposed to be ongoing throughout the design process.

The problem analysis aims at identifying what the main problems are and establishing the cause and effect relationships between these problems. The key purpose is to ensure that the actual "root causes" are identified and subsequently addressed in the project design, not just the symptoms of the problem(s). There are two main approaches that can be used to help give focus to the problem analysis, namely: (i) the "focal problem" method, whereby development problems (or constraints) are brainstormed by the participants, a core or focal problem is identified, and the cause and effect analysis then pivots around the focal problem; or (ii) the "objectives oriented" method, whereby a broad or high level development objective is specified at the start of the analysis, and constraints to achieving this objective are then brainstormed, analysed and categorised as either cause or effect. Both approaches are regarded to be equally valid, and which to use is largely considered to be up to individual preference and circumstances.

When the main problems and the cause and effect relationship between them have been identified, it is time for the stakeholder analysis. This phase essentially aim at answering whom these problems actually impact on most, and what the roles and interests of the different stakeholders might be in addressing the problems and reaching solutions. Such stakeholders might include, when legal and judicial interventions are discussed, *inter alia* the government, judicial institutions, commercial groups, and human rights-oriented NGOs. The stakeholder analysis can further help to devise strategies to counter the kind of political and bureaucratic opposition to reform discussed in Chapter 4.4.1. It is also known that the identification and appropriate involvement of the relevant target groups or beneficiaries in project design and implementation are critical factors in promoting sustainability.

An objective analysis should be performed after the stakeholder analysis has been completed. While the problem analysis aims to illustrate the "negative" cause and effect relationship between problems, the objective analysis aims to illustrate the "positive" means and ends relationship between objectives. Once such positive statements have been articulated, it will also be possible, in theory, to check whether the statements are sufficiently clear and unambiguous, if the links between each statement are logical and reasonable, if the risks to achieving the objectives and to have sustainable outcomes appear to be manageable, etc. The culmination of the objective analysis is often the presentation and circulation of the proposed objective ("tree") structure for further comment and feedback among local stakeholders and other parties concerned.

It may then be time to enter into a detailed discussion on the potential merits and difficulties associated with different possible reform and assistance modalities. For example, what combination of interventions is most likely to bring about the desired results? What are the likely immediate and recurrent cost implications of different possible interventions, and what can be realistically afforded? The assessment of different approaches is believed to be helped by the identification of a number of assessment criteria against which the alternatives can be ranked or scored. Such criteria could include *i.a.* the expected benefits to target groups; sustainability of the benefits; total cost and recurrent cost implications; financial and economic viability; contribution to institutional strengthening and management capacity building, etc. Even among the most devout disciples of the LFA methodology, there is recognition that the development of sensible assessment criteria for legal and rule of law interventions is often very difficult, as these areas are "qualitative" almost by definition.

The results of the logical framework analysis are presented, and further analysed, through the development of a logframe matrix providing a graphic illustration of the basic project design.[134] The matrix has four columns and usually four or five rows, depending on the number of levels of objectives used to explain the means-ends relationship of the project. The vertical logic identifies what the project intends to do, clarifies the causal relationships, and specifies the important assumptions and uncertainties (or risks) beyond the project manager's control. These assumptions are particularly important to consider in planning for legal and justice sector projects in unstable political environments or projects that require the cooperation of a number of stakeholder groups with diverging agenda. The horizontal logic defines how project objectives specified in the project description will be measured, and the means by which the measurement will be verified.

As already mentioned, the identification of good indicators for achievement in the area of law and justice (beyond merely counting the number of new laws, etc.) poses many difficulties, but some guidance may be found in the popular "SMART" (Specific, Measurable, Attainable, Relevant, and Timely) characteristics. Specific means that key indicators need to be specific and to relate to the conditions the project seeks to change. Measurable means that quantifiable indicators are preferred because they are precise, can be aggregated and allow further statistical analysis of the data. Attainable means that the indicator (or information) must be attainable at reasonable cost using

134 For real-world examples, see *e. g.* www.restorativejustice.org/rj3/Full-text/Uganda/

an appropriate collection method. Relevant means that indicators should be relevant to the management information needs of the people who will use the data. Timely means that an indicator needs to be collected and reported at the right time to influence management decisions. The different costs of collecting the information needed to verify success or failure must also be considered. Some indicators may for example give the information ideally wanted, but require the investment of too much time, work or money.

It should be noted that the enthusiasm for the LFA in the donor community is rarely matched among the recipients. This is problematic because inherent in the LFA are ideas of participation and inclusiveness, and if the recipients are not committed to the approach, much of the logic on which it rests instantly falls. In order to help stakeholders better understand the potential benefits of the LFA and use it in project planning and reporting, assistance providers organise customized training courses for local policy-makers and project staff.

4.4 BUILDING POLITICAL OPINION

4.4.1 DEMAND AND LEADERSHIP

It should come as no surprise that assistance programs are easier to promote and implement if they are built around a shared vision among the assistance providers, the domestic political leadership, and other stakeholder groups about what the goals of the process are and how to get there. The degree of "success" or "failure" in introducing legal concepts borrowed from abroad is similarly linked to the extent to which the domestic leadership manages to maximise incentives and remove disincentives to popular acceptance and invocation.[135] Prior to committing resources to a specific reform initiative, assistance providers may consequently want to assess the level of domestic commitment or "ownership" (Chapter 4.3). Should the assessment indicate that there is commitment, then donors may proceed to discuss

[135] An issue that has crucial importance for establishing political opinion, but falls outside of the scope of this book, is fair and free elections. Elections are the key means of legitimising the legislature and government, and thus also the normative instruments emanating out of these bodies. In practice, the degree of legitimacy conferred on the legislature depends on the nature of the elections and on the type of representation required. While it is commonly believed that elections should be held as soon as possible in transition societies to legitimise new power structures, experience from many such environments indicates that pressure to hold elections before other basic institutions are in place can sometimes backfire on their credibility and otherwise be detrimental to the greater process of political, economic and judicial reform. It is further important to remember that elections should not be heralded as the end of the transition, but rather as an entry-point for shifting focus and support to developing the capacity of administrative and judicial institutions, amongst other priorities.

with local counterparts specific goals, principles and assistance modalities. On the other hand, if the demand for reform is deemed to be weak or merely rhetorical, the most sensible conclusion would be to step out of the process, or, if the moral or political rationale for pushing ahead is very strong, consider strategies for changing prevailing negative opinions and building demand.

The "second generation" of governance reforms, with its emphasis on human rights and "social" issues, has been instrumental in changing the understanding of "demand" and "ownership" from being preconditions for support to something that can be generated from the outside, and infused in the donor community much optimism as to what such strategies can accomplish.[136] There are many means to this end, ranging from grass-roots dialogue and participatory assessments to straightforward conditionality. Although soft and inclusive grass-roots approaches have always been surrounded with much sympathy in the donor community, there is growing recognition that they are resource-demanding and long-term. The focus is instead on building top-level constituency for reform objectives by introducing new structures of political and financial incentives. It has been mentioned that international organisations and donor agencies frequently seize on the window of political opportunity that accession procedures provide to push for specific reforms that the candidate countries may neither want nor believe in. "Structural adjustment programs" and policy-lending initiatives may similarly include arrangements where the release of loans are conditioned on certain legal and judicial reforms.[137] Among the best known examples are the conditions attached to the International Monetary Fund's financial rescue packages for Thailand, Indonesia and South Korea in the wake of the Asian financial crisis in 1997-1999, where the borrowing governments had to itemize in so called Letters of Intent which specific legal reforms they should be taking in return for support.

Before discussing the pros and cons of conditional assistance, it should be noted that it is often difficult to determine whether a specific reform, *e.g.* the adoption of a law or establishment of a new judicial or administrative agency, is actually the result of a conditional arrangement or not. National governments may be reluctant to admit

---

136 Kerry Rittich (2004 p. 13) points out that it is a hallmark of "second generation" governance reforms to take account of the way power balances shift when governance is dispersed across society.

137 During the 1970s a notion emerged that ideology and overarching concerns with equitable distribution of wealth cemented severe "imbalances" in the economies of many developing countries. To address these problems the development community urged that programmes of "structural adjustment" should be undertaken and redirected a significant amount of financial assistance to support such programmes. The ensuing assistance agreements were often combined with certain "performance criteria" or other requirements that had to be fulfilled before new loans and payments could be released. These criteria have traditionally been financial and quantitative, but the trend goes towards the inclusion of more and more qualitative governance-related conditions. Generally, see Gelb 1993; Larsson 1994; Ljunggren 1993b; Shihata 1991 and Rittich 2003.

to caving in to international pressure. The international financial institutions may simultaneously refute accusations that they stipulate or purchase reforms, but rather argue that the purpose of their work is to help implement domestic policies they too believe will work, while refusing to spend their principals' (member states) money on policies they think will not work.[138]

There is thus sense in regarding the process as a bargaining situation in which both parties have a strong interest at maintaining the assistance at a high level, but while the donors wish to maximise the policy implications of the assistance, the recipients often wish to minimise them.[139] The bargaining power that the recipient country can mobilise would then be one factor influencing the presence and content of conditional arrangements. It is symptomatic that Laos, a land-locked country with a very small economy, agreed to implement what could be regarded as a blueprint of a World Bank/IMF reform agenda within the economic area, including the adoption of what is popularly referred to as "World Bank Laws", while Vietnam, with expectations of being the next "tiger" and greater bargaining power, took the liberty of declining assistance from the international financial institutions on a number of occasions, particularly in governance-related reform projects.[140] Clearly, the degree to which countries accept conditions and comply with them is also influenced by their perception of the compliance monitoring performed. It seems that in many cases the monitoring has been perceived to be lax enough to allow the making of casual promises.

In other situations, perceptions matter more than facts. In the wake of the financial crisis in Indonesia, the IMF's insistence on having a group of international experts with a hands-on role in the drafting of a new Law on Bankruptcy and establishment of a new Bankruptcy Court, and on having this law and court fast-tracked through parliament, provoked massive political controversy and worked to entrench an already existing erroneous local notion that any such new law and court were established solely for the benefit of foreign creditors at the expense of local debtors. The ensuing problems in implementing this structure were enormous. William Neilson finds it difficult to imagine how anyone could think that a bankruptcy court constructed under such premises could ever be successful in asserting itself and work independent of the greater Indonesian political and legal surround.[141]

The Indonesian example reminds that laws constitute an important means of allocation power and resources to different social groups, and that distributive

[138] Shihata 1991.
[139] Larsson 1994 p. 30.
[140] de Vylder 1993 p. 7.
[141] Neilson 1999 pp. 7-8.

struggles among stakeholders below, besides and outside of the government tend to be commonplace in conjunction with legal reforms.[142] The range of groups with means and incentive to resist or redirect the implementation of reform initiatives has proven to be vast, comprising *inter alia* politicised labour unions, state or collectively owned enterprises, companies that benefit from monopolies, and various mafia-like constellations. Even the judiciary and prosecution may need to be convinced about the necessity of reform, or they may resist the effort because of the threat to their current power and privileges the proposed reforms seem to pose. For example, the socialist-inspired and omnipotent Procuracy have sought to exploit the widespread perception that crime is on the rise in many formerly socialist countries as a means to resist its transformation into a conventional prosecution office.[143]

Another frequently mentioned reason for assessing and promoting domestic ownership and lead is that the sustainability of any reform effort depends on the willingness of the hosting government to ultimately assume the responsibility for its long-term implementation, including the costs. For example, the logic behind the recent change from supporting various forms of *ad hoc* judicial training in developing and transition countries to helping to establish judicial training centres and other "permanent" structures is essentially that such centres are believed to provide for more sustainable results. While it could reasonably be argued that it should be a responsibility for any government to make sure that there is a properly established and funded judicial training structure in place, donor have been disappointed to note that many governments have often been slow, or unwilling, to assume the administrative and financial responsibility for sustaining them after establishment, and that many centres have experienced serious problems in retaining their staff, maintaining facilities, and in providing any kind of training services. In some cases, frustrated donors have therefore decided to cut out the government and instead provide support to NGOs to operate the centres. Here too, the long-term sustainability of the arrangement may be questioned.[144]

The prospects of building and maintaining political opinion for reforming laws and institutions in a certain direction are determined by a variety of factors. It has already been mentioned (Chapter 2.6) that history suggests that the form of "relationship" or "community" targeted is a factor of special relevance. Generally, the more "instrumental" the situation or community is, the greater are the prospects for success.[145] It would consequently be easier to build and maintain broad-based consensus for attempts at reforming trade and customs regimes than reforming aspects

142 Rittich 2004 p. 5; Nelken 2001 p. 49; Dezalay & Garth 2002a pp. 246-250.
143 Dietrich 2000 p. 9.
144 Id. pp. 15-16.
145 See *e. g.* Levy 1954 p. 244 and Cotterrell 2001 pp. 82 and 87.

of family law, etc. The reasons are difficult to pin down, but there seems to be reason in Roger Cotterrell's argument that it is the combination of relatively weak social bonds and other informal constraints in these situations or communities on one hand, and the perceived need for strong and technical law on the other, that creates fertile ground for quick and widespread reception and invocation of new ideas and concepts.[146] While such theories may say something about the potential effectiveness of a contemplated initiative, development planners also need to be aware of their policy implications. Theories about what is likely to be embraced and refuted have in many cases led assistance providers to focus on assumed "apolitical" aspects of law (*e.g.* commercial law and "regulatory law") rather than issues that could incite debate about values or beliefs (*e.g.* family and penal law).

As mentioned in Chapter 2.3, a generally expressed commitment to "the rule of law" has sometimes been accepted by donors as evidence of a shared vision of law and justice, also comprising politically sensitive issues such as human rights. However, the definition of the rule of law is almost always shaped by battles between rivalling local groups whom understand the central role of the concept in structuring state power. A donor that explicitly or implicitly sanctions the presented definition thus lends strong support to the promoters of that specific definition.[147] At the same time there is nothing that says that that specific group is the most progressive, human rights sensitive, or otherwise most worthy of support. Particularly among those remaining regimes that still confess to some form of socialism, much effort is spent on developing a "newspeak" that gives the rule of law a meaning akin to traditional concepts of "socialist legality" and rule *by* law as a means to enhance the capacity of the administration and judiciary to produce outcomes that substantially reflect Party objectives.[148] John Gillespie points out that successfully mobilising international support for such definitions can work as a "vaccination" to forestall more far-reaching changes.[149]

Assistance providers that agree to support domestic reform policies aiming at establishing some form of delimited rule of law, *e.g.* as a means to provide for greater legal formalism in commercial matters, need to be aware of the conspicuous political and technical difficulties involved in promoting and maintaining different "legal

---

146 Cotterrell 2001 p. 87.

147 Dezalay and Garth 2002a pp. 246-250; Gillespie 2004 p. 147.

148 Clarke, D. 1999; Gillespie 2004; and Peerenboom 2004. The former Vietnamese Prime Minister Vo Van Kiet is often quoted as having urged that "*there must be a complete change from bureaucratic management to running the nation by law.*" The 1992 Vietnamese Constitution (Art. 4) accordingly stipulates that all organisations of the Party "*operate within the framework of the Constitution and the law*". Art. 12 stipulates that the state administers society "*by means of law*", that all state agencies "*must seriously observe the Constitution and the law*" and that all infringements of the lawful rights and interest of collectives and individuals "*shall be dealt with in accordance with the law*".

149 See Gillespie 2004 p. 159, footnote 65.

paradigms" for different sectors of society. There is reason to believe that shared commitment to one consistent definition of the rule of law is a minimum requirement of any viable legal and judicial reform policy.[150]

4.4.2 CRITICAL DIALOGUE AND CIVIL SOCIETY SUPPORT

4.4.2.1 Motivations and agenda

While legal and judicial reform (rule of law promotion) has long been treated as a separate development task, essentially insulated from the greater donor project of promoting democracy and participatory development in transition and developing countries, there is reason to believe that rule of law projects would be more politically consistent, and thus effective, if issues of legal and judicial organisation were regarded as inherent aspects of democratic practice.[151] Governments and international organisations already have a long tradition of criticising problems in other countries with a bearing on law and justice, and various transnational NGOs, either acting individually or in coalitions bound together by shared values, are becoming increasingly active and effective in exposing problems and persuading national policy makers to take action.[152] The *fatwa* on Salman Rushdie in Iran, Brazil's unilateral decision to manufacture AIDS/HIV drugs in violation of international intellectual property rules, and the reluctance to abolish the death penalty in many countries, are examples of issues that have spurred systematic, co-ordinated and long-term international criticism.

A key component of effective critical dialogue strategies is the "framing" of problems and remedies in ways that are amenable to legal and judicial action. A well-know example is the reframing by a network of women's and human rights organisations of the practice in many African and some Middle Eastern countries of what was neutrally called "female circumcision" into the criminally laden term "female genital mutilation".[153] Another is the framing of the repression of the political opposition and the judiciary in Zimbabwe as a breach of international law and human rights: International organisations and foreign governments have repeatedly pointed out that as a member of the United Nations, the African Union, the Southern Africa Development Community, and a number of other international and regional bodies,

150 See Chapter 2.2-2.3.
151 McInerney 2004 p. 6.
152 Sikkink 2002 pp. 38-40, 46.
153 Id. pp. 42-43.

Zimbabwe is bound to adhere to the rules and principles of these organizations. It is similarly underlined that as party to a number of specific international instruments, notably the ICCPR and the ICESCR, Zimbabwe must uphold and respect the guarantees enshrined in these instruments, among them that all persons are to be equal before the law and entitled to equal protection of the law, and that any person whose rights or freedoms are violated shall have an effective judicial remedy. As a member of the United Nations, Zimbabwe is further reminded that the 1985 United Nations Basic Principles on the Independence of the Judiciary and the 1990 Basic Principles on the Role of Lawyers provide that each member state should organize and administer justice in accordance with the UDHR, ICCPR and ICESCR, and that there are a number of specific principles by which member states should seek to guarantee the independence and proper roles of their judiciaries and lawyers in the administration of justice.

The British Commonwealth and many of its member countries have similarly pointed out that as a member of various Commonwealth bodies and instruments, notable among them the Harare Commonwealth Declaration of 1991 and the Latimer House Guidelines of 1998, Zimbabwe has explicit obligations to safeguard and promote judicial independence, rule of law and human rights. Many international NGOs concerned with legal and judicial issues, have joined the chorus and stressed in various fora that internationally recognized standards are being violated. For example, after having noted that the 1982 IBA Minimum Standards of Judicial Independence are routinely ignored, the International Bar Association has engaged in a critical discussion with the regime on the status of the judiciary, the role of lawyers, and access to justice-related issues.[154] The few remaining independent domestic NGOs pursue the same strategy but also include in the argument violations of important domestic laws and constitutional provisions, notably the articles in the 1979 Constitution providing for a formally independent judicial system and a judiciary enjoying security of tenure.[155]

While alliances between donor governments, international organisations and progressive civil society actors can often be effective in promoting human rights and

---

[154] In particular, the IBA has criticised the attempts by the regime at silencing the criticism and concern expressed by the principal professional organization for lawyers, the Law Society, with references to the guarantee for lawyers to enjoy freedom of expression, belief, association and assembly enunciated in Art. 23 of the 1990 Basic Principles on the Role of Lawyers.

[155] The 1979 Constitution of Zimbabwe, Chapter III, contains a detailed Declaration of Rights that sets out which "fundamental rights and freedoms of the individual" are to be protected (subject to specific limitations contained in the Constitution). Among these are a number of basic rights recognized internationally as fundamental human rights, notably the right for individuals to "the protection of the law" (to be afforded a fair hearing within a reasonable time by an independent and impartial court, etc), and specific guarantees for the protection of the independence of the judiciary (members of the judiciary shall not be subject to undue direction or control, etc.).

rule of law agenda, they may also create perceptions of a subversive coterie or conspiracy, acting to disorient and eventually overthrow the regime. As a consequence, the local members of such alliances, whether individuals or civil society organisations, stand the risk of being treated as agents of hostile forces. In Zimbabwe, new legislation restricting the rights of civil society has been adopted. Although these instruments violate both the spirit and content of important international conventions and domestic laws, civil society organizations are reluctant to challenge these enactments in court as this would carry the risk that the government decides to withdraw from these conventions, or directs its destructive energy against the little that remains of an independent judiciary.

In situations like this, assistance providers end up walking a tightrope: On one hand, support to civil society could help to give vulnerable groups and political outsiders a voice, expose the illegitimacy and incompetence of the regime, and make the political alternatives known to a greater group. On the other hand, loud-voiced foreign criticism of "domestic" issues, combined with visible support to reform-oriented local constituencies, could "prove" arguments of repressive regimes that there is an international conspiracy or similar aiming at overthrowing them, and thus expose these constituencies to danger.

4.4.2.2 Protection strategies

Assistance providers seeking to build or change political opinions in difficult environments need to combine the empowerment of progressive constituencies with the creation of protective arrangements to ensure their mere survival should a worst-case scenario become reality. The creation of such arrangements requires both ingenuity and discretion. Besides the "conventional" strategies discussed below, various forms of covert assistance within the realms of applicable laws and established practices may be required. The detailed modalities of such assistance will not be discussed here, but recent accounts of experiences of supporting reform-oriented civil society actors in South Africa under Apartheid,[156] and in other countries with similarly difficult political conditions, suggest that helping local NGOs to "mutate" (*i.e.* go from being a voluntary organization to being a trust to being a consultancy firm to being a regional body), or to move their key programs and resources beyond government reach in other countries, can be effective strategies. Donors may also help to set up legal protection funds and similar arrangements for civil society actors, independent media, and other likely targets of repression.

---

156 Sellström 2002.

Among the open and conventional ways to protect local individuals and organisations are to help break their isolation and facilitate their integration into regional and international structures. For example, assistance providers may help attorneys, journalists, academics and others to link up through study tours, networking conferences, joint initiatives and other efforts designed to strengthen regional professional ties and civil society ties generally. As an example can be mentioned the UNDP support for the establishment of a Southern African Development Community Judicial Secretariat in Johannesburg that helps to enhance the integrity and independence of the battered judiciaries in the region.[157] The support of the CoE and EU to facilitate the participation of Eastern European judges and prosecutors in various European networks is another initiative to the same end. Sometimes such technical initiatives are not enough. Donor countries and organisations may then need to demonstrate to the regime that the working environment of civil society attracts their attention, and that unless the regime proves its good intentions, governance-oriented support programs will be suspended or terminated. Should the situation be deemed very serious and acute, the donor community may threat to terminate all support, including essential humanitarian aid.

4.4.2.3 Civil society and the rule of law

In countries where there is a free civil society, assistance providers may choose among a range of strategies for empowering NGOs and other civil society institutions as centres for alternative leadership and catalysts for legal and political change.

Assistance providers have a long history of helping NGOs and professional organisations develop capacity to provide topical training (human rights, democratic practice, etc), facilitate and promote debate, and guard the interests of their members and other important yet vulnerable groups in society. For example, in Zimbabwe, the donor community has sought to empower the main professional body, the Law Society, to serve and protect lawyers who venture seriously into public interest work. A more ambitious and directly political approach is to help create "movements" through the building of networks among various civil society actors with a shared purpose and ethos. These networks can be maintained either through formal arrangements like umbrella organizations and confederations, or more informally through the holding of joint seminars and conferences, issuing of joint statements, etc. Key elements of such approaches are to help civil society actors develop good lobbying skills and to

---

157 There is a common view among civil society representatives in Southern Africa that the "peer pressure" exerted by regional actors within fora such as NEPAD and SADC on governments in the region to undertake or refrain from specific actions has often been more effective than its international equivalent.

teach them to make the most of the opportunities media publicity provides. For example, NGOs may be helped to develop agenda strategies for interesting local and international media in revealing human rights and rule of law problems, or to report "success stories" in the legal and judicial area. Assistance providers may also help reform-oriented NGOs develop skill to analyse and expose problematic features of proposed legislation and to present "best practice" alternatives.

Experiences from many development and transition societies demonstrate that NGOs can often be effective in subtly introducing and "mainstreaming" new perspectives on human rights and rule of law within formal agencies. However, there are different schools as to whether civil society actors should be supported to directly engage the judiciary. One school favours the idea of working with the judiciary, seek to break its isolation, and imbue it with new skills and ideas,[158] while another argues that the judiciary is a "superstructure" in a class of its own, and should be left to formulate its own needs and actions. It should be noted that "outsiders" (civil society, academia, etc.) and "insiders" (judges, prosecutors, Ministry of Justice) have often rather disparate opinions about what the judiciary already knows, needs to know, and can meaningfully absorb. While the "outsiders" often describe it as an unmitigated disaster with ignorant, biased and corrupt judges running the errands of the government or party, the insiders frequently tend to paint a too rosy picture.

4.4.2.4 Commitment and capacity in NGO-cooperation

Some assistance providers live under the false assumption that civil society represents the perfect opposite to the authoritarian, repressive and corrupt state. However, the reality is that some civil society organizations are created not because their founders are true believers or see a real need for their services, but because they see an opportunity to enrich themselves at the expense of the credulous donor community.[159] The expertise these organizations possess is not in justice sector reform, human rights or any other desirable field, rather in writing proposals and reports full of appealing rhetoric. Civil society support must therefore be carefully positioned to target actors that do possess the skills and integrity required, and to avoid those who are incompetent or merely opportunistic.

In principle, the burden of proof should always lay on the individual organisation seeking support: It should reasonably be required to demonstrate that it has the status under law, organisation, and people, needed to seriously address the task. However,

---

158 The 1993 Vienna World Conference on Human Rights calls on states to introduce human rights into their institutions.

159 Dietrich 2000 p. 11.

when donors are pressured to spend budgets and have few potential implementers to choose from, this principle is frequently and seriously compromised with. The problem seems particularly pronounced when a new crisis or "political flavour" have suddenly appeared on the donor agenda, and there are no established procedures or counterparts to rely on, as was the case when trafficking in human beings was made a major donor priority a few years ago.

At the same time, assistance providers have a political, legal and moral responsibility to the tax-payers and voluntary contributors to actively investigate how their funds are used. NGOs may typically be established either as public voluntary organisations (PVO) pursuant to national laws providing for such organizations, or as trusts through a trust deed. In many states trusts are less transparent and consequently both more difficult to audit for donors (but also to manipulate and infiltrate for governments) than more "democratic" traditional PVOs. Whether a PVO or a trust, the charter of the organisation is the first thing to examine, and it should provide as a minimum a consistent policy on issues of democracy, governance and rule of law. The board or trustees, and other people representing the organization, should further be able to speak confidently about these issues. Good trustees are also important for the operational effectiveness and efficiency of the organization. Assistance providers therefore need to be careful about transitions in leadership, especially if these take place in times of crisis or as the result of conflicts within the organizations, or if there is a risk that they are the result of attempts at government manipulation or infiltration. The presence of proper governance and management tools (procedures for policy making, mechanisms for dispute resolution, etc.) is yet another important factor to consider.

4.5 SETTING THE STRUCTURE: CONSTITUTIONAL AND LEGAL REFORM

4.5.1 PROBLEM IDENTIFICATION, AGENDA SETTING AND DRAFTING

The main rationale for including in rule of law programs the processes by which legislative agenda are set, laws are drafted, debates are framed and entertained, etc. is that these processes are of fundamental importance for the legitimacy, effectiveness and sustainability of any enactment.[160] Donors may for example argue that active and critical public participation in the process of law-making will augment the likelihood

160 Neilson 1993; Waelde and Gunderson 1994; Seidman and Seidman 1994; and Tanner 1995.

of support for the draft law, which, in turn, will contribute to greater respect, compliance and invocation of the final law.[161] In other situations, they may admit the cognitive difficulties for a small group of experts (whether domestic or international) to determine *ex ante* appropriate legal solutions for a given country, sector or subject matter,[162] and therefore argue in favour of less state-centred and more inclusive approaches to problem identification and norm-making.

It is true that historically, many effective norms, particularly with regard to civil and economic relationships, have emanated from sources outside the realms of the states and legislatures. For example, during the industrialisation of Europe, a period during which many key concepts were codified, governments recognised the private sector's customary trade practices as efficient and well established and gave them the force of law so that breaches could be prosecuted and penalised.[163] This policy was effective and efficient since instead of trying to shape reality to its wishes, the state sanctioned real-world practices that had already proved acceptable and effective. It also provided continuity between the traditional and the modern systems of norms and helped to maintain the self-consciousness of the nation or the group. It is thus hardly surprising that some current commentators of processes of legal and judicial reform argue that as much as possible of the "established" or "traditional" system should be retained.[164] National lawmakers may similarly argue that attempts to regulate "new" aspects of civil and commercial life should be based on existing or historical paradigms. In Vietnam, it is officially stated that "national characteristics" should be at least implicitly considered in the drafting of new legislation.[165]

The dilemma is that often there is very little of adequate traditional and historical models to be found and revived. For example, the dynasties of China and Vietnam, with their predominantly negative view of commerce, spent little effort on promoting rules and institutions for commercial litigation, and the informal mechanisms that evolved to make up for the lack of formal rules were often too *ad hoc* and fragile to be viable over time.[166] Many systems of traditional norms have also been disrupted

161 Legal and Judicial Reform: Strategic Directions 2003 p. 36.

162 McInerney 2004 pp. 9-11, 15.

163 Stein 1984; Tigar and Levy 1977.

164 For example, Waelde and Gunderson (1994 pp. 362-363) argue that "*If the independent republics* [of the former Soviet Union] *are to complete a legal framework for capitalist market economies, their best chance of achieving legitimacy is to retain as many existing norms as are compatible with such an economic system and develop the legal principles missing or neglected in the old system in a manner compatible with what is retained from the old system.*" Regarding matters of continuity and the relevance of pre-communist legislation in the Central and Eastern Europe generally, *see* Fogelklou 1997a p. 270 and Johnsson 1997 pp. 127-131.

165 The "National Characteristics Model" essentially suggests that sources of law can be found in local commercial practice and cultural values. Gillespie 1996 pp. 397-398 and 405.

166 For examples from China and Vietnam, see Marr 1981 p. 28.

and distorted by colonialism, fragmented along rural-urban divides, or rendered socially irrelevant for other reasons. Further, the rare attempts that have been made to retain allegedly "traditional" concepts within systems of otherwise "modern" or "rational" norms have often resulted in inconsistencies and confusion.[167]

The extent to which imposed colonial concepts of law and justice can serve to inspire and legitimise contemporary law-making is similarly limited. In many former colonies there is a rooted notion that the colonial law served the interests of the occupier only, and should not stand model for any current attempts at social engineering.[168] Much of this law is also sinking into oblivion as the lawyers trained in the colonial administration die away, libraries are shattered, implementing institutions reformed, etc.

Hernando de Soto and others have pointed out that spontaneously developed "informal" practices may sometimes provide temporary solutions to immediate problems and could, potentially, work as models for regulation.[169] However, it is characteristic for such practices that they evolve primarily to compensate for lacks and lapses in the existing framework of formal rules, and as such don't provide optimal solutions. It is also difficult to formally recognise some presumed effective informal practices within the legal system, *e.g.* "hut transfers" (meaning the selling primitive fixtures as a means of informally transferring the underlying land), and at the same time refuse to recognise other practices that in the eyes of ordinary people appear equally effective and justified, *e.g.* to build and operate a restaurant on the sidewalk.[170] Of course, this does not mean that informal practices should always be refuted as models when new structures are contemplated. Rather, unprejudiced observation of how these inherently dynamic and flexible conceptions evolve and operate can contribute important ideas and impulses to policy-makers struggling to find new solutions to contemporary and pressing problems.

---

167 For example the stipulation in the 1995 Vietnamese Civil Code that the "family household" is a legal entity *sui generis* with a capacity for civil intercourse parallel with physical and legal persons. Vietnamese commentators admit that this construction seems strange from a "*purely legal and technical perspective*", but argue that the Civil Code should be looked upon as a reflection of a long tradition of promoting the household as an economic and social entity. See *e.g.* Hoang The Lien 1996 pp. 24-25.

168 Marr (1981 pp. 308–315) argues that no experience more defined the nature of the Vietnamese revolutionary leadership than prolonged detention in colonial prisons.

169 On the evolvement of formal rules as extensions of informal rules and vice versa, see de Soto 1989 *in extenso*; North 1990 pp. 86–91.

170 In many countries inspired by socialism, ownership of land for commercial use, and consequently also transfer of ownership of such land, is not legally recognised. However, installations on the land may be owned and sold, so huts are erected on unused land in order to acquire legal protection for the possession and to facilitate transfer.

Another factor influencing the identification and adaptation of models is the growing recognition that the path of legal reform is not, and cannot be, determined by domestic factors alone. It has already been stressed in Chapter 2.4 and 2.5 that membership of international bodies and conventions, international trade, and an increasing international and regional interdependence in general, create external and internal expectations that the legal and judicial system should be harmonised with international law practices in general and with the laws of neighbouring countries and trading partners in particular.[171] It should therefore come as no surprise that similarities in political and economic conditions between countries often inspire law-makers to scrutinize each others' system with special care.[172] The need to take more active part in regional and international affairs have also helped national law-makers to overcome some of the guardedness that initially prevented objective scrutiny and assessment of different comparative models.[173] Foreign observers of the Vietnamese experience, on the rare occasions that they have had an insight, have often been surprised by the ease with which drafting groups have been able to re-evaluate what they have already drafted in the face of criticism or a new thought.[174] It is also notable that despite the trauma of the "American War", Vietnamese lawmakers show few signs of being biased against US concepts and advice.[175] It is recognised, albeit not always enthusiastically, that Vietnam, like the other countries along the Pacific Rim, cannot resist the continuous process of globalisation in which the United States is the prime mover.

Little is known with certainty about the behind the scenes-adaptation of foreign model concepts to local situations and problems. Foreign experts seldom or never participate in the actual drafting, and local lawmakers have often an interest in making it appear that new enactments are the genuine result of their own efforts. Judging from the resulting laws, lawmakers often cut out certain elements of model laws that they find appropriate, while rejecting others.[176] A disadvantage with this technique is the

---

171 Ajanant 1996 pp. 131-132; Gillespie 1995 p. 115 and 1996 pp. 403–404; Doan Trong Truyen 1996 p. 3; Le Minh Thong 1997 pp. 19 and 22; Neilson 1998 *in extenso*; and Ngo Ba Thanh 1993 pp. 81–83.

172 Cohen 1990 pp. 43–44 and Gillespie 1995 p. 90.

173 Nguyen Van Tam (1994) explains how various models for organising the new Vietnamese administrative courts were discussed and evaluated. For a general discussion, *see* Cohen 1990 pp. 44–45; Gillespie 1995 pp. 90–91; Le Minh Thong 1997 p. 19; and Tran Son 1994 p. 36.

174 In spite of limited experience, international isolation and scarce resources, Vietnamese lawmakers have managed to avoid many of the pitfalls that have occurred in other countries undertaking similar legal reforms, *e.g.* China. For example, while the Vietnamese regulated all forms of foreign investment in the 1987 Law on Foreign Investment, China regulated different form of investment in different laws. Vietnam also placed the State Commission on Co-operation and Investment, at the time the agency responsible for approving foreign investment contracts, apart from other line ministries with interests in the matter, while China incorporated its equivalent into the Ministry of Foreign Economic Relations and Trade, with a problematic relationship to other ministries as the result. Brahm 1990 p. 42 and Cohen 1990 p. 46.

175 On the Star-program, see Chapter 2.4.

176 For a similar observation, see Falk 1997 pp. 115-116 and Rose 1998 p. 105.

difficulty involved in assembling the pieces into a coherent whole, and the ensuing risk of developing a system or sectors of a system with fragmented and conflicting provisions. The evaluation of the content and interaction of isolated fragments from many different systems also requires technical skills and time, factors that are in scarce supply in many developing and transition countries. In an attempt to circumvent or at least reduce such problems, some countries have begun to draft comprehensive codes that are believed to be easier to put into place.[177] Although basically a good idea, the implementation of such codifications puts a formidable burden on already stretched judicial machineries.

Assistance providers have found that its is often difficult to create political opinion among law-makers and other insiders for reforming the processes of problem identification, agenda setting and legislative drafting. Alan Watson may be right that for these chief "controllers" of processes of legal change, the means for creating law and the sources for legalising and justifying law are something given, or almost "something sacrosanct".[178] Often they stress the complexity of these processes and then assert that a specialised elite only, which happens to be found within their own group, possesses the technical skills needed to handle them. Particularly in the shrinking group of socialist countries, most bills are thus still conceived in Party bureaus, passed to state executive offices staffed largely by Party members (most ministries host a Party unit, often with a neutral name, which scrutinises all significant plans and operations), and then submitted to the legislature, which is also heavily dominated by Party members. Participating non-Party experts are normally requested to prove political correctness and subjected to recurrent loyalty checks. The political leadership may also commission, or otherwise encourage, research that supports the favoured policy. While there is very little opportunity for groups outside the Party and bureaucracy to propose alternative views and solutions,[179] various politicised mass organizations may frequently be consulted, and controlled public opinion polls conducted, to create an image of a democratic process and add legitimacy to the initiative.[180]

However, the process is rarely completely controlled or internalised. Various domestic agencies with their own very distinctive missions and peculiarities frequently seek to influence it with whatever means they have at their disposal. Murray Scot Tanner's

177 Vu Mao 1996 pp. 17-18.

178 Watson 1985b p 119.

179 Jeong 1997 p. 167; Porter 1993 pp. 160–164; and Sidel 1993 pp. 223–228. The Vietnamese Law on the Promulgation of Legal Documents (art. 22) stipulates that "*The law and ordinance-elaborating program shall be worked out on the basis of the Party's lines and policies, the strategy on socio-economic development, defence, security and the State managerial requirements in each period while ensuring citizen's rights and obligations.*"

180 Porter 1993 pp. 153–160; Rose 1998 p. 101.

observations of the process of lawmaking in China are illustrative. Tanner argues that it is more accurate to describe the politics of agenda-setting, debate and drafting as a less structured interplay of more or less independent "streams" of policy making elements: "*[...] governments constantly face a stream of problems, some of which are viewed as urgent or ripe for solution at any given time, and others which go largely ignored for long periods. Meanwhile, other parts of the system, sometimes in response to these problems and sometimes independently, also produce a stream of available policy and/or legislative proposals (that is, potential 'solutions'). Any of these legislative proposals could be used to address one or more of the currently recognized problems in the system. And the chief advocates of a given policy alternative frequently do not care which problem, so long as their pet proposal is adopted. The system also has continually shifting political power balances or 'moods,' or 'cycles' which reflect key leaders' current policy dispositions. [...] Major decisions take place only under relatively rare and auspicious circumstances, such as when a given problem is perceived as urgent and solvable; when one of the available policy solutions is simultaneously viewed as suitable and acceptable; when the leadership's political mood (or balance of power) is propitious for attacking the problem with that preferred solution; and when an appropriate opportunity or vehicle for ratifying such a choice is at hand.*"[181] Analysts and donors have noted that important forces for breaking deadlocks and speeding up the process seem to be sudden shifts in leadership politics and strong interventions by top leaders, but also foreign political pressure and prospects of obtaining aid.[182] In other cases, disagreements between equally strong parties must resolved through attenuating compromises, in which much precision and substance may be lost.

It is common that once a law has been adopted, the actors rejoin battle to define how the provisions of the law are to be interpreted, what sub-laws should be drafted, and how the law should be administered. Even the agencies principally responsible for promoting and drafting the law may use this stage to alter its content. It is not only the highest echelons that fight over these matters. Middle and low-level agencies and officials may also seek to influence the implementation. Donors have noted that the capacity of these actors to attenuate and thwart reforms that run counter to their interests, for example by introducing internally inconsistent implementation instructions. Even when the obstruction is not organised, the combined effect of many such actions often suffice to bring the original initiative to nothing.

---

181 Tanner 1995 pp. 43-44.

182 Dezalay & Garth 2001.

4.5.2 CONSTITUTIONS AND CONSTITUTIONALISM

The preceding description of closed and dysfunctional legislative processes suggests that a constitutional reform, or at least a serious attempt at reasserting the existing constitutional order and constitutionalism as the governing paradigm, is often called for. Constitutionalism is here understood to mean both a classical outline of the offices of the state and their functions, and a "modern" stipulation of the normative limits of state power and a guarantee of the rights of individuals.

It is sometimes regarded a dilemma that periods of radical change are difficult to reconcile with any traditional concept of constitutionalism as a principle for legitimising and binding an enduring political order.[183] But instead of conceptualising constitutionalism as an end stage and something that preserves *status quo*, donors seem to regard constitutionalism as a means of facilitating continuous and controlled renewal. Reforming the constitutional provisions on law-making is similarly difficult in countries where there is a one-party monopoly. In China, Vietnam, Laos, for example, the embrace of market economy and rule of law principles is not predicated on an official rejection of socialism and party rule as obsolete or intolerable. Instead, the official rhetoric maintains that Marxism-Leninism and the thoughts of "great leaders" (Mao, Ho Chi Minh, *et. al.*) are still the guiding principles and that "erroneous" viewpoints must be combated.[184] The question which body that should be targeted for support thus becomes politically loaded. While assistance providers in the typical case would point to the logic of building capacity within the constitutionally designated body, the legislature, the Party may resist this option because it sees its direct involvement in law-making as a way of restoring the legitimacy it has recently lost. Where donors have managed to convince the regime (Party) of the logic of focusing on the legislature, they have often found themselves supporting a controlled "rubber stamp" institution. In spite of these difficulties, there are strong reasons to continue to work systematically to build capacity in legislatures, not least because improvements in skills and capacity help to make them politically stronger vis-à-vis other competing bodies, among them the Party. Investments in developing their administrative apparatus (the "office" of parliaments and similar bodies) are also likely to pay off once the authoritarian regime has collapsed, as there will then be an organisation in place to help the new and hopefully more legitimate legislature realise its ambitions.

183 Teitel (2000 p. 191) argues that constitutions and constitutionalism in such periods stand in a "constructivist" relation to the prevailing order in the sense that they are both constituted by the prevailing political order (backward-looking) and constitutive of political change (forward-looking).

184 Ngo Ba Thanh 1993 pp. 91-92 and 100–101; Le Minh Thong 1997 p. 19; and Pham Hung 1995 p. 20.

Less politically complicated to address is the common situation where a legislature is properly in lead but lacks the capacity to pursue critical legislative projects. Assistance providers respond to such problems by offering a range of support modalities, some structured to strengthen the legislature generally and some designed to facilitate a specific legislative project (for example adaptation to the *acquis* and practices of international and regional organisations such as the WTO, EU, and CoE).

Many of the support modalities offered by the European Commission to facilitate rule harmonization in transition countries in Central and Eastern Europe have grown out of the Phare program launched in 1989. The initial focus of this program was on matters closely related to the economy, with only very few references to human rights, rule of law, or other political objectives. However, as the participating countries one after one expressed their wish to eventually join the European Union and adhere to its fundamental principles, Phare developed into an instrument for the realisation of specific political, economic and legal goals, among them the rule of law. The support process was divided into specific steps, the first of which was to establish a strategic plan for the effort. The next step was the preparation of a work programme, followed by a project design phase, including as the main component the writing of terms of reference. Then tendering, contracting and monitoring followed on. The extent of local ownership and lead in these processes was debatable, perhaps understandably so as the goals was harmonisation to a pre-determined set of binding rules. Notably, the requirements regarding the administration and monitoring of this support were sometimes so complicated and resource-demanding that the European Union had to provide a separate line of support help recipient governments cope. For the countries of the former Soviet Union (apart from the Baltic States which were covered by Phare), the EU Tacis program offered various forms of support, including support to legal and judicial reforms.

The Council of Europe similarly provides support to new and aspiring member countries in Europe and parts of Asia to harmonize their laws and legal practices with the European Convention on Human Rights and other CoE instruments.[185] Depending on the topic, these support projects are implemented either by the Directorate General of Legal Affairs or the Directorate General of Human Rights. The European Commission for Democracy through Law (popularly The Venice Commission) is an independent advisory body under the CoE providing guidance on constitutional issues to states involved in constitutional reforms, consolidation of democratic institutions

185 At the Council of Europe's Vienna Summit in October 1993, the participating heads of state and government casted the Council of Europe as the guardian of "democratic security", founded on human rights, democracy and the rule of law.

and related questions. The European Commission for the Efficiency of Justice similarly seeks to improve the efficiency of justice agencies in the member states by helping to carry out assessments of problems and remedies, introducing new knowledge and management tools, and promoting better relations between the courts and the public. Under the Directorate General of Human Rights, the Human Rights Co-operation and Awareness Division pursues a range of human rights-oriented initiatives, comprising compatibility studies, legislative drafting assistance, and training and awareness activities.

Sometimes the conclusion of bilateral trade agreements and similar is combined with support modalities. For example, the implementation of the US-Vietnam Bilateral Trade Agreement (BTA) is facilitated by the USAID-sponsored "Support for Trade Acceleration" (STAR) program. This program, which was requested by the Government of Vietnam, is designed to be "demand-driven", *i.e.* to focus on issues identified by the Vietnamese agencies responsible for the implementation of the BTA in Vietnam. The support is essentially provided in the form of help with assessing the conformity with the BTA of Vietnamese legislation; organizing topical training workshops, policy seminars and study tours; and facilitating publication and translation of reference materials. The program management of STAR is made up of a team of local and international experts, including four expatriate lawyers and economists, seven Vietnamese professional and administrative staff, and a group of expatriate and Vietnamese lawyers and economists who work on part-time basis. The primary Vietnamese counterpart is the Office of the Government, which also manages an inter-agency Steering Committee of more than 10 ministries and state agencies.

The role of constitutional courts in changing constitutional paradigms, laws, and judicial practices should not be forgotten. In the transition from authoritarian rule in Eastern Europe, a great deal of the burden for establishing new understandings of modern constitutionalism, the rule of law, and the administration of justice came to devolve on the judiciary, particularly the evolving constitutional courts. First, as these courts often emerged out of a system of centralized state power, their very establishment defined a break with unacceptable political practices. Second, providing access to constitutional courts through litigation enabled an embryonic form of participation in the fledgling democracy. Third, where the constitutional courts were vested with mandates to engage in judicial review, they emerged as guardians of the new constitutional order.[186] This process has been relatively expedient as the courts have not been paralysed by the kind of political battles that often plague new legislatures.

---

186 Teitel 2000 pp. 22-23.

4.5.3 CONSISTENCY AND CO-ORDINATION

That many socialist, post-socialist and developing countries are still characterised by a pronounced sector-by-sector administration of society and host a multiplicity of organs with competence to pass binding norms create great difficulties in effectively co-ordinating various aspects of legal and judicial reform. In the group of post-socialist countries, the retreat of the Party from direct involvement to more subtle ways of influencing the processes has created a situation where new agencies and alliances of agencies compete to assume the supreme supervisory role that the Party once had.[187] It should therefore come as no surprise that the implementers of the reforms, *i.e.* courts and other judicial agencies, are often confused as to what are the valid law and preferred practice. The potential role of supreme courts and constitutional courts in bringing clarity to the situation is often limited, as judicial bodies in many such countries are either still formally prevented from interpreting laws and cases or ruling on matters of judicial organization, or have not had time to develop the skills required.[188] At the end of the day, detailed secondary legislation such as instructions and guidelines, in some cases even mere political statements, often prevails over actual laws.

Assistance providers have supported some reasonably successful attempts at drafting legislation that bring order and structure to the situation, as for example the 1996 Vietnamese Law on the Promulgation of Legal Documents. This law formally designates the National Assembly (and its Standing Committee) as the principal producers of laws, ordinances and resolutions, and stipulates that these instruments are formally superior to instruments enacted by other administrative and judicial agencies. Another significant stipulation in the law is that important matters pertaining to external and internal relations, defence and security, the organisation and operation of the state apparatus, and a number of other specifically mentioned areas, are to be regulated in law. This provision limits the possibility for lower bodies with normative competence to issue conflicting provisions within these areas, although the Government is retaining the right to issue decrees in matters *"which are extremely necessary*

187 In Vietnam the rivalry between the National Assembly, the Government and the Supreme People's Court is considerable. An early attempt by the Ministry of Justice to bring order to the huge volumes of secondary legislation, where the idea was that neither the Government nor the Law Committee of the National Assembly should accept a draft which had not first been properly reviewed by the Ministry, failed because the Ministry lacked the means and authority to influence the other line ministries and other central agencies.

188 This position may be ascribed largely to the rejection of the theory of constitutional separation of powers by Marxist-Leninist legal theorists, who instead insist that the power to supervise and "explain" the application of the law should be vested in the legislature as the supreme legal expression of the will of the ruling class. For a general discussion, see Costea 1990; David & Brierley 1985 pp. 237-239; and Dicks 1995 p. 86.

but which have not gathered enough conditions for the elaboration of laws and ordinances". A number of donor agencies have similarly pushed for, and offered support to, reforms of the processes for promulgation and publication and new legislation. This strategy was probably instrumental for inclusion in the Law on the Promulgation of Legal Documents of a provision that all legal documents enacted by the National Assembly, the Government, the Prime Minister and other central authorities must be published in the Vietnamese Official Gazette.

4.6 INSTITUTIONAL REFORMS

4.6.1 LAW IN ACTION

From the assistance providers' perspective, supporting legislative and law reform is appealing because it is relatively cheap, expeditious, and produces tangible results. However, the next step in the sequence, the building of judicial institutions, is perceived as being difficult, time-consuming and extremely resource-demanding. At the same time, there is no doubt that poor implementation is a widespread and serious problem in most developing and transition countries.[189] Experiences from Cambodia, Rwanda, BiH, Kosovo, East Timor and other post-crisis environments also show that the legal and judicial institutions are among the first to collapse in situations of unrest and among the most difficult to rebuild.

There are signs that assistance providers are slowly reacting on this recognition and beginning to shift the focus of their support from legislative and law reform to various aspects of implementation and administration of justice.[190] For example, the WTO has adjusted its priorities to reflect the conclusion in the Doha Development Agenda that successful trade law reform depends on technical assistance to institution and capacity building.[191] Much of the recent work of the Council of Europe in new member states and candidate countries similarly focuses on improving the independence and capacity of the judiciary. The World Bank similarly finances projects in Armenia, Georgia and other places that aim at making the judiciary more independent, efficient and accessible. Among the many components of these projects are help to put in place

---

189 Brunetti, Kisunko and Weder 1997a p. 19; The State in a Changing World 1997 p. 36.

190 Another important component of justice sector reform, namely law enforcement (police) reform, is discussed in the context of state building in Chapter 5. The essence of the "Security First" argument presented there – that rule of law and respect for human rights are hardly possible without basic conditions of law and order – is equally valid for developing and transition countries.

191 Footer (2003 pp. 109-110) critically argues that there is a difference between rhetoric and reality: Most technical assistance directed at facilitating trade law reform is still focusing on normative change and mimicking norms already in place in developed countries.

a new organisational structure; outline the division of labour; develop principles for self-governance; reform principles for hiring and firing, introduce modern court administration systems; reform judicial training; and improve enforcement of court decisions.

4.6.2 ALTERNATIVES TO COURTS

It is sometimes argued that the kind of formalism and almost "mechanical" implementation often associated with European and North American judicial structures cannot be meaningfully reconciled with the different social, cultural, and economic "matrix" of many developing and transition countries. This argument seems particularly popular with regard to East and Southeast Asian societies.[192] Others criticise attempts at creating court-centred systems on the ground that the fees, red tape and corruption associated such systems will work as a prohibitive transaction cost and put financially weak parties at a disadvantage. Yet others point to the enormous amounts of money required to attain tangible and sustainable results, and argue that there must be more efficient ways of using scarce resources.

Clearly there are numerous possible alternatives to courts and other forms of formal adjudication, but the combined effect of a number of global trends such as increasing legal and human rights literacy, eroding religious and social taboos, more frequent international contacts, rising volumes of trade, greater complexity of the transactions, and membership of international and regional organizations, spur enormous demand for formal yet independent institutions that can resolve disputes with direct reference to authoritative and publicly known rules.[193] There is also much lingering scepticism in many post-socialist countries about what, if any, role informal quasi-judicial organisations could play in a system based on democracy, market economy and the rule of law.[194]

---

192 For example, John Gillespie (1999 p. 128) builds on the argument made by Vietnamese commentators that the primary reason for the limited success of the new Economic Courts (in terms of the number of cases settled) could be the change from state management (through the Economic Arbitration Organization) to adversial contest, and suggests (*id.* pp. 128 and 130) that this is one important factor calling into question "*neo-liberal assumptions regarding the centrality of courts to market transactions*" and that "*[...] it is far from certain that that neo-liberal legal institutions are needed to resolve domestic commercial disputes. It is equally possible that informal and non-state institutions, more in tune with particularised trading networks will expand to perform this function.*"

193 See *i.a.* Blair and Hansen 1994; de Soto 1993; *From Plan to Market* 1996; Gray, C. S. 1991; Gray, C. W. 1993 and 1997; Lateef 1992; and Nalin 1994.

194 This notion is impressed by the previous amalgamation of legal and socio-political functions in various quasi-judicial organisations such as community boards and state arbitration structures. Bergling 1999 pp. 134-138.

That changes in the political and economic universe create demand for new institutions for dispute resolution is no novelty.[195] Economic scholarship has long embraced the idea that the institutions that structure and govern exchange develop along similar and predictable paths. In its earliest form, typically a small village, exchange takes place without formal written rules and third party enforcement. This is made up for by repeat dealings, cultural homogeneity and a dense social network of informal rules. The costs of transaction in this context are low, but because specialisation and division of labour are rudimentary, transformation costs are high. As the size of the market grows the transaction costs increase sharply because the dense social network is replaced by new and alien partners and more resources must be devoted to measurement and enforcement. There may still be no formal rules or institutions for third party enforcement, but moral precepts etc. can impose standards of conduct that help to reduce the costs of transacting. This stage is also typically when the state begins to take a role in the protection of businessmen and trade, *e.g.* through the promotion of merchant codes, since the links between higher volumes of trade and greater revenue potential become apparent. The third level of exchange includes the creation of capital markets and the development of firms with large amounts of fixed capital. In this world of impersonal and complex transactions, personal ties and other voluntary constraints are no longer effective. At this last stage, international and regional structures have also emerged to support and supervise international trade and intercourse, and the distinction between what is "domestic" and "international" becomes blurred.[196]

This schematic description suggests that it is changes in the relative costs of formality and informality that drive the increasing formalisation of transactions and dispute resolution. A number of other studies similarly underline that the extent to which people in developing and transition countries use the services of courts and other formal fora primarily depends on the real and perceived "costs" (in terms of time, money and other resources) associated with litigation.[197] It is consequently not moral, religion, or some other soft factor, that primarily determine whether courts are in demand or not, rather rational calculations as to costs and benefits. While a high rate of litigation may not be a quality *per se*, Katharina Pistor and Philip Wellons' comparative study of the relationship between law and economic development in six Asian countries suggests that there is a relationship between economic growth and a higher rate of commercial and administrative litigation.[198] Edward Epstein and other observers of the most dynamic economy in the region, China, have similarly noted

195 See *e.g.* Eggertsson 1996; Libecap 1996; North 1981 and 1990; Rosenberg & Birdzell 1986; and Stone, Levy and Paredes 1996.

196 North 1990 pp. 34-35 and 120-130.

197 de Soto 1989 pp. 131–172; Epstein 1994 p. 39; and Waelde & Gunderson 1994 pp. 370-371.

198 Pistor and Wellons 1998 pp. 168–169.

that greater economic freedom has made Chinese people more willing to view their world in terms of individual rights and to litigate to protect those rights.[199]

Policy makers in many developing and transition countries have noted that a new aspect of adjudication and enforcement has surfaced in the context of transition from state ownership and central planning to diversified ownership and decentralised decision-making: If state and private enterprises are to operate in a competitive environment, it must be ensured that they operate under roughly the same set of constraints regardless of where they operate and who the owners are, or the system risks reverting to the problematic combination of specific directives and *ad hoc* bargaining that necessitated reform in the first place.[200] Only courts of general jurisdiction have the necessary authority to issue binding orders cutting across such bureaucratic and territorial boundaries and capacity to maintain consistency in decision-making. It has already been mentioned that international trade, international conventions (for example the ICCPR and the 1958 New York Convention on Recognition and Enforcement of International Arbitration Awards), membership of international and regional bodies (WTO, CoE, *et. al.*), and an increasingly global environment in general, also create external and internal expectations that the institutions for dispute resolution and enforcement should conform reasonably well to international standards and their institutional equivalents in neighbouring countries (Chapter 2.4). Yet another recognition that makes courts attractive to national governments is that such systems improve the expedience of their own rule: If the system works as it should, norms enforced by courts are not as attenuated as norms enforced by alternative bodies such as local governments because of the lower number of layers between policy-making (law) and policy-implementation (litigation).

4.6.3 RESTRUCTURING JUDICIAL AGENCIES

4.6.3.1 Adjustment or overhaul

To an even greater extent than the drafting of new laws, the prospects of reforming and strengthening courts and other judicial agencies are determined by a greater "surround" of historical, political, economic and cultural factors, as well as an

---

199 Epstein (1994 pp. 38-39) shows that from 1982 to 1991, *i.e.* the initial phase of the Chinese economic reform effort, the number of civil cases taken to Chinese courts annually more than doubled and economic cases more than quadrupled. At the same time, the number of settlements successfully mediated by the Chinese courts fell from its usual high of about 90 per cent of cases to between 70 and 80 per cent. Throughout the eighties this was accompanied by a decrease in cases taken to the quasi-judicial Chinese People's Mediation Committees.

200 Clarke D. C. 1995 p. 66; Trung Duc 1994 p. 20.

"interior" of agency-specific habits and practices. This does not mean that reform architects should always seek to maintain continuity and consistency. Rather, there is experience to suggest that the inherent conservatism of these institutions and their staff (sometimes motivated by self interest) risks reducing deliberately piecemeal or gradual reforms to nothing. The greatest problem for assistance providers may therefore be to ensure a sufficiently comprehensive departure from a problematic past and present: In spite of the recognition among Vietnamese policy makers already in 1986 that the administrative and judicial structure was unable of providing essential services, the 1992 and 1994 reforms of the court organisation were matters of adjustment rather that overhaul.[201] Among the few significant changes were the establishment of special Economic Chambers (Courts) within the system of general People's Courts for handling disputes relating to commerce, and that judges were to be appointed instead of elected (the term in office was still five years and the requirement to protect "*socialist legality*" and "*the socialist regime*" remained). These optimistically introduced islands of the rule of law did little to change the greater paradigm of "*a socialist rule of law state*", and the initial enthusiasm for the initiative in business community and the general public soon faded. Other transition and developing countries that have viewed judicial reform as a natural continuation of political and constitutional reform and proceeded to more radically and comprehensively reform their judicial systems, for example Estonia, Poland and even Georgia, are commonly regarded to have faired better. It seems that high-level and broad-based commitment to comprehensive reform is essential for breaking up vested interests and introducing new and better organisational structures and work processes.[202]

4.6.3.2 Political independence and professional integrity

International organisations and donor agencies emphasise judicial independence for many reasons. The most frequently mentioned is that human rights and the rule of law cannot exist without a judiciary that interprets and applies laws and regulations in an impartial, predictable and transparent manner. Another is that independent and consistent application of justice is seen as instrumental for private business activity, and thus for economic growth. Many other aspects of the greater processes of democratisation, economic liberalisation, etc. are also believed depend on the existence of an independent judiciary to check on threats the by corruption, organised crime, and other undesirable and potentially dangerous side-effects of greater freedom.

---

201 Nicholson 1999 p. 317.

202 With regard to reforms of private legal practice, it often seems enough that that the powers in being takes a neutral stance and creates a level playing field. Dezalay and Garth (2001 pp. 243-244) mentions as a example the emergence of corporate law firms with a global presence.

The abstract and qualitative nature of the concept of judicial independence renders the choice of definition important. There is still some variation between assistance providers, but most policy documents elaborating on the issue include language that defines an independent judiciary as one that delivers judgements that are respected and enforced by the legislative and executive branches; receives an adequate appropriation from the legislature; and is not compromised by political attempts to undermine its impartiality. Sometimes a distinction is made between "individual" independence and "institutional" independence. Individual (or "decisional") independence is understood to comprise both a substantive dimension, *i.e.* that judges are allowed to perform the judicial function subject to no authority but the law, and a personal dimension, *i.e.* that judges are guaranteed job tenure, adequate compensation and security. Institutional independence refers to the operation of the judiciary and comprises matters of political status and resources in the broad sense, such as the position of the judiciary in the constitutional hierarchy and the processes by which court budgets are determined and allocated.[203] Yet another important aspect of judicial independence (sometimes regarded as part of individual independence above) is knowledge. This aspect is discussed in Chapter 4.6.3.3 below.

The abstract and multidimensional nature of the concept also makes the development of agreed standards or methods for assessing judicial independence difficult, but there is some methodological and country-specific guidance to be found in various databases and indexes. The most authoritative source may be the materials emanating out of the ICJ-affiliated Centre for the Independence of Judges and Lawyers (CIJL), essentially because the CIJL enjoys the prestige of an international quasi-judicial body and bases its work to assess and promote judicial independence on the equally authoritative UN Basic Principles on the Independence of the Judiciary and the UN Basic Principles on the Role of Lawyers.[204] Freedom House carries out recurrent surveys in a number of developing and transition countries of various aspects of democratic governance, including the rule of law and judicial independence. The results are presented in the annual "Countries at the Crossroads" publication.[205]

---

203 Legal and Judicial Reform: Strategic Directions 2003 p. 26.

204 Among other things, the CIJL intervenes with governments in particular cases of harassment of jurists; observes trials which impact upon judicial independence or where lawyers are targeted; conducts fact-finding missions to countries where the functioning of the judiciary is under serious threat; organizes seminars to promote the UN instruments providing for judicial independence; and publishes country reports documenting cases of harassment and persecution of judges and lawyers throughout the world.

205 The 2005 edition of the "Countries at the Crossroads: A Survey of Democratic Governance" features reports on no less that 60 key countries that are at a crossroads in determining their political future: Afghanistan, Algeria, Angola, Armenia, Azerbaijan, Bahrain, Bangladesh, Bhutan, Bolivia, Burkina Faso, Cambodia, China, Colombia, East Timor, Ecuador, Egypt, Eritrea, Ethiopia, Georgia, Guatemala, Haiti, Honduras, Indonesia, Iran, Jordan, Kazakhstan, Kenya, Kyrgyzstan, Laos, Libya, Malaysia, Mauritania, Morocco, Mozambique, Nepal, Nicaragua, Nigeria, Pakistan, Paraguay, Peru,

That promoting judicial independence almost by definition means changing power balances makes it an assistance topic particularly conditioned on top-level political "backing" or "will".[206] Assistance providers need thus make sure that the reform objectives and methods are carefully anchored among national political elites and as many other influential stakeholders as possible. At the same time, assistance providers need to be aware that often it is these very political elites that are supposed to surrender part of their power (and presumably sources of income) to the judiciary. Another related problem is to determine who the local addressee or beneficiary of this kind of assistance should be: While the supreme objective of the assistance is basically to isolate the judiciary from the contaminating influence of political and executive bodies, it is still the political and executive organs of the state that control these processes and sit on the resources necessary for the implementation of any reform initiative.

Another sensitive yet necessary aspect of sustainable strategies for building judicial independence is to screen out those judges and other judicial officials who do not possess the integrity, skills or other professional qualities required, or are associated with past abuses. The foreign input in this area often consists of helping to develop professional standards and establish vetting mechanisms operating on objective and lawful criteria. While other aspects of democratic, economic and human rights reform are often conditioned on the quick removal of the unfit, assistance providers may need to hold back and stress that the new vetting processes should be different from the wholesale purges practiced in some countries (involving sweeping dismissals based on party affiliation, political opinion, or association with a prior state institution) and function in a manner respectful of both the sensitivities of the general public (including the victims of injustices) and of the human rights of those under scrutiny.[207] The new processes introduced should accordingly include safeguards to ensure that parties under investigation are notified of the case against them, are allowed to contest the case, and have the right to appeal an adverse decision to a court or other independent body.

The discussion on vetting demonstrates that inherent in the concept of judicial independence is the idea that there should be corresponding accountability mechanism. It is not least for this reason that issue-specific support activities should always be developed as part of comprehensive legal and judicial reform strategies. Another aspect of effective and sustainable independence strategies is to make sure that there is external pressure (from the legislature and executive) that the internal control

Philippines, Qatar, Russia, Rwanda, Sierra Leone, Sri Lanka, Swaziland, Syria, Tajikistan, Thailand, Tunisia, Turkey, Uganda, Ukraine, Uzbekistan, Venezuela, Vietnam, Yemen, Zambia, and Zimbabwe.

206 Legal and Judicial Reform: Strategic Directions 2003 pp. 27 and 30.

207 See *e.g.* UNSG Report S/2004/616 p. 18.

mechanisms in courts and other judicial organs work as they should. Assistance providers are increasingly helping civil society actors, mass media, bar associations, ombudspersons, anti-corruption agencies, think tanks, and other bodies concerned with human rights and the rule of law to develop capacity for monitoring judicial integrity and other important aspects of judicial performance.[208]

The processes by which justice sector and court budgets are determined and made available profoundly impact on the institutional and individual independence of courts and judges. Historically, court budgets have consisted mainly of personnel costs, while providing for construction and maintenance of buildings and other facilities has often been the responsibility of other branches of the state or simply ignored. As a result, the physical infrastructure has often been inadequate or completely lacking. While some assistance providers are of the view that scarce donor resources could do more good in other less "capital-intensive" areas than construction, the World Bank, Sida, and a few others, have supported the building of court houses, procurement of office equipment, and installation of information technology, when such issues have posed serious bottlenecks to other aspects of legal and judicial reform.[209] A more philosophical reason why donors should not categorically refute the idea of supporting the building and renovation of court buildings and other physical infrastructure is the effects of such efforts on popular perceptions of judicial status, power and capacity. The image of the courts and judiciary, just like any other branch of the state, is to a great extent determined by outward and easily observed factors such as the location and condition of buildings, etc.

4.6.3.3 Developing professional skills and knowledge

A number of studies from developing and transition countries show that among the most important reasons why people hesitate to bring matters to the courts is that they are not certain that the judges can fairly and accurately comprehend and adjudicate their problems.[210] Part and parcel of any sustainable judicial reform policy is therefore to ensure that there is a sufficient number of adequately trained and committed jurists to operate the judicial institutions.

The explosion of interest in law in many transition and developing countries has lead to a number of new law-schools of varying quality springing up. Many of these are in fact technical schools, for example in fishing or engineering, that have added law

---

208 The balancing of judicial independence and accountability in an anti-corruption context is discussed in Chapter 4.6.5.

209 Legal and Judicial Reform: Strategic Directions 2003 p. 31.

210 Brunetti, Kisunko and Weder 1997a p. 19; The State in a Changing World 1997 p. 36.

to the curricula to attract tuition-paying students. This development is problematic because there are rarely sufficient physical and human resources to sustain these schools. Neither are there any working central means for accreditation and quality control. The market may ultimately ensure the "survival of the fittest", but meanwhile scarce resources are scattered further and obviously unfit graduates produced. Another issue is that students may gain entry and take grades not on merit, but by paying bribes or relying on contacts. This form of corruption is problematic because it introduces a culture of corruption into the legal system from the very beginning and thus undercuts advances made in other parts of the legal and judicial sector.

While it is in the universities that the quantity and quality of the resource-base is ultimately determined, most donors are directing their support to address the enormous need for complimentary training for already practicing judges, prosecutors and law enforcement officers. Training in this sense means much more than conveying new knowledge about the black-letter law. For judges, prosecutors and law-enforcement officers whom have received their education and acquired their professional skills in a deeply politicised environment, the adaptation to a new professional role in a more democratic and transparent society poses a formidable technical and ideological challenge. Even seemingly straightforward and uncomplicated concepts like to be "indebted" or have a "right" may be difficult to comprehend and apply. Judges and prosecutors must further suddenly disregard the social status, revolutionary merits and other subjective characteristics of the parties, and instead define the issue between them more narrowly and legally, and perhaps even deliver an uncomfortable either/or decision.[211] Further, the rapid introduction of many new laws and legal practices brings the tacit dimension of much legal knowledge into focus. Assistance providers have realised that while it is relatively easy to explain the content of a law, it is much more difficult to convey the intangible skills that make new laws operative and effective, for example the techniques for analysing, weighing, writing and otherwise communicating legal arguments.[212]

The enormous need for training cannot be met even with expanded donor effort. At the same time, assistance providers have noted that singling out certain professions or categories of jurists (*e.g.* judges) for training may not have significant impact on

211 Consider the following statement by the President of the Vietnamese Supreme People's Court, Pham Hung (1995 p. 20): "*[T]he People's Courts have always based themselves on the political tasks, and closely collaborated with the law enforcement agencies, under the leadership of the Party and through their original court sittings, have made a major contribution to the timely and effective repression of the counter-revolutionaries, spies, commandoes and reactionaries of all colors engaged in sabotaging the revolution.*"

212 McInerney 2004 p. 19.

the overall performance of the justice sector and may even impede reform.[213] The reason seems to be that the overall performance of the sector depends on effective and equal interaction between the different categories of jurists, *i.e.* that a sufficient number of competent prosecutors present cases to a sufficient number of competent judges, etc. Even in situations where resources are scarce, training initiatives thus need to encompass actors outside of the core judiciary, including in particular independent lawyers or "the bar". Another reason for emphasising independent lawyers is the relationship between the quality of their services and the effective protection of citizen and human rights. The rapid increase in demand for commercial legal services in the wake of transition is yet another factor prompting the transfer of new legal skills to the bar. Assistance providers working with this group of lawyers often begin with helping them understand and perform their new functions in a liberalised and competitive environment, *i.e.* what it means to protect the interests of clients, what the legal and ethical standards of conduct are, and what constitutes conflict of interest. Another frequently addressed matter is the regulation of entrance into the profession and the development of disciplinary procedures.

Many training initiatives were initially centred on the organising of shorter seminars (led by foreign experts flown in for the occasion) in conjunction with the adoption of new pieces of legislation, reforming of institutions, ratification of international instruments, etc. However, as the topical and capacity-limitations to this approach became apparent, the major assistance providers shifted focus to help the recipient countries establish and operate their own "permanent" training structures. The status, form and organisation of the ensuing structures vary considerably between countries, particularly between civil law and common law countries. Most Commonwealth countries have adopted as a first precept that the overall control and direction of judicial training should be in the hands of the judiciary, while the majority of civil law countries have favoured constructions where training is provided by a separate entity established specifically for this purpose, such as a judicial training centre or institute.[214] The EU, Sweden, Germany and other donors have thus helped the civil law countries Estonia and Latvia to establish centres geared at providing training and otherwise helping to improve the professional knowledge of judges, court employees, bailiffs and other legal professionals. The potentially sensitive relationship between the centres and the "parent" Ministry of Justice is regulated in agreements according to which the ministry delegates, and the centres undertake to perform, specified training activities. Besides providing various forms of training, the centres also host conferences and seminars on topical legal and judicial issues, often in cooperation with different international institutions and in the framework of international projects.

---

213 Legal and Judicial Reform: Strategic Directions 2003 p. 41.

214 Id. p. 28.

To be effective and ensure sustainable results, assistance strategies to build and empower national training structures must comprise a range of structural and institutional components. In the structural sphere, assistance providers need to support initiatives to assess and adjust the rules and regulations that govern professional training and the division of tasks and responsibilities between various training institutions; staff management reforms (reviewing and reforming rules and principles for hiring, firing, promoting, discipline, etc.); and information management reforms. In the institutional sphere, assistance providers need to support to the elaboration of sector/agency-specific training plans and curricula; development and introduction of new training methods; training of trainers; creation of teaching materials; and improving foreign (essentially English) language skills to facilitate cross border communication and comparative research. The American Bar Association's Central European and Eurasian Law Initiative (CEELI), through its many local offices across Europe and Eurasia and network of American and European jurists, is among the most active in implementing activities in the area of professional training for different categories of jurists.[215] A particular priority is to help the fledgling local bar develop its own training programs covering new areas its members need to master, such as trial advocacy skills and law practice management.

That supporting training now often equals to helping to build training institutions does not mean that the era of *ad hoc* efforts is over. Parallel to long-term institution-building activities, most assistance provides continue to facilitate training on various topics that are perceived to be pressing, and for which domestic capacity is deemed to be lacking, such as the prevention of organized crime, trafficking in human beings, etc. Many formerly closed or socialist countries also benefit from training activities designed to facilitate membership of international bodies and participation in the international political dialogue. Such activities may have a focus on how to incorporate international norms, perform supervisory functions, etc.

4.6.4 REFORMING ENFORCEMENT

A World Bank-commissioned survey comprising 69 developing and transition countries and 3 600 respondents points out that poor implementation of judgements is a widespread and serious problem: over 70 per cent of the respondents said that they

---

215 CEELI is a public service project of the American Bar Association (ABA). It is established to advance the rule of law by supporting the law reform process in Central and Eastern Europe and the former Soviet Union. The CEELI field offices cover *inter alia* Albania, Armenia, Belarus, Bosnia and Herzegovina, Bulgaria, Croatia, Georgia, Kazakhstan, Kyrgyzstan, Macedonia, Moldova, Montenegro, Romania, Russia, Serbia, Slovakia, Tajikistan, Ukraine and Uzbekistan.

did not believe that judgements would be fairly and efficiently enforced.[216] One of the most urgent aspects of judicial sector reform is thus to help developing and transition countries reform and empower the structures for enforcement of judgments and decisions.

At the same time, attempts at reforming enforcement encounter a range of political, legal and institutional problems for donors and hosts alike. The most palpable is perhaps scarcity of resources. Enforcement is a hands-on activity that requires staff (bailiffs and others), storages, vehicles, registers, and many other things that neither donors nor hosts can afford in sufficient numbers. The political problems are more intangible. Politicised courts may for example be expected to be particularly solicitous towards state bodies and state-owned enterprises, or influential commercial actors generally. It may also be understood that enforcement alone should not be stressed to the neglect of other factors.[217] In other cases government agencies may see the courts as just another bureaucracy with no more authority than *e.g.* the Telecommunications Administration or the Post Office.[218] In countries with strong regions and weak centres, or long traditions of de-centralised administration, various forms of local protectionism may further exacerbate the problems. An official or agency in one district may for example not help to enforce a judgement in favour of a plaintiff in another district, especially if a court outside the first district has delivered the judgement. Among the institutional problems can be mentioned that finding and seizing property are often difficult when official records of who owns what are missing or unreliable. Such information may also be difficult to obtain from banks and other key institutions operating under a competitive regime and anxious to show that their loyalty rests primarily with the customers.

It is only recently that international organisations and development agencies have begun to systematically address enforcement as a distinct "topic". One reason for the slow and hesitant engagement may be that enforcement as an institution and capacity-building topic appears late in the justice sector reform sequence (see Chapter 4.2).

---

216 Brunetti, Kisunko and Weder 1997a p. 19; *The State in a Changing World* 1997 p. 36. Regarding the relationship between enforcement and economic development in general, see Clarke D. C. 1995 pp. 65–66; Gray, C. S. 1991 pp. 2–5 and 20–23; Gray, C. W. 1991 pp. 763-764; North 1990 pp. 54–60; and Waelde and Gunderson 1994 pp. 360-361. It is an oversimplification to say that insufficient means for enforcement is always bad. It can be the case that business transactions are made difficult by an obsolete or otherwise inappropriate substantive law, but that lax enforcement allows effective institutional substitutes to evolve that mitigate the costs that otherwise would have been imposed by the inefficient laws, see *e.g.* Stone, Levy and Paredes 1996.

217 The Vietnamese Minister of Justice Nguyen Dinh Loc (1995 p. 21) argues that enforcement measures are to be undertaken "*[…] with the care and direction of the local Party Committees and administration, and with the support of the Vietnam Fatherland Front and its member organizations*".

218 Clarke D. C. 1995 p. 79.

Another may be a perception among assistance providers that the quantitative aspects of the problem cannot be meaningfully addressed without the infusion of enormous resources. It may also be the case that reforming enforcement is not regarded primarily or purely a justice sector project, but rather something that could as well be regarded as an aspect of public administration reform.

The donor initiatives range from narrowly designed interventions to remedy specific technical problems (*e.g.* the absence of reliable records of who owns what) to integrating enforcement as a topic in comprehensive justice sector or public administration reform programs. In the framework of such programs, donors are addressing the political aspects of the problem by supporting workshops for lawmakers and others discussing the functions of enforcement agencies in market economies, the importance of orderly liquidating loss-making enterprises, and need to protect the interests of creditors, etc. The structural aspects are addressed by providing support to the drafting of new laws, harmonization of existing national rules to international standards, and other initiatives to create a transparent and predictable normative framework. In the area of institution-building, donors have long supported training and various analytical efforts to identify problems and remedies, but are now opening up for supporting the development and introduction of new registers, communication systems and other "hard" matters.

4.6.5 ADDRESSING JUDICIAL DISCRETION AND CORRUPTION

What is labelled corruption in a given environment depends on the nature of the state, its constitution and laws, prevailing views on politics and morality, and many other things. It is thus virtually impossible, and hardly even meaningful, to seek a precise and commonly accepted definition (outside of the area of criminal law). For the purpose of facilitating a structured discussion of corruption in an assistance context, it is sufficient to define corruption as a matter of conscious deviation from formal duties and accepted norms for private advantage.[219]

The reasons why governments and assistance providers emphasise corruption are equally manifold. One reason is that a number of studies show a clear negative correlation between the level of corruption and both investment and economic growth in countries worldwide.[220] Another is that there is little doubt that corruption

219 On definitions and strategies generally, see Anger 2004 and Sandgren 2005.

220 The State in a Changing World 1997 pp. 102-103; Brunetti, Kisunko and Weder 1997a, 1997b, and 1997c.

undercuts the ability of the state to implement laws and policies in other areas not specifically related to the economy, as it creates incentives to keep norms and practices complex, opaque and arbitrary. Yet another is the recognition that corruption is a serious problem within the legal and judicial organs themselves, rendering them ineffective in fighting the phenomenon in other branches of the state.[221] Further, assistance providers, civil society groups and NGOs have noted that human rights abuses tend to be particularly serious and frequent in corrupt societies, and that weak and vulnerable groups such as women and ethnic minorities tend to be the most seriously affected. The final and most dramatic observation is that unfettered corruption can lead to fragmentation of weak states even state collapse.[222]

The IFIs and aid agencies have also their own internal reason for taking corruption seriously, notably that corrupt insiders in recipient countries siphon off money for loans and development aid at its destination, and thus make assistance programs less effective. So called sector and budget support modalities, which channel development money via the budget of the recipient state, are believed to be particularly vulnerable (see Chapter 4.8). Donors and international organisations are similarly aware of the political bad-will that surrounds corruption and corrupt countries, and afraid that perceived lenience in addressing such conditions will impact adversely on the organisations' reputation. The indexes of corruption in different countries produced by the Berlin-based NGO Transparency International and other organisations thereby come to impact on the size and specific direction of assistance and loans.[223]

It is sometimes suggested that there should be significant differences between various kinds of corruption, for example between "greasing" corruption, which is supposed to be predictable and function like a transaction cost, and blocking corruption, which is believed to be unpredictable and cause uncertainty. It may for example be argued that if the bureaucracy that acquires a bribe seeks to maximise bribe income and shares it among all its members, the person paying the bribe is subjected to low uncertainty, although possibly to high bribes. If the corruption within the bureaucracy is not organised, on the other hand, the payer is subjected to more uncertainty and perhaps

221 Brietzke 2002 p. 115; Goodpaster 2002 pp. 96-97.

222 de Soto (1989 p. 13) and Karlström (2003 p. 23) point out that the development of informal practices outside the boundaries of state control means that the state is forced to enter on a path of steady retreat which undermines its social relevance, sometimes to such a degree that it is unable to execute even modest objectives.

223 Transparency International publishes two indices of the degree of corruption in countries in the world: The Bribe Payers Index (BPI) measures the supply side of corruption, *i.e.* the probability that companies in a given country pay bribes in connection with business. The Corruption Perception Index (CPI) makes an annual ranking list of some 100 countries on the basis of how people representing the country's trade and industry, its academics, and risk analysts, perceive the degree of corruption in the country.

also to blackmail from different officials. There are some indications that for a given level of corruption, countries with more predictable corruption tend to have higher investment rates, but even here, the corruption has serious adverse impact on economic performance. World Bank studies show that no matter how high the degree of predictability of corruption in a country, the rate of investment would be significantly higher were it less corruption.[224] There is further the risk that countries that have achieved high rates of economic growth despite serious corruption find themselves paying a higher price in the future as corruption feeds on itself and creates a widening spiral of illegal payoffs until ultimately development is undermined and years of progress are reversed.

Assistance providers thus see themselves essentially unrestrained by relativist and scholarly arguments in analysing and addressing corruption in host countries.[225] Rather, the post Washington consensus dogma is clear on the point that the introduction of a new paradigm of "clean" governance is part and parcel of any successful political, economic, legal and human rights reform policy, and anti-corruption measures often form part of the conditionality for loans made to developing and transition countries.[226] Additional endorsement is found in a number of international and regional instruments, among them the 2003 OECD Convention on Combating Bribery of Foreign Officials in International Business Transactions and notably the 2003 UN General Assembly Convention Against Corruption.

The UN Convention emphasises four elements of effective anti-corruption strategies: prevention, criminalization, international co-operation and asset recovery.[227] An entire chapter of the Convention is dedicated to prevention, with measures directed at both the public and private sectors. These include model preventive policies, such as the establishment of anticorruption bodies and enhanced transparency in the financing of election campaigns and political parties. States must endeavour to ensure that their public services are subject to safeguards that promote efficiency, transparency and recruitment based on merit. Once recruited, public servants should be subject to codes

224 The State in a Changing World 1997 p. 103

225 Sandgren 2005 pp. 265-266.

226 On the views of the World Bank, see Anger 2004 pp. 19-26; Buscaglia & Dakolias 1999 p. 1. For a commentary and critique, see Goodpaster 2002 pp. 97, 104-105; Jayasuriya 2002 p. 24; and Lindsey 2002 p. 7.

227 After intense lobbying by some member countries, the General Assembly recognized in 2000 that an effective international legal instrument against corruption (independent of the United Nations Convention against Transnational Organized Crime) was needed. The responsibility for drafting the instrument was given to an *ad hoc* committee under the UN Centre for International Crime Prevention, Office for Drug Control and Crime Prevention in Vienna. The Convention Against Corruption was finally adopted by the General Assembly by Resolution 58/4 of 31 October 2003 and needs 30 ratifications to come into force.

of conduct, requirements for financial and other disclosures, and appropriate disciplinary measures. Transparency and accountability in matters of public finance must also be promoted, and specific requirements are established for the prevention of corruption in the particularly critical areas of the public sector, such as the judiciary. It is also recognized that preventing public corruption requires an effort from all members of society at large. For this reasons, the Convention calls on countries to promote actively the involvement of non-governmental and community-based organizations, as well as other elements of civil society, and to raise public awareness of corruption and what can be done about it. The Convention further requires countries to establish criminal and other offences to cover a wide range of acts of corruption, if these are not already crimes under domestic law. The Convention goes beyond previous instruments of this kind in criminalizing not only basic forms of corruption such as bribery and the embezzlement of public funds, but also trading in influence and the concealment and laundering of the proceeds of corruption. Offences committed in support of corruption, including money laundering and obstructing justice, are also dealt with.

By signing the Convention, countries agree to cooperate with one another in every aspect of the fight against corruption, including prevention, investigation, and the prosecution of offenders. Countries are bound by the Convention to render specific forms of mutual legal assistance in gathering and transferring evidence for use in court. Countries are also required to undertake measures which will support the tracing, freezing, seizure and confiscation of the proceeds of corruption. It is also a major breakthrough that countries by signing the Convention agree on asset-recovery. This is a particularly important issue for many developing countries where high-level corruption has plundered the national wealth, and where resources are badly needed for reconstruction and the rehabilitation of societies under new governments. Reaching agreement on this chapter involved intensive negotiations, as the needs of countries seeking the illicit assets had to be reconciled with the legal and procedural safeguards of the countries whose assistance is sought. Several provisions specify how cooperation and assistance will be rendered. In the case of embezzlement of public funds, it is stipulated that the confiscated property shall be returned to the state requesting it.

Membership of international and regional bodies such as the EU or NAFTA, is increasingly conditioned on the presence of effective anti-corruption strategies. Sometimes these organisations also offer to assistant in the implementation of such strategies. For example, anti-corruption strategies were and are central elements of the large EU-financed Phare, Tacis and CARDS-modalities aiming at facilitating various aspects of economic and political transition in Eastern Europe and the republics of the former Soviet Union (see Chapter 4.5.2).

What specific strategies that assistance providers employ to address corruption is largely determined by their respective perspectives on the phenomenon.[228] According to a historical-political perspective, corruption should be understood as a natural, perhaps even inevitable, phenomenon in a certain phase of the political, social and economic development of a society. A donor may from that conclude that there are no "quick fixes", but a chance that the degree of corruption will be reduced as society develops towards greater specialisation, legal sophistication, etc. The response strategy would then be to refrain from specific anti-corruption activities, but rather seek to speed up the processes of economic and political reform generally. Another perspective is that corruption is attributable to individual behaviour (moral failure) within a given legal and political framework. The remedy would then be to help put in place criminal sanctions for unacceptable behaviour. Yet another perspective is to understand corruption as a result of erroneous economic policy (in the typical case a policy that emphasises planning and price control), and then to focus on deregulation, privatization, competition, etc. The related "good governance" argument, finally, is to underline the tendency of resource-weak states to overstretch their institutional capabilities and thereby create for themselves a climate fertile to corruption. The suggested cure in this case would be to promote a state that is smaller in scope, but more effective in its core functions.

Another critical factor for the choice of strategy is of course how national policy-makers think of the phenomenon. Whether and to what extent the domestic leaderships are genuinely concerned varies, but democratic governments whose political survival depend on a perception of being "clean" have reasonably a stronger incentive to take the problem seriously than authoritarian regimes with a vested interest in the *status quo*. Members of the latter category are also notorious for trying to throw suspicion on outside initiatives to highlight and address problems of corruption and to argue that anti-corruption programs are ethnocentric and colonial.[229] Another argument has a bearing on the existence of double standards. Asian governments in particular have pointed out that practices such as lobbying and campaign financing seem to be acceptable in Western capitals but regarded as corrupt when practiced in the East or South. Yet another defense is that anti-corruption seems to be about "blaming the victim", *i.e.* locating responsibility in local elites at national level, whereas, these critics claim, the actual responsibility should lie with international organisations, multinational corporations, aid agencies, and others disorienting local

---

228 For an overview, see Anger 2003 pp. 19-45 and Karlström 2003 p. 10-19.

229 Lindsey 2002 pp. 1-3; Taylor 2002 pp. 37 and 40-41.

practices and introducing new temptations. Kennedy and Lindsey point out that although these arguments are often "anti-Western" rather than "anti-anti-corruption", and as such off the point, they point to the importance of carefully framing projects in terms that don't provoke unnecessary sensitivity.[230] If assistance providers fail in this, there is a risk that important national stakeholders refuse to be associated with the assistance providers and their intrusive programs.

However, even authoritarian regimes have rational self-interest reasons to take corruption seriously. There are many historical examples where popular disgust with corruption has eventually turned into revolutionary discontent.[231] These governments are also aware of the negative relationship between high levels of corruption and low levels of aid and investment. A number of authoritarian states are consequently turning to international organizations and donor agencies for help in formulating and implementing anti-corruption strategies.[232]

Many national governments prefer a reactive and carefully delimited approach, the first step of which is to embrace the idea of corruption as a matter of criminality or individual moral failure, and consequently to order more prohibitive legislation and stiffer criminal sanctions (including the death penalty). However, these regimes have often realised that such strategies are neither very effective nor efficient (supervising, investigating, prosecuting and punishing every incident of corruption require enormous resources, especially when the law enforcement and judicial structures are themselves corrupt), and do not appeal to the human rights-sensitive donor community. A similarly more realistic attitude has emerged with regard to political campaigns appealing to "purity" or "morality", where even the Chinese and Vietnamese regimes seem to fear that such propaganda may rather galvanise popular notions of Government and Party hypocrisy.

Another strategy has been to regard corruption as a transitional phenomenon, *i.e.* to argue that the rapid growth in administrative and judicial corruption should stem from temporary regulatory problems in the administration of the state in conjunction with the changeover from state ownership and central planning to private ownership and decentralised decision making. The preferred "quick fix" has accordingly been

---

230 Kennedy 1999 pp. 457-458; Lindsey 2002 pp. 15, 17-18.

231 Schwarz (1996 p. 18) refers prominent Vietnamese Party leaders who describe internal corruption as a bigger threat than the many perceived foreign and domestic enemies who would like to drive the Party from power. The Vietnamese leadership has accordingly deemed the problem with corruption a "national disaster."

232 For example, Vietnam turned to the UNDP for assistance in developing the comprehensive Public Administration Reform Program (PAR), which has among its core priorities to curtail corruption within the various branches of the state.

to reduce the opportunities for taking bribes and other forms of undesirable behaviour by speeding up the changeover and removing the jurisdiction of official agencies over potentially profitable matters.[233] Another key component in this strategy has been the introduction of "anti-corruption laws" that formally lock bureaucrats out of the marketplace and provide for accountability. However, many such national and international strategies have similarly fared poorly, much because of national ambivalence surrounding some of the key assumptions underlying them with regard to the proper relationship between political parties, state bureaucracies, the judiciary, and society.[234]

In other cases, donors have supported national efforts at creating anti-corruption commissions and similar bodies in hope that such unpolluted entities would be able to begin afresh and take the lead in fighting corruption. For example, the international financial institutions and donor agencies supported Indonesia in hastily creating many ostensibly independent regulatory commissions from 1999 onwards, among them the Anti-corruption Commission.[235] While the origins of such strategies have often been in domestic ambitions to demonstrate that problems of corruption are taken seriously, assistance providers have experienced that the same domestic policy makers have not always been clear on the purpose and proper organisation of such bodies, or been willing to give them the mandate and resources required, with conflicts over jurisdiction and resources with the "ordinary" courts and law enforcement as the result. In the Indonesian case, there was never consensus on the political objectives of the Commission, its organisation, or funding, which meant that it began its life seriously handicapped.[236] Neither have such bodies been very effective in a coordinating or advisory capacity: their mandates have rarely or never been strong enough to make competing agencies listen, and they have often ended up on the losing side in the "palace wars" that regularly and inevitably erupt when vested interests are challenged.[237]

At this point, national governments have little option but to go along with essence of the Post-Washington Consensus idea that the fight against corruption is conditioned on profound political, legal and institutional reforms, particularly the introduction of some form of authoritatively defined division of power between the legislative, executive, and judicial branches of the state (albeit not necessarily "Western-style" democracy), and giving the various branches means to hold the other accountable for

233 Goodpaster 2002 pp. 104-105.
234 Gillespie 2002 pp. 168-169, 185-186.
235 Assegaf 2002 pp. 128-130; Brietzke 2002 p. 120.
236 Assegaf 2002 p. 136.
237 Id. p. 136.

their decisions. Governments have also needed to accept that the existence of a legitimate legal and political order depends on the idea that the ruled and the rulers obey the same rules.[238] A large number of constitutions in transition and developing countries throughout the world have consequently been changed in recent years to reflect the principles of "law-based," "legal" or "constitutional" government. The actual transformations have also frequently included the removal of the monopoly of the communist Party in political life, introduction of checks and balances, and the restructuring and reinforcement of the judicial system.[239]

However, when authoritarian regimes call for the rule of law, what they actually mean is often a carefully delimited version of rule *by* law as a way of limiting the room for discretion in the execution of official functions and enhancing the capacity of the judiciary and administration to produce outcomes that reflect top-level objectives (Chapter 2.3).[240] For example, the 1992 Vietnamese Constitution (Arts. 4 and 12) stipulates that all organisations of the Party "*operate within the framework of the Constitution and the law*"; that the state administers society "*by means of law*"; that all state agencies "*must seriously observe the Constitution and the law*"; and that all infringements of the lawful rights and interest of collectives and individuals "*shall be dealt with in accordance with the law*".

Given the limited success in pursuing criminal and structural strategies in isolation, it is not surprising that so-called "trust and governance" prescriptions addressing corruption both as a failure of institutions and as a problem of trust are attracting increasing attention among donors and hosts alike. In essence, these prescriptions add to the Post-Washington Consensus dogma about making judicial institutions stronger in their core capacity, the idea that an internalisation of a higher degree of trust as obligation and confidence could help to transform courts and other judicial institutions into "clean zones" in otherwise difficult environments, able of setting an example for others.[241] A primary issue in trust-based approaches is the identification of a

---

238 Adelman and Centeno 2002 pp. 142, 154 and 158.

239 See Chapter 3.2.

240 The former Vietnamese Prime Minister Vo Van Kiet is often quoted urging that "*there must be a complete change from bureaucratic management to running the nation by law.*" At the same time, the Communist Party's self-assumed constitutional role as the "*force leading the State and society*" and "*vanguard of the Vietnamese working class*" remains unchanged (Constitution 1992, art. 4). Doan Trong Truyen 1994 pp. 30-31 and 1996 p. 4; Nguyen Duy Gia 1997 p. 20.

241 Braithwite (1998) argues that societies work better when two kinds of mutually constituting and reinforcing trust are maximized: trust as confidence (the expectation that someone will do what we want) and trust as obligation (people accepting that they have obligations and acting to honour them). This latter definition comes close to the legal definition of trust. In essence, Braithwite argues that the more people are trusted to behave in a trustworthy way, the more they are likely to do so. At the same time, Taylor (2002 p. 46) and Braithwite (1998 p. 367) critically point out that it is

distinct target group, which is willing and capable of assuming the role of moral example and regulatory model. The legal profession has attracted particular attention in this respect, much because in its archetypical incarnation, it is believed to display important characteristics such as control over entry into the profession, a shared ethos, and ability to regulate itself.[242] Anti-corruption policy makers have been particularly attracted by the built-in incentives in this model of organisation: The profession has a strong incentive to maintain a high quality of regulation and police its members well, because if the government and society at large recognize the professions ability to do so, it will eventually be able to make a "claim to legitimacy", *i.e.* say that it should be given a formal monopoly to perform specific functions in society as long as it follows the professional ethics and otherwise acts altruistically. Further, if lawyers as a profession can police themselves, then potentially they could also function as watchdogs, strategically placed between government and non-government entities, looking for corrupt behaviour in society in general.

The dilemma is that as of present, very few developing and transition states have anything like a legal profession that meets, or will soon be able of meeting, these criteria. Rather, the legal profession often consists of fragmented and competing clusters of occupational groups with some form of legal training as the only common denominator. Further, the mere circumstance that a profession has the capacity to develop its own rules and self-police its members does not guarantee that the members will actually be less inclined toward corruption. There are many examples that lawyers are not ethical or moral simply because they are lawyers or trained in law. Rather, professionals comply with the ethical rules of their group because the rules are reinforced in various ways: by collegial pressure, gossip, informal and formal sanctions, etc.[243] Yet another problem is the "other-worldly" nature of the legal profession, which sometimes shrouds it in mystery and sets the stage for suspicion and misunderstanding. Self-regulation and internal control could result in even more secrecy and become a cloak behind which members of the profession could safely conceal illegal and corrupt acts.[244] Further, it should be remembered that self-regulation is hardly possible without official endorsement and a degree of state regulation. Autocratic regimes may not want to take the risk that such alternative structures evolve into something that may eventually pose a threat to the political paradigm.[245] This explains why countries

difficult to think of any institution in any society that remains completely virtuous or free of undue influence over time. For this reason, it may be necessary to institutionalise some distrust in regard to all institutions so that their various "pathologies" can be checked by the strength of other institutions.

242 Brietzke 2002 p. 119; Taylor 2002 pp. 38 and 40.

243 Taylor 2002 pp. 38-39.

244 Dakolias and Thachuk 2000 p. 361.

245 Taylor 2002 p. 38.

such as Belarus, China, Vietnam and Cuba have been careful to preserve the technocratic nature of the legal profession. Rather than building on existing groups of professionals in such countries, assistance providers may therefore need to begin with promoting the formation of the kind of professions needed.

A first step in facilitating the creation of a profession may be to suggest reforms of the principles for entry. The norms and procedures for judicial appointments are particularly important but also sensitive in this respect. While competitive judicial and civil service examinations have often been suggested as a way of providing for a profession with the right formal and personal qualities, there is rarely a sufficient number of properly educated people to choose from. It has also been repeatedly proven that there are ample opportunities to manipulate such examinations. A system based on entrance examinations must further be combined with effective means to sustain performance after recruitment, such as clear criteria for upward mobility and rewards for meritorious service. Without such a structure, judges and prosecutors will worry as much about pleasing their superiors and other influential people as performing their duties.

There are other possible ways of making the identification and appointment of judges more transparent and less partisan, and of ensuring a degree of accountability in their work. Judges may for example be elected and re-elected. While some may argue that decisions made by ill-informed voters do not necessarily ensure that the better candidate wins, elections may be combined with programs to provide voters with systematically collected and processed information on the legal and administrative skills, integrity and impartiality of candidates. Where such programs already exist, the data frequently come from internally compiled statistics and surveys of court users, including attorneys, police, jurors, litigants, etc.[246] Public hearings are another means to the same end. Assistance providers may also seek to promote the introduction of internal auditing and systematic compilation of judicial statistics as a way of facilitating non-intrusive performance supervision. Such statistics may answer whether judges try cases within stipulated time limits, what the appeals ratio is, how many cases that are reversed on appeal, but also provide data on internal matters such as court budgets and expenditures, staff management, etc.

Trust as confidence and obligation needs to be maintained also after appointment. One means to this end is a healthy *esprit de corps* that conveys a common understanding about what is desirable and undesirable behaviour, imposes self-discipline and helps to uphold the honour of the respective professional group. Mechanisms for control, accountability, public participation, and other matters related to openness

---

246 Dakolias and Thachuk 2000 p. 387.

and transparency, have already been mentioned as important, but there may also be scope for "softer" approaches. In Slovakia, CEELI and the U.S. Department of Justice organized a conference in October 2002 for 50 Slovak judges, prosecutors and police with the purpose of creating a baseline understanding on what is public sector corruption and how to investigate and prosecute it. In Georgia, CEELI assisted the judiciary in adopting a new Code of Ethics for Judges in 2001 and soon thereafter joined forces with the Georgian Judicial Training Center and Judges of Georgia Association in developing and implementing an ethics training program for judges. The trainers, who were themselves Georgian judges, presented to the participants hypothetical situations that involved ethical issues. Those judges who were deemed to have demonstrated sincere commitment to the principles discussed in the course were then selected to take part in a later Integrity Management Workshop aiming at empowering them as a leading group in upholding the integrity and independence of the judiciary.[247] In other cases, assistance providers have helped to identify and promote positive models. For example, donors have helped Vietnamese policy-makers to analyse what made the Singaporean bureaucracy able of developing in a short time into a group well known for its competence and conscientiousness.

While there is a relationship between salary levels, motivation and corruption, promoting salary reforms has proven difficult.[248] Judicial salaries in many developing and transition countries are too low to allow judges to support themselves without extra income (and lag too far behind what the private sector can offer) but donors need to be careful not to promote initiatives that lead to inconsistencies in the general salary structure (as has been the case in Bosnia and Herzegovina and other places, see Chapter 5.5.4) or put a too heavy burden on the local taxpayers. Sector support, as discussed in Chapter 4.8, may carry the possibility for managing such problems.

Assistance providers have noted that promoting improvements in the reporting on corruption is often an effective strategy for building pressure for accountability. Where there is widespread confusion about what is acceptable and what is not, good reporting help to educate officials and ordinary citizens alike about new laws and intended behavioural norms.[249] It may similarly help turning an apathetic and resigned public opinion into one that speaks out and demands change.[250] Good reporting further helps to create and maintain loyalty to the state among uncorrupted officials: If officials

---

247 http://www.abanet.org/ceeli/areas/anticorruption.html

248 It should be mentioned that some studies of the relationship between wages and corruption in the civil service suggest that the relationship linkage may not be as strong as is often assumed. For example, Van Rijckeghem and Weder (1997) suggest that where the wages are low in general, the level of wages may be of secondary importance, as potential bribes dwarf wage income.

249 Holmes 2002 pp. 57-58.

250 Dakolias and Thachuk 2000 p. 380.

never hear that corrupt colleagues get caught and exposed, they may think that they themselves can engage in improprieties with impunity.[251] The most common means to help "the reporters" improve their reporting is various forms of awareness and training activities targeting journalists, academics, progressive civil society actors, etc.

While the formal authority to monitor and sanction arbitrary or corrupt use of public power is typically placed with law enforcement bodies, independent anticorruption commissions or ombudsmen, assistance providers are aware that independent mass media may also have political and economic incentives to expose corruption and other violations of rule of law principles. For example, within the narrow limits sanctioned by the Party, and with reservations for the possibility that it has been used or manipulated, the business press has already assumed an important watchdog role in China and Vietnam, and there are signs that domestic officials are much more cautious about misusing official power in the face of such exposure. In this sense, there is reason to believe that support to mass media carry much greater prospects of contributing to curtailing corruption and exposing other irregularities than has previously been assumed.

4.7 ACCESS, INFORMATION AND ASSISTANCE

Legal reforms are essentially pointless unless the "users" of the system, the general public, are aware of the new laws and can seize on the opportunities they provide. At the same time, it is well known that radical overhauls of the legislation and the implementing institutions have rendered the system difficult to both understand and access in many developing and transition societies. Structural and capacity-building reforms should therefore be combined with, or followed by, efforts to explain and open up the system.

Access to justice can be discussed in three parts: improving access to existing services; expanding access to facilitate or encourage use of dispute resolution mechanisms by non-traditional users (for example marginalized groups); and creating new legal standing to advance the interests of classes of individuals. Besides institutional and capacity reforms, access to justice strategies need thus also include a normative component, *i.e.* the changing of laws and norms that prevent certain groups (race,

[251] There is also the sensitive question whether assistance providers should facilitate show trials and similar demonstrations of right and wrong. While there are some benefits of making examples of serious cases of corruption, particularly in that it helps to convince the public that the government and judiciary are dedicated to eradicate the phenomenon, such approaches also carry the risk that important human rights and rule of principles are compromised for the sake of pedagogy. Dakolias and Thachuk 2000 p. 366.

gender, children, etc.) from accessing the system, and can therefore be politically controversial. An authoritative regime or a leading political group may for example not favour the idea of allowing or helping people challenge government policies in court. In other instances, local policy makers may see little point in spending resources on helping groups that are politically and economically irrelevant, for example mountainous tribes that neither vote nor control assets of any value. Assistance providers may here point out that access to justice is a right protected by human rights treaties and other instruments to which most countries are parties, and that the state has a legal obligation to provide the institutional arrangements necessary to exercise this right.

Assistance providers define access to justice in different ways, and target different aspects of the concept, depending on the construction of their respective mandates and programs. For example, while the UNDP supports issues of access in the broad sense (both the capacity to seek remedy and to provide remedies), the World Bank has traditionally focused on those aspects of access that are believed most important for promoting economic recovery and development. As of recent, the Bank has widened the scope of its engagement to include a range of general empowerment issues.[252] Other assistance providers, meanwhile, target other topical and country-specific problems. The range of activities comprise the introduction of private and court-annexed alternative dispute resolution mechanisms, developing citizen education programs, waiving normal fees, facilitating *pro bono* representation, supporting publicity campaigns, producing legal information materials in indigenous languages, creating legal databases, and establishing traveling courts.

Parallel to the work of the IFIs and bilateral agencies, various NGOs and other civil society actors play a crucial role both in highlighting issues and in pursuing reform projects. Many NGOs focus on increasing the dissemination to the general public of legal and human rights materials, establishing and supporting legal clinics and consultation bureaus, and providing for other legal aid and advocacy mechanisms. Some strategically placed NGOs have managed to establish themselves as pseudo-consultants implementing traditional technical assistance projects with funding from bilateral agencies. For example, Legal Aid of Cambodia (which is established to "*assist in the construction of a more civil society and a more just legal system based upon respect for human rights, equal justice and the rule of law, and to ensure that high-quality legal services are made available to the most vulnerable segments of Cambodian society*") receives funding from no fewer than the Netherlands Organization for Development Cooperation (Novib); Oxfam Great Britain; Embassy of Finland; Asia Foundation; European Union through Danchurch Aid; the Cambodia Office of the UN High

[252] Legal and Judicial Reform: Strategic Directions 2003 p. 41.

Commissioner for Human Rights; Save the Children Norway; American Center for International Labor Solidarity; Lawyers for Lawyers Foundation; ICCO; and the Soros Foundation. In Zimbabwe, where the high level of inflation has eroded the financial underpinnings of the existing legal aid system to an extent where hardly any lawyer is prepared to accept the nominal remuneration offered, a number of development agencies similarly offer support to various domestic organisations pursuing access-oriented programs. For example, the non-governmental Legal Resources Foundation is supported to run a paralegal program as a "comfort zone" for people before they access the formal court system.[253]

4.8 SECTOR AND BUDGET SUPPORT

A new modality for channelling support to justice sector reform is "Sector (Budget) Support" or "Sector Wide Approaches Programs" (SWAP). In essence, SWAP is a donor reaction to the problems of fragmentation and lack of domestic ownership often associated with traditional project support, and an attempt at offering a "holistic" alternative that provides better conditions for genuine national ownership and strategic planning. The core idea is that the recipient government and as many assistance providers as possible should unite around one sector policy and pool all their resources into a facility (fund) that allocates resources to priority projects within the sector as identified by the host government.

In Uganda, the Government and various ministries and agencies within the justice sector came together in 1999 to form the Justice, Law and Order Sector Reform Programme (J/LOS) with a mission of "*enabling all people in Uganda to live in a safe and just society*". 11 donors, among them Denmark, Sweden, United Kingdom, Austria, Ireland, Netherlands, Norway, Germany, United States of America, the World Bank and the European Union Delegation, responded favourably to this initiative and decided to pool money into a special facility according to a basket funding formula. The main focus of the program is to reform the commercial and criminal justice systems. The specific policy objectives are stated as fostering a human rights culture, promoting the rule of law, securing access to justice, amending all discriminatory laws, reducing crime, promoting new methods for crime prevention, encouraging grass-root and civil society participation, and strengthening the structures for commercial justice.

---

[253] The overall objective of the Legal Resources Foundation of Zimbabwe is to promote a democratic environment based on the rule of law and human rights. The Foundation has Legal Project Centres in the five major cities in Zimbabwe and 20 rural Legal Advice Centres. A range of donors help to fund LRF's activities, among them CIDA, USAID, the Netherlands, Sida, DANIDA, Finland, European Union, Oak Foundation, Friederich Naumaum Foundation, British High Commission, International Bar Association, Norwegian Embassy and the Konrad Adenauer Foundation.

There may not be as much domestic ownership and lead in all such initiatives as the concept of SWAP suggests. The roots of the Ugandan initiative are to be traced back to the 1996 joint IMF/World Bank "Highly Indebted Poor Countries" initiative, a modality designed to encourage reforms of the structures for economic activity (essentially private business) in return for debt relief, thus helping developing countries meet their financial obligations while simultaneously retain sufficient means to realise priority reform initiatives. The money thus "rescued" from lenders (approximately USD 90 million annually for Uganda) was put in a Poverty Eradication Fund, and when surveys in the end of 1990s pointed out justice, law, and order as key concerns, and particularly access to justice and lack of security for individuals and property,[254] these conclusions were reflected in the Poverty Eradication Action Plan elaborated by the Government. The final step was to make resources from the Poverty Eradication Fund available for addressing them.

The guideline for the specific efforts under the Ugandan J/LOS is the Strategic Investment Plan (SIP), "owned" by stakeholders and adopted by the government and the donors together. The SIP focuses on three themes as derived from the Poverty Eradication Action Plan, namely access to justice, efficiency and effectiveness of justice, and quality of justice. Decisions regarding the orientation of the SWAP-facility support, and regarding the allocation of resources, are taken by a Technical Committee in which all the participating institutions are represented (the Ministry of Justice and Constitutional Affairs, the judiciary, the Ministry of Internal Affairs, the prison service, the police, the Department of Immigration, the Directorate of Public Prosecutions, the Judicial Services Commission, the Uganda Law Reform Commission, the Ministry of Local Government, etc.), together with the donors. The donors also meet in a specific Donor Group, which convenes once per month to discuss the progress of legal and justice sector reforms and the future focus of the program. The cooperation between donors, the Technical Committee, and the respective institutions, is coordinated by a Donor Liaison Group, which meets twice per year. The National Council for Justice, Law and Order executes high-level supervision of the whole effort at legal and judicial reform and provides political support and policy guidelines.

As an example of a concrete reform initiative under the program can be mentioned the "Chain-Linked Initiative", aiming at improving the efficiency of the administration of justice. It was launched as a pilot project in 1998 in the district of Masaka with the purpose of conveying to the participants the image of the justice sector as a chain where all agencies are linked together and mutually dependent, thus helping to create a better understanding for the need of improving inter-agency communication and

[254] For example "Particiapatory Poverty Assessment Project in Uganda, 1998-1999"; "Uganda Integrity Survey 1998"; and "Uganda Poverty Status Report 1999".

coordination. The project is officially described as successful and having spurred similar initiatives in 29 other districts. Among the most important improvements as a result of the initiative is a significant reduction in the time offenders spend is detention and prison.

It too early to draw final and general conclusions regarding the effectiveness and efficiency of SWAP in legal and justice sector reform, but it is clear that the political and economic situation within the country greatly conditions the prospects for success and failure. As a stable political environment and baseline consensus around common goals and policies are essential for putting a SWAP-structure in place, SWAP is hardly an alternative in environments characterised by fragmentation and rivalry. Disappointing experiences from Vietnam and other countries also indicate that if the lead agency does not enjoy sufficient trust among the other stakeholders or lack the political and bureaucratic refinement to maintain an image of a transparent and inclusive decision-making process, SWAP will reach a deadlock. Further, as funds are channelled via the general state budget, corruption must be under control and strong supervision and accountability mechanisms in place. There are indications that donors have often underestimated this aspect of SWAP, with the consequence that funds have been wasted and the corruption nourished further.[255] SWAP thus seem most appropriate in the rare situations where there is good government and genuine commitment to a comprehensive reform plan, but its implementation is made impossible by lack of resources.

255 Anger 2004 p. 48.

5. INTERNATIONAL ADMINISTRATION APPROACHES

5.1 INTRODUCTION

The most ambitious attempts at promoting legal and justice sector reforms are made in the context of "state building" in countries or territories recently devastated by war or haunted by gross human rights violations.[256] Sometimes this effort is labelled as "security sector reform" because of its initial focus on reforming the organisations that have the authority to use force, or order the use of force, as well as those civil structures that are responsible for their management. However, the project is greater than that and comprises many other legal and judicial components and counterparts essential for the long-term political, economic and social viability of the state and society.

One component of this effort that will be only briefly touched upon is "transitional justice". The concept refers to a combination of policies that post-crisis countries implement to address past human rights violations in order to guarantee accountability and facilitate reconciliation in the future. These specific activities may be both judicial and non-judicial. Transitional justice may also indirectly encompass institution and capacity-building elements in that the success of judicial strategies depends on the reviving and sensitizing of courts, prosecution agencies and other judicial institutions.[257] The linkages between law (the rule of law) and sustainable peace are also articulated in the concept of "human security", which emphasises individual human rights as the fundament of international order. Human security thus encompasses not just the achievement of minimal levels of material needs, but also

---

256 There is an increasingly accepted delineation between state building and the related issue of nation building. While state building refers to the creation or strengthening of institutions, and is something that outside agents are believed to be able to contribute to, the term nation building as it is used in the international debate refers to the creation of a community bound together by a shared history and culture, something which is recognised to be beyond the power of any outside agent to achieve. Fukuyama 2004 p. 134.

257 Some commentators argue that the retributive and restorative aspects have received more attention by the international community than rebuilding and enhancing collapsed or weakened justice systems, essentially because of the higher moral and justice imperatives associated with the former aspect and the costs and difficulties associated with the latter. Bassiouni 2002 pp. XV and XVIII; and Kritz 2002 p. 59.

the security of people in the broad sense, *i.a.* their physical safety, their economic and social well-being, and their human rights and fundamental freedoms.[258]

The responsibility to lead the project of state building is typically trusted to so-called "international territorial administrations" or "transitional administrations" with an executive mandate from the Security Council to lay the groundwork for a new a supposedly better structure of governance and law. These administrations are also supposed to provide interim governance services until the political situation is stable enough to allow a transition of political leadership to local bodies. The United Nations Transitional Authority in Cambodia (UNTAC) may be regarded as the first in the row of such "modern" executive UN missions.[259] Subsequent examples include the United Nations Mission in Kosovo, the United Nations Mission in East Timor, the United Nations Mission in Sierra Leone, and the United Nations Mission in Liberia. The discussion below will focus on the international efforts to promote legal and judicial reforms in Cambodia, Bosnia and Herzegovina, Kosovo and East Timor/Timor-Leste,[260] while the most recent and on-going missions in Sierra Leone and Liberia will only be touched upon.[261]

At the level of administration, these bodies are, as the acronyms indicate, formally to be regarded as UN peacekeeping missions, and fall as such under the administrative responsibility of the UN Department of Peacekeeping Operations in New York (DPKO). The authorisation of these missions under Chapter VII of the UN Charter, and the practice of vesting them with the authority to take "*any measures necessary*" to attain the goals of the relevant resolutions and peace agreements, allow them to address problems in the legal and justice sector with a range of tools not available in the context of conventional rule of law programs. They may for example impose

258 See UN Secretary General report "In Larger Freedom: Towards Development, Security and Human Rights for All", A/59/2005.

259 Historically, the League of Nations and the United Nations have undertaken to perform various governance and judicial functions in states and territories on a number of occasions. The Mandates System basically allowed the League of Nations to authorize individual states to administer the former colonies and territories of the nations defeated in WWI. After WWII, the Trusteeship System was established under Chapter XII and XIII of the UN Charter placing territories under the administration of fully developed states acting on their behalf as trustees.

260 The province and territory formerly known as East Timor became Timor-Leste upon independence on 20 May 2002.

261 UNAMSIL's original 1999 mandate was essentially to help implement the Lome Peace Agreement and comprised traditional peace-keeping tasks. The mandate was expanded in 2000 by Security Council Resolution 1289 (2000) to include assisting the Sierra Leone Government to restore law and order throughout the country. In the case of Liberia, Security Council Resolution 1509 (2003) was adopted to facilitate the implementation of the Comprehensive Peace Agreement, and UNMIL was authorized right from the beginning to re-establish the rule of law in Liberia by means of police and justice sector reforms.

legislation, substitute themselves for non-working local bodies, order the removal of obstructionist officials from office, or otherwise use force to expedite the process.

Behind this construction is an assumption that the local political interlocutors are either insufficiently committed, or too weak, to constructively and effectively lead the reconstructive effort. It is regarded symptomatic to conflict and post-conflict environments that there is no strong and organised domestic constituency pressing for justice and the rule of law. Rather, various competing groups, whether representatives for embryonic political parties or leaders of lingering militias, are believed to compete for control over the way justice is administered, or seek to prevent justice from being administered at all. Other stakeholders, comprising disparate elements such as crime syndicates, religious groups, and various parts of the state and local administration, are similarly suspected of having a vested interest in a perpetuated conflict and a judicial system working at their mercy.

At the level of UN politics, this forceful approach to state building and rule of law promotion has been made possible by two contemporary developments, namely the post cold-war rapprochement of the superpowers and the simultaneous disintegration of states, primarily but not exclusively among the group of formerly socialist countries. The Security Council is no longer automatically divided along ideological lines and paralysed by its veto powers, and the violent collapse of various authoritarian regimes provides it with plenty of work.[262] The current Secretary General, Mr. Kofi Annan, has also advocated a more committed and forceful UN policy in regard to human rights and the rule of law, and thus helped to elevate these topics on the Security Council agenda.[263] Yet another factor behind the recent elevation of law and justice on the international agenda is the realisation that chaotic environments, to which category weak and failed states must be counted, are excellent breeding grounds and bases of operation for terror groups.

While lack of national ownership is the *raison d'etre* for these missions, it is also the most influential factor conditioning their success. There are many critical accounts emanating out of international organisations, NGOs and thinks tanks underlining that "state building" as an international project has proven much more difficult and resource demanding than initially assumed (none of the efforts so far is described as an unqualified success story), and frequently they attribute the most serious problems

262 Österdahl 1997 p. 241.

263 Corell 2004 p. 339. This greater UN interest in issues of rule of law visualises *i.a.* in the so called Millennium Report of the Secretary General (www.un.org/millennium/sg/report/full.htm) and the Millennium Declaration of the Declaration of the General Assembly (General Assembly Resolution A/RES/55/2.

to lack of such ownership and lead.[264] The emerging view is consequently that even in difficult political environments, the maximum authority possible (within the conditions stipulated by local capacity and context) should be vested with local stakeholders at any given time, and that a minimum of popular and political acceptance is indispensable for all stages of the transition to gain foothold and be consolidated.[265]

Another factor conditioning success and failure is the way the mission mandates are formulated. In spite of the normative character of "state building" as a project, these are often vague and ambiguous. There are many reasons why the empowering Security Council resolutions and peace treaties often lack sufficient detail on important issues. One is that it is simply impossible for the Security Council to know or predict exactly what consecutive steps the implementation of the peace agenda will need to entail. Another is that there may be short-term political utility in being deliberately vague on some points: For example, what countries would have accepted to contribute to the implementation of the Dayton Agreement in Bosnia and Herzegovina if they had been aware of the enormous resources its implementation would require, and what countries would have agreed on the international presence in Kosovo if the "final status issue" had needed to be addressed right away ? Among the corresponding prices to be paid was the erosion of local trust and growth of suspicion: because the Security Council avoided the spectrum of issues related to the greater question of status (democracy, minority rights, etc), Kosovars started to question the real motives of the Security Council and UNMIK: Was the mission deployed to promote self-determination and human rights, or was there another, hidden, agenda? Another was the costs of uncertainty and perpetuated debate. For example, what political system should the constitution of Kosovo provide for, what rights should the laws protect, how should the police set its priorities, etc?[266]

The conditions for success and failure are also influenced by the resources made available to the missions. It is well known that only fractions of the amounts of voluntary aid committed to international crises reach their destination, and that disbursements are often irregular and late. In other cases, the estimates of what the peace effort needs to comprise may be unrealistically low. There may even be a strategy of obfuscating the level of contributions actually needed in order not to scare hesitant nations away from the table and thus increase the political and financial burdens of

---

264 Chesterman 2003; "Strengthening the Security-Development Nexus: Assessing International Policy and Practice Since the 1990s" 2004; Wilde 2001 and 2002.

265 It may be argued that these international administrations, just like trusteeships under Chapters XII and XIII, should be seen as perform their governmental functions "in trust", *i.e.* in the interest of the country or territory in question, and not primarily in the interest of the United Nations or other outside stakeholders. Stahn 2001 p. 112.

266 Chesterman 2003 p. 3; Ehrenreich 2003 p. 2294.

the others.[267] In other cases, the goals set may be artificially and unrealistically high, thus making the "marginal cost" of reaching them impossible to bear. Simon Chesterman points out that particularly when the UN itself assumes a governing role, there is a temptation to demand the highest, and thus most costly, standards of democracy, human rights and rule of law.[268] A system by which a greater part of the costs was covered by assessed contributions (in a way similar to the system that currently covers the expenses of "traditional" peacekeeping operations) would probably lead to more realistic assessments of missions capabilities and prove to be more manageable.

5.2 INTERNATIONAL ADMINISTRATION AND INTERNATIONAL LAW

A number of legal issues impact on the scope, organisation and modalities of UN-sponsored efforts at rebuilding the legal and judicial sector in conflict-ridden societies. For example, what kinds of entities are these administrations, what is the extent of their authorities, and how to hold them accountable for their actions?

It should first be established that that although international (UN) administration in the wake of a military intervention bears many similarities to military occupation, the principles of international humanitarian law regarding the rights and duties of an occupying power with regard to the temporary administration of territory are not applicable as far as UN operations under Chapter VII are concerned.[269] This view is derived from important differences in the identity of the agent, the nature of the presence, and the tasks at hand. For example, while there is no expectation or obligation for a state occupying another to further the creation of something new and supposedly "better", a UN administration is deployed for the very reason of promoting reconstruction, democracy, human rights, rule of law, etc., and expected to do so in the best interest of the population of the state or territory.[270]

---

267 This aspect was considered by the authors of the Brahimi Report (Report of the Panel on United Nations Peace Operations, para. 59). It was concluded that missions with inadequate resources should not be created at all because such a strategy would risk leading member states into believing that they are doing something useful for countries in crisis, when they are in fact agreeing to contribute to something which is impossible and will result in a waste of human resources, time and money.

268 Chesterman 2003 p. 7.

269 The 1907 Hague Regulations and the Fourth Geneva Convention of 1949 provide, *inter alia*, that the occupying power is required to "*take all the measures in his power to restore, and ensure, as far as possible, public order and safety, while respecting, unless absolutely prevented, the laws in force in the country*".

270 The main obligation of an occupant is to administer the territory and to respect the existing law, unless absolutely prevented from doing so. Hague Regulations, Art. 43; Fourth Geneva Convention, Arts. 64 (1) and (2).

The applicability of the rules governing Trusteeships in Chapter XII and XIII of the UN Charter is similarly doubtful.[271] Although the Trusteeship System was originally created to guide former territories toward self-government and independence, it is explicitly stated that the System can only be applied to three different categories of territories: the former Mandate Territories (the former colonies and dependent territories of the German and Turkish empires); territories detached from enemy states after WWII (such as the Italian colony of Somaliland); and territories voluntary placed in the system by the states responsible for their administration. The wording of the UN Charter (Art. 78) also explicitly prohibits application of the Trusteeship System to UN member states because of the violation of the principle of sovereignty equality this would entail. With the independence of the last trusteeship territory completed in 1994 (Palau), the Trusteeship Council has suspended operation. While it may be possible under the Charter for member states to voluntarily place parts of their own territory under the System (violation of sovereign equality would not be an issue in this case), there has been little interest in this option both within and outside the UN. The only time this option was discussed in earnest (with regard to Somalia in 1993) the idea was soon given up because of the seemingly insurmountable political difficulties associated with it.

The normative framework for international (UN) administration is instead to be found in Chapter VII of the UN Charter (*Actions with Respect to Threats to the Peace, Breaches of the Peace, and Acts of Aggression*), and in mission-specific Security Council resolutions under Chapter VII. Formally speaking, such administrations are to be regarded as peacekeeping missions (the implications of this label are further discussed below). In some cases, the Security Council has also provided *ex post* endorsement of peace treaties providing for the presence of an international authority in a post-crisis environment, as for example with UNTAC in Cambodia and the High Representative in Bosnia and Herzegovina. This construction rendered the High Representative in Bosnia and Herzegovina the categorization of "hybrid international territorial administration". It is not uncommon that in addition to the Chapter VII resolution, there are various agreements between the UN and the "host government(s)" to provide for a secure and effective working environment. Such instrument may be anything between Status of Forces/Mission Agreements, *i.e.* treaties regulating the legal status of the international military and civilian presence, to memoranda of understanding and similar documents regulating everyday affairs. Strictly speaking, if the international presence is provided for under Chapter VII, such agreements are neither legally possible nor necessary since Chapter VII activities by definition are not based on consent and agreement with the territorial state.[272]

---

271 For a detailed discussion, see Stahn 2001 pp. 116-120.
272 Bring 1998 p. 949.

The political difficulties of obtaining a Security Council resolution under Chapter VII providing for an international administration are typical for the general weaknesses and defects of the UN system of collective security, *i.e.* if one or more of the permanent members of the Security Council opposes a particular aspect of the mission or the mission in its entirety, there will either limitations in its mandate or no mission at all. The political battles in the UN and other diplomatic fora preceding the deployment of UNTAC, UNMIK, UNTAET, etc. have been both fierce and sophisticated, and the respective parties have not hesitated to use the most drastic political, legal, and economic arguments available. While those in favour of the deployment of an international administration have tended to stress the political and moral responsibility of the international community to ensure that the fundamentals of human rights and rule of law are put in place, those opposing such initiatives have underlined both the challenge to sovereignty equality posed by such interventions and the enormous costs and risks they involve. It should be noted that those states that have systematically abstained or voted against resolutions providing for UN interventions in crisis environments have often had dubious human rights and rule of law records.

While the UN Charter does not explicitly mention international administration, the deployment of such bodies is seen as the logical and anticipated consequence of an earlier decision under Chapter VII to intervene on humanitarian grounds. Before discussing this "second generation" of peace-keeping missions, it should be mentioned the essentially internal nature of many humanitarian crises does not prevent the Security Council from taking action. Although Art. 2(7) of the Charter has always excluded action under Chapter VII from the principal prohibition of UN intrusion into the *domaine réservé* of individual nations, the Security Council seems to be promoting an even more reduced significance of the concept of internal affairs. The first indication of this trend came with the actions taken to protect the Kurds in Iraq under the landmark Resolution 688 of 5 april 1991, where the Council explicitly says that Article 2(7) has been duly considered and found not to constitute a barrier to action.[273] The language of the preamble of Resolution 940 (1994), providing for the multinational operation in Haiti, even suggests that the most important fact for the Council to come to its decision to intervene was the fundamentally internal matter that the *de facto* government refused to step down in favour of the democratically elected President Aristide.[274] After this, the Security Council has expressed similar

[273] By labelling the persecution of Kurds and its ensuing consequences as threats to peace and security the Security Council actually points out that the definition of "peace" in Chapter VII should be understood to be far broader and deeper than the absence of war between two or more states, and that any political, economic and military enforcement measure under Chapter VII may be considered in such situations. Ruffert 2001 p. 617; Österdahl 1997 pp. 243 and 264.

[274] The Security Council consequently authorised member states to form a multinational force and to use all necessary means to prompt the resignation of the illegitimate regime and facilitate the return of the elected President and the restoration of the legitimate authorities of the Government of Haiti.

support for intervention in a number of other essentially internal conflicts, for example Somalia, Rwanda, Kosovo and East Timor.

The most evident proof of a "second generation" of peacekeeping operations in which government, law and justice issues formed integral parts, came with the United Nations Transitional Authority in Cambodia (UNTAC).[275] Security Council Resolution 745 (1992), which endorsed the 1991 Paris Accords, conferred upon the mission "*all powers necessary to ensure the implementation of [the] Agreement*" (Art. 6) and authorised the UN Special Representative to carry out a range of legislative and governance tasks. The SRSG was also explicitly empowered to overrule any decision of the Cambodian factions that he deemed inconsistent with the Accords and to remove obstructionist Cambodian officials from office and insert UN personnel in any executive capacity.

In 1993, only two years after the deployment of UNTAC in Cambodia, the UN undertook to assume full control of the collapsed state of Somalia. This time the UN engagement was not sparked by a peace settlement, but rather by a perceived need among the member states to bring peace and order to a country in chaos. Security Council Resolution 814 (1993), passed under Chapter VII of the Charter, thus enumerated among the tasks of the expanded United Nations Operation in Somalia (UNOSOM II) to ensure the consolidation, expansion and maintenance of a secure environment throughout the country, and to re-establish the Somali police forces and judicial and penal systems. Resolution 940 (1994) providing for a multinational operation in Haiti similarly reiterated the "*[...] commitment for the international community to assist and support the economic, social and institutional development of Haiti*".[276] The emphasis was thus not "peace" in the narrow sense of the word, rather restoration and consolidation of a particular system of governance and administration.[277]

A more difficult test for the UN came with the conflict in Bosnia and Herzegovina, where the members of the Security Council failed to reach consensus around a common peace-enforcement policy. The first relevant Security Council Resolution, 770 (1992), merely calls "*[...] upon States to take nationally or through regional agencies all measures necessary to facilitate in coordination with the United Nations the delivery by relevant United Nations humanitarian organizations and others of humanitarian assistance to Sarajevo and wherever needed in other parts of Bosnia and Herzegovina*".[278]

275 Together with the UN missions in Namibia, El Salvador, Angola and Mozambique.
276 Security Council Resolution 940 (1994), preamble para. 7.
277 Österdahl 1997 p. 269.
278 Security Council Resolution 770 (1992) para. 2.

Not until the "General Framework Agreement for Peace, GFAP, (popularly "Dayton Agreement") had been concluded by the leaders of Croatia, Bosnia and Herzegovina, and the Federal Republic of Yugoslavia, Franjo Tudjman, Alija Izetbegovic, and Slobodan Milosevic in 1995, did the international community manage to unite around the idea of providing a sort of peace implementation mechanism for the new-born state of Bosnia and Herzegovina (BiH). Pursuant to Annex 10 of the GFAP and the endorsing Security Council Resolution 1031 (1995), the High Representative was then given the typical powers to impose legislation, substitute himself for local authorities, and perform other governance functions to ensure the implementation of the GFAP.

Soon thereafter, the Security Council again invoked Chapter VII in Resolution 1037 (1996) to establish the United Nations Transitional Administration for Eastern Slavonia, Baranja and Western Sirium (UNTAES). This mission was created to provide for a peaceful reintegration of the collapsed Republika Srpska Krajina into Croatia after the war, while at the same time securing the human rights of the Serb minority living in the area. The military and civil mandates of the mission were concentrated in the hands of a United Nations Transitional Administrator, who governed the territory until Croatia could resume full control in 1998.

The next manifestation of growing international commitment to the concept of state-building came after the eleven-week NATO air campaign had forced the Federal Republic of Yugoslavia to agree to withdraw all military and security forces from the province of Kosovo. On June 10, 1999, only a day after the suspension of the campaign, the Security Council adopted Resolution 1244 (1999), establishing the United Nations Interim Administration in Kosovo (UNMIK).[279] What made this Resolution so significant was that the Security Council used its powers under Chapter VII to actively shape the system of governance within the territory, and thus clearly manifested that the organization of the government and judiciary need not be the exclusive prerogative

[279] The fact that the FRY was not a member state of the UN at the time of adoption of Resolution 1244 (in 1992 the UN Security Council had rejected the claim by the FRY to continue automatically the membership of the former Socialist Federal Republic of Yugoslavia) gave rise to the issue whether the UN Security Council was empowered to address enforcement measures under Chapter VII against a third party. Zimmermann & Stahn (2001 pp. 439-440) point out that while such a power is hardly consistent with the classical principles of international law enshrined in Article 34 of the Vienna Convention on the Law of Treaties (*pacta tertiis* rule), article 2 para. 6 of the UN Charter directs the organisation to secure – as far as possible – that non-member states do not disturb international peace and security (although without obliging them to abide by enforcement measures of the Security Council). In practice, the Council has not refrained from addressing resolutions under Chapter VII to "*all states*". There is also some support for the assumption that the Council now enjoys powers vis-à-vis third states by virtue of international customary law. In the case of Kosovo, the problem lost much of its practical significance when the FRY gave its approval to the establishment of UNMIK within the framework of Resolution 1244 and FRY was accepted as a new member of the UN on November 1, 2000.

of the territorial state (on some previous occasions the Council had identified basic and fundamental injustices within national systems, for example in South Africa, Haiti and Rhodesia, but it had never before prescribed specific remedies as to their elimination, nor vested with itself the mandate to implement them). The Resolution also made specific determinations concerning the status of Kosovo within the FRY based on the general understanding that a state does not have unrestricted decision-making power towards its people and sub-entities. The Security Council referred, in particular, to the need to develop self-government and substantial autonomy in Kosovo, knowing that this would require significant re-arrangements in the constitutional system of FRY, and even potentially pave the way for independence.[280]

The most ambitious example of direct United Nations territorial administration so far is the United Nations Transitional Administration in East Timor (UNTAET), established by Security Council Resolution 1272 (1999) in the aftermath of the referendum for independence in the former Indonesian province. The Security Council made UNTAET fully responsible for the administration of East Timor during its transition to independence, and gave the Special Representative of the Secretary General the power to exercise all legislative and executive authority, including the administration of justice. Such sovereign powers had never been vested with a UN administration before (in the cases of Eastern Slavonia, BiH and Kosovo, the states of Croatia, Bosnia and Herzegovina and Serbia had retained *de jure* sovereignty of the territory). It is also worth noting that UNTAET deemed itself to have the power to conclude grant agreements with multilateral organizations, designating the mission and East Timor as "recipient".[281]

The UN approach to state building in Afghanistan represents a counterpoint to East Timor in many ways. After the 11 september 2001 terrorist attack on the United States by the Afghan-based Al Qaeda group, the Security Council expressed its support for the efforts of the Afghan people to replace the Taliban regime. Soon thereafter, the Northern Alliance with support from the United States and other countries managed to overthrow it with military force. In order to help the new Afghan state find its form and assume control, the United Nations organized a meeting among prospective political leaders and other stakeholders, eventually resulting in the 2001 "Bonn Agreement on Provisional Arrangements in Afghanistan Pending the Re-establishment of Permanent Government Institutions". In Resolution 1383 (2001) the Security Council endorsed the Bonn Agreement and declared its willingness to take further action to support the interim institutions established therein. Among the most important features of the Bonn Agreement was the establishment of an Interim

[280] Zimmermann & Stahn 2001 p. 441.
[281] Chopra 2000 pp. 30-31; Zimmermann and Stahn 2001 pp. 434-435.

Authority consisting of an Interim Administration, a special Independent Commission for the convening of the Emergency *Loya Jirga* (Pashtu for grand council), and a structure of courts. The Agreement further specified the convening of a Constitutional *Loya Jirga* to adopt a new constitution. The next step by the Security Council was to adopt Resolution 1401 (2002) providing for the United Nations Assistance Mission in Afghanistan (UNAMA) to better integrate and coordinate the work of the various UN agencies in the country, their Afghan government counterparts, and national and international NGO partners in implementing the principles of the Bonn Agreement and otherwise providing for a democratic Afghanistan. Unlike in the preceding missions, the mandate of the SRSG is thus limited to direct and coordinate the work the various UN agencies in Afghanistan, while political leadership and ultimate executive authority remain in the hands of the Afghan Administration. Among the specific tasks entrusted to the UNAMA was the promotion of the rule of law.[282]

Although the Security Council has been careful to underline that the situations and responses in Cambodia, Bosnia and Herzegovina, Kosovo, etc. are unique, the number of very similar "unique" decisions indicates the emergence of a practice or principle that intervention on humanitarian grounds should typically be followed by the deployment of a UN interim administration empowered to create a legal and administrative structure able of preventing such crimes in the future. There may also be a sense of moral obligation to treat similar situations in similar ways.[283] At the same time, critical voices suggest that the circumstance that the Security Council has on several occasions authorised state-building missions under Chapter VII should not be interpreted as conclusive evidence of its authority to do so. The different approach of the UN in Afghanistan seems to have reinforced this view.

Whether and under what circumstances the Security Council may engage in reshaping legal and judicial structures is an issue surrounded by much controversy. Article 24 of the UN Charter lays down the basic principle that "*In order to ensure prompt and effective action by the United Nations, its Members confer on the Security Council primary responsibility for the maintenance of international peace and security, and agree that in carrying out its duties under this responsibility the Security Council acts on their behalf.*" Regarding the limits of the authority thus vested in the Security Council, the same article merely stipulates that "*In discharging these duties the Security Council shall act*

---

282 The mandate and structure of UNAMA are specified in the Report of the Secretary-General on the Situation in Afghanistan and its Implications for International Peace and Security, dated 18 March 2002. Among the other tasks of UNAMA are preventing and resolving conflicts; building confidence and promoting national reconciliation; monitoring the political and human rights situation; investigating human rights violations; and maintaining a dialogue with Afghan leaders, political parties, civil society groups, institutions and representatives of the central authorities.

283 Österdahl 1997 p. 270; Zimmermann and Stahn 2001 pp. 437-438.

in accordance with the Purposes and Principles of the United Nations." It is thus for the Security Council itself, and ultimately the International Court of Justice, to determine the limits of the Council's mandate under the Charter.[284] The absence of a specific reference in the UN Charter to state-building can consequently not be regarded a significant obstacle for the deployment of an international administration with a governance mandate.[285] The International Commission on Intervention and State Sovereignty even argues that the "*responsibility to rebuild*" is an operational necessity and moral imperative once a decision to undertake a military intervention on humanitarian grounds under Chapter VII has been taken, and that reconstructive efforts should be seen as an integral part of any intervention.[286] Other commentators of UN politics similarly argue that pursuit of such objectives as security in isolation of coherent state building strategies, encompassing the rule of law, is at best a waste of resources.[287]

It is nevertheless uncertain what the exact limits are of the authority of the Security Council and its missions to direct constitutional, legal and judicial changes countries and territories under UN administration, and regarding what mechanisms there should be to hold the missions and their staff accountable when these limits are transgressed. Broadly speaking, the arguments range from suggesting that the Security Council and its bodies, when acting under Chapter VII, can never act *ultra vires*, to suggesting that it is evident that any legitimate exercise of legislative or executive authority in the interest of the countries concerned requires that the missions themselves submit to a set of internationally accepted constraining rules.

Although it must be assumed that a wide and robust mandate was exactly what the Security Council had in mind when establishing these missions, it seems obvious that it never intended to vest them with unlimited powers or to put them "above" internationally accepted principles of law and human rights. Rather, it is almost axiomatic that as a legal subject deriving its authority from international law, an international administration cannot be above that law, but must function within the framework of an international legal order including in particular those norms

---

284 In "Certain Expenses of the United Nations", 1962 ICJ REP. 151, 168 (July 20), the ICJ stated that actions taken by the Security Council should not be regarded *ultra vires* as long as they are "*appropriate for the fulfilment of one of the stated purposes of the Organization.*"

285 Some commentators metaphorically argue that the concepts of peace-keeping and international administration should have their origin in an unwritten "Chapter VI½" between Chapter VI and VII. The advocates of the VI½-idea argue that it is legally defensible because even if based on consent, peace-keeping and international administration signify a more ambitious level of UN involvement than anything provided for in the Chapter VI. See for example Bring 1998 p. 946.

286 International Commission on Intervention and State Sovereignty, 2001, paras. 2.32, 5.1-5.6.

287 Chesterman, Ignatieff & Thakur 2004 p. 9.

and laws developed and endorsed by the UN itself.[288] Further, the very purpose of the international administrations – to build up post-civil-war societies based on democracy, human rights and rule of law – can hardly be achieved if the missions are simultaneously perceived to constantly violate these very principles. If the parallel to a trusteeship is accepted, it may also be argued that an international administration is the servant of both an international and a local legal order. The limits of its authority must accordingly be defined both by the purpose of the mission (reconstruction) and its obligations towards the inhabitants of the administered state or territory.[289]

The circumstance that the governance functions are essentially carried out by entities (international organisations, UN missions, etc.) that are not subjects to international law *senso stricto* does not fundamentally change this assumption as the UN Charter obliges UN bodies to act in conformity with universally accepted standards of human rights. The specific mandates assigned to the missions also provide for the applicability of international law. There is further reason to assume that the human rights treaties in force in the administered country or territory before the international take-over continue to apply, also in relationship to the new authority, since the rights enshrined in these treaties belong to the persons living in the territory notwithstanding changes in government. Moreover, the application of customary law to non-state entities seems particularly plausible in the context of international administrations because the administering authority assumes functions which are, under normal circumstances, exercised by the state.[290]

In the strategic report "*The rule of law and transitional justice in conflict and post conflict societies*", the Secretary General seeks to establish once and for all that "*The normative foundation for our [UN] work in advancing the rule of law is the Charter of the United Nations itself, together with the four pillars of the modern international legal system: international human rights law; international humanitarian law; international criminal law; and international refugee law. This includes the wealth of United Nations human rights and criminal justice standards developed in the last half-century. These represent universally applicable standards adopted under the auspices of the United Nations and must therefore serve as the normative basis for all United Nations activities in support of justice and the rule of law.*"[291] The Secretary General continues to explain that: "*These standards also set the normative boundaries of United Nations engagement, such that, for example, United Nations tribunals can never allow for capital punishment, United*

288 Österdahl 2002 pp. 909-911.

289 Stahn (2001 pp. 138-139) consequently suggests that normative guidelines for the exercise of UN governmental powers may be found in the "*magna charta*" of principles applicable to trusteeship administrations in Art. 76 of the UN Charter.

290 Id. p. 139.

291 UNSG Report S/2004/616 p. 5.

Nations-endorsed peace agreements can never promise amnesties for genocide, war crimes, crimes against humanity or gross violations of human rights, and, where we are mandated to undertake executive or judicial functions, United nations-operated facilities must scrupulously comply with international standards for human rights in the administration of justice."[292]

Although international administrations seem to be bound by international law in most significant respects, there are few effective mechanisms to check on the legality of their actions. Rather, by virtue of their broadly defined mandates and the lack of international political interest in supervising their actions, the missions are practically unfettered in their daily governing and norm-making capacities and have on many occasions created instruments that have been inconsistent with international as well as national norms, or made decisions that have violated fundamental principles of human rights. An often mentioned example in the legal and judicial area is UNMIK Regulation 2000/6 on the Appointment and Removal from Office of International Judges and Prosecutors. While international and regional instruments applicable in Kosovo such as the ICCPR and the ECHR spell out the conventional and virtually universally accepted meaning of the concept of an independent judiciary, this Regulation contains almost no safeguards against their removal from office. In fact, their removal does not even require a specific procedure, merely a decision of the SRSG which may be based on such indeterminate grounds as "serious misconduct" or "failure in the due execution of office" (Section 4.1). The very same vague criteria apply to the removal from office of national judges and prosecutors, although in this case the SRSG shall "consult" the Advisory Judicial Commission before rendering a decision.[293]

Considering that these missions are formally peace-keeping missions, the absence of review mechanisms is hardly surprising. The drafters of the UN Charter must have hosted a view enforcement measures under Chapter VII would not be effective unless the avenues for legal challenge were kept very narrow. The difficult real-world conditions under which the international administrations of the last decades have been established and deployed (massive violations of human rights, political unrest, fragmentation, etc.) also help to explain why review has remained a matter of secondary importance. Each of these projects has furthermore been conceived as "temporary" and "interim", why few have seen reason to bother too much about carefully formulating rules and principles for something that will not last and may not recur. The absence of review mechanisms may also be attributable to lingering traditional notions in international law and politics concerning the status and roles

292 Ibid.

293 Stahn 2001 pp. 152-161.

of states and international organizations: States administer territory, while international organisations monitor human rights, etc. The former activity requires regulation, while the second does not. Ralph Wilde points out that this traditional notion of a division of responsibilities seems to influence the application of national law to these two actors, particularly with regard to issues of immunity, and to produce peculiar results. OHR, UNMIK and other international administrations are thus granted immunity for all their activities just like international organisations, while they actually perform traditional state functions.[294]

No matter the reason, the absence of effective review mechanisms is problematic in many respects, foremost among them that it may constitute a violation of human rights obligations under the UDHR, ICCPR, ECHR and national law to allow for judicial review.[295] Another is the perception of hypocrisy their absence creates.[296] Recent domestic and international developments demonstrate the explosiveness of the matter. In the path-breaking "Law on State Border Service Case", the BiH Constitutional Court boldly established its competence to rule on the "constitutionality" enactments by the High Representative by arguing that the Constitution of BiH confers on the Court the right to control the conformity of any law with the Constitution, regardless of the identity of its author.[297] If also flows from this decision that if the specific instrument is found to be inconsistent with the Constitution, then the legislator ought to be free to proceed to amend it.[298] At the same time, the Court concluded that the powers of the High Representative under Annex 10, the relevant Security Council resolutions and the Bonn Declaration are beyond its review. In Kosovo, UNMIK was quicker to realise the political sensitivity of the issue and act proactively. The most important initiative was the SRSG decision in 2000 to set up the institution of the Ombudsperson and give it jurisdiction to receive and investigate complaints from "*any person or entity in Kosovo concerning human rights violations and actions constituting an abuse of authority by the interim civil administration or any emerging central or local institution.*"[299]

294 Wilde 2001 pp. 457-458.

295 UDHR Art, 10; ICCPR Art. 14(1); and ECHR Art. 6 (1). The wording of these provisions leaves some doubts as to whether they merely contain procedural guarantees in relation to judicial proceedings or whether they also grant a right to a judicial procedure, but it seems increasingly accepted that the right of access to court forms part of the fair trial guarantee. The Constitution of BiH, Annex 1, Art. 1; and UNMIK Regulation 1999/24, Section 1.3, similarly leave no doubt that international principles of human rights, including the right to access to court, apply in BiH and Kosovo respectively.

296 Stahn 2001 pp. 138, 143; Wilde 2001 pp. 458-460.

297 Constitutional Court of BiH, Decision No. U 9/00 of 3 November 2000.

298 For an analysis, see Stahn 2001 pp. 168-170.

299 UNMIK Regulation 2000/38 Section 3.1.

5.3 TOPICS AND PRIORITIES

5.3.1 OVERVIEW

The general directions for the work of the UN interim administrations are typically spelled out in the relevant Security Council resolutions and peace treaties. Certain policy documents and strategic reports, such as "An Agenda for Peace", the "Brahimi Report", and the "Report on the Rule of Law and Transitional Justice in Conflict and Post-Conflict Societies", also provide some guidance on the broader political goals and principles of contemporary peacekeeping and state-building.[300] Beyond that, it is essentially for the Special Representative, sometimes in consultation with the Security Council or some *ad hoc* international consultative body, to decide on specific work priorities and sequences.

Strategy making and co-ordination for the various stages of state-building have improved over the years and several mechanisms have been developed to help determine sequences, funding needs and long-term reconstruction plans, such as Comprehensive Post-Conflict Needs Assessments, dedicated donor conferences, and the Consultative Group Mechanism (Afghanistan). Still, however, the sequencing and prioritisation of reform topics tend to be determined by practical necessities, such as the resources available and the timelines stated, rather than careful deliberation. It is also notable that to the extent there are plans and strategies, these seem often to have been elaborated to address the challenges of the previous mission, rather than the novel circumstances of the current situation.

The first point on the mission agenda has typically been to provide for basic conditions of law and order by establishing emergency law enforcement structures. The immediate wake of a conflict is often marred by an outburst of violence, such as killings, looting, rape and a general break-down of public order, and the "Security First" argument suggests that basic conditions of law and order need to be established before any other aspect of reconstruction can be meaningfully pursued. Failure to provide for such fundamentals in the initial phases of the mission is also believed to erode public trust in the international agenda and presence generally.[301] Often such initial services need to be performed by an international military presence ("peace-keepers"), with all

300 "An Agenda for Peace: Preventive Diplomacy, Peacemaking, and Peace-Keeping", Report of the Secretary General pursuant to the statement adopted by the Summit Meeting of the Security Council on 3 Jan. 1992. UN Doc. A/47/277-S/24111; "Report of the Panel on United Nations Peace Operations", UN Doc. A/55/305 – S/2000/809; "Report of the United Nations Secretary General on the Rule of Law and Transitional Justice in Conflict and Post-Conflict Societies", UN Doc. S/2004/616.

301 Marenin 2005 p. 5.

problems of variations in competence, commitment and mandate that construction entails.

When missions decide to provide for emergency law enforcement services, they also commit themselves to taking the process a step further in the justice chain by default, because there is little point in providing for law enforcement unless there is some form of judicial structures to deal with the perpetrators once identified and apprehended. Besides police officers, they need therefore provide for a framework for detention, investigation, prosecution, trials of first instance, and sentencing.[302] A special problem in providing for such services is that some cases may be so politically sensitive and technically complicated (typically war crimes and other serious human rights violations) that neither the national authorities nor the missions have the capacity to properly handle them. Rather than inviting to a parody of justice, the international community may therefore either refer these cases to special international tribunals, or empower the missions to create *ad hoc* domestic regimes to the same end. Where there is a UN Security Council Resolution providing for an international administration in a specific country or territory, the creation of an alternative domestic jurisdiction may already be within the mandate of the Special Representative. The jurisdictional relationship between local courts and such superior or parallel mechanisms may then be regulated in a special document with the force of law.[303]

There is strong evidence that such national or international fora can play an instrumental role in laying the ground for peaceful co-existence and recovery:[304] That individuals are not left alone with experiences of officially endorsed oppression and suffering, but rather allowed and encouraged to tell their stories to commissions or tribunals, is a first step to convincing them that they dare hope for protection of life and integrity in the future. Psychologists argue that this *"transport of pain"* from the private to the public sphere is among the most important cognitive and emotional steps in the process of truth disclosure and reconciliation.[305] Criminal tribunals and Truth Commissions can further help to break vicious circles of perceived humiliations and calls for revenge. There are numerous examples illustrating that in societies with histories of recurrent outbreaks of violence, popular myths of humiliation and defeat have greatly contributed to shape identity at both the individual and the collective levels, and that the resulting "collective memories", false as they may be, have

302 Strohmeyer 2001 pp. 47-48.

303 Pursuant to an agreement reached in February 1996, popularly dubbed "the Rules of the Road", the former warring factions in BiH agreed not to arrest persons on suspicion of war crimes until ICTY had reviewed files of the charges against them.

304 The rapidly growing doctrine on this topic, and "Transitional Justice" generally, comprise important works by Bassiouni (2002); Caplan (2005); Chesterman (2003); Coliver (2000); and many others.

305 Sveaass and Lavik 2000 p. 49.

maintained destructive psychological tensions into the following generations. For example, Serbian historical myths about the defeat of the Serbian army and death of Prince Lazar at battle of Kosovo Polje in 1389 are still factors making a peaceful settlement of the status of Kosovo difficult.

The next point in the sequence has been to ensure the presence of a constitutional and legal framework that facilitates both the operation and of the international administration and the emergence of viable domestic legal and administrative structures. This task has been addressed both in terms of helping or harnessing domestic agencies to create new legal instruments, and in terms of mission-internal legislative efforts when the local political climate has been deemed disabling. However, before making any comprehensive attempt at codifying law and principles for the fledgling state, the missions have needed to map the already existing law of the land. The identification and classification of the "applicable law" in these countries and territories have not been easy, neither technically nor politically.[306] The presence of conflicting and confused notions of about the law, even among local jurists and policy-makers, have led to frequent disputes regarding the validity of even the most basic instruments and which instrument that should prevail in the event of collision. Not least those laws governing fundamental issues such as law enforcement and conflict resolution have been subject to hot contestation. When new laws have been contemplated, there have similarly been domestic groups of varying size and influence trying to block them by challenging their constitutional validity. It seems that the experiences gained in Bosnia and Herzegovina, where the High Representative was taken by surprise by the sophistication of many such challenges, have highlighted to the UN and subsequent missions the importance of a constitutional perspective, even with regard to "interim" instruments.

In defending their instruments and actions, the international administrations have in most cases taken a point of departure in commonly accepted and publicly known international law principles. The essence of this policy is that the international administrations should be characterised as subsidiary organs of the Security Council (UN Charter Art. 29) or at least of the UN as a whole (Art. 7[2]) and that the new legislation should be considered UN law derived from the powers of that organisation. Regulations enacted by the SRSG should accordingly be regarded as international legal acts and as enjoying direct applicability in the country or territory.[307] This assumption

306 For examples from Kosovo, see Brand 2001 p. 470. Regarding East Timor, see Chopra 2000 and Ehrenreich 2003.

307 For example, by virtue of the Security Council and SRSG regulation, the "laws" that should be applied in Kosovo for the time being are UNMIK Regulations and, in the event a subject has not been regulated by UNMIK and there is no other relevant provision in Kosovo law, the rules applicable in Kosovo on 22 March 1989. See UNMIK Regulation 1999/24 Section 1 and Regulation 1999/1 Section 3. For a commentary, see Zimmermann and Stahn 2001 p. 443.

also finds support in the fact that prior to being issued by the SRSG, each new legal instrument should be reviewed from a "constitutional" and human rights perspective by the Office of Legal Affairs at the UN Secretariat in New York.[308] The international administrations have also been careful to made references in conjunction with new enactment to the rules in the respective resolutions according to which all powers – legislative, executive and judiciary – are vested in OHR, UNMIK, UNTAET, etc. Ruffert suggests that an alternative to regarding these legal systems as extensions of the UN legal system applicable within BiH, Kosovo, etc. would be to describe the unique fabric of laws and regulations as *"the law"* of the respective country or territory.[309] This perspective finds some support in the unique character of the legal framework of the territories, in the many points of contact with Yugoslav and Indonesian law, and regarding Kosovo specifically, the peculiar status of the territory under public international law.

After having ensured the presence of a framework of basic rules, the missions have proceeded to build judicial and prosecutorial institutions. The perceived lack of constructive national leadership in the initial phases of the reconstructive effort has prompted the missions to impose fundamental yet provisional structures in order to facilitate interim judicial services and to create a basic foundation for later efforts to create something more sustainable in an inclusive process. The court structures of Kosovo and East Timor are typical examples of this policy. In other cases, for example Bosnia and Herzegovina, the overall structure of institutions has already been authoritatively laid out in a peace treaty or similar document. While institutional reorganisation should typically be followed by capacity building, the missions have often been surprisingly irresolute, and consequently unsuccessful in, addressing this topic. A particularly complicated issue has been to ensure that the people operating the institutions, notably the judges and prosecutors, have possessed the professional and moral qualities required. The international administrations have experimented here with a range of trust-based and coercive approaches to promoting disclosure and the removal of "rotten apples".[310]

Post-crisis environments are typically characterised by conflicts and confusion as to what rules that apply and how to access them. There is consequently a great need for

---

308 Corell 2004 p. 339.

309 Ruffert 2001 p. X.

310 Sveaass and Lavik (2000 p. 43) underline that in countries and territories traumatized by human rights abuses and impunity, the processes of renewal and reconciliation will not begin unless there is social accommodation and confidence-building between affected individuals and communities. The judiciary is a crucial facilitator of such processes, but if its members have been tools in the conflict and actively contributed to violations of fundamental human rights and rule of law principles, they can hardly be effective in this capacity unless their credibility as impartial and efficient adjudicators of conflicting claims is first restored.

various forms of legal information, aid and assistance services. The last step on the mission agenda has accordingly been to promote various aspects of access to justice. Having realised the lack of resources and experience in this reform area, the missions have often sought to encourage and empower others to take the lead in this work, particularly international and local NGOs and other civil society actors.

5.3.2 BACKGROUND, MANDATE AND OPERATIONAL FRAMEWORK

5.3.2.1 United Nations Transitional Authority in Cambodia

After seizing power in 1975, the radically communist Khmer Rouge immediately proceeded to destroy all key aspects of the largely French-inspired Cambodian administrative and legal system. Courthouses, the law school, and all other legal institutions of significance were torn down and converted to other uses. In order to ensure the permanence of their revolution, the Khmer Rouge spent particular efforts on killing or otherwise removing from Cambodia all people with higher education. Scholars and NGOs with insights into Cambodian matters estimate that of the 400–600 legal professionals working in the country prior to the 1975 revolution, as few as six to twelve were alive and still in Cambodia when Vietnamese troops brought the terror to an end in 1979.[311]

The point of departure for the international engagement in the reconstruction of the country was the 1991 Agreement on a Comprehensive Political Settlement on the Cambodia Conflict ("Paris Agreement"), signed by the four major warring factions (of whom three had fought for various kinds of socialism), as well as by 19 nations, including all the members of the UN Security Council and ASEAN. The Paris Agreement provided for the Supreme National Council (SNC) as the interim national government of Cambodia, but also designated a special body, the United Nations Transitional Authority in Cambodia (UNTAC) to supervise the implementation of the Agreement. The mandate of UNTAC thus came to include both traditional peacekeeping tasks (supervise the cease-fire and military withdrawal, etc.) and a range of governance tasks including the operation of an interim civil administration in parallel with the SNC structure.[312] The Mission was divided into several components with distinctive roles. The supervision and reform of the judicial and penal structures belonged to the human rights component, together with a human rights education

---

311 Donovan, D. 1993.

312 Agreements on a Comprehensive Political Settlement of the Cambodia Conflict, Arts. 2-3 and Annex 1, Sec. B-E.

programme, general human rights oversight of all existing administrative structures, and the investigation of allegations of human rights abuses occurring during the transitional period.

The Mission had to comply with the "advice" of the Supreme National Council only if the SNC was unanimous in its view or if its President (Prince Sihanouk) spoke on its behalf; and the advice was consistent with the objectives of the Agreement as determined by the chief of UNTAC. This meant that is the SNC was unable to articulate an opinion and provide an advice, the Special Representative could act as he wished.[313] The many similarities between this construction and the principles laid out for the implementation of the peace agreement in Bosnia and Herzegovina in 1995 (Chapter 5.3.2.2) enforce the view that the UN was the original architect of the governance structure to which the Cambodian factions consented, and creates an impression that the UN must have considered this model at least moderately successful in Cambodia as it was revived only four years later for application in another war-torn part of the world.

The explicit commitment in the Paris Agreement to the establishment of a liberal political regime and independent judiciary made it possible for UNTAC to emphasise human rights and rule of law topics in the dialogue with the SNC and other national stakeholders. The Mission could also be explicit on the point that these principles should be put at the forefront in the work to create a new constitution to be adopted after the first free elections in May 1993. In spite of an impressive turnout (90 per cent), the election resulted in an uneasy coalition government between the royalist party (FUNCINPEC) and the major communist party (CPP). The vast majority of officials in the administration also remained loyal to the previous Vietnam-supported government, which gave the CPP an immediate upper hand over the FUNCINPEC in directing the orientation and implementation of future legal and judicial reform policies.[314]

The 1993 Constitution of the Kingdom of Cambodia nevertheless came to mark the beginning of a new era for Cambodia as a modern state and the conclusion of the UNTAC mandate. Pursuant to the Paris Agreement, it stipulates that the Constitution is the supreme law of the land and provides a long list of human rights to be protected in a manner consistent with relevant international instruments. Among these rights is an entitlement to have a independent court adjudicate and enforce these rights. Even after the end of the governance mandate and departure of UNTAC, the international community has continued to provide conditional assistance to promote certain aspects

313 Id., Annex 1, Sec. A, para. 2.

314 Neilson, K. 1996 p. 8.

of the Paris Agreement and the 1993 Constitution. In 1995 and 1996, the Cambodian government received warnings from the United States and France, two of its largest donors, that failure to fight large-scale trafficking, curb political corruption, and implement the rule of law generally, could affect the level of future aid.[315] Cambodia's application for most-favoured nation trading status with the US was also held back because of doubts about the human rights situation in the country.[316] In recent years, the UN and many countries and NGOs have engaged in an assertive dialogue with Cambodia to promote and facilitate war-crimes trials against the Khmer Rouge leadership.

5.3.2.2 High Representative to Bosnia and Herzegovina

Fighting in Bosnia and Herzegovina came to an end on 11 October 1995. From that date until 20 december 1995, forces of the United Nations Protection Force (UNPROFOR) monitored a ceasefire put in place to allow for the peace negotiations being held in Dayton, Ohio. The negotiations in Dayton eventually resulted in a peace treaty, the General Framework Agreement for Peace (GFAP) signed in Paris on 14 december 1995 by the leaders of Croatia (Franjo Tudjman), the Federal Republic of Yugoslavia (Slobodan Milosevic), and the Muslim population Bosnia and Herzegovina (Alija Izetbegovic). The GFAP was subsequently endorsed by Security Council resolutions under Chapter VII of the UN Charter.[317] The Agreement and its 11 annexes cover a broad range of issues, including military aspects of the peace settlement; regional stabilization; delineation of an Inter-entity Boundary Line between the Federation of Bosnia and Herzegovina and the Republika Srpska; holding of democratic elections; human rights; assistance to refugees; and an International Police Task Force. The signatories pledged full cooperation with "*all entities involved in the implementation plan*", including the International Criminal Tribunal for the Former Yugoslavia (ICTY) at The Hague.

GFAP Annex 10, "Agreement on Civilian Implementation of the Peace Settlement", provides for two *ad hoc* bodies: the High Representative and the Peace Implementation Council (PIC). The PIC, which consists of representatives for the principal countries and organisations involved in the peace process, and its Steering Board, are tasked to oversee and issue political guidelines for the work of the High Representative. The PIC,

---

315 In the fall of 1995, large-scale trafficking in narcotics was reported with high level military and government personnel implicated. The US threatened to place Cambodia on its Major Narcotics Country list. Once on that list, Cambodia would have to demonstrate that it had taken "legal and law-enforcement measures to prevent and punish public corruption". If it could not, the US would consider halting most bilateral assistance and voting against multilateral assistance.

316 Neilson, K. 1996 p. 18.

317 Security Council Resolutions 1031 (1995); 1144 (1997); and 1256 (1999).

in turn, has conferred upon the High Representative to act as "final authority" in interpreting the GFAP. Although it may be argued that the joint administration of BiH through national and international authorities cannot be placed in the direct context of second-generation peacekeeping, essentially because the High Representative is not a UN body *senso stricto*, the GFAP and the Security Council Resolutions provide for a "hybrid" model of UN administration where the High Representative performs functions comparable to those exercised by the "proper" UN missions in Kosovo and East Timor.[318]

Although the general authorities of the High Representative are formally constructed to be exercised jointly with the constitutional organs of the state of BiH, the combination of Security Council endorsement and delegation of PIC authority (the so called "Bonn Powers") allows the High Representative to decide and implement policies as he deems appropriate in order to uphold and implement the principles of the GFAP, including imposing decisions and laws and removing obstructionist officials.[319] When performing such functions within the realms of the competence of local agencies, the High Representative may, just like the UN Special Representatives in Kosovo and East Timor, be seen as functionally substituting himself for failed or un-cooperative local organs.

Between 1995 and 2002, the High Representative shared important aspects of the peace-implementation and state-building project with the United Nations Mission in Bosnia and Herzegovina (UNMIBH).[320] UNMIBH, which was headed by a Special Representative of the Secretary-General, essentially functioned as an umbrella for many different UN agencies responsible for issues such as humanitarian relief, de-mining, refugee return, etc. Three UNMIBH bodies or programs specifically targeted legal and judicial issues: the Human Rights Office, the Judicial System Assessment Program (JSAP), and the International Police Task Force (IPTF). The mandate of the Human Rights Office included investigation of human rights violations by law enforcement agents; designing remedial measures to correct such violations; and monitoring and ensuring the implementation of the corrective measures.[321] JSAP was mandated to monitor and assess the court system in Bosnia and Herzegovina, as part of the overall programme odf legal reform under the overall coordination of the High Representative.[322] Teams of international and national lawyers were deployed in various parts

[318] Stahn 2001 p. 136.

[319] Since Dayton, the somewhat vague and undefined authority of the OHR has been supplemented by the decisions of Peace Implementation Council (PIC) meetings, most notably Sintra (30 May 1997) and Bonn (10 December 1997).

[320] Established pursuant to Security Council Resolution 1035 (1995).

[321] Established pursuant to Security Council Resolution 1088 (1996).

[322] Established pursuant to Security Council Resolution 1184 (1998).

of BiH to carry out regular and thematic assessments of various aspects of judicial and prosecutorial work. Their reports were made the basis for recommendations for action to the High Representative.[323] At the end of 2000, the responsibility for assessing the state of affairs within the judiciary was transferred to a new body under the Office of the High Representative: the Independent Judicial Commission.

Given the nature of the conflict in Bosnia and Herzegovina, it is understandable that human rights and the rule of law were placed high on the reconstructive agenda. It was for example stipulated in the GFAP that BiH should be a democratic state operating under the Rule of Law and that the state and entity governments (Federation and Republika Srpska) should ensure the highest level of internationally recognized human rights standards and fundamental freedoms. However, the transformation of this language into reality has proven very difficult. 10 years after the GFAP, ethically motivated discrimination, serious corruption, and general lawlessness remain enduring features of BiH political and judicial life.[324] Some of the problems are attributable to lingering elements of communism, central planning and isolation,[325] while others stem from the physical and psychological aftermath of the war, and yet others from the peculiarities of the GFAP.

The stipulation in the GFAP what the state and entity judiciaries should look like, and what the exclusive competencies of the state, entity and cantonal legislatures are to create new rules and institutions, have been both a blessing and a curse for the High Representative. On the positive side is that the construction has provided a least common denominator, agreed upon by all parties in a binding treaty, of which basic judicial institutions that should exist at each level and who that should carry the legal and financial responsibility for their proper functioning. On the negative has been that it etched in stone the processes and tools by which the legal and judicial reform project should be pursued and allowed few or no adjustments along the way, thus preventing

323 JSAP also assisted in the development of a review mechanism for judicial and prosecutorial positions (see Chapter 5.3.5.2).

324 The Wall Street Journal Central European Economic Review (December 1998 – January 1999), with the help of a group of international economists, ranked 27 countries in the region as a place to do business. One of the ten analyzed categories was "Rule of Law". While BiH tied for 24th place overall with Albania, it was ranked 26th in the Rule of Law category, ahead of only Tajikistan. Other countries which comprised part of the former Yugoslavia received more respectable rankings in the category with Slovenia as number 4 and Croatia as number 8.

325 Although not a monolithic structure, socialist Yugoslavia was characterized by an inefficient and heavily politicised administration and judiciary. There was also a considerable element of nepotism and corruption. The wars of 1991-1995 brought immense physical and intellectual destruction to the country and society, and eventually the fragmentation of Yugoslavia essentially along ethnic divides. A number of skilled members of the legal profession was also killed, forced to seek refuge or better opportunities abroad, or prevented from returning to their previous jobs on political or ethnic grounds.

progressive political actors from implementing structures that are objectively necessary to make the system work, but not explicitly provided for in the GFAP. Even the High Representative with his far-reaching powers has needed to be sensitive to this imperative: too creative interpretations of the GFAP could put the fragile consensus that surrounds it, and consequently the entire idea about continued existence of BiH as a unified state, in peril.

After three years of virtual standstill in the legal and judicial area, the June 1998 Luxembourg Peace Implementation Council Meeting and the December 1998 Madrid PIC called for expanded judicial reform efforts coordinated by the High Representative. An OHR-chaired Judicial Reform Working Group, comprising the principal international organizations, was formed to provide for policy-making and co-ordination of reform initiatives. Among the participating agencies were the European Commission, the Council of Europe, the Organization for Security and Cooperation in Europe, the United Nations Judicial System Assessment Program, and a group of specialised non-governmental organizations.[326] Another consolidation took place in March 2001 when the High Representative created the Independent Judicial Commission to lead the implementation of all internationally promoted judicial reform initiatives in BiH (see below).[327]

5.3.2.3 *United Nations Mission in Kosovo*

Security Council Resolution 1244 (1999) providing for the United Nations Mission in Kosovo (UNMIK) called upon the mission to "*provide transitional administration while establishing and overseeing the development of provisional democratic institutions to ensure conditions for a peaceful and normal life for all inhabitants of Kosovo*".[328] In plain language this meant that UNMIK was tasked already from the beginning to perform a virtually unlimited range of interim administrative functions; maintain civil law and order; and promote the development of sustainable and presumably better domestic governance and judicial structures for the future. The only significant limitation flowed from the absence of a final status agreement regarding the future status of Kosovo, making it necessary for UNMIK to refrain from taking any measures in the political, structural and institutional spheres that could create a *fait accompli* and thus prejudice such an agreement.[329]

326 Among the NGOs, the American Bar Association – Central and Eastern European Law Initiative (ABA-CEELI) has played an important role in promoting judicial reform initiatives, particularly reforms aiming at reforming the structures for private legal practice.

327 Decision No. 94/01 On the Establishment of the Independent Judicial Commission.

328 Security Council Resolution 1244 (1999), para. 10.

329 Zimmermann and Stahn 2001 pp. 443.

An important feature of UNMIK was the "pillar" structure. With the problems of conflicting and overlapping international agenda in BiH in fresh memory, the United Nations and the major other international and regional organisations decided to bring basically the entire international presence in Kosovo under the arches of UNMIK in four topical pillars.[330] The first of them, the Humanitarian Assistance Pillar led by the UN High Commissioner on Refugees, was phased out at the end of the emergency stage in June 2000. In May 2001, a new Pillar I was established, this time comprising efforts in the area of "Police and Justice" and operating under the direct leadership of the United Nations. Pillar II was tasked to deal with the related area of "Civil Administration", also under the direct leadership of the United Nations. Pillar III was formed to deal with "Democratization and Institution Building" and led by the Organization for Security and Co-operation in Europe.[331] Pillar IV, finally, took on to promote "Reconstruction and Economic Development" under the leadership of the European Union. A Special Representative of the UN Secretary General was appointed to preside over the entire UNMIK structure and co-ordinate the work in all four pillars with the help of an Executive Committee consisting of the heads of the respective pillars. It may be argued that the division of labour between the pillars with regard to legal and judicial reform has not been entirely clear. For example, how to delineate between police and judicial issues in Pillar I and the generally framed topics institution-building and human rights in Pillar II, including among other things the training of police officers, members of the judiciary and civil servants?

The local counterpart of UNMIK in the inception period was the Kosovo Transitional Council, a body established by UNMIK in 1999 and intended to "shadow" the international administration until elections could be held. The Council initially consisted of six Kosovo Albanians, two Kosovo Serbs, one Muslim and one Turk, but grew to 36 members in 2000. In December 1999, UNMIK established the Interim Administrative Council as part of the Joint Interim Administrative Structure. This body was tasked to advise the SRSG on laws and policy and share management of the province generally. It consisted of four local and four international representatives, but it soon became apparent that the local members were often inclined to put their partisan loyalties first.

330 Security Council Resolution 1244 (1999) para. 5 and Annex 2, para. 3.

331 A specific department of the OSCE Mission in Kosovo was designated to pursue "Human Rights and Rule of Law" issues. Its officers were deployed in more than a dozen field offices and regional centres across Kosovo, with the primary duty to monitor and report of human rights violations. Although the mandate originally given by the OSCE includes the "protection" of human rights, the mission in Kosovo has been reluctant to get involved in individual cases. See Brand 2001 p. 485.

Following the elections in 2001, these and other authorities were transferred to the Provisional Institutions of Self-Government (PISG). Certain so-called "reserved powers" were retained by the SRSG, among them authority over the legal and justice sector. The next step was taken in april 2005, when tentative attempts were made to create the equivalents of Ministries of Justice and Interior. The establishment of such bodies had long been considered impossible as they would provide the Kosovo territorial government with the outward trappings of a sovereign state, and thus risk to anticipate a final status agreement.

5.3.2.4 United Nations Transitional Administration in East Timor

An attempt to describe the international presence in East Timor (after 2002 Timor-Leste) must reach as far back as 1960, when the General Assembly added the territory to its list of so called Non-Self-Governing Territories. After the colonial power Portugal had withdrawn in 1974, fighting soon erupted between those who favoured independence and those who advocated integration with Indonesia. In 1976, after many failed attempts to establish a provisional government and a popular assembly that would determine the status issue, Indonesia intervened militarily and annexed East Timor as its 27th province. The UN reacted by declaring this integration as unlawful, and both the Security Council and the General Assembly called for Indonesia's withdrawal. Beginning in 1982, at the request of the General Assembly, successive Secretaries-General held talks with Indonesia and Portugal aimed at resolving the status issue. In June 1998, Indonesia eventually proposed limited autonomy for East Timor within the Republic of Indonesia. After this opening, the talks made rapid progress and resulted in a set of agreements between Indonesia and Portugal, signed in New York on 5 May 1999. The most important component of these agreements was that the two governments entrusted the Secretary General with organizing and conducting a "popular consultation" in order to ascertain whether the people of East Timor accepted or rejected special autonomy for East Timor within the Republic of Indonesia. In order to carry out the consultation and other matters flowing from the 5 May Agreement, the Security Council authorized the establishment of the United Nations Mission in East Timor (UNAMET).[332]

After the consultation had produced an overwhelming "no" to autonomy within Indonesia (effectively meaning "yes" to independence),[333] pro-integration militias, at times with the support of elements of the Indonesian security forces, launched a

[332] Security Council Resolution 1246 (1999).

[333] On the voting day, 30 August 1999, some 98 per cent of the registered voters went to the polls and decided by a margin of 94,388 (21.5 per cent) to 344,580 (78.5 per cent) to reject the proposed autonomy and begin a process of transition towards independence.

campaign of violence, looting and arson throughout the entire territory. The Secretary General and the Security Council tried various diplomatic efforts to halt the violence and pressed Indonesia hard to meet its responsibility to maintain security and order. Indonesia eventually accepted the deployment of a multinational force (INTERFET) to restore peace and security in East Timor, protect and support UNAMET in carrying out its tasks, and facilitate humanitarian assistance operations. In conjunction with this, Indonesian armed forces, police and administrative officials began their final exit from the territory.

On 28 september, Indonesia and Portugal, at a meeting with the United Nations, reiterated that the authority over East Timor would be transferred to the United Nations and that *ad hoc* measures were required to fill the gap created by the early departure of the Indonesian civil authorities. Shortly thereafter, on 25 October, the United Nations Security Council approved Resolution 1272 (1999) which established the United Nations Transitional Administration in East Timor (UNTAET). Unlike the preceding UNAMET, which had been placed under the UN Department of Political Affairs and essentially geared at facilitating elections and otherwise prepare the political structures for transition, UNTAET was regarded a peacekeeping mission and as such placed with the Department of Peacekeeping Operations (DPKO). Some commentators argue that this change in organisational belonging led to discontinuity in strategies and plans, loss of leadership, and eventually a new mission culture more impressed with the traditional imperatives of peacekeeping than the modern concept of state-building.[334] Other choose to describe UNTAET as the successor of the multinational peace-keeping force INTERFET, or as an attempt at combining the capacities of INTERFET and UNAMET to better match the multidimensional challenges of simultaneous peacekeeping and state building.

UNTAET was mandated to exercise all legislative and executive authority during the transition to independence.[335] The Resolution also tasked UNTAET to lay the foundation for legal and judicial structures that would outlive the international presence. The civilian side of the mission consisted of a governance and public administration component; a civilian police component (up to 1,640 civilian police); and a humanitarian assistance and rehabilitation component. The transitional activities of the mission were initially financed essentially by pledges of more than USD 520

---

334 Chopra 2002 p. 28.

335 Specifically, Resolution 1272 (1999) conferred upon UNTAET the responsibility to provide security and maintain law and order throughout the territory of East Timor; establish an effective administration; assist in the development of civil and social services; ensure the coordination and delivery of humanitarian assistance, rehabilitation and development assistance; support capacity-building for self-government; and to assist in the establishment of conditions for sustainable development.

million, made at a donor meeting in Tokyo in december 1999. In July 2000, UNTAET launched the first mechanism for co-governance with the East Timorese. While both the national and international members of the joint cabinet were appointed by the SRSG, the idea was to gradually replace the international members with East Timorese as local capacity developed. The law enforcement and justice portfolios were among the last to be relinquished by the SRSG.

UNTAET was better prepared and equipped than both OHR in Bosnia and Herzegovina and UNMIK in Kosovo to help the territory under administration integrate into the most important international and regional structures. Notably, the Mission was vested with an explicit mandate to "*conclude such international agreements with states and international organizations as may be necessary for the carrying out of the functions of UNTAET in East Timor*".[336] This mandate was also interpreted to give UNTAET a proactive role in securing the best possible conditions for East Timor's economic survival, *i.a.* by negotiating and concluding the 2001 Timor Sea Arrangement on behalf of East Timor. This "Timor-friendly" document governs the relationship between Australia and East Timor with regard to petroleum operations in the Timor Sea, and provides East Timor with a potential source of enormous income.

Critical commentators have pointed to the paradox that although the conditions for local participation in the formulation of polices and instruments were more favourable in East Timor than in preceding UN missions (in the sense that the armed hostilities were essentially over, the local population fairly united and represented by a sensible interlocutor, the UN welcomed, etc.) the UN decided to base its policies on assumptions of distrust and obstruction and to use modalities more resonant to a war-like environment. Jarat Chopra goes as far as to suggest that rather than trying to render itself obsolete as soon as possible, UNTAET resisted Timorese participation in order to safeguard the UN influence, and that UNTAET's implicit agenda bore the ominous hallmarks of a typical UN "exit strategy" by avoiding committed engagement in problem-solving.[337] Other commentators point out that a gap soon developed between the UN *de jure* authority and the provisional national government's *de facto* control, particularly outside the capital, and that on many occasions, well-organised local stakeholders seemed to be able to push the UN ahead and force the mission to work reactively.

It may be true that the UN Department of Peace-Keeping Operations in New York and UNTAET were late in realizing the important differences between Kosovo and

---

336 Security Council Resolution 1272 (1999), para. 4.

337 Chopra 2000 pp. 28, 31-32.

East Timor in regard to local commitment to the peace agenda and capacity to constructively participate in it. However, the international community may also have perceived that the many and profound "capacity gaps" in East Timor made it necessary to invent most state-level functions from scratch and continue to operate them in the interim period. Many accounts bear witness of discussions among UNTAET staff whether to act so as to maximise output by performing line-function or to promptly incorporate poorly trained local staff in policy and decisional fora and in this way ensure a degree of national ownership, but also inadvertently delay the establishment of critical governance and security structures. UNTAET soon shifted from consolidating power in its own hands to relinquishing power and working systematically on the creation of sustainable national structures. The National Consultative Council was soon replaced with a National Council composed of selected and supposedly respected representatives of local civil society. The joint local and UN cabinet, the East Timor Transitional Administration, was also allowed to take over many governance functions from the UN Special Representative.

After independence in 2002, the UN continued to maintain a presence in Timor-Leste through the United Nations Mission of Support in East Timor (UNMISET) to ensure the security and stability of the new-born state.[338] The Report of the Secretary-General on the United Nations Transitional Administration in East Timor identified among the areas in the greatest need of sustained international attention law enforcement and justice. It was noted with particular concern that the number of judges and prosecutors remained very low and that judgements were often arbitrary and erroneous.[339] Among the capacity building programs requested of UNMISET, there were accordingly one on "Stability, Democracy and Justice" and another on "Public Security and Law Enforcement". In 2005 the international presence was re-organised again. The new United Nations Office in Timor-Leste (UNOTIL) was similarly mandated to ensure the consolidation and viability of essential state functions.

5.3.2.5 United Nations Assistance Mission in Afghanistan

In some significant respects the international presence in Afghanistan represents a reversal or counterpoint to the international governance structures developed for BiH, Kosovo and East Timor. Although war-torn and otherwise disrupted, Afghanistan remains a sovereign state, and the role of the UN is essentially to advise and otherwise empower the fledgling national government. This policy, the "light foot print approach", traces its roots to the strategic Brahimi Report, and aims at encouraging

338 Established pursuant to Security Council Resolution 1410 (2002).

339 Report of the Secretary-General on the United Nations Transitional Administration in East Timor 2001 p. 3.

Afghans to assume effective ownership of the reconstruction of the country.[340] It may also have been a matter of making virtue of necessity, as the experiences of overstretching mission capabilities in the various UN missions in the 1990s were in fresh memory. The UN may further have hoped that inviting and encouraging member states to be more active would make them willing to accept greater responsibility for the implementation of the peace agenda and the long-term sustainability of the new structures of Afghanistan. In spite of the 'light foot print', the UN influence on matters of governance has been considerable and among the highest placed of its priorities have been human rights and the rule of law.[341]

The history of UN engagement in Afghanistan is a long one. After the Taliban had taken Kabul in September 1996 and executed the former President Najibullah, the Security Council called on all Afghan parties to end the hostilities and engage in a political dialogue aimed at achieving national reconciliation.[342] The Council also repeated its concern that the conflict provided fertile ground for terrorism and drug trafficking. However, fighting continued between the Taliban and Northern Alliance groups between 1997 and 2000. In July of 1997, the Secretary General appointed Lakhdar Brahimi as his Special Envoy for Afghanistan and tasked him to consult with interested and relevant countries and parties and to make recommendations to the UN on possible peacemaking activities.[343]

Following the terrorist bomb attacks on United States embassies in Nairobi and Dar-es-Salaam in August 1998, the Security Council adopted resolutions that repeated its concern at the continuing presence of terrorist groups in the territory of Afghanistan and demanded that the Taliban stop providing sanctuary and training for such organizations and that all Afghan factions cooperate in bringing indicted terrorists to justice.[344] In October 1999, citing the failure of the Taliban authorities to respond to this demand, the Security Council applied broad sanctions (among other things the freezing of funds owned or controlled by the Taliban) under the enforcement provisions of the UN Charter. The Security Council also pointed out in a resolution that Usama bin Laden had been indicted by the United States for the embassy bombings and demanded that the Taliban should turn him over to the appropriate authorities to be brought to justice.[345] The Council further expressed grave concern

340 Report of the Panel on UN Peace Operations, A/55/305-S/2000/809.

341 Report of the Secretary-General on the Situation in Afghanistan and its Implications for International Peace and Security, 18 March, 2001.

342 Security Council Resolution 1076 (1996).

343 Special Envoy Brahimi convened a series of informal meetings with what became known as the "Six plus Two" group, composed of the six States bordering Afghanistan (China, Iran, Pakistan, Tajikistan, Turkmenistan and Uzbekistan) plus the United States and Russia.

344 Security Council Resolutions 1193 (1998) and 1214 (1998) respectively.

345 Security Council Resolution 1267 (1999).

at the seriously deteriorating humanitarian and human rights situation (forced displacements of civilian populations; summary executions; abuse and arbitrary detention of civilians; violence against women and girls; etc.).

In spite of these resolutions and other diplomatic efforts, the conflict continued essentially unabated until the end of 2001. Throughout this period, the international community had little other option but to try to ensure that the victims of the war and turmoil received at least of minimum of food, shelter and protection. At the same time, the political and security problems caused frequent interruptions in the flow of humanitarian assistance, and various crises required the temporary departure of UN and non-governmental aid workers. In the late 1990s, there was a series of natural disasters further worsening the situation.

After the 11 September 2001 terrorist attack on the United States by the Afghan-based Al Qaeda group, the Security Council expressed its strong support for the efforts of the Afghan people to replace the Taliban regime. At the diplomatic level, the UN also began to prepare the ground for a new inclusive government. On 3 October, the Secretary General reappointed Lakhdar Brahimi, who had resigned two years earlier, as his Special Envoy for Afghanistan. On 12 november, the "Six plus Two" group met again in New York under the chairmanship of the Secretary General, agreeing on the need for a broad-based and freely chosen Afghan government and pledging continued support for various UN humanitarian efforts. On 27 november, a conference on Afghanistan's reconstruction sponsored by UNDP, the World Bank and the Asian Development Bank, opened in Islamabad. Over 300 participants attended, including many from Afghanistan. The issues discussed included human rights, the role of women, education, and public health. A further donor conference, focusing on the immediate and longer-term needs of the country, was held in Berlin in early December.

At about this time the Northern Alliance was entering Mazar-e-Sharif, Herat and then Kabul, thus putting an end to the Taliban regime. In order to consolidate and empower the new interim structures for the new Afghan state, the United Nations organized a meeting among prospective Afghan political leaders and other stakeholders in Bonn, leading up to "The Bonn Agreement on Provisional Arrangements in Afghanistan Pending the Re-establishment of Permanent Government Institutions". In Resolution 1383 (2001), adopted immediately after the conclusion of the Bonn Agreement, the Security Council endorsed the Agreement and declared its willingness to take further action to support the interim institutions established therein.

Among the most important features of the Bonn Agreement was the emphasis on national ownership of the reform process, visualized *inter alia* in the immediate establishment of a national Interim Authority consisting of an Interim Administration with Hamid Karzai as the Chairman, a special Independent Commission for the convening of the Emergency *Loya Jirga* (Pashtu for "grand council", a traditional forum in which tribal elders come together and settle affairs), and a structure of regular courts. Annex 1 to the Bonn Agreement explicitly stated that "*[t]he participants in the UN Talks on Afghanistan recognize that the responsibility for providing security and law and order throughout the country resides with the Afghans themselves*".[346] The Agreement further specified the convening of a Constitutional *Loya Jirga* to prepare and adopt a new constitution for Afghanistan. The Transitional Administration was mandated to establish a Constitutional Commission to assist the Constitutional *Loya Jirga*.

On 20 December 2001, the Security Council authorized the establishment of an International Security Assistance Force (ISAF) to help the Interim Administration maintain security in Kabul and its surrounding areas.[347] Special Representative Brahimi also moved to Kabul to commence his activities in support of the new Administration. At the same time, the first of the ISAF troops were deployed, under British control.[348] The next step was the establishment of the United Nations Assistance Mission in Afghanistan (UNAMA) in March 2002 to better integrate and coordinate the work of the various UN agencies in the country, their Afghan government counterparts, and national and international NGO partners.[349] The SRSG leading UNAMA is formally in charge of all UN activities in the country, including legal and justice sector reforms, but has no formal authority over the Afghan Administration. Under the SRSG, two Deputy SRSGs are responsible for Political Affairs, and Relief, Recovery and Reconstruction, respectively. There are also Special Advisors on Human Rights, Gender, Drugs, Rule of Law, Police, Military and Demobilization issues.

In line with the Bonn Agreement and later the Petersberg Agreement, special commissions were formed for advancing reforms within justice, human rights, and the civil service. The Judicial Reform Commission were supposed to work "from below" and with a close eye at the Constitutional Commission to promote the establishment of a legal and judicial system that connects "modern", "traditional" and Islamic elements. An important task was also to act as clearinghouse and information broker between the established Afghan institutions, and between these institutions and the donor community. All members of the Commission were Afghan, but they interacted frequently with foreign advisors, donors agencies and their consultants.

---

346 Agreement on Provisional Arrangements in Afghanistan Pending the Re-establishment of Permanent Government Institutions (5 December 2005), Annex 1.

347 Security Council Resolution 1386 (2001).

348 To raise sufficient means for this undertaking, the International Conference on Reconstruction Assistance on Afghanistan was held in Tokyo in January 2002, resulting in pledges of over USD 4.5 billion.

349 Established by Security Council Resolution 1401 (2002).

Since its inception, the Commission has facilitated or implemented various studies and surveys, training of young judicial professionals, reviews of laws, and helped in information and awareness campaigns. Critical commentators have described the Judicial Reform Commission as a structure set up to substitute for a strategy. While the idea was to have a neutral body identifying and facilitating reforms cutting across political and bureaucratic boundaries, they point out that the Commission has neither had the political skills to overcome institutional and personal tensions among the established permanent institutions, nor the mandate to effect real changes. It has also been disputed whether the Commission should focus of facilitating implementation of existing strategies, or on the identification and implementation of new reform objectives. The Commission has similarly been unable of influencing those issues with relevance for the legal and judicial sectors that formally fall within the realms of the other commissions, for example budgetary, organisational and management reform in the civil service.[350]

Another special feature of the international presence in Afghanistan is the "lead nation approach" whereby specific donor governments have taken responsibility for leading the international support efforts in specific topical area. The responsibility for assisting in the countering of production and trade in narcotics rests with the United Kingdom; rebuilding the armed forces with the United States; demobilization and reintegration with Japan; rebuilding the police force with Germany; and rebuilding the justice system with Italy. This *de facto* "delegation" to individual governments to make plans and provide for implementation in an entire sector largely explains why there has been no comprehensive strategy for the rule of law and so few efforts at co-ordinating law and justice-related initiatives. The lack of shared vision, and a consistent strategy to attain it, may in turn explain the apparent problems in creating popular confidence among local stakeholders and the population at large in the international community's ability to effectively promote reforms in this area. There is also tentative experience to suggest that the lead nation concept weakens the sense of national accountability and ownership, and thus works to offset the essence of the light foot print approach.

The Bonn process formally ended with the inauguration of the Afghan National Assembly on 19 December 2005. At this point, Afghanistan had a new constitution, an elected president, a government, a parliament, and provincial councils. However, the international engagement did not end. In January 2006 a number of governments and international organisations met in London to discuss the plans and principles for a future international engagement in Afghanistan. The participants agreed on a document called the Afghan Compact, laying out a framework for a partnership-based "holistic" engagement with the country to consolidate democratic institutions,

---

[350] Assistance to Justice and the Rule of Law in Afghanistan 2004.

stimulate the economy, and enforce the law. In the judicial and law enforcement area, the Afghan Compact is particularly concerned with the introduction of a clear and transparent process for the appointment of senior judges, prosecutors and chiefs of police. The Compact will also reflect the needs identified in the comprehensive needs assessment of the justice sector being undertaken by the Afghan Ministry of Justice, for example with regard to ways of maintaining a role for traditional justice mechanisms within the political and constitutional framework of the new Afghanistan.[351]

A cross-cutting issue in reforming the laws, institutions and practices in Afghanistan has been to reconcile traditional justice mechanisms and modern liberal standards of human rights and the rule of law. Historically, the reach of the formal system has been rather limited, and in the Bonn Agreement and ensuing documents, the Afghan people expressed its will to retain many aspects of traditional law and justice within the framework of the new state. This aspiration may in part be regarded as a reflection of trust and confidence in the local and traditional, in part to the alien nature of the new and formal, and in part to sober scepticism of the capacity of the state and its agents to dispense fair and timely justice throughout the country. It is also possible that Afghan policy-makers are not always aware of the institutional alternatives and the possibilities they offer. For the lead nation, Italy, this means that a key challenge is to ensure that traditional justice mechanisms meet international human rights standards and to create interest and demand for "modern" or "international" alternatives where needed.

5.3.3 EMERGENCY LAW ENFORCEMENT AND CRIMINAL JUSTICE

5.3.3.1 United Nations Transitional Authority in Cambodia

The idea behind the presence of an UNTAC civil police component in Cambodia was to help assure Cambodians that the language in the Paris Agreement about human rights and the rule of law was going to be transformed into reality. Much of the daily work of the 3,600 UNTAC civilian police thus came to focus on the supervision or control of local police activities and on providing various forms of general and topical training.[352] Such training comprised, *inter alia*, basic police methods, traffic control, human rights observance, criminal law, criminal investigation, crime prevention, and

---

351 Justice for All 2005.

352 Priority in the initial deployment of UNTAC police and human rights resources was given to areas were Cambodian refugees and displaced persons were being resettled.

riot control. Special instruction and training was also provided to police officers and judges in the implementation of the new penal code.

The UNTAC police further undertook independently a large number of investigations into serious crimes, particularly those considered to be politically or ethnically motivated. In some cases, the UNTAC police could hand over sufficient evidence for the Special Prosecutor to issue a warrant. In other cases where political action was needed to address systemic problems, the Special Representative could raise the matter either formally with the SNC or more informally in private meetings with party leaders. However, there were neither means nor mandate for the UNTAC police to seriously and systematically address the atrocities of the Khmer Rouge regime.

5.3.3.2 High Representative to Bosnia and Herzegovina

The international community was never directly involved in providing for law enforcement in Bosnia and Herzegovina (with the exception of arrests and investigations ordered by ICTY, see below). The international emphasis was instead on promoting and facilitating reforms of existing police structures on state, entity and cantonal level. The GFAP placed the responsibility for police reform with the UNMIBH International Police Task Force (IPTF). Its tasks thus included, among other things, monitoring law enforcement activities and facilities (including associated judicial organizations, structures and proceedings); advising and training law enforcement personnel; facilitating local law enforcement activities; assessing threats to public order and advising on the capability of law enforcement agencies to deal with such threats; and advising domestic authorities on the organization of effective civilian law enforcement agencies. After having noted the great problems faced by IPTF in effectively promoting these goals within its original mandate, the Security Council expanded the mandate and increased the number of staff on the ground several times throughout the mission term.[353] After the conclusion of UNMIBH in the end of 2002, the European Union Police Mission (EUPM) took over many of the tasks of IPTF.

The efforts to reform the police in BiH encountered some serious political, legal and cultural difficulties. The autocratic Yugoslavian regime had needed a loyal and forceful instrument of control, which meant that the various police forces of Yugoslavia and the republics had developed into organizations primarily concerned with matters of state security, executive protection, border services, and "order" in general. There was

[353] For example, Security Council Resolution 1103 (1997) endorsing the Secretary-General's recommendations relating to international policing in the city of Brcko. This Resolution provided for an increase in the strength of IPTF by 186 civilian police personnel, taking into account the fact that the Brcko arbitration award called for the monitoring, restructuring and retraining of the police in the Brcko area with an intensity far beyond that in other parts of the country.

also the paramilitary Ministry of Interior Special Police (commonly MUP), which units could be assigned to support territorial defence and maintain control of the interior of the country in times of war, martial law and unrest. The MUP was armed with rocket-launched grenades, large calibre weapons, light armour, and in some cases tanks and anti-aircraft guns. During the war of 1992-1995, the three ethnic groups quickly co-opted their respective regular police and MUP-forces and used them to perform a range of paramilitary functions, sometimes functionally integrated into regular military units. The standard uniform of the police in this time was often a slightly modified version of the fatigue uniform of their military counterparts, and their basic weapon the distinctly military AK-47 assault rifle. There was also an influx of new officers with little or no police training to boost the ranks.[354]

That the GFAP provided for *de facto* entity and cantonal-level monopoly on law enforcement meant that even after the conclusion of the armed hostilities, the ethnic groups could continue to rely on their "own" police in a low-intensity war of control and repression. Having realised the political fragmentation of the police and the lack of commitment to the GFAP, the IPTF tried as a first measure to create some sort of consensus with local stakeholders around a description of problems and their potential remedies. Another initial priority was to change the primary focus of the police from the security of the state or ethnic group to the security of the individual. Generally, the best results were achieved in addressing institutional and quantifiable matters, such as restructuring police administrations and downsizing the total number of police officers.

Later into the mission, the IPTF promoted structural initiatives such as the establishment and training of a State Border Service; a Bosnia and Herzegovina police contingent for duty in UN peacekeeping missions outside the former Yugoslavia; and a Judicial (Court) Police force to provide better physical protection for members of the judiciary, witnesses and other people participating in trials and investigations, and improve the enforcement of court decisions. The Judicial Police initiative was difficult to promote also within the international community, as there was concern that some of the functions of the Judicial Police (*i.a.* to "secure information" and conduct searches and seizures) would risk to duplicate the mandate of the existing police. There was also concern that the creation of a new police structure would send the wrong signals in a country which only recently had begun to reduce its traditionally heavy police presence.

In order to help the reformed police institutions deliver better services, the IPTF launched various training initiatives to ensure that all police officers had the knowledge

[354] According to a 1996 IFOR study, over 80 % of the Federation police officers had fewer than 6 years of experience, and in many cases their background was of military or paramilitary character.

and personal qualities their work in a democratic state required. IPTF's mandatory core training program, which resulted in what was popularly referred to as "IPTF certification", consisted of three courses: a two-day information course that explained the restructuring and its aims; a three-week transition course that was essentially a condensed version of a police academy course focusing on basic policing skills; and a one-week human dignity course that provided a "modern" view of the role of the police officer in society.[355] Officers who failed to meet the criteria and standards required for final certification were disqualified from the process and their right to exercise police powers was withdrawn. IPTF and UNMIBH also assisted Federation and RS authorities in establishing police academies in Sarajevo and Banja Luka and in developing new police training curricula. Although the policy was to encourage minority candidates to attend the training, and to ensure that the training was provided by a multi-ethnic staff, a high number of minority candidates left the academies in response to real and perceived ethnical discrimination from their local instructors and fellow candidates.

Although not law enforcement institutions *sensu stricto*, *ad hoc* tribunals merit discussion in this context because of their important indirect contribution to the establishment of basic conditions of peace and stability in war-torn societies. When the UN Security Council in the midst of the conflict in BiH decided to create the International Tribunal for the Prosecution of Persons Responsible for Serious Violations of International Humanitarian Law Committed in the Territory of the Former Yugoslavia since 1991 (ICTY), it confirmed both that justice and punishment are important parts of peace and reconciliation, and that such matters belong to the Security Council's field of competence.[356] A similar *ad hoc* structure, the International Criminal Tribunal for Rwanda, was established soon thereafter to try persons accused

[355] Important components of these courses were developed by, and implemented in cooperation with, the U.S. Department of Justice's International Criminal Investigation Training and Assistance Program. The Swedish National Police Board (in cooperation with IPTF and Ministries of Internal Affairs and the Police Academies in Sarajevo and Doboj) also developed a training program in conflict resolution for local police instructors, with financing from the Swedish International Development Co-operation Agency. Under a specific training mandate, IPTF provided specialized training in fighting organized and drug-related crime, crowd control and major incident management.

[356] It is stated in the empowering Resolution 827 (1993) that the Tribunal's sole purpose is to prosecute "*persons responsible for serious violations of international humanitarian law*" and thereby to "*contribute to restoration and maintenance of peace*" (para. 2 and preambular para. 6). Geographically and temporally, the crimes tried by ICTY must have been committed on the territory of the former Yugoslavia since 1991. The jurisdiction is limited to natural persons, thus excluding organisations, political parties, administrative entities or other legal subjects regardless of their role in past and present crimes. It should be noted that many legal issues now before the Tribunal have not been tried in a international judicial fora since the Nuremberg and Tokyo trials. Examples of important legal decisions made by the ICTY include clarifications of the application of the Geneva Conventions, the further development of the command responsibility doctrine, and the interpretation of rape as a form of torture and a crime against humanity.

of genocide and other grave violations of international humanitarian law committed in Rwanda during 1994.[357] The explicit categorization of war crimes and crimes against humanity as "threats to peace", and the establishment of the Tribunals under Chapter VII of the Charter, further meant that the decisions became binding upon all UN members and that the road was open to create supporting institutions and processes as needed.[358] In addition, the establishment of the Tribunals demonstrated that the Security Council considered itself in a position to rule on the quality and feasibility of present and future institutional alternatives, national as well as international. In the case of ICTY, the Council signalled that it did not consider the domestic courts and law enforcement agencies of Croatia, Bosnia and Herzegovina, the FRY, etc. able of fairly and effectively adjudicating these kinds of sensitive and high-profile cases.[359]

The ICTY judges and prosecutors are judicially independent of the UN and national governments. The Tribunal also employs police officers, crime experts, political analysts, translators and many other professional categories to assist in investigations and the ensuing trials. The conduct of the trial draws on both the civil law and common law systems, and elements of the adversarial and inquisitorial procedures are combined. The Rules of Procedure and Evidence guarantee that the proceedings adhere to internationally recognised principles of fair trial.[360] There are also rules and routines for providing assistance and protection to witnesses before, during and after the proceedings. There is an ICTY Detention Unit in The Hague where the accused are held following their arrest and until the completion of the proceedings. Sentences, with life imprisonment as the maximum, are served in one of the States that have signed an agreement with the United Nations to accept persons convicted by the ICTY.

Although judicially independent, the ICTY must rely heavily on various forms of international cooperation in order to successfully carry out its mandate, particularly in the stages of arrest and investigation (for example in the collection of evidence and the transfer of accused persons). States and international organizations have generally been willing to offer such assistance when needed, for example in the relocation of sensitive witnesses and the enforcement of sentences. The Tribunal has also depended on the good will of individual states for securing funding, staff and political clout.

---

357 Established pursuant to Security Council Resolution 955 (1994).

358 Österdahl 1997 p. 253.

359 While the "Rules of the Road" that regulate the relationship between ICTY and the national courts allow the national courts concurrent jurisdiction over serious violations of international humanitarian law, they also stipulate that ICTY can claim primacy over national courts and take over any national investigation or proceeding if would be in the interest of international justice.

360 For example the presumption of innocence, the right to be tried without undue delay, the right to examine adverse witnesses and the right of appeal.

The concrete results of the work of ICTY and ICTR have fanned interest and support for the establishment of similar *ad hoc* fora in other conflict situations as far apart as Sierra Leone and East Timor, and for the International Criminal Court. The positive effects on public opinion may have been even greater had it not been for the failure of ICTY to bring to justice some of the most notorious suspected war criminals, and the limited success in eradicating certain misconceptions about its purpose and work methods among people in the region. Many Serbs and Croats, in particular, are still convinced that the ICTY is biased against their communities and Christianity, but willing to turn a blind eye to atrocities committed by Muslims.[361] The ICTY was relatively late in realizing the importance of countering such perceptions of bias and illegitimacy, but eventually launched active outreach programs and activities (among them a series of hour-long programs on ICTY produced and broadcasted by the EU-funded Open Broadcast Network) to establish a more accurate image of the Tribunal and create more realistic expectations as to what it could and could not do within its mandate and available resources.

It has proven important that international courts and tribunals have a working strategy for supporting domestic efforts to investigate and try serious and sensitive crimes. That ICTY gives clearance to local courts in BiH to try war-crimes cases, but does not exercise its right to supervise such trials (largely because of a decision not to devote scarce resources to what were viewed as secondary tasks) has resulted in a situation where technically difficult and politically sensitive cases are tried by inexperienced and easily manipulated local judges. It is even conceivable that people suspected of serious crimes have sought to take advantage of this situation to create a procedural hindrance for a later, more thoroughly prepared, trial.

5.3.3.3 United Nations Mission in Kosovo

Besides establishing a civilian administration for Kosovo, Security Council Resolution 1244 (1999) also mandated the military Kosovo Force (KFOR) to ensure "*public safety and order*" until the international civil presence, the UNMIK Police, could take responsibility for this task.[362] In response to escalating violence and crime, KFOR soon started to carry out large-scale arrests to restore public peace and order to the territory. Once deployed and operative the UNMIK Police also used its executive powers to maintain law and order. As neither the domestic courts nor ICTY could process all these arrests, this strategy soon led to a backlog of several hundred detainees, many

361 Coliver (2000 pp. 20-21) mentions as an example that many Serbs find it insulting that Alija Izetbegovic was allowed to hold Presidency, while Radovan Karadzic was forcibly expulsed and indicted.

362 Security Council Resolution 1244 (1999) para. 9(d).

of them held for serious crimes such as arson, violent assault and murder, and some for grave violations of international humanitarian and human rights law.

In this situation, KFOR and the UN administration had to choose between releasing the detainees (with the bad-will and potential for unrest that would entail) or immediately proceed to provide for emergency judicial structures. Attracted by the demonstration effect of trials, UNMIK decided to make an attempt at the latter and to base the interim structure on the local courts of general jurisdiction. In order to help the courts deal with the extraordinary caseload, and hopefully also balance existing loyalty ties between the regular judges and local political groups, the SRSG appointed temporary local judges and prosecutors whom would be able to hear cases all over the province. However, it soon became apparent that these teams were unable to meet demands due to lack of experience and status. UNMIK then decided to give itself the right to appoint an international judge as a member of any three-judge panel in local courts.[363] Neither was this initiative enough to prevent ethnic bias and corruption from influencing the judgements, as the two local judges typically did not hesitate to outvote their international colleague.[364]

After the idea of establishing a special "Kosovo War and Ethnic Crimes Court" had been briefly considered and abandoned (essentially because of the risks for overlaps with ICTY and the enormous costs involved), a new approach to international supervision and participation was adopted, consisting of a new regime by which any part to a prosecution, at any stage in the proceedings, could petition the Department of Justice for appointment of an international prosecutor or investigating judge, or the assignment of the case to a "Special Panel" of one local and two international judges (with one of the international judges presiding). Following a recommendation by the Department of Justice, it was then for the SRSG to finally decide whether the specific case warranted this special treatment and to appoint the prosecutor and the members of the Special Panel.[365] Predictably, the members of the local legal community (particularly the Kosovar Albanians) did not greet this UNMIK initiative favourably, much because of a perception of not having been included in the decision. International and regional organisations concerned with issues of human rights and rule of law also criticized the lack of clear and objective criteria for deciding which cases that should qualify for assignment to a Special Panel, and even expressed concerns that the procedure for assignment and disqualification of the international judges could

363 UNMIK Regulation No. 2000/6 of 15 February 2000 on the Appointment and Removal from Office of International Judges and International Prosecutors.

364 Kritz 2002 p. 73.

365 UNMIK Regulation No. 2000/64 of 15 December 2000 on Assignment of International Judges/Prosecutors and/or Change in Venue.

shed the independence of the judiciary in doubt.[366] As of 2005, Kosovo judges and prosecutors were still not involved in cases of serious crimes. While the employment of international judges was of some use in processing the backlog of cases and in dealing with sensitive crimes that otherwise might have been unfairly judged, their participation also had the negative effect of relieving pressure on local stakeholders to promptly and properly address institutional problems in courts and prosecution agencies. The long-term capacity-building effects of the international participation would also have been greater if mentoring and training had been made explicit parts of the international judges and prosecutors assignments.

Although the rationale for the infusion of international judges was to ensure independence and impartiality, the authority of the SRSG and UNMIK over these judges and the cases they would hear soon became a source of concern, first among external commentators and later within the mission itself. In order to defuse suspicions of taking the issue of judicial independence lightly, the UNMIK Department of Justice established two accountability mechanisms, the Kosovo Judicial and Prosecutorial Council to oversee the appointment of judges and prosecutors (paradoxically, the Council was not given authority over international staff), and the Judicial Investigation Unit to look into accusations of improper behaviour in the judiciary. Critical commentaries and insider reports describe the evolution of the participation of international judges and prosecutors in local trials as haphazard and crisis-driven, and argue that more could have been done to ensure sustainable results of their presence.[367] In a recent initiative, the new Kosovo Special Prosecutor's Office established to deal with high-profile cases has been assigned international prosecutors specifically tasked to provide their local colleagues with hands-on training.

A technical problem in the operation of the emergency and hybrid systems in Kosovo was the lack of a recognised and acceptable framework of criminal and criminal procedure laws. The interim solution was to use the criminal procedure laws of the Federal Republic of Yugoslavia as the basis for the prosecution and trial, but to apply only those provisions of these laws that corresponded to recognized international human rights standards (*e.g.* the ICCPR and the ECHR). It soon became apparent that the general weakness of the system made this solution untenable. For example, the number of detainees by far exceeded the number of available lawyers in the territory, thus making it practically impossible to accord initial judicial hearing to all detainees within seventy-two hours of their arrest.[368] The political sensitivity of this issue, and the recognition that the mission could not realistically maintain the interim structure

366 Kritz 2002 p. 74.

367 Hartmann 2003 p. 13; Finding the Balance 2002 pp. 1, 8-9.

368 Strohmeyer 2001 p. 55.

in the long run, elevated the rebuilding and empowerment of domestic law enforcement even higher on the UNMIK agenda.[369]

5.3.3.4 United Nations Transitional Administration in East Timor

Although the official political understanding was that the Government of Indonesia would continue to have responsibility for law and order in the territory of East Timor until authority was formally transferred to the UN, conditions were chaotic and violence rampant at the arrival of the UN peace-keeping force INTERFET. The mission thus found itself compelled to immediately provide for emergency law enforcement functions to ensure a degree of law and order.

This task could hardly be achieved without arresting a number of people involved in acts that posed serious threats to peace and security. While apprehending these people proved relatively straightforward for the military force, INTERFET was neither mandated nor prepared to carry out the next step, *i.e.* to provide for emergency judicial functions. The Mission thus had little option but to hand over most of these persons to the remaining civilian authorities, who in turn promptly released them. As it became clear that the domestic judicial authorities were basically dysfunctional, and that no significant improvements could be expected in the short term, the Mission needed to proceed to establish basic, short-term provisions for preventive detention and other essentials of law enforcement and criminal justice. These provisions remained effective until October 1999, when the Detainee Management Unit was established as an interim judicial system pending the re-establishment of legitimate civil authorities.[370] The INTERFET staff operating the DMU based their decisions on Indonesian law. The successor mission UNTAET came to inherit the backlog of arrests and detentions made by INTERFET, but also needed to deal with the growing number of people apprehended by the subsequently deployed UN civil police force for various kinds of ordinary crimes.[371] Parallel to this, UNTAC needed to address the physical reconstruction of court buildings, archives, and other essentials of a working judicial system.[372]

The separate regime for dealing with the most serious human right violations in East Timor (genocide, war crimes, and crimes against humanity) came to be differently

369 Id. p. 49.

370 Notably, the legal authority to establish this interim structure was essentially derived from the framework for administering occupied territories set out in the Fourth Geneva Convention, although it was known that this instrument did not technically apply since the Indonesian government had consented to the deployment of INTERFET.

371 Strohmeyer 2001 p. 51.

372 Id. p. 50.

structured and more "local" than the ICTY-based approach of BiH and Kosovo, and more similar to the originally contemplated model for Cambodia. The core in this regime was the Special Panels for Serious Crimes (SPSC), composed of two international and one local judge, initially established within the District Court in Dili and later relocated to the Court of Appeals.[373] There was also a hybrid prosecutorial body, the "Serious Crimes Unit" (SCU), with both international and local prosecutors, to deal with the investigation and prosecution of these types of crimes.[374] The principal reasons for emphasising domestic prosecution and trials seem to have been the ambition to make the most of the pedagogical and demonstration effects, while simultaneously avoiding the laborious work of building opinion and seeking mandate for an international alternative.

Although the SPSC structure was essentially a response to lack of national capacity, it too suffered from a range of capacity-related problems. In the beginning, the lack of pre-trial detention facilities compelled the release of a number of detainees. The lack of office equipment, IT, etc. has also restrained the SCU. For a long time, the SPSC and SCU have further been dependent on international (UN) assistance and seconded experts for their functioning. Not only have the overall capacity of these bodies been low, it has also been unevenly distributed. While the SCU had at least some basic resources to draw on and could ask for help from the international community when needed, legal representation for the accused had to be found among the utterly small number of Timorese public defenders, whom also were known to often lack the skills and experience the task required. In response to such problems, a group of international jurists formed the Defense Lawyers Unit in 2002 and managed to create a formal affiliation with the SPSC structure. After having prosecuted more than 50 cases (most resulting in convictions) the SCU completed its mandate in June 2005, and the responsibility for prosecuting serious crimes was then placed with the regular prosecutorial structures.

5.3.3.5 United Nations Assistance Mission in Afghanistan

It was clear from the outset that the international community had neither the ambition (strategy) nor the resources to maintain law and order throughout Afghanistan. Still

---

373 Their exclusive jurisdiction of the Special Panels over the crimes of genocide, war crimes, and crimes against humanity (and the crimes of torture, murder and sexual offences if committed between 1 January 1999 and 25 October 1999), was provided for in UNTAET Regulation 2000/15, Section 10, and formulated with the 1998 Rome Statute of the International Criminal Court as the model.

374 Established by UNTAET Regulation 2000/16. Kritz (2002 p. 71) mentions that the new prosecution mechanism was developed largely in isolation by international experts and UN staff, and as a result its announcement was initially received with little enthusiasm, even hostility, by the remaining members of the East Timorese judiciary and prosecution. See also Linton 2001 p. 150.

today, former warlords and local commanders empowered by the trade in drugs continue to challenge the ability of the Afghan Government, and the international civil and military apparatus supporting it, to spread its executive powers to the whole country and effectively restore law and order. In some cases, the Government and the international presence have even formed temporary alliances with such warlords, thus granting them a degree of superficial international legitimacy and simultaneously undermining the fledgling local police and judiciary.

Hope is instead invested that the legitimate local authorities, inspired by Kabul (where the International Security Assistance Force and local bodies provide for a basic level of security) and helped by the donors, will gradually be able to expand control and perform essential security, law enforcement and justice functions throughout the country. However, this strategy too is being slowed down or reversed by the very conditions it seeks to address: factional fighting, drug wars, and lawlessness in general. Various acts of strategic violence, notably political murders targeting government ministers, also work to preserve a climate of insecurity and uncertainty and adversely impact on the reform process generally.

The international community may have arrived at a point in Afghanistan where it needs to rethink its optimistic policy on security, or the entire state building project risks to collapse. As an international military presence throughout Afghanistan remains unfeasible, the first point on the agenda would need to be the creation a non-factional Afghan armed force and national police that are both committed and equipped to seize effective power. The Special Representative is already lobbying donor governments and international organisations to make adequate financial resources available for this project. A small but encouraging sign is that there is now a Police Academy in Kabul offering training to a large number of cadets of different ethnicities. Germany, the lead donor in the area of law enforcement, is helping the Academy along by providing support to curricula development, field-training programs, acquisition of non-lethal equipment, rebuilding of facilities, and notably salaries. At the multilateral level, the UNDP has established the Law and Order Trust Fund of Afghanistan as multi-donor funded facility to support the re-emergence of the regular Afghan Police Force as the unchallenged law enforcement agency throughout the country.

5.3.4 CONSTITUTIONAL AND LEGAL REFORM

5.3.4.1 United Nations Transitional Authority in Cambodia

The main factors determining the course of legal and judicial reform in Cambodia were the Paris Agreement and the ways the Special Representative used his pseudo-legislative, executive and judicial powers in response to actions and inaction by the national authorities in implementing Agreement.

The explicit commitment in the Agreement to establish and consolidate conventional principles of democracy and division of power was regarded by the mission as a mandate to push for a range of initiatives in the area of legal and judicial reform, including the drafting of a new constitution consistent with these principles.[375] As a matter of first priority, UNTAC pushed the interim government to accede to a number of international human rights conventions, including the ICCPR and the ICESCR, thus establishing a lower threshold for rule of law and human rights standards in ensuing national enactments. The accession to the ICCPR also brought with it an obligation for the national authorities to immediately provide for effective remedies for violations of rights, something which in turn presupposed the establishment of an independent judiciary and other essential elements of fair criminal trials.[376]

While UNTAC initially relied heavily on foreign experts in the formulation of reform strategies and drafting of instruments, the Mission staff soon realised the need to include and consult Cambodian jurists when important pieces of legislation were drafted. At the same time, such inclusive and consultative approaches were made difficult by the very low number of domestically trained jurists still alive and in the country. Of those few, the majority was also unfamiliar with many fundamental concepts of international law and human rights law. For this small group, the Paris Agreement actually represented a confusing turnaround; the goals and models for the reconstruction of the Cambodian legal system were no longer socialist and Vietnamese, as had been the case after the Vietnamese invasion, but rather democratic and "Western". They were also confused by the change of advisors: the Vietnamese went home and in came the multinational UN Mission, various bilateral agencies, a plethora of international NGOs, and their consultants. Yet another difficulty for the Mission and the participating Cambodians alike was the lack of recognizable and appealing country models: Vietnam lacked a system that held up to international scrutiny; Thailand wrestled with the reputation of having an organised but corrupt legal system; Singapore was too autocratic; etc. Among the more innovative yet unrealistic suggestions that circulated at the time was that returning refugees would help to model new laws and institutions on the structures that had evolved to govern social life in the Cambodian refugee camps in Thailand.

375 According to the Paris Agreement, the Constitution should, *inter alia*, include a provision establishing its role as the supreme law of the land, a long list of human rights to be protected in a manner consistent with relevant international instruments, and a guarantee that there should be courts to adjudicate and enforce these rights. Annex 5, Arts. 1, 2, 4, and 5.

376 ICCPR, Arts. 3, 14 and 26.

The need to base the 1993 Constitution on the ambitious principles of the Paris Agreement meant that the drafters had to stipulate standards and conditions that the political and judicial authorities could not possibly meet at the time of enactment, for example in regard to the independence of the judiciary and the protection of human rights. However, merely codifying the unsatisfactory *status quo* at would have sent the wrong signals and made ensuing efforts at restructuring and strengthening other laws and agencies virtually impossible.[377]

5.3.4.2 High Representative to Bosnia and Herzegovina

The statement in the GFAP and the annexed BiH Constitution that Bosnia and Herzegovina should display the characteristics of a modern constitutional democracy were intended to signal to national and international authorities to proceed with far-reaching and profound legal reforms. However, in want of a shared vision and common strategy, the OHR and the other international agencies only managed to promote piecemeal and minimal changes in the first years after Dayton. Many such reform initiatives were also successfully obstructed by local spoilers. Perhaps the rigidity of the GFAP, and particularly the statement in it that the highest international instruments of human rights (ECHR, UDHR, ICCPR, ICESCR, etc.) should be the highest laws in the land,[378] lulled the international community into a false sense of accomplishment and security. Further, as the GFAP its annexes did not explicitly point out whether or not a specific national instruments corresponded to these high standards, the OHR was immediately tangled in the laborious work of scrutinizing all previously valid legislation in BiH and defending its decisions on this matter.

Another factor that made law reform difficult was the unclear and problematic division of responsibilities between the State of Bosnia and Herzegovina and the two entities (Federation and Republika Srpska). Article III:1 of the BiH Constitution specifies the responsibilities of the joint state institutions as foreign policy; foreign trade policy; customs policy; monetary policy; finances of the institutions of BiH; immigration and refugee policy; international and inter-entity criminal law enforcement; communications policy; inter-entity transportation; and air traffic control. The remainder of Article III deals with relationships between the entities and the joint institutions, the most important statement being: "*all governmental functions and powers not expressly assigned in this Constitution to the institutions of BiH shall be those of the entities.*"[379] Unlike most other states, the State of BiH thus has no unified army or police force,

[377] Kathryn Neilson (1996 p. 8) describes that there were representatives of the new constituent assembly whom initially set about drafting the constitution in secrecy and tried to omit a number of the requirements set out in the Agreement, including provisions for an independent judiciary.

[378] GFAP Annex 4, Constitution of BiH, Preamble.

[379] Id. Article III:3(a).

does not raise any significant taxes, relies on a judiciary with very limited responsibilities, and hosts a legislature that is essentially prevented from formulating laws without the approval of the entities. For the High Representative, this construction meant that initiatives to promote further co-operation and integration by means of state level law would almost inevitably be challenged on constitutional grounds by domestic constituencies with a stake in the *status quo*. Examples of such tactics included the attacks on the international initiatives to introduce a common license plate, a common passport, a border (police) service, and a state-level court. The entities, on the other hand, are best described as *de facto* mini-states within a very loose and uneasy confederation. Notably, there is no domestic enforcement mechanism capable of compelling them to implement state-level decisions.

The High Representative nevertheless proceeded to impose a number of critical state level laws and institutions on an interim basis.[380] Paradoxically, it seems that this policy reduced the domestic incentive to take responsibility for the future well-being of the nation even further and left the staunch nationalist parties in a politically comfortable position. Even if they would happen to share the view that a specific law needed to be adopted, they could safely block it and thereby remain loyal to their nationalist agenda, knowing that it would be imposed anyway by the already unpopular High Representative. Thus OHR/Council of Europe working groups and specially designated international experts ended up formulating policies and drafting laws that should rightly have been conceived by the democratically elected representatives of the people of Bosnia and Herzegovina. A related problem is that the refusal to participate in drafting betrayed the national law-makers of the chance to develop the skills needed to one day effectively represent their countries in international and regional bodies such as the Council of Europe, the European Union, ASEAN, and WTO.

This problem of ownership and capacity "sucking out" is not unique to BiH, but rather a common feature of international efforts to build a common home for rival factions in post-crisis environments. The international administrations in Cambodia and Kosovo have similarly needed to recourse to doing the job themselves on many occasions.

The potential role of the Constitutional Court of Bosnia and Herzegovina in reforming the legal framework has been reduced by factional fighting and systematic obstruction

---

380 *Inter alia* Law on Citizenship; Law on the Policy of Direct Foreign Investment; Law on the Flag; Law on the Seal; General Law on the Privatisation of Companies and Banks; Law on Telecommunications; Law on the State Hymn; and Law on Administrative Taxes. It should be mentioned that many important laws have been passed without imposition, among them the Law on Foreign Debt; Law on the Central Bank; Law on Foreign Trade Policy; Law on Customs Policy; Law on Customs Tariffs; Law on the Official Gazette; Law on Immunity; Law on the Council of Ministers and Ministries; and Law on Travel Documents.

too. Paradoxically even the High Representative has been rather cautious in encouraging the Constitutional Court in making dynamic interpretations of the GFAP and other fundamental instruments (see Chapter 5.2). The Court, in its capacity of supreme guardian of the BiH Constitution, has exclusive jurisdiction over sensitive jurisdictional disputes between the institutions of the state and the entities.[381] It is also vested with appellate jurisdiction over issues under the BiH Constitution arising out of judgments of any other court. In spite of the fact that there are both national and international judges in the Court (six nationals representing the different peoples of BiH balanced by three international members), it took almost four years from the signing of the GFAP until it dared and could review the first appeal of a decision of a lower court. Attempts at reforming the jurisdiction and organisation of the court, or even appointing a new judge, continue to provoke great political controversy and intrigue. Efforts to improve the institutional capacity of the court are similarly made difficult by the problem of securing adequate funding from hostile or indifferent budgetary organs. Without the political and financial support of the international community, the court would hardly be functioning at all. Such support has been provided by OHR, CoE, ABA/CEELI and EC/Phare, including essentials such as the payment of the salary of a member of the Court Registry.

The seemingly insurmountable political and legal obstacles in reforming and activating the Constitutional Court have spurred the international community to explore the conditions for creating an alternative and partly supplementary "State Court" to perform essential judicial functions at the state level, including war crimes trials. Once again, the rigid format of the GFAP and the BiH Constitution has made such efforts difficult. In the absence of an explicit provision allowing for additional courts or other agencies at the state level,[382] the High Representative has needed to fall back on interpretations made by the Madrid PIC and the Venice Commission, suggesting that the GFAP and the annexed Constitution in fact contain an implicit mandate for the High Representative to establish additional state-level bodies in response to established constitutional needs, as for example the effective exercise of the constitutional competencies of the state of BiH and upholding the respect of fundamental human rights and rule of law principles in the entire country.[383] After having failed to create

381 GFAP Annex 4, Article VI:3.

382 The BiH Constitution also provides for a Human Rights Chamber with many traits of court (its decisions are final and binding and cannot be appealed), but this body is not formally regarded part of the regular court system. Discussions have long been entertained whether the jurisdiction on all final appeals in human rights cases should be transferred to a single body at the state level, preferably the Constitutional Court, in order to resolve problems of overlapping competencies and to provide for a more efficient use of scarce judicial resources.

383 The Venice Commission identified three special courts that BiH should be constitutionally required to set up: a permanent election jurisdiction which would issue final decisions on all kinds of electoral disputes at the state, entity and cantonal level (subject to review of constitutional issues by the BiH

majority for the State Court initiative in the BiH Government and Parliament, the High Representative finally imposed the law providing for the Court of Bosnia and Herzegovina in november 2000. Its trial panels consist of three judges of which two are international and one, the presiding judge, is Bosnian. It was also decided in 2003 that War Crimes Chamber should be established within the State Court to meet the demand for local capacity to try such cases. Critical commentators have pointed out that this jurisdiction at least in part overlaps what should typically be the prerogative of the BiH Constitutional Court and ICTY.[384] Whether the court has the political and judicial strength to assert its right to decide on these issues is a different issue. It can only be noted that the recruitment and training of judges, hiring of administrative staff, identification of office premises, procurement of equipment, etc., have proven very difficult and taken much longer time than anticipated, much due to lack of local commitment to this essentially internationally promoted initiative.

The absence of clear and accepted hierarchy of norms (between old and new, national and international, etc.), and the ensuing problems in identifying the "applicable law", preserved much unnecessary uncertainty and tension and made the implementation of the peace agenda difficult. The High Representative relatively late realised the explosiveness of the matter, and had then to fight the battles of what law that should prevail without the support of authoritative statements and established practices. In essence, the High Representative legitimized his enactments and decisions with references to the powers vested with him by the GFAP, the PIC (the "Bonn Powers") and the endorsing Security Council Resolutions. In order to minimise the risk for future conflicts regarding the right to create legal instruments and institutions as needed, and to simultaneously promote a degree of local ownership, the High Representative also became more careful to anchor legislative initiatives in broad-based working-groups with both local and international members, hold public hearings, and carry out information campaigns, etc.

In a situation where the appointed representative of the international community exercises the authority normally attributed to the sovereign, the theoretical point of departure must reasonably be that his powers are legally and morally combined with corresponding obligations towards both the inhabitants of the respective country or

---

Constitutional Court); a BiH administrative court which would deal with all aspects of disputes arising from any act or omission of BiH administrative authorities, insofar as they constitute a criminal penalty or immediately affect any individual's personal or economic rights (a definition derived from ECHR Article 6 jurisprudence); and a high criminal court to deal with offences provided for in criminal legislation which, when committed by persons appointed to government or political office at the state level, cannot be tried by entity courts.

384 With regard to the BiH Constitutional Court, for example the right to take a final position on the implementation of state laws and international treaties or the right to assess the legality of individual and general enforceable administrative acts adopted under state law.

territory and the territory as such.[385] Already at the time OHR and SFOR were established, a practice was developing of regarding human rights as an integral component of every UN field mission, in particular UN peacekeeping operations. Recent UN policy documents, among them the Brahimi Report and the Rule of Law and Transitional Justice Report, have provided further endorsement for this assumption.[386] In addition, the concept of automatic succession into human rights treaties suggests that the human rights guarantees enshrined in treaties applicable in the respective countries and territories before the establishment of the international administrations continue to be binding upon the High Representative or SRSG and his agents. Human rights treaties and similar instruments accordingly form an integral part of the *acquis* of the territory, which is not and cannot be affected by the fact that an international entity takes over certain administrative and judicial responsibilities. An alternative way of reaching the same result is to argue that the universal instruments in question constitute documents of a constitutional character adopted on the basis of Article 55 of the United Nations Charter, which define the core of human rights standards binding at least the organization itself. In fact, very few advocates of humanitarian intervention and international administration, whether inside or outside the UN system, would contest the legal and political necessity for the UN and UN-affiliated bodies to carefully adhere to international human rights in their operations, although some critics may argue that the prioritisation between different areas or aspects of human rights and rule of law in their everyday work may not be ideal.[387]

The High Representative has nevertheless been unwilling to admit legal challenges to his decisions, whether in international or domestic fora, essentially on grounds that his office was established as a body *sui generis* by virtue of a peace treaty, and as such meant to be above the local law and outside the formal ranks of the UN. Should this argument be accepted in its entirety, then scrutiny by the International Court of Justice (ICJ) would only be possible in the somewhat unlikely event the United Nations should first decide that the High Representative was indeed a UN body, and then decide to refer a case relating to his activities for a non-binding advisory opinion.[388] The Security Council would similarly be practically prevented from exercising any kind of daily managerial authority over the High Representative. The circumstance that the Security Council authoritatively endorsed the GFAP structure would also make it improbable

385 Zimmermann and Stahn 2001 pp. 442-443, 445.

386 Report of the Panel on United Nations Peace Operations, A/55/305 – S/2000/809; Report of the United Nations Secretary General on the Rule of Law and Transitional Justice in Conflict and Post-Conflict Societies, S/2004/616.

387 For example, some commentators point out that the strong focus on minority protection in UN peace-keeping and state-building efforts has somehow obscured other, equally important but more structural issues, such as ensuring that there are effective procedural guarantees in judicial and administrative matters. Brand 2001 p. 466.

388 Statute of the ICJ, Art. 34.1 and Art. 65.

that it would suddenly line up with those groups resisting its implementation.[389] That the "final authority" power granted to the High Representative formally applies "in theatre" only, *i.e. vis-à-vis* the organs of BiH and other national and international organisations working in BiH, could be seen as an opening for bringing violations of the European Convention on Human Rights before the European Court of Human Rights in Strasbourg, but such strategies are made impossible by jurisdictional problems (the High Representative is not a state, BiH does not fulfil the criteria for membership of the Council of Europe, etc.).

There are many reasons why the matter of mission accountability was not attributed much attention at the time the international presence in BiH was created, and why the High Representative has not been very proactive in providing for review mechanisms. The most important is of course that the High Representative was created *ad hoc*, in response to an acute crisis, with a multitude of nations and organizations with different agenda and traditions involved in the process. The structure was furthermore conceived to be "temporary" and "interim", and few saw any reason to bother too much about carefully formulating rules and principles for something that will not last and may not recur. However, the values and principles thus grafted to the peace implementation structure are difficult to credibly reconcile with the greater goal of promoting democracy, rule of law and human rights, and there is a risk that that the establishment of a regime under which only the locals are held accountable creates perceptions of paternalistic system of "us" and "them".[390] Predictably, national judicial bodies such as the BiH Constitutional Court are increasingly favouring the idea that while the final authority of the High Representative to interpret the GFAP may be unchallengeable in BiH, the constitutionality of his enactments and their conformity to international and regional instruments are not (see Chapter 5.2).[391]

5.3.4.3 United Nations Mission in Kosovo

Security Council Resolution 1244 (1999) gives the SRSG sweeping powers "*[...] to change, repeal or suspend existing laws to the extent necessary for the carrying out of his functions, or where existing laws are incompatible with the mandate, aims and purposes of the interim civil administration*", and "*[...] to issue legislative acts in the forms or regulations*" to remain in force until repealed by the SRSG or suspended by rules issued by the institutions established under a political settlement. The enormous discretionary powers of the SRSG to create new laws are thus conditioned by the imperatives that

389 Wilde 2001 pp. 455-457.

390 Wilde 2001 pp. 458-460.

391 BiH Constitutional Court Decision No. U9/00 of 3 November 2000 on the Law on State Border Service.

Kosovo is not a state and that the future status of the territory has not been decided.[392] The SRSG must be particularly careful not to take any measure that creates a *fait accompli* or otherwise anticipates the results of the domestic political process. All UNMIK instruments are accordingly considered as transitory and interim instruments that cease to be binding once the final status for Kosovo has been agreed upon and divergent rules adopted by the legitimate new authorities.[393]

The SRSG nevertheless needed to provide as a matter of first priority a foundational "pseudo-constitutional" framework outlining the division of powers between international and local bodies, the hierarchy of international and local norms, legal and administrative procedures, etc.[394] As UNMIK had been established by the Security Council and the SRSG was named by the Secretary General,[395] the SRSG could plausibly argue that the his office should be characterised as subsidiary organs of the Security Council or at least of the UN as whole, and that these new rules should be considered to have the dignity of directly applicable UN law derived from the powers of that organisation.[396] A less politically expeditious but perhaps more legally accurate alternative to describing the new legal framework as an extension of the UN legal system exclusively applicable within Kosovo, would have been to describe the elaborate fabric of laws and regulations as "the law" of Kosovo. This perspective finds support in the peculiar status of the territory under public international law, the unique character of the legal framework of Kosovo, the interferences with Yugoslav law, and the "principle of continuity". It should also be remembered that the establishment of UNMIK as "the only legitimate authority" and the subsequent adoption of specific regulations by the SRSG did not coincide with any complete departure from the pre-existing legal order of Kosovo as part of the Socialist Federal Republic of Yugoslavia and its successor the Federal Republic of Yugoslavia.[397]

On the thorny issue of the status of the Yugoslavian legislation applicable in Kosovo prior to the arrival of UNMIK, the SRSG initially decided that the laws that applied prior to the adoption of Security Council Resolutions 1244 (effectively the pre-1999 laws of Kosovo) should continue to apply insofar as they conformed with internationally recognized human rights standards and did not conflict with the Security

392 While Security Council in Resolution 1160 (1998) and 1199 (1998) reaffirmed the territorial integrity of the FRY (thereby indirectly endorsing that Kosovo is not an independent state), Resolution 1244 (1999) leaves the FRY with very limited real authority over Kosovo.

393 Zimmermann and Stahn 2001 p. 444.

394 Already in July 1999 the SRSG handed down Regulation No. 1999/1 (Section 1, para. 1) reiterating and concretising his own powers, stipulating *inter alia* that "*all legislative and executive authority, including the administration of the judiciary*" shall be in the hands of the Special Representative.

395 Charter of the United Nations, Art. 29 and 7[2] respectively.

396 UNMIK/REG/1999/1, Section 3; UNMIK/REG/1999/24, Section 1.

397 Zimmermann and Stahn 2001 p. 443.

Council's mandate to the Mission or any subsequent regulation promulgated by the Mission.[398] In spite of good practical reasons for coming to this decision (avoiding a legal vacuum in the initial phase of the transitional administration, allowing the cadre of local lawyers to continue practice in a recognizable legal universe, etc.) it prompted vigorous protests by Kosovar politicians and lawyers who argued that many elements of the previous order, particularly in the area of criminal law, were tools of repression and should as such be summarily abrogated.[399] Confronted with threats of boycotts, strikes and the like, and worried over tendency of Albanian judges to move forward with proceedings based on the officially invalid pre-1989 law which they tended to favour as having been passed with the approval of the Albanian-dominated Kosovo parliament before Yugoslavia ended Kosovo's autonomy, UNMIK suddenly decided to change its policy on this fundamental issue. Without further comment or motivation, a new UNMIK Regulation thus declared that the law applicable in Kosovo would henceforth be the pre-1989 law insofar it was consistent with international human rights standards.[400]

Another problem immediately emerged as this decision was not combined with any guidance as to what parts of the pre-1989 law that should be regarded as inconsistent with such international standards, or procedures to be followed in the event of a possible conflict. It was thus for the international and national jurists in Kosovo to determine *ad hoc* whether or not a specific provision of the old order conformed to the new standards, and in the event of collision substitute conflicting local elements with suitable international norms. Many Kosovar lawyers had neither the motivation nor the skills this task required. It was also difficult to obtain from the disorganised government current and consolidated compilations of enactments and other things necessary for performing this task. Any effective international input to this work further required the translation of large volumes of texts into English. Rosa Ehrenreich points out that ironically, the pre-1989 laws that were so dear to the Kosovar Albanian community were actually far less consistent with international human rights standards than the post-1989 Yugoslavian or Serbian law they had so vehemently rejected.[401] Rather than risking chaos in the interpretation and application of the law, UNMIK, eventually decided to conduct a comprehensive and systematic review of all domestic legislation pivotal to the greater task of state-building, and to explicitly amend or supersede those elements of the old order that were inconsistent with international

---

[398] *"The laws applicable in the territory of Kosovo prior to 24 March 1999 shall continue to apply in Kosovo insofar as they do not conflict with standards referred to in Section 2, the fulfilment of the mandate given to UNMIK under Security Council Resolution 1244 (1999), or the present or any other regulation issued by UNMIK"*. UNMIK/REG/1999/1, Section 3.

[399] Strohmeyer 2001 pp. 58-59.

[400] UNMIK/REG/1999/24, Section 1.

[401] Ehrenreich 2003 pp. 2292-2293.

law and UNMIK regulations.[402] Thus, something resembling a hierarchy of norms for Kosovo began to evolve, comprising the UN Charter at the top and the relevant Security Council Declarations under it, then the "constitutional" regulations and the other SRSG regulations, and the SRSG decisions on specific matters at the bottom. In the beginning of the mission, UNMIK included references in conjunction to virtually every new enactment to the specific empowering provisions in the Security Council Resolution and the constitutional framework.[403] These references were helpful in explaining the nature of the evolving legal universe and served an important "client" interests in the sense that they constituted an admission that the SRSG was bound by a framework of superior rules limiting his discretionary powers.

In order to ensure a degree of local ownership in the legal and judicial reform process, UNMIK established a number of consultative bodies such as the Judicial Advisory Council, the Interim Advisory Council and the Legislative Advisory Council, and sought to promote acceptable representation for the many different ethnic, cultural and religious stakeholders within them. The Kosovar members were in the typical case lawyers, academics and political figures that could be trusted to have a fairly constructive outlook. It was further hoped that the inclusion of people with first-hand knowledge of local conditions and preferences would make the identification of problems and remedies easier, and provide legitimacy to the new legal and administrative structures of Kosovo. Sometimes this worked more or less as hoped, but frequently quarrels broke out over who could claim to represent the people, how to describe past and present problems, what the ultimate goals of the reform process were, etc. In some cases, these bodies were boycotted entirely by one group or another.

The inclusiveness strategy faltered on more substantive issues too. Ehrenreich reports that not infrequently, for instance, Albanian participants would express the view that there should be no Serb judges at all since all Serbs were war criminals, or that the property code should give all Serbian property to Albanians since it had been stolen from them in the first place several hundred years ago, or that revenge killing of Serbs by Albanians should be treated more leniently than other kinds of killings.[404] A frustrated and disappointed UNMIK eventually responded by dismissing many of these advisory bodies and shifting back to making key decisions in office and above the heads of the rival ethnic groups. Although both complicated and delaying, the potential gains of the inclusiveness strategy motivated UNIMIK to try and try again. There were also some symbolically significant success stories. For example, the JIAS-structure, in which each Administrative Department (reconstruction, teaching, telecommunications, etc.)

---

402 Strohmeyer 2001 p. 59.
403 UNMIK/REG/1999/1, Section 1(1).
404 Ehrenreich 2003 pp. 2294-2295.

was co-headed by a Kosovar and an UNMIK representative, finally managed to establish a revenue administration and pass a genuine Kosovo budget. The Interim Administrative Council, with its composition of eight members of different nationality and ethnicity, similarly managed to initiate regulations and promulgate policy guidelines for a number of politically sensitive areas.

Although the legal and political imperatives surrounding the issue of mission accountability were essentially the same in Kosovo as in BiH (democratic governance and effective human rights-protection *vis-à-vis* effective international administration in an explosive environment) UNMIK arrived at the conclusion that a more proactive and accommodating strategy was to be preferred. The greater preparedness to put these issues up for discussion in Kosovo was partly attributable to fresh memories of the political sensitivities they had aroused in BiH, and partly to an evolving practice of regarding human rights as an integral component of every UN peacekeeping operation, visualised by the explicit proclamation in Resolution 1244 (1999) providing for UNMIK (the construction for UNTAET is similar) that the international administration must adhere to human rights principles as laid down in a series of universal and regional declarations and treaties (the Universal Declaration of Human Rights, the UN Human Rights Covenants, the European Convention on Human Rights, etc.).[405] At the centre of the UNMIK policy was recognition that with the far-reaching powers of the SRSG come corresponding legal and moral obligations towards both the inhabitants of Kosovo and the territory as such.[406] The SRSG also confirmed in a regulation that apart from other universal standards, the specific guarantees enshrined in the two International Covenants and the European Convention on Human Rights would fall within the category of rights to be protected and promoted by UNMIK, thus further endorsing that UNMIK as an organisation was bound to comply with these instruments too.[407]

However, the binding force of these instruments does not comprise the enforcement mechanism provided for in the respective covenants, treaties and charters as long as Kosovo is not a state.[408] For example, accession to the European Convention on Human Rights is open to Council of Europe members only, and membership of that

405 Security Council Resolution 1244, paras. 11(j) and (k). The inclusion of human rights concerns in all mission mandates finds support in several important UN policy documents on issues of peace keeping and state building, among them Report of the Panel on United Nations Peace Operations, A/55/305 – S/2000/809; Report of the United Nations Secretary General on the Rule of Law and Transitional Justice in Conflict and Post-Conflict Societies, S/2004/616. For a detailed discussion, see Brand 2001 and Ruffert 2001.

406 Zimmermann & Stahn 2001 pp. 442-443.

407 UNMIK/REG/1999/24 of 12 Dec. 1999, Section 1(3).

408 Brand 2001 pp. 465 and 476; Ruffert 2001 p. 623.

organisation is open only to states.[409] The widespread bias and corruption in the regular courts of Kosovo similarly make it politically impossible for the SRSG to grant them jurisdiction over the actions of the Mission. In addition, established principles of public international law and specific UNIMIK regulations confer upon UNMIK and its staff immunities similar to those typically enjoyed by accredited diplomats.[410] In order to counter suspicions that the confessions to high standards of human rights are merely rhetorical, the SRSG has established an Ombudsperson with jurisdiction to investigate complaints from any person and entity in Kosovo concerning human rights violations and actions constituting an abuse of authority committed by national and international actors alike.[411] This measure does not affect the final authority powers of the SRSG or provide any mechanism to force the SRSG to change his decisions,[412] but helps to deflect criticism that UNMIK should be willing to set and enforce high standards for the work of local bodies, but not to apply them to its own actions.[413]

Issues of external representation and treaty-making power must be considered when legal and judicial reform strategies for territories under international administration are formulated, not least because membership of international and regional structures is a very strong reform incentive. At the same time, issues of statehood and other aspects of status often pose serious problems for those seeking to seize on the opportunities accession processes provide. In regard to Kosovo, the international legal status of the territory is characterised by the recognition of FRY's *de jure* sovereignty on the one hand, and the exclusive UN administration powers on the other. Resolution 1244 (1999) does not expressly vest UNMIK with foreign affairs powers, but there are strong reasons to read the mandate to contain an implied power to represent the territory *vis-à-vis* third states, not least since such a power seems indispensable for establishing the kind of relations with both international organizations and neighbouring states the fulfilment of the mandate presupposes.[414] UNMIK has also *de facto* concluded international agreements with the territory's neighbouring states and other third parties in various areas, ranging from economic cooperation to the repatriation of Kosovars. Any such implied legal personality must in the normal case be assumed to be limited to affairs that are directly linked to the mandate of the respective state-building mission.

---

409 ECHR, Art. 59; Charter of the Council of Europe, Art. 4.

410 UNMIK Regulation 47/2000 on the Status, Privileges and Immunities of KFOR and UNMIK and their Personnel in Kosovo.

411 UNMIK/REG/2000/38.

412 Constitutional Framework, preamble, para. 9; and Section 12.

413 Zimmermann and Stahn 2001 p. 448.

414 Zimmermann and Stahn 2001 pp. 448-450. Ruffert (2001 p. 630) speaks of "functional" legal personality.

5.3.4.4 *United Nations Transitional Administration in East Timor*

In order to facilitate the transformation of the territory of East Timor into the new state of Timor-Leste, the transitional administration and its local counterparts basically had to create a new legal and constitutional framework from scratch. As a first step, the SRSG established the National Consultative Council (NCC) with 11 East Timorese and four UNTAET members to formally guide and oversee the development and application of the various interim regulations needed to administer the territory in the transitional phase, including those pertaining to the administration of justice. However, the establishment of the NCC was not combined with any delegation of authority. Rather, the SRSG retained the right to decide any significant policy issue and to substitute himself for the NCC and other joint and local organs when he deemed necessary.[415]

As the situation consolidated, and after having been criticized for not allowing meaningful local participation in the articulation of important legal and administrative instruments,[416] UNTAET began in earnest the process of reorganizing itself to resemble more closely the future organs of East Timor and to gradually increase the direct participation of the East Timorese in policy and executive fora. In October 2000, a National Council was established to replace the former National Consultative Council as the nucleus of a future legislative assembly. It comprised 36 members from East Timorese civil society, businesses, political parties, NGOs, and the territory's 13 districts. The Council was given the right to initiate or modify regulations by simple majority, but the power of final decision remained with the Special Representative.[417] An inner circle or cabinet was also named by the Special Representative and functioned as a kind of government under his supervision. East Timorese were appointed to five of the nine portfolios similar to ministerial tasks (internal administration, infrastructure, economic affairs, social affairs, finance, justice, police and emergency services, and political affairs), but the justice portfolio belonged to the four that were still to be headed by senior UNTAET officials.

On 30 August 2001, the voters went to the polls again, this time to elect an 88-member Constituent Assembly. Shortly thereafter, a new all-East Timorese Council of Ministers with 24 members was sworn into office. These bodies were now expected to make laws

---

415 UNTAET/REG/1999/1 on the Authority of the Transitional Administration in East Timor, Section 1.1.

416 Linton 2001 p. 136; Chopra 2000 p. 33. Chopra (*ibid.*) writes that "*[... SRSG] de Mello brought with him an inner circle from the Balkans, whose members projected a blunt, bullying style, when both the veterans of UNAMET and the traumatised Timorese would have responded better to modesty and genuine concern.*"

417 UNTAET/REG/2000/24, Sections 2, 4 and 10.

and govern East Timor during the remaining transitional period. The Constituent Assembly signed into force the Territory's first Constitution on 22 March 2002, which among other things provided basic principles for the formation and operation of an independent justice system and prosecution. The Assembly finally transformed itself into the country's first proper parliament and legislature on 20 May 2002.

As regards the issue of applicable law in the transitional period, the SRSG stipulated that "*Until replaced by UNTAET regulations or subsequent legislation of democratically established institutions of East Timor, the laws applied in East Timor prior to 25 October 1999 shall apply in East Timor insofar as they do not conflict with the standards referred to in section 2, the fulfilment of the mandate given to UNTAET under the United Nations Security Council resolution 1272 (1999), or the present or any other regulation and directive issued by the Transitional Administrator.*"[418] The decision to continue to apply the Dutch-based civil law of Indonesia was surrounded with much controversy. Suzannah Linton suggests that part of the objection may have stemmed from a lack of appreciation that UNTAET was simply a transitional administration and that the choice of what law that would eventually be applied after its departure would be for the elected representatives for the new state to make. At the same time, Linton points out, if UNTAET had really maintained that its enactments were truly interim and that the authorities of the new state would one day rule on the matter, then UNTAET should have done much more than symbolical efforts to provide for real consultation with the East Timorese in matters pertaining to the applicable law in the interim period.[419]

UNTAET Regulation 1999/1 does not provide for international instruments to have direct effect in East Timor, but Section 3.1 states that existing laws should be read subject to international instruments and in the light of UNTAET's mandate and the normative instruments issued by the SRSG. No systematic efforts were made by the Mission to review the entire body of old legislation in the light of the international law and UNTAET's mandate. Like in Kosovo, it was instead essentially for the people applying the law (either international lawyers insufficiently acquainted with East Timor or local lawyers unaccustomed to their new professional roles) to make the difficult determination whether an old instrument conformed to international human rights norms and UNTAET regulations. There were many worrying examples of how this played out in practice, also in matters touching on sensitive principles such as *nulla poena sine lege* and *ne bis in idem*.[420]

---

[418] UNTAET/REG/1999/1, Section 3.1.

[419] Linton 2001 pp. 137, 177-178.

[420] Id. p. 137.

A long awaited transitional Criminal Procedure Code providing detailed regulations on the various stages of criminal proceedings was finally introduced by UNTAET regulation in september 2000.[421] This Code was instantly criticised for containing a mix of civil and common law concepts and for being a mishmash of provisions borrowed from the different legal systems of the international draftsmen. Linton describes that when it was presented to the East Timorese for "consultation" shortly before the National Council was to meet and debate it, the local jurists expressed the view that they had once again been systematically excluded from all fora and processes where important decisions were made. By taking a strong and consistent position on the issue, they even managed to make UNTAC accept a new procedure for consultation in legislative drafting.[422]

5.3.4.5 United Nations Assistance Mission in Afghanistan

The Bonn Agreement provided for an interim legal framework that would apply in Afghanistan until the democratically elected representatives of the people could adopt a new constitution. The interim framework essentially consisted of the pre-1964 Constitution and existing laws and regulations (to the extent that these instruments were not inconsistent with the Bonn Agreement or with international legal obligations to which Afghanistan is a party.[423] This construction reflected the hope among the drafters of the Bonn Agreement that returning to the principles of the relatively stable and peaceful pre-1964 period would provide a way of avoiding the sensitive and controversial aspects of the Taliban and socialist legal regimes and simultaneously maintain a degree of continuity in political and legal affairs.[424]

The process of building political opinion for a "permanent" constitutional structure began with the 2002 *Loya Jirga*. Prior to its initiation, teams organized by the Special Independent Commission for Convening the *Loya Jirga*, accompanied by some 50 UNAMA staff and international monitors, travelled all over the country in order to explain the process and the ensuing constitutional reforms and elections.[425] During the actual *Loya Jirga*, which was held between 12-19 June 2002 in Kabul with 1,500 elected delegates participating, UN personnel and international observers assisted in

---

[421] UNTAET/REG/2000/30.

[422] Linton 2001 p. 174.

[423] The Bonn Agreement thus incorporates only the international legal obligations to which Afghanistan is a party, rather than the entire corpus of "internationally recognized human rights standards" as in Kosovo and East Timor.

[424] Chesterman 2002 pp. 9-10.

[425] The Special Independent Commission for the Convening of the Emergency Loya Jirga was established in January 2002. On 7 February, at its inauguration, Hamid Karzai, Chairman of the Interim Administration, made it clear that his administration would fully respect and safeguard the independent status of that Commission.

the monitoring of voting and counting to ensure that there was no discrimination and that procedures were followed.

While unprecedented in Afghanistan in terms of democracy and transparency, the *Loya Jirga* process was not without difficulties. Some were of a logistic nature since access to a number of districts was inhibited by geography or weather conditions. Other problems related to the state of insecurity that existed due to tensions or open conflicts between tribes and local commanders in some regions. The UN also noted that a broader problem resulted from the very success of the process itself: its obvious importance prodded certain elements to seek political legitimacy through it. There were many attempts by local commanders and authorities in different regions to control the outcome of the selection process by money, intimidation or other tactics. Incidents in approximately one dozen districts were deemed serious enough by the Special Independent Commission to warrant the cancellation of some district elections.

The UN and the international community provided logistical support (transportation, communications, premises, etc.) to the Special Independent Commission and the *Loya Jirga* process. Contractors were called upon to prepare eight election sites, while the German Agency for Development Cooperation helped to rehabilitate part of the Polytechnic Institute in Kabul and installed several tents to house the *Loya Jirga* itself. In collaboration with the Afghan Ministry of Women's Affairs, UNAMA also conducted an introduction course for the women delegates to the *Loya Jirga* and provided advice and assistance to them throughout the process. At the end of the *Loya Jirga*, Chairman Karzai was elected by secret ballot as President of the new Transitional Administration and immediately started to put together the Cabinet of the Transitional Administration.

A nine-member Constitutional Drafting Commission was formally inaugurated in November 2002. The Commission was chaired by the Vice-President and made up of Afghan legal scholars and jurists. The Commission started to work on the new constitution with the 1964 constitution as the starting point. The UN through its good offices supported the work of the Commission, for example by assisting in establishing its Secretariat and in raising international support for other vital tasks and functions.

5.3.5 COURT REFORM AND JUDICIAL APPOINTMENTS

5.3.5.1 United Nations Transitional Authority in Cambodia

After the atrocities of the Khmer Rouge regime, it was natural that UNTAC put human rights protection high up on the reform agenda and pushed the interim Cambodian government to quickly adopt laws and approve principles relating to the legal and judicial system, particularly penal law and penal procedure. On 10 September 1992, the SNC adopted the cornerstone Provisions Relating to the Judiciary and Criminal Law and Procedure Applicable in Cambodia during the Transitional Period. This instrument in many ways reflected UNTAC's ambition of promoting a system that safeguarded high standards of human rights and rule of laws without completely revamping local laws and legal practices. Although the name of the instrument indicates that it was never intended to be a permanent feature of the Cambodian legal system, it remained the primary criminal law in force for a long time.

The Provisions begin with stating that the independence of the judiciary should be guaranteed, and specifically mention that the standards against which the degree of independence should be measured are those spelled out in the UN Basic Principles on the Independence of the Judiciary. The Provisions further provide for a conventional hierarchy of courts and rules of jurisdiction, comprising *inter alia* an Appeals Court and an improved Supreme Court with the power to review legislation. The Provisions also authorize the establishment of an independent Bar Association, but recognizing the small number of attorneys in Cambodia, permit anyone with secondary school education or members of the family to represent accused persons. While being instrumental for the reform of the Cambodian legal system, the Provisions also created immediate difficulties for the fragmented and fragile courts and prosecutorial agencies. Kathryn Neilson mentions that enforcement of the new penal law was almost impossible in the absence of competent legal counsel and a judiciary familiar and comfortable with the concept of judicial independence.[426]

Even more significant for the future organisation and composition of the judiciary was the forward-looking 1993 Constitution of the Kingdom of Cambodia. The international community had successfully promoted the idea that the new Constitution should reflect not only the norms and principles outlined in the Paris Agreement, but also the highest international standards of human rights and rule of law. This meant that a clear benchmark was created against which any future enactment or institutional reform should be assessed. Particularly important was the stipulation that the legislative, executive, and judicial powers should be separate, that the judiciary should be independent and impartial, and that judges and prosecutors should be appointed by the Supreme Council of the Magistracy, under the chairmanship of the King.[427] The Constitution also included a long list of human rights to be protected, with references to relevant international human rights instruments.[428]

---

426 Neilson, K. 1996 pp. 7-8.

427 1993 Constitution of the Kingdom of Cambodia, Arts. 51, 21, 109 – 116.

428 1993 Constitution of the Kingdom of Cambodia, Arts. 31-50.

Another cornerstone in the building of a new judiciary was laid with the adoption of the 1994 Law on the Organization and Functioning of the Supreme Council of Magistracy. This initiative provoked some initial controversy, particularly among human rights groups, as it permitted the Minister of Justice to be a member of the Council and thus risked to undermine the separation of the executive and the judiciary. Other groups were not happy with the fact that all the other members of the Council had to be recruited from the cadre of sitting judges and prosecutors, the vast majority of whom were loyal to one of the established political parties. Representatives of the royalist party in particular argued that some of their sympathisers in the judiciary and prosecution should be identified and appointed to allow a more balanced representation. The dominant communist party, on the other hand, logically retorted that if appointments were made solely on this basis, they would be purely political and not conducive to an independent judiciary.[429]

5.3.5.2 High Representative to Bosnia and Herzegovina

Although the High Representative and the other leading international organisations in BiH had received strong international endorsement at the 1998 Madrid PIC for gearing up their efforts to reform the justice sector, it soon became apparent that the conditions for fast-tracking judicial reforms were no better than for any other aspect of the state-building effort. The combination of a "weak" centre (State) with little more than a nominal role in the administration of justice on the one hand, and strong entities (Federation and Republika Srpska) with diverging political agenda made harmonising and consolidating efforts particularly difficult, at least as long as the GFAP was to be respected. There were also the 10 cantons of the Federation (some dominated by Croats, some by Bosnians, and some mixed) with a considerable degree of constitutional autonomy, veering off in different directions in matters pertaining to law and justice. The combination of a weak State and strong sub-state entities also created problems of unequal access. For example, the Croat-dominated cantons could introduce laws and practices that deprived citizens of these cantons of their right to an appellate review beyond the canton in the Federation Supreme Court. In practice, an ethically homogenous (Croat) judiciary would thus try criminal matters in all instances, with all real and perceived risks for ethically motivated discrimination that entailed.

The High Representative and UNMIBH made many attempts to address such problems of inconsistency and resulting bias, for example by promoting with national and local politicians the idea of a unified court structure for the ethically and politically divided Herzegovina-Neretva Canton and City of Mostar. After almost three years of fruitless

---

429 Neilson, K. 1996 p. 12.

dialogue and nine months of intensive negotiations, a frustrated High Representative eventually imposed in August 1998 laws providing for a unified structure of courts in these areas. Although this initiative did not reach the root causes of the problem, it did eliminate the parallel structures and facilitated the establishment of a properly constituted Cantonal Court. Faced with this fact, Croat and Bosnian political factionists soon shifted their attention to ensuring the greatest possible representation in the unified court structure, but here too, the High Representative eventually managed to promote an agreement on the staffing of the respective courts. The efforts to reform the equally fragmented system of minor offences courts in the Federation were similarly resisted by local law enforcement and judicial authorities who sought to preserve a judicial alternative to formalistic criminal procedures when people of their own ethnicity were charged of serious ethically motivated crimes. The centralised structure and absence of cantons in the Republika Srpska reduced the problems of fragmentation and inconsistency, but also made it easier for the ruling party to execute political control of the judiciary.[430] The impression is that the problems of political interference in judicial matters were at least as serious as in the Federation.[431]

The efforts to reform the prosecution services of the entities and cantons were similarly made difficult by old habits and systematic political obstruction. For example, the important principle of the new Federation and RS rules on criminal procedure that the public prosecutor should have a more active role in ensuring justice and procedural fairness (including supervising that the police respect the rights of individuals who are questioned, searched or detained) collided with an entrenched notion that the role of the prosecutor was secondary to both the investigating judge and the police. Both the judges and the police had thus an interest in resisting the reform. The high hopes invested in the right of the Federation Prosecutor to prosecute persons suspected of certain "Federal crimes" (and to order cantonal prosecutors to do so) as a means to address the unwillingness or inability of local prosecutors to pursue cases involving ethnically motivated violence and serious economic crime were similarly shattered by criminal-political alliances, etc.[432]

430 The system of regular courts consists of the RS Supreme Court in Banja Luka, district courts, basic courts, and minor offences courts. The division of material competencies between them is similar to the Federation.

431 The District of Brcko, with the status of a "District directly under the State" should have laws and judicial structures different from the entities, but seems to be gravitating towards the Republika Srpska.

432 In an unprecedented move in 2000, the Federation Prosecutor ordered a deputy to the problematic town of Drvar to investigate why the local prosecution did not function and why the appointment of new, supposedly more competent and energetic, municipal prosecutors was repeatedly obstructed by nationalist parties and groups.

The lack of effective cooperation between the law enforcement, administrative and judicial authorities of BiH and the entities challenges not just the idea of BiH as a state, but also critical aspects of human rights and rule of law. While some progressive and pragmatic courts and law enforcement agencies tried to mitigate for the lack of formal inter-entity co-operation by developing informal practices for issues such as the service of summons and recognition of documents over the entity line, the lack of a clear legal basis for such practices led to arbitrary availability and uncertainty. Pushed by the OHR to come up with more reliable and sustainable solutions, the Ministers of Justice of the Republika Srpska and the Federation signed the 1998 Memorandum of Understanding on the Regulation of Legal Assistance between the Institutions of the Federation of Bosnia and Herzegovina and the Republika Srpska, which provided for procedures, largely controlled by the entity ministries of justice, for tracing of witnesses, service of subpoenas, and investigations at-the-scene, etc. The ministries were also requested to issue further binding instructions and draft legislation as necessary to fully implement the Memorandum, but whereas the Federation submitted a first draft of instructions, no action was taken by the Republika Srpska. Neither was there much interest in pushing for such instruments among the members of the ethnically divided judiciaries. The international community thus decided to pursue a more assertive policy, involving pushing the collective BiH Presidency to use its power to "facilitate inter-entity coordination" under Article III:4 of the BiH Constitution to establish the Commission on Inter-Entity Legal Cooperation. The eight permanent members of the Commission (one appointed by each BiH Presidency member, two from each entity, and an OHR-appointed chair) were given the power to draft concrete provisions for the implementation of the Memorandum and to address any other future need that could arise in this area. However, after having met for an inaugural session and two subsequent working sessions in 1998 (at which some recommendations regarding accessibility and exchange of documents, land records and court files were given) further sessions were suspended during the september 1998 BiH elections pending confirmation of its role and composition, and the Commission has not met again since.

In order to regain strength and momentum in justice sector reform, the High Representative decided in the beginning of 2000 to establish the Independent Judicial Commission for Bosnia and Herzegovina (IJC).[433] The IJC was mandated to provide opinions and advice in judicial reform and rule of law issues to the High Representative and other international organisations, but also directly to the Federation and Republika Srpska ministries of justice, members of the judiciary, etc. The Director of the IJC could recommend to the High Representative the use of his coercive powers, *e.g.* to

433 The decision to take this course was made in accordance with the directives of the Peace Implementation Steering Board in Lisbon in May 2000 and endorsed by UNMiBH, OSCE and CoE.

impose legislation or remove officials from office, including judges. The Director could also decide upon actions to be taken on the basis of powers authorized by the High Representative.

It soon emerged as a core task for the IJC to ensure that the "judicial service laws" enacted in 2000 (the Federation Law on Judicial and Prosecutorial Service and the Republika Srpska Law on Courts and Courts Service and Law on Public Prosecutor's Office) were effectively implemented as part of a strategy to sever the political influence over the judiciary and prosecution, and to ensure that all judges and prosecutors henceforth had the professional qualities their positions required.[434] The essence of the this new structure, as it was originally conceived, was that the responsibility for reviewing judicial appointments and professional performance should be removed from the political parties and placed with trusted peers, *i.e.* other supposedly impartial and competent Bosnian judges and prosecutors. Special judicial and prosecutorial commissions (Federation) and councils (RS) were thus established, consisting of 7-13 *ex officio* and elected members of the entity judiciaries and prosecution services (typically the chairmen of the supreme courts, the highest entity prosecutors, etc.). All councils/commissions duly held their inaugural sessions and took up working through the information on the merits of individual judges and prosecutors submitted to them by the international community and the general public. In this work, the commissions and councils were supervised and assisted by the Independent Judicial Commission.

While this initiative enjoyed strong support from many members of the local judiciary and prosecution, the entity political and executive organs were not equally enthusiastic. Their lack of practical commitment resulted in difficulties for the commissions and councils in securing adequate funding, recruiting competent people, and other matters. As a result, the review proceeded much slower than anticipated and much of the initial enthusiasm that had surrounded the initiative soon disappeared. The number of judges and prosecutors that were actually removed from office also turned out to be suspiciously low, only three in the year of 2001. After many less than successful attempts at revising the laws and giving the commissions and councils more "bite" by means of institutional support, the international community arrived at the conclusion in 2002 that a more forceful approach was called for, including requiring basically all sitting judges and prosecutors to reapply for their position (or another position within the judiciary or prosecution) in competition with other qualified candidates, thus providing for a comprehensive examination of the entire judiciary and prosecution service.

---

434 The RS laws were passed by the RS National Assembly in May 2000, and the High Representative imposed the Federation law in June the same year.

The responsibility for reviewing the applications was initially placed with state and entity level High Judicial and Prosecutorial Councils created by the High Representative specifically for this purpose. These bodies, and the Independent Judicial Commission overseeing their work, were merged into one unified structure in 2004 to ensure consistency and synchronicity in judicial reform throughout the country. The new High Judicial and Prosecutorial Council (HJPC) consists of 13 local and three international members, all appointed by the High Representative. Besides the ambition to speed up judicial reform generally, the establishment of the HJPC was also spurred by a decision of the European Union that BiH would not be allowed to enter into negotiations on a Stabilisation and Association Agreement before a single structure had been established. In conjunction with the establishment of the HJPC, the High Representative also imposed far-reaching changes to the laws establishing the rules of jurisdiction for courts at various levels, thus providing for a more homogenous and centralised judicial organisation.

Another component of the judicial reform package was the introduction of a reformed salary structure. There had always been an assumption, locally as well as within the international community, that the poor performance and inclination towards corruption among judges and prosecutors were partly attributable to the vastly insufficient salaries. The powers of the High Representative to formulate and impose policies in all areas were therefore used to introduce a more attractive salary structure. While regular Federation judges used to be paid amounts ranging from KM 800 to KM 1,500 per month (in basic step with prosecutor salaries), and RS judges and prosecutors as little as 432 KM per month, the new structure provided for salaries beginning at KM 2,500. Not surprisingly, the entity and cantonal budgetary organs argued that they had no means to pay the new salaries and procrastinated in making the necessary funds available. Other categories of high-ranking civil servants, among them ambassadors, heads of administrative agencies, and under-secretaries of state, also started to argue that they should be paid at comparable or even higher levels. Although it has become apparent that this reform will never be fully implemented unless the international community agrees to provide support to the justice sector budget, the international community still refuses to do so.

5.3.5.3 United Nations Mission in Kosovo

Unlike in BiH, justice sector reform was immediately recognised by the international community as being vital to promote security, human rights protection, economic reconstruction and other central aspects of the peace-building agenda in Kosovo. Once deployed, UNMIK could therefore immediately proceed to create a framework of laws and regulations providing for various types of courts, prosecution agencies and other key elements of a working justice sector.

Although UNMIK was technically at liberty to depart from any pre-existing order, the SRSG did not see a new system as an end in itself. The template for the reformed judiciary and prosecution in Kosovo was accordingly structured essentially along the lines of the previous Kosovo autonomous province of the Federation of Yugoslavia, with a basic three-level structure of municipal courts, five district courts and a supreme court. The system also included minor offences courts. However, there was no doubt that the principles underpinning their work should be radically reformed to correspond to the highest international and regional standards of human rights and rule of law. This "revitalisation" of existing institutions in an environment of scarce resources proved much more time-consuming and difficult than anticipated. Among the most difficult obstacles were lack of commitment to the idea of a multiethnic judiciary among local jurists and politicians, ethnic and political biases, and widespread and accelerating corruption. Finding and hiring staff that had the substantive skills and moral qualities required also proved difficult. As late as 2002, the Supreme Court only consisted of an Ad Hoc Court of Final Appeal acting as an appeal body in criminal proceedings.[435]

Despite the prioritisation of justice sector reforms, the SRSG was slow to use his authority to appoint new, and supposedly better, local candidates to key judicial and prosecutorial positions. Strohmeyer suggests that the reason for the slow approach was a wish to depart from the flagrant politicisation of judicial appointments that had characterized the previous regime and now clearly demonstrate that all new appointments, and particularly the initial appointments, were characterised by objectivity, transparency, and other core traits of good process: There should be no doubt that capable candidates had been identified; selections made in accordance with objective and verifiable criteria and merit, matters of political and ethnic balance duly considered; etc.[436] A more cynical interpretation is that the SRSG made virtue out of necessity. The limited resource base made it necessary to screen refugee camps in country and abroad for candidates, spread word by mouth, activate civil society/NGO channels, and undertake other complicated and lengthy efforts, before any decisions could be made.

In order to ensure a degree of domestic ownership over the appointment process, the SRSG created the Advisory Judicial Commission (initially called the Joint Advisory Council on Provisional Judicial Appointments) to take the lead in identifying and proposing candidates for judicial positions. This body initially comprised two Kosovar Albanians, one Muslim Slav, and one Serb (all of whom had previous experience in the administration of justice in Kosovo), and three international lawyers from different

---

435 Brand 2001 p. 480.

436 Strohmeyer 2001 pp. 51-52.

international organizations. The majority of the members was thus local experts and empowered to overrule the international members. There was an ambition to reduce the international membership of the commissions further as local capacity evolved, thus making it easier for a completely domestic mechanism to evolve. In essence, the Commission was designed to receive and process applications from persons whom had the formal qualifications (a law degree minimum), make a selection of the candidates on the basis of merit, and make recommendations on appointments to the SRSG.

The formation of the Commission provoked much political sensitivity, particularly among hard-line members of the Kosovo Albanian community. The Serb and Muslim Slav members were even subjected to serious intimidation and harassment on several occasions.[437] Strohmeyer argues that such reactions should have been anticipated, given the political turmoil that prevailed, the weak support of the general principles of the agreement among many groups, and particularly the problems inherent in meeting the mission goal of ensuring ethnic "balance" in all fora when there was so few competent lawyers from which to draw.[438]

In spite of the difficulties, the Commission managed to propose a number of judges and prosecutors (55 in the initial months) for appointment *ad interim* by the SRSG. The SRSG also made clear to them that their appointments could be renewed after a period of trial and observation. However, this relative success was overshadowed by the parallel exodus of Serb judges, often as a result of intimidation from Albanian colleagues. The problems of ethnic bias in judicial matters also seemed to be on the increase, supposedly as a result of the shifting power balances in the judiciary and prosecution service. Yet another set-back came when it was noticed that several of the newly appointed judges and prosecutors had neither the skills nor the integrity needed to deal with the wide range of sensitive and complicated cases brought before them. Rather than taking the risk of replacing them with a new set of untested appointees, the SRSG decided to place international judges to work alongside the local judges, first at the Mitrovica District Court and later all over Kosovo.[439] Neither did this measure suffice to compensate for the lack of capacity and integrity. Numerous independent assessments and UNMIK, OSCE and NGO-reports maintain that the justice system

437 Strohmeyer (2001 p. 52) mentions that the Serb member was evicted form his apartment after only a few days in office. He then joined the general Serb exodus to Serbia proper and was threatened with death if he returned. For his part, the Bosnian member was immediately accused of having collaborated with the previous Serb-dominated regime in Kosovo. One of the Kosovar Albanian experts, who had been the last president of Kosovo's abolished Supreme Court, was considered to stand for the old Yugoslav order and was criticized for his involvement in the trials of Kosovo Albanian leaders in previous the strikes and demonstrations.

438 Id. pp. 52-53.

439 Brand 2001 p. 480; Chesterman 2002 p. 5.

of Kosovo was still unable of providing the kind of safeguards traditionally associated human rights and the rule of law.[440]

5.3.5.4 United Nations Transitional Administration in East Timor

The international administration in East Timor spent considerable resources on promoting a functioning judiciary and prosecution service. The SRSG formally established a number of basic agencies in 2000, among them the Office of the Prosecutor General, courts of first and second instance, a legal aid agency ("defender service"), and penitentiary institutions. While the eight new District Courts were intended to form the backbone of the system, lack of trained judges (the Indonesian policy had been to refuse to appoint East Timorese to judicial or prosecutorial office) and scare resources overall made it necessary to grant the Dili District Court interim jurisdiction throughout the entire territory.[441] Still today, the Dili court retains a *de facto* leadership role in the judicial structure of East Timor.

As indicated, the identification and appointment of suitable candidates for judicial and prosecutorial positions presented the most serious difficulties in the capacity-building effort. In order to make the most of the little that was, and to ensure a degree of local ownership in this important reform area, the SRSG decided to establish the Transitional Judicial Service Commission to take the lead in staffing the new judiciary.[442] This *ad hoc* organ comprised three East Timorese and two international lawyers. Among its tasks were also to draft the instruments needed for the new agencies to work, including codes of ethics for the judiciary and prosecution, and to act as a disciplinary body to review complaints of misconduct. Unlike in Kosovo, the establishment and composition of the Commission did not provoke much political sensitivity.[443] The members of Commission could essentially proceed undisturbed with the tasks of designing and conducting the interview and selection process.[444] On the recommendation of the Commission, the SRSG eventually appointed the first eight East Timorese judges and two prosecutors in January 2000, and gave them full authority to exercise their responsibilities from the moment of appointment.

The wisdom of rapidly appointing local judges and prosecutors instead of relying on international judges and prosecutors in the first critical phase of the state building effort in East Timor has been contested. Critics particularly mention that the pre-

440 Brand 2001 p. 480.

441 UNTAET/REG/2000/11.

442 UNTAET Regulation 1999/3 on the Establishment of a Transitional Judicial Service Commission.

443 Strohmeyer 2001 p. 52.

444 Within two months after the establishment of the new judicial organs, over sixty East Timorese jurists had formally applied for judicial or prosecutorial positions. Chesterman 2002 p. 7.

appointment training of this first batch of judges and prosecutors was confined to a week, and that as a consequence thereof, many of them proved to lack both the skills and integrity needed to adjudicate complicated and sensitive cases in a volatile legal and political environment.[445]

On the other hand, the SRSG was aware of the myriad of predictable and unpredictable problems that other UN missions (particularly UNMIK) had experienced in inserting international lawyers in domestic structures, notable among them the tendency to reduce the local incentive to assume responsibility for essential judicial functions. It was also obvious that the Mission could not afford to administer parallel or joint structures at that point in time. Further, the SRSG could not wait any longer to establish a domestic mechanism to address the backlog of cases involving people whom had been arrested and detained by the initial international military and police presence. On a more technical level, another reason to emphasize local structures may have been that UNTAET (like UNMIK before it) considered that immediate involvement of local lawyers would help to prevent, or minimize, any disruptive effect on the judiciary once the limited international funds earmarked for financing international lawyers inevitably dwindled and forced their withdrawal. However, most important was the perceived political need to quickly create an appearance of a complete domestic legal system.[446] Strohmeyer points out that this need to a large extent was the result of expectations and lobby among human rights-oriented people and groups in the wake of the international intervention.[447]

5.3.5.5 United Nations Assistance Mission in Afghanistan

After decades of war, chaos and terror in Afghanistan, the creation of respect for human rights and the rule of law was made a main priority of Afghan administration and the international organisations supporting it. A key element in this effort was to establish and empower a structure of courts and prosecution agencies. President Hamid Karzai formed in November 2002 the Judicial (Reform) Commission and tasked it to lead the reform work. The Commission consisted of Afghan nationals only and was mandated to rebuild the justice system (courts; prosecution service; law enforcement authorities; correction services authorities; and legal education and training establishments) in Afghanistan "*in accordance with Islamic principles, international standards, the rule of law and Afghan legal traditions*", but commentators suggest that the International Administration had a great role in outlining its specific

[445] Linton 2001 p. 134.
[446] Id. p. 134.
[447] Strohmeyer 2001 p. 54-55.

mandate and operating procedures.[448] The Commission was also tasked to conduct a human resources survey and to work out programs for the selection and training of judges and other law officers. All these functions should be carried out in cooperation with the UN and the donor community.

Various assistance programs were directed at supporting the legal and judicial reform efforts promoted by the Commission and other actors in Afghanistan. The most important among the initial international initiatives was the UNDP program "Rebuilding the Justice Sector of Afghanistan".[449] This program was designed to work closely with the Judicial Reform Commission and to facilitate the creation of a justice sector that could promote and consolidate Afghanistan's long-term social and economic development. The international community also decided for a system of "lead nations" to ensure long-term international commitment to important sector-reform projects. Italy assumed the role of "lead country" in providing support to the justice sector, which meant that the Italian Government took on to maintain donor interest in the sector, raise sufficient resources for key reform initiatives, and otherwise support the reform agenda. Germany similarly assumed the role of lead nation with regard to law enforcement reform.

As a first step toward improving coordination and communication among the different actors in the justice system, the UNDP Project supported the Judicial Reform Commission in clarifying the roles and functions of the most important legal and judicial organs in the country. This effort comprised conducting a survey of organizations operating at the central and regional levels of the system, covering essential data such as jurisdiction, organisational structure, staffing, financing, etc. The Program also sought to promote clarity and consistency in the creation and application of laws by cataloguing, indexing and helping to disseminate various kinds of formal and informal (customary) normative instruments.

The specific commitment in the Bonn Agreement to respect and promote fundamental human rights made UNAMA and the other assistance providers emphasise human rights matters in their discussions with the Afghan authorities and in the allocation of resources to various national reform programs. Among the priority topics were the empowerment of the Afghan Independent Human Rights Commission (established in the Bonn Agreement as the national institution in charge of defining the Human Rights agenda in Afghanistan); facilitating protection activities for the most vulnerable segments of the population (such as returnees, internally displaced persons, women

448 Chesterman 2002 p. 11.
449 UNDP AFG/03/001/01/34.

heads of households and unaccompanied minors); and establishing structures for monitoring and investigating human rights abuses.

More recent institutional reform activities, and the support directed to them, have essentially been guided by the Judicial Reform Commission and the recommendations of the Comprehensive Needs Assessment ("Justice for All"). The general principle for all reforms remains that the Government is in lead and that initiatives should be implemented through normal political and administrative processes. The specific reform plan comprises reforming the central institutions (the Supreme Court; the Ministry of Justice; the highest prosecutorial authority); restructuring the Faculty of Law and Sharia and its curricula; establishing judicial training mechanism; and the physical rehabilitation of courts, prisons and other critical infrastructure in Kabul and the provinces.

5.3.6 CAPACITY BUILDING AND ACCESS CREATION

5.3.6.1 United Nations Transitional Authority in Cambodia

In Cambodia, the principal tool for capacity building in the legal and judicial sector was training and other forms of transfer of knowledge. This meant that parallel to the kind of topical (human rights and rule of law) training called for by the Paris Agreement, the international community also provided various forms of basic skills training for different categories of legal and judicial professionals and support staff to make them more effective in their professional capacities. The UNTAC Human Rights Component early launched a major program of training for judges, prosecutors and defence lawyers. Training sessions for civil servants, representatives for activist groups, and others concerned with law and justice issue broadly, were also undertaken in almost every province. A number of bilateral assistance providers soon followed with their own training programs, some of them aiming at improving basic judicial skills, and some with a focus on topical issues such as aspects of human rights, organized crime, and corruption.

The assistance providers experimented with a variety of approaches to transfer of knowledge. Some programs sought to facilitate fast and direct exchange of knowledge by placing foreign lawyers and judges in a number of provinces to work with the provincial agencies and their staff as mentors or trainers.[450] Other programs placed advisors with the Ministry of Justice and other key agencies, and sought to promote

[450] The UN Centre for Human Rights Judicial Mentor Program and the International Human Rights Law Group Court Training Project.

the establishment of a comprehensive training program for new judges. Yet other projects aimed at building a cadre of paralegals as a means of circumventing the problems caused by the desperate dearth of trained defence lawyers.

5.3.6.2 High Representative to Bosnia and Herzegovina

It soon became apparent that besides providing for sensible legislation, a workable judicial reform strategy for the new state of Bosnia and Herzegovina also needed to comprise efforts to strengthen and open up key legal and judicial institutions at state, entity and cantonal level, and improving the structures for providing legal assistance and aid.

The international efforts to this end were challenged on many levels. On the philosophical and conceptual level, the Yugoslavian heritage of passive defence counsels overshadowed by active investigative judges died hard. The first versions of the modernized Republika Srpska and Federation criminal procedure codes did little to change this basic position. They also maintained that mandatory defence, *i.e.* that the competent court had to ensure that the accused was represented by counsel, was required only in a narrow range of cases (such as when the accused was deaf or mute, or if a very long sentence could be pronounced). As these laws did not provide the kind of judicial safeguards required of a country aspiring for membership of the Council of Europe and eventually the European Union, the international community continued to press for further amendment until drafts were presented that provided for a system more akin to modern European equivalents. At the same time, there was a widespread belief in the international community that although the laws were essentially good, problems of political will and lack of resources would make implementation very difficult.

The natural starting point for capacity building would have been to ensure the accuracy and proper circulation of the state, entity and cantonal Official Gazettes. However, many legal and judicial agencies either could not afford to subscribe to the relevant gazettes or preferred to rely on the gazettes of neighbouring countries such as Croatia and Serbia and Montenegro. Further, some law-making agencies on lower (cantonal) level reportedly did not bother with duly publishing their enactment in the relevant gazette. There were thus no guarantees that laws were properly promulgated and disseminated, let alone read. Confronted with such problems, and reluctant to subsidize subscriptions, the OHR and a range of assistance providers started to explore other avenues to ensure the presence of vital legal information throughout the country. A notable initiative by the OSCE was the distribution of a compilation of the most essential BiH laws (modelled after the Swedish "Law Book", a commercial publication widely used in Swedish courts and legal agencies) to all regular judges and prosecutors in BiH.[451]

At a more mundane level, attempts at improving the capacity and accessibility of the system was frustrated by the lack of qualified and motivated people, particularly defence lawyers. The scarcity of skilled counsel was partly attributable to lingering restrictive and formalized requirements for legal practice. Under law, the right to represent people in court was effectively reserved for members of the relevant bar association. The situation was complicated further by the existence of essentially ethnically divided bar associations in both entities, which made cross-boundary practice virtually impossible.[452] The initial attempts by the international community to create a unified bar associations, or even an umbrella organization, rendered little success, except that the "Bosnian" and "Croat" associations in the Federation felt compelled to begin a process of slow and cautious rapprochement as a result of intensive lobby and encouragement of ABA-CEELI and the High Representative.

It was also necessary to ensure that the general public could readily access important laws and human rights materials. Without such access, the "subjects" or "consumers" of the system could not benefit from the protection and opportunities the new and supposedly better laws provide. After many initial problems, mainly stemming from similarly indifferent or negative attitudes among domestic politicians and agencies, the considerable international efforts spent on inproving access to such materials eventually started to pay off. The overall public awareness of international human rights standards (*e.g.* as provided by the UN conventions and the ECHR), and of specific individual entitlements according to domestic legislation, began to increase, as demonstrated by the steadily rising number of grievances being submitted to the courts and human rights institutions. Among the many initiatives in this area can be

---

[451] The BiH Law Book contains some 250 state and entity level legal instruments, structured in nine law topical areas. The laws are printed in the language in which they were originally promulgated. OSCE has similarly pursued a Legislation Commentary Project that produced a series of commentaries on the application of the entity laws on criminal and administrative procedure, and other cornerstone laws.

[452] Before the war, each of the republics and autonomous provinces of former Yugoslavia had separate bar associations, joined in the Union of Bar Associations of Yugoslavia. The associations adopted their own statutes and other by-laws. The Bar Association of Bosnia and Herzegovina continued its existence after BiH was recognized as an independent state in 1992. The existence of one unified bar association eventually became synonymous with aspirations by influential Bosnian lawyers to keep BiH unified, but this pan-BiH association was not recognized by authorities in Republika Srpska, which instead promoted the passing of an entity Law on Legal Practice in October 1992. This law required RS citizenship for membership in the association. Similarly, the Croatian Defense Council in 1993 adopted a law and a decree on legal practice for the territory of the (then) Croatian Republic of Herzeg-Bosna that determined that attorneys from the territory should be organized in the Bar Association of the Croatian Union of Herzeg-Bosna, and that legal counselling as a professional activity could only be exercised under conditions set out in the law and decree mentioned.

mentioned that OSCE disseminated topical materials and established reading rooms in various locations around the country; SFOR CIMIC produced human rights public information material; CoE donated a Human Rights library to the Human Rights Center of the University of Sarajevo (on the condition that it be accessible to the public); UNHCR and OHR produced and distributed a range of human rights and general legal materials, etc. Bilateral donors have channelled even greater resources to a range of local organisations active in this area.

Like in Cambodia before it, the international effort to build capacity and access largely centred on training. After the conclusion of the GFAP, a number of NGOs were quick to provide or facilitate human rights-related training to members of the judiciary, prosecution service and law enforcement. Soon thereafter, the major international organisations followed suit. Many of the initial efforts took the form of shorter seminars where Bosnian and international experts met to exchange experiences and discuss alternative solutions to current and pressing problems. After the limits of *ad hoc* training had become apparent (expensive, too short to be effective, etc.), and the need for a more systematic and comprehensive approach recognised, the international organisations and many NGOs began to promote the establishment of self-sustaining domestic structures (judicial training centers and similar) able of providing recurrent and advanced training on a variety of subjects to all members of the judiciary and prosecution. Behind the shift to long-term institution-building were also the expectations created by the reforms of the procedures for the appointment of judges and prosecutors: The assistance providers had concluded that if these reforms should succeed in bringing about a new and better breed of judge and prosecutors, they need to be combined with efforts to ensure that those that pass through the needle-eye get to benefit from systematic and advanced professional training on important aspects of BiH law, international law, and practical legal and judicial work. After having repeatedly failed to convince national policy-makers on the importance of establishing a permanent structure for judicial and prosecutorial training, the High Representative imposed in May 2002 legislation establishing such centres as domestic bodies. The stated objective of the Centres is to ensure that training programs for judges and prosecutors are designed and implemented in the light of the requirements of open-mindedness, competence and impartiality normally associated with exercise of judicial and prosecutorial duties.

In response to the call of the 1998 Madrid PIC for even greater international efforts to open up the justice system, the international community has similarly sought to transform the Benefits Commission (a body established jointly by OSCE and CoE in 1997 to help Bosnian clients with money to afford local representation) into a domestic agency under BiH law. The most common reasons for seeking the assistance of these centres were problems related to property ownership, employment discrimination, social policy issues, juvenile crime and pensions rights. Particularly in property and refugee-return related fields these centres also served as a valuable means of gathering information and oversight of the implementation of new laws.

5.3.6.3 United Nations Mission in Kosovo

In Kosovo, the introduction of large volumes of new legislation, including a new adversarial criminal procedure, coincided with the exodus of a large part of the former judiciary and prosecution. Further, there was no system of legal assistance and aid to help the traumatized population understand and seize on the opportunities the new legislation provided. UNMIK thus needed to immediately launch efforts to maintain at least minimal capacity within courts and prosecution, and to make sure that people could and dared use their services.

A key issue was to identify a sufficient number of qualified lawyers of different ethnic background to perform the functions of judges, prosecutors and defence lawyers, and convey to them by means of training the philosophical and legal fundamentals of the new justice system, particularly the new criminal procedure.[453] As UNMIK did not have the resources to do this itself, the greater donor community needed to be activated. Many international and regional agencies working in Kosovo were already providing training to different categories of jurists, but as many of these initiatives had had a specific focus on human rights-related topics, trafficking in human beings, organised crime and other "hot" issues, the UNMIK effort also involved reorienting existing projects to target general legal and judicial skills.

At the same time, it was obvious that many lawyers in Kosovo considered such "basic" or "general" professional training to be somewhat patronizing. For their part, the training received in the Yugoslavian universities was perceived quite adequate for all but the most contemporary and complex issues at hand. Strohmeyer mentions that the international agencies promoting training also needed to deal with the peculiar problem that some Kosovar Albanian lawyers, particularly those schooled during the decade (1989-1999) of *de facto* "parallel" systems of Yugoslav/Serbian and Kosovar Albanian law and legal training, reacted extremely cautiously to the whole idea of training for fear that the revelation of the inadequacy of their experience and skills would disqualify them for judicial office or provide an advantage to those who had "collaborated" with the previous regime.[454] Some initiatives aiming at providing general and basic skills thus needed to be dressed up to look like training in aspects of international and regional law and practice (*e.g.* ICCPR and ECHR implementa-

453 Strohmeyer 2001 p. 55.

454 Id. p. 56.

tion), so as to provoke less sensitivity. Already in 1999, UNMIK and its partners arrived at the conclusion that any sustainable capacity-building strategy for Kosovo needed to comprise the establishment of a judicial training centre able of providing recurrent and systematic training along the lines of many other countries in the region. An embryo to such an institution was provided by UNMIK regulation.

The Kosovo Police Service School was run by the OSCE with input from the US International Criminal Investigative Training Assistance Program. That the School so quickly became operative and got to benefit from sustained international assistance were largely attributable to the novelty of UNMIK's law enforcement mandate. Initially the training focused almost exclusively on technical skills (securing crime scenes, investigative skills, weapons training, etc.), but like in BiH it soon took on a normative dimension as well, comprising human rights issues, democratic policing, community policing, and other components aiming at transforming the police from a security organisation into a public service institution.

5.3.6.4 United Nations Transitional Administration in East Timor

The lack of local capacity and experience with self-governance in East Timor presented UNTAET and the international community with considerable problems, both in administering the territory *in interim* and in facilitating the development of sustainable structures for the new state of Timor-Leste. In particular, there were worries that without broad-based and meaningful participation of East Timorese where laws were drafted and decisions made, the resulting structures would neither be legitimate nor sustainable. There was also concern that the Mission would overstretch itself as it inevitably slipped into managing more and more of local government tasks. Capacity building was thus elevated on the mission agenda, from being regarded a matter of secondary importance and something that could be addressed by the development community (as had been the case in Bosnia and Herzegovina and Kosovo), to something that needed to be prioritized and initiated immediately.

The initial focus of the capacity building effort was on training key categories of state functionaries, among them judges, prosecutors and government lawyers.[455] The apparent insufficiency of the training given to the first batch of local judges and prosecutors appointed by the SRSG, and the ensuing problems of unpredictability and inconsistency in the application of UN and local legal instruments, had also made it clear that there were no quick fixes to the problem. Rather, there needed to be

455 Various local NGOs (such as the local civil rights organization Yayasan Hak) could help to fill some immediate capacity gaps in the legal system, in particular in the provision of legal assistance. Chesterman 2002 p. 8.

"permanent" structures able of providing systematic and recurrent training, and the scope of the training needed to extend beyond conventional legal and judicial topics to comprise basic concepts of democracy and the rule of law, and the role of the legal profession in promoting and protecting such concepts in a transitional environment.[456]

UNTAET proceeded to develop a three-tiered approach to training consisting of a series of one-week, compulsory "quick impact" training courses for becoming judges, prosecutors, and public defenders; mandatory ongoing training for already active judges, prosecutors, and public defenders; and a "mentoring scheme" in which a pool of experienced international legal practitioners served as "shadow" judges, prosecutors, and public defenders without actually exercising judicial power.[457] Linton mentions that sometimes such on the spot advice and assistance were perceived by local judges and prosecutors as attempts at interference or at least supervision from the side of the UN interim administration, and consequently ignored or greeted with suspicion.[458] The Mission was also aware that shorter training programs organised from the outside were neither sustainable nor an effective in meeting to enormous demand for new lawyers, and thus began to promote the establishment of a permanent judicial training structure for East Timor similar to a judicial training centre.[459]

In planning for the successor mission UNMISET, the UN identified a number core state functions for which the new state of Timor-Leste lacked national capacity and for which the international community could continue to provide interim solutions, either in the form of seconded international staff to perform line functions or in the form of mentoring and training. Following Security Council authorization, a number of "stability positions" were created in the framework of the Civilian Support Group initiative, among them 14 positions in the area of legal/justice. The nature of the support provided varied depending on the unique needs and capacities of the host institution, but often comprised institutional and organisational capacity building components such as formalization of rules and procedures, management reforms, and human resources development. The human capacity building effort was largely centred on knowledge transfer by means of on-the job-training. While in other sectors (such as public administration) such capacity building initiatives soon reflected in a diminishing need for foreign advisors and mentors, the need or foreign experts to perform both in-line functions and training rather seemed to increase in the legal and judicial sector. The relative failure of the capacity building efforts in this area were believed to be at least in part attributable to the one-to-one, individual-level approach

---

456 Strohmeyer 2001 p. 55.
457 Chesterman 2002 p. 7; Strohmeyer 2001 pp. 55-56.
458 Linton 2001 p. 135.
459 Strohmeyer 2001 pp. 55-56.

to training, and a number of bilateral assistance providers therefore joined in a three-tier approach to institutional capacity building emphasising skills and knowledge, systems and processes, and attitudes and behaviours.[460] However, as of today, the East Timorese justice system continues to rely on international advisors to perform key in-line and training functions. The Judicial Training Centre program similarly depends on foreign input, although the elements of "training of trainers" is steadily increasing and may eventually result in East Timorese jurists taking over the training function from their foreign colleagues.

As of recent, UNOTIL has begun to transform the Mission's technical advising to a more long-term and comprehensive development assistance framework. It is hoped that bilateral donors will take over much of the responsibility for funding and administrating the secondment of experts to various Timor-Leste legal and judicial agencies. A new Consultative Group comprising the major actors in the justice sector, a number of assistance providers, and civil society representatives, has been formed with the aim of enhancing government ownership and leadership, facilitating the development of new approaches and methods, and providing for co-ordination and consolidation of international efforts in the sector.

5.3.6.5 United Nations Assistance Mission in Afghanistan

In Afghanistan, the principal responsibility for capacity building and access creation rests with the 11 Afghan members of the Judicial Reform Commission in line with the "light footprint" approach. Much of Commission's attention has been devoted to establishing a national structure for systematic and recurrent training of judges, prosecutors and other categories of legal personnel. The Commission has also prioritised the related area of creating teaching and information materials, and making them accessible to professionals and laymen alike.

While security considerations have prevented the international community from engaging in the promotion of comprehensive capacity and access-creation programs throughout the country, there are a range of international initiatives to support the Commission in its important work. For example, the UNDP has tried to meet the objectives of the Commission by launching a training program targeting various categories of legal and judicial professionals from Kabul and the regions, supporting the production of research and reference materials, and otherwise empowering

[460] The joint UNDP/Government of Timor-Leste Capacity Development Coordination Unit program "Strengthening the Justice System in Timor-Leste" continues to develop various support functions by means of training interpreters, court clerks and prison guards, and by helping the respective institutions define their mandates and work processes.

teaching and training institutions. More recently, USAID has contracted the University of Washington Asian Law Center to assess and promote new curricula with the mentioned faculties and to help them develop teaching materials reflecting the changing legal landscape of Afghanistan. A particular area of attention for the international support to legal and judicial reform in Afghanistan is to ensure gender equality and a more prominent role for women throughout the judicial system.

A particular challenge is to build capacity for the administration of law and justice in the provinces and districts, where neither national authorities nor the international military presence have effective control of the security situation. An Italian effort to this end is the Provincial Justice Initiative. This project aims at reactivating lingering formal criminal justice structures in a number of provincial capitals by means of capacity building, essentially training. With the help of this initiative, some 150 local judges, prosecutors, and other categories of jurists have been trained by Afghan trainers, mainly in Kabul, for three months in criminal justice topics so far, but the initiative is currently being expanded to comprise further provinces and more people. The initiative also comprises monitoring and access creation components, and the provision of basic office equipment and vehicles to the targeted regional justice bodies. The immediate and independent effects or this initiative, without basic conditions of law and order in place, may not be very palpable. On the other hand, initiatives of this kind are instrumental in creating awareness and a feeling of being included among the members of the legal profession, and thus in the creation of a shared "ethos"and understanding of what justice is and what it means to be a jurist in the new Afghanistan.

6. CONCLUSIONS

6.1 IDEOLOGIES OF DEVELOPMENT AND STATE BUILDING

The history of integrating legal and judicial reform into the projects of development and state building may be described as a succession of dominant ideas and dogma. In the development project, the optimistic modernization theories of the Law and Development Movement were soon replaced with theories of path dependency. In the 1980s these theories had to yield to concepts of "good governance", and most recently, there are signs that the overt instrumentality of the "Washington consensus" is being replaced by a more value-laden "post Washington-consensus" idea of governance and law comprising doctrines of the rule of law, human rights and what is called "the social". Inherent in the current dogma is a belief that laws and institutions that promote and support democracy, human rights, etc. are not just an expected consequence of reaching a higher level of economic development, but also instrumental in inciting and powering processes of economic development to the benefit of all.

A similar trend can be discerned in the context of post-conflict reconstruction, where the traditional concept of peace-keeping as a matter of maintaining *status quo* has been replaced with an idea that sustainable peace depends on success in addressing the underlying causes of conflict. Multifunctional "international administrations" are therefore mandated to "take all means necessary" to build states based on democracy, the rule of law and human rights. Inherent in this idea is that justice, peace and democracy cannot be meaningfully promoted in isolation, but are mutually reinforcing imperatives.[461] Among the most palpable side-effect has been relieving local stakeholders of the political responsibility for the future well-being of the nation or territory, and the tendency to "capacity sucking out". Afghanistan may be indicative of yet another paradigm shift, where the UN instead of assuming responsibility for important governance and judicial functions have decided for a "light footprint" approach and geared itself to consolidate and strengthen historical and existing national structures to the extent they conform to basic universal concepts of human rights and the rule of law.

[461] UNSG Report S/2004/616 pp. 1-2.

At an abstract level, the projects of development and state building are fuelled and directed by the greater processes of "internationalisation" or "globalization". Governments, assistance providers and international organisations assume that such processes, particularly when involving membership of international and regional organisations such as the WTO, EU and ASEAN, are conditioned on far-reaching legal and judicial harmonization.[462] Both projects thus contain an element of "end of history" triumphalism, where assistance providers base their policies on the assumption that responsiveness to universal and regional principles of law and justice is in the enlightened self-interest of elites and populations everywhere.[463]

No less significant for the integration of law into development and state building ideologies is the emergence of new potent agents of change. It is apparent that the way laws and institutions travel between countries and cultures cannot be explained with references to the ideas and actions of states and development agencies only. The international scene is also populated by a range of change agents above, below, besides and within states such as NGOs and regional organizations, and "parts" of states such as legislatures, courts and regulatory agencies. These actors form coalitions and networks with similar institutions in other countries and thus allow for an exchange of ideas as well as concrete norms and practices. Such networks also work to socialize members of a "rule of law community" through the transmission and reinforcement of "metanorms" such as judicial independence, regulatory transparency and public participation.[464] On the private side, multinational corporations (national companies with foreign subsidiaries) are similarly giving way to transnational corporations (corporations with diffuse national belonging and specialised facilities all over the world, producing for a global market). These transnational corporations and their advisors generate their own norms and push for favourable or at least uniform and recognizable standards wherever they operate.[465]

Interestingly, the variations in identity, ideas and formal justifications between the actors do not produce corresponding variations in how they implement their respective activities. Allowing for the evident differences in the size of programs and projects, there is considerable similarity in the kind of activities being sponsored (needs assessments, expert advise to law makers, topical training, study tours, conferences, resident advisors, acquisition of information technology, production of information materials, etc.). That some large assistance providers and international organisations are moving into what they call comprehensive, integrated, or holistic programs, means

---

462 Footer 2003 pp. 109 and 112.

463 Orth 1998 p. 80. The end of history idea plays a central role in Francis Fukuyama's 1992 book "The End of History and the Last Man".

464 Slaughter 2002 pp. 18-19.

465 Dezalay & Garth 1996; 2001; 2002a; 2002b.

little more than the pursuit of multiple objectives by combining an equal or greater number of conventional project components.[466] Many such programs are similarly characterised by a common sequence of first prioritizing the building of broad-based political opinion or "ownership" for the general objectives of the reform process, then drafting and adoption of new laws and other normative instruments, followed by institution building to ensure there are agencies able of transforming the language of the law into reality, and finally access creation to ensure that the "users" of the system can benefit from the opportunities the laws provide.[467] Behind this sequence is recognition that reform programs focusing on just one dimension or aspect of law and justice have not brought satisfactory and sustainable results, while programs that have reached over the entire sequence and sector have generally fared better.[468]

There remains much tension between the paradigms of local ownership and lead on the one hand, and promotion of a certain "Western", liberal or democratic concept of law and justice on the other. A popular way of managing this tension has been to promote the rule of law as a politically neutral concept or least common denominator around which donors and hosts with different outlooks on politics, human rights etc. should be able to unite. This policy is problematic for many reasons, particularly that there is no way of knowing that donors and hosts share a common understanding of what the rule of law means or for what reasons it is being promoted, with goal conflicts within projects as outcome. There seems to be a casual assumption among assistance providers that somewhere in international law or human rights law, there must be an authoritative and detailed definition, but international law is a field primarily concerned with relationships between states and provides surprisingly little specific guidance as to what should be regarded as the "international" or "universal" idea of the rule of law.

Perhaps the strategic 2004 UN Secretary General report "The rule of law and transitional justice in conflict and post-conflict societies" will help to put the rule of law in a policy framework. According to this report, the UN confesses to the principle that "*The normative foundation for our work in advancing the rule of law is the Charter of the United Nations itself, together with the four pillars of the modern international legal system: international human rights law; international humanitarian law; international criminal law; and international refugee law. This includes the wealth of United Nations human rights and criminal justice standards developed in the last half-century. These represent universally applicable standards adopted under the auspices of the United Nations and must therefore serve as the normative basis for all United Nations activities*

466 Hammergren 2003 p. 306.
467 Chesterman 2002 p. 1.
468 UNSG Report S/2004/616 p. 9; Hurwitz & Studdard 2005 p. 3.

in support of justice and the rule of law."[469] On the issue of how these norms relate to local notions of law and justice, the UN argues that: "*United Nations norms and standards have been developed and adopted by countries across the globe and have been accommodated by the full range of legal systems of member states, whether based in common law, civil law, Islamic law, or other legal traditions. As such, these norms and standards bring a legitimacy that cannot be said to attach to exported national models, which, all too often, reflect more the individual interests or experience of donors and assistance providers than they do the best interests or legal development needs of host countries.*"[470] The translation of the all-encompassing nature of this definition into assistance agreements, mission mandates and specific activities poses an enormous political and technical challenge. There is much evidence to demonstrate that "UN" "international" or "universal" concepts are not apolitical or uncontroversial per definition. Rather, there are countless examples of national governments and others arguing that any pursuit of a "universal" concept of law and justice is a challenge to their sovereignty and "uniqueness".

That the rule of law remains controversial and insufficiently theorized does not mean that the concept lacks utility. Rather, it has inherent qualities as a political declaration because its core elements, however defined, are minimum requirements of any decent society.[471] Assistance providers should therefore spend more effort on analysing its normative foundations, legal and institutional implications, and most effective technical assistance vehicles. Empowered with this knowledge, it would be easier to join with local stakeholders in assessing country-specific needs, setting up realistic goals, formulating effective projects, maintaining focus in implementation, and determining success and failure. Such analysis would also underscore the need for patience. The accumulation of appropriate constitutional norms, professional cultures, and personal characteristics for the rule of law in Europe took long time, and there is little reason to expect that the process should be much faster in other places.[472]

6.2 THE WAY LAW TRAVELS

It is not certain that law is always used where it should be used. The orientation of support initiatives is rather indicative of where the assistance providers consider the prospects for success in transplanting and otherwise diffusing legal concepts the greatest, and on what factors they base their considerations. It appears that in the first

469 UNSG Report S/2004/616 p. 5.
470 Ibid.
471 Peerenboom 2004 pp. 9, 13 and 34-35.
472 Orth 1998 pp. 79-81.

decades of international engagement in this area, older and conventional comparative law doctrines on differences in the prospects of successful reception and implementation between different substantive areas of law, exerted considerable influence on donor policy. These doctrines typically suggest that among the more likely to travel well should be the areas of law that are essentially "technical" or "instrumental" in nature, for example the law of commerce. At the other extreme should be strongly religiously or historically anchored ("affective") areas of law, such as family law and land law.[473]

While ideas that instrumental areas of law are easier to address from the outside still linger, an increasing number of contemporary projects seek to target rather affective aspect of law and society. This is not surprising. Inherent in the influential good governance paradigm is that law (as an institution) matters and that outsiders can meaningfully help "good law" take root in new environments. A range of new actors above, below, within and besides states, notable among them international human rights-oriented NGOs, also persistently and successfully lobby for international attention to their respective fields, whether free speech, animal rights or gender equality. So-called "mirror theories" of law and social change (essentially suggesting that law always and consistently reflects the current political, economic or social conditions of society) are not easily reconciled with contemporary donor thinking. Rather, for assistance providers to accept such theories and simultaneously try to induce change from the outside would be impossible by definition.

Further, assistance providers no longer believe that the mechanisms of legal change are, or should be, controlled "internally" within the political and legal system by conservative and autonomous elites (lawmakers, government lawyers and others). Most donor strategies rather rest on the assumption that the assistance is provided in response to a broad-based domestic demand for a specific type of reform, as expressed either by a democratic legislature or by some other actor with broad popular support. Contemporary donor policy is similarly emphasising inclusiveness, *i.e.* seizing

473 See for example Levy 1950; and Watson 1974; 1977; 1985a; 1985b; and 1991. Cotterrell (2001 p. 82) argues that that the prospects of success or failure are related to which form of law or "community" that the specific transplanted or borrowed concept has a bearing on. He derives from Max Weber's four pure types of social action (traditional, affective, purpose rational and value rational) four types of pure communities (instrumental, traditional, community of beliefs, and affective community) and argues that while the prospects of successfully introducing foreign or international concepts are often good with regard to matters that address instrumental communities, the prospects are much slimmer with regard to affective ditto. Other researchers have made different observations. For example, Andrew Harding (2001 p. 213) notes with regard to the retention and survival of transplanted laws in Southeast Asia (essentially laws imposed by colonial administrations) that "*the more public law is, the more it has diverged from Western law; but the more private or commercial law is, the less it has diverged.*"

on the views and knowledge of a wide range of legal, political, and religious groups, as a means to determine that problems really exist and that the proposed remedies will actually be helpful in addressing them.[474] This expansion of the range of change agents also makes it possible implement reforms with other means than before. For example, the "legal profession", "human rights lawyers", "younger judges", and other groups joined together by shared values and experiences may be empowered to pursue their own reform agenda more or less independently of the national government. While such strategies are often the only option in politically "difficult" countries, assistance providers need to be aware that such groups too are affected by problems of self-interest, corruption and political manipulation.

There are different schools as to whether assistance providers should expect and encourage civil society actors to act as intermediaries between the international community and the domestic legal and judicial elites. One school favours the idea of encouraging NGOs to work directly with the judiciary and thus help to imbue it with new ideas and skills, while another argues that the judiciary should be regarded a "superstructure" in a class of its own and as such be left to articulate its own needs and seek assistance where and when it deems appropriate. There is no definite right or wrong on this point, but it can be noted that civil society actors have in many cases successfully contributed to reforming, sensitizing and empowering weak judiciaries, for example by facilitating various networking and training initiatives.

With regard to the prospects of combining elements of different legal "families" or "cultures" in the same system, for example common law and civil law concepts, most assistance providers host a notion that this need not be as problematic as often assumed. Apparently there is awareness of the global trend, also comprising developed and advanced jurisdictions (Quebec, Louisiana, South Africa, etc.) of borrowing and successfully combining elements of both traditions. The pragmatic notion is that the real issue is substance rather than form.[475] It should be noted that donors operating out of common law countries (USAID, DfID, AusAid, *et al.*) frequently rely on experts from civil law jurisdictions such as Sweden and the Netherlands when implementing projects and activities in civil law countries. When problems have actually occurred in combining civil law and common law concepts in reform projects, they have often been attributable to simple misunderstandings, language errors, ignorant or insensitive experts, etc., rather than some kind of structural incompatibility.[476]

[474] For example Fukuyama 2004 pp. 115-116.

[475] Fogelklou 2000 p. 103; Rose 1998 p. 105; and Waelde & Gunderson 1994 pp. 372–373.

[476] Bogdan 1997 p. 78.

6.3 THE CRAFT IN PRACTICE

Many assistance projects centre on the assumption that the natural point of departure and necessary condition for any strategic reform efforts is the creation of good law. Would this assumption be accepted, then assistance providers should actually begin at an even more profound level; with promoting constitutional amendments to ensure sufficient "alignment" between the foundational rules governing the state and the ulterior goals of the assistance. However, assistance providers and their technical experts seem to be of the view that overt advocacy of constitutional changes could easily be perceived as intrusive and provocative, and consequently host a rather high level of tolerance as to what degree of "alignment" that is required. Inconsistency between constitutional norms, the regular laws, and the goals of the assistance is thus not regarded an absolute impediment. The situation is of course regarded differently where the state itself seeks help in redefining its ethos and organisation. In the immediate wake of the collapse of the communism in the Soviet Union and Eastern Europe, assistance providers such as the EU, CoE and OSCE were quick to launch comprehensive constitutional reform projects in the new democracies.

Policy makers are also struggling with the dilemma that constitutions (and constitutionalism as a concept) are both backward-looking (legitimising the *status quo*) and forward-looking (constitutive of the process of change). A popular formulae as to how this problem can be resolved in periods of radical change is to conceptualise constitutionalism as a way of facilitating a continuous yet orderly improvement of the organisation of the state and its relationship to the individual.[477] Even where UN state-builders have been explicitly instructed by the Security Council to implement a certain vision of a good state (the most clear-cut example being Resolution 1244 (1999) where the Security Council used its powers under Chapter VII to construct virtually from scratch a new structure of government and justice for Kosovo) there has been self-restraint. The missions have been careful to explain the normative context, follow an established procedure, and not to go further than perceived absolutely necessary.

Whether an international initiative to introduce or reform a legal concept in a developing or post-crisis society deserves to be labelled successful depends on the definition of success. If the donor agencies would confine their ambitions to facilitating the introduction of new laws as positive rules (a quantitative criteria), then many programs would easily qualify as successful. On the other hand, if the desired outcome is a specific result or "impact", in the starkest case conditions identical to those in the donor country (a qualitative criterion), then the number of successful projects would

[477] Teitel 2000 p. 191.

obviously be much lower. The prevailing view among assistance providers on what constitutes success and failure, and thus on how "good" projects need to be, seems to be rather sober and pragmatic: It is recognised that new laws modelled on foreign concepts will almost always develop in ways that do not parallel developments in their original society, and that this needs to be anticipated and accepted as long as the results of their interpretation and invocation are basically positive from a human rights, rule of law or economic effectiveness point of view. There are also other salient features of legal and judicial reform that make the determination of what works and what does not difficult. For example, legal and judicial reforms are often means to other ends (democratisation, poverty reduction, etc.) and the exact casual relationships are difficult to establish. Yet another is that rule of law reform is a long term-process where the effects are slow and gradual, meaning that changes on the ground may be initially imperceptible and difficult to interpret.[478]

The international administrations are often compelled to measure success and failure against the more categorical standards spelled out in the relevant Security Council resolutions and peace treaties, stipulating for example that the "highest possible standards" of human rights and rule of law should prevail. Not surprisingly, many independent evaluations of their success to date have been negative. The circumstance that the end goals have been set with little or no regards for the marginal costs of reaching them, or for their sustainability after "exit", has not been considered particularly extenuating.

Once the law has been reformed, one would have expected assistance providers to proceed with equal enthusiasm to build capacity within the courts, prosecution agencies and other implementing institutions. However, this task has attracted much less attention, perhaps because of a notion that any serious attempt at building capacity would require massive resources, and that to an even greater extent than the drafting of new laws, the conditions for success are determined by a difficult "surround" of historical, political, economic and cultural factors beyond the reach of any assistance provider.[479] The notable exception is training. Inherent in virtually all legal and judicial reform strategies is the idea that the actions therein must comprise efforts to ensure that there is a sufficient number of adequately trained and committed professionals to operate the judicial system. While many initial efforts in this area were *ad hoc* and focused on training key groups in new aspects of substantive law (*i.e.* property or human rights law), donors are now shifting the focus to the establishment of permanent domestic training structures such as judicial training centres able of

[478] Hammergren 2003 p. 297.
[479] Chesterman & Ignatieff & Thakur 2004 p. 2.

continuously adjusting to new training needs, developing general and topical curricula, and facilitating the elaboration of teaching materials.

Some assistance providers continue to provide, or in some cases even require, *ad hoc* training on topical issues that are perceived to be pressing and for which the host country is deemed to lack capacity. In many instances, the "pressing need" is actually to be found within the donor country itself. This is evidenced by the circumstance that many such initiatives have a focus on criminal phenomena with cross-border or international implications, such as money laundering and trafficking in drugs and human beings. The donor rationale is simply that unless the recipient is sensitized to their existence and helped to address them, there will be adverse effects also in the assistance providers own country or region. While the risk of conveying "too much" knowledge is limited, assistance providers need to be aware that many parallel and uncoordinated initiatives targeting the same small elite groups divert attention from important everyday tasks and create much unnecessary confusion and overlap.

Institution and capacity building in post-war settings poses an additional set of problems. The international administrations may for example need to deal with problems of massive and systematic destruction of the physical infrastructure, falsification of records and registries, displaced (or dead) judges and prosecutors, etc. While the UN missions in Kosovo and East Timor were relatively quick in passing legislation that reformed key aspects of the previous judicial organisation, they were less successful in the ensuing task of making the restructured courts and prosecutions agencies actually work. Among the reasons for the slow progress were insufficient resources, uncertainties and conflicting views as to how far their mandates allowed them to go in "micromanaging" local institutions, and not least poor concepts of the essentially "developmental" tasks of reforming institutions and building capacity.

The international administrations in Cambodia, BiH and Kosovo and East Timor have also needed to struggle with the dilemma of combining the seemingly incompatible and mutually undermining tasks of being *"the highest authority in theatre"* and performing line legal functions on the one hand, and promoting local ownership and a truly independent judiciary on the other. This dilemma has been most pronounced where internationally appointed jurists have sat on the bench in local courts and prosecution agencies alongside with local colleagues, as in Kosovo and East Timor. The long-term impact of such constructions is too early to assess, but tentative observations suggest that without a shared commitment to new paradigm of law and justice, the devolvement of responsibility to national counterparts is difficult or even impossible. The envisaged opportunity for knowledge transfer and monitoring similarly tends to be circumscribed by lack of time. The international judges and prosecutors have simply been too busy with the preparation of their own cases to be effective in any such capacity.[480]

The apparent difficulties in reforming courts and other formal institutions in developing and post-crisis states have spurred interest in some circles in the potential role of informal alternatives such as customary courts, mediation bodies, and similar. Although intellectually interesting, there are normative and common-sense reasons to continue to focus on formal norms and agencies, at least as long as resources are scarce and knowledge of the standards by which the alternatives operate is limited. Supporting the unknown is not just a violation of good development practice, but could also work to condone and perpetuate unacceptable practices. Assistance providers need to remember that there are a number of binding or strongly compelling international and regional norms making it necessary for governments and donors to ensure that certain quality standards are met in the administration of justice.[481]

While many donor policy documents confess to the importance of ensuring that the "ordinary man", the business community, members of "vulnerable" or "underprivileged" groups, and other "users" of the system, are aware of their rights under the law and can readily access judicial services, the level of resources committed to this reform topic remains modest. It may be the case that assistance providers think that as long as the groundwork of law and institutions is not perfectly in place, it is too early to commit to these issues in earnest. Assistance providers are also frequently heard arguing that they don't have the organization and tools to effectively engage in the "grass root" aspects of access creation and information dissemination.

The preferred course of action is consequently to trust other actors, essentially international and local human rights-oriented NGOs, to take the lead in this area. As a spin-off, some NGOs have in a short time developed into sophisticated international lobbyists for their respective fields and succeed in raising their own organizational priorities on the international donor agenda. There are signs that the relationship between the NGO community and the assistance community is developing towards an uneasy symbiosis in which each is depending on the other for political and financial survival: Those NGOs who adapt to the donor flavors of the day are flooded in money and praise, while those who guard their agenda more carefully risk being left out in the cold. The main problem with NGO-based strategies is nevertheless sustainability. Opening up the system is a long-term task, and it may be doubted whether NGOs dependent on voluntary and irregular contributions are able of carrying it to an end.

---

480 Caplan 2005 p. 63

481 Kritz 2002 p. 80.

6.4 CO-ORDINATION AND SPECIALISATION

While the preceding chapters have demonstrated that effective approaches to legal and judicial reform should ideally be based on comprehensive strategies developed in participatory processes, the reality is that international and regional organisations, donor agencies and international NGOs often drive different and even conflicting agenda within the same country. Improved mechanisms for the organisations and coordination of international initiatives are therefore of the essence. There is still no established "hierarchy" of international and regional organisations (beyond the regimes provided under Chapters VII and VIII of the UN Charter) or other formal support for having one organisation unilaterally dictating the agenda of others. Reform agenda and projects comprising efforts by more than one organisation must therefore be formulated on a voluntary basis, and conflicts of competence between the participating organizations resolved in a consensual process.[482]

In the area of peace and state-building, voluntary arrangements providing for a division of labour according to the priorities and strengths of respective participating organisations have become increasingly popular in the last decades. In Kosovo and East Timor, there were agreements and eventually Security Council endorsement that the various international and regional organizations should work in the fields in which they had the most experience and expertise, but under the leadership of the Special Representative of the Secretary General. The OSCE was accordingly responsible for media issues, democratisation, elections; CoE for human rights promotion and constitutional issues; EU and WB for economic reconstruction; and the UN agencies for civil administration transitional justice mechanism. In Afghanistan, where the international community stopped short of engaging in governance functions and instead geared itself to consolidating and empowering key national structures, designated "lead nations" are expected to perform a similar role. Italy, the lead nation in the area of justice, is thus expected to develop strategies, mobilise donor interest and provide coordination and oversight for this area of international engagement. Tentative observations suggest that this construction is fraught with a range of political, conceptual and technical problems, notable among them that the degree of progress in a sector is made dependent on the competence, commitment and resources of the respective lead nation.

There is a similar trend towards specialisation along the lines of comparative advantages in development co-operation, but the lead nation concept is neither politically possible nor practically feasible in this context. The primary reason is the

---

482 Ruffert 2001 p. 619.

challenge it would pose to local ownership and "lead", and possibly to state sovereignty. Another reason is problems of oversight and capacity. Experience from pursuing sector reform projects in the Balkans, Vietnam and other places suggests that no single organization is currently capable of effectively managing all aspects of a comprehensive sector reform strategy on its own. In want of an established division of labour or hierarchy between donors, the key means to provide for such specialisation is high-level and multi-party agreements. Sceptics warn that such modalities are still far from perfect. Linn Hammergren writes: "*Despite high-level meetings where cooperation and coordination are promised, with a few notable exceptions, in-country donor cooperation at its best means staying out of one another's way. At its worst, it begins to look like the dark side of political campaigns, high-stakes sport matches, and industrial races for a larger market share. [...] The worst cases are natural outgrowths of the organization's incentive systems, occurring with neither the direct encouragement not the knowledge of higher-ups.*"[483] Effective co-ordination also presupposes the inclusion of initiated local stakeholders in fora where projects are formulated and information exchanged. Without their participation, there will never be good matching of needs and resources, or alignment with local plans and preferences. In principle, the earlier local stakeholders can make a substantial contribution, the more appropriate the designated goals and the more effective the assistance.

Although development dogma are ephemeral and regularly reinterpreted, law and judicial organisation are likely to stay high on the international agenda. Behind this assumption is the observation that "good law" is no longer just a means to other ends, but also accepted as an end in itself.[484] For example, the World Bank now includes criminal law and justice within its programs on grounds that high levels of crime are not just a disincentive to investment but also disproportionately affects the poor, women and other vulnerable groups, and prevent these groups from meaningfully participate in economic, social and political activities conducive to economic growth.[485] The efforts spent on establishing conceptual and practical links between strategic international (UN) instruments such as the Millennium Declaration and An Agenda for Peace reinforce the assumption that the major international organisations and assistance providers will continue to work in this area for a long time to come.

It is encouraging to note that issues of strategy and methodology are attributed increasing attention, and that there is recognition that this area of international engagement entails managing some important dualities and contradictions, for example between promoting a specific vision of "good" or "just" law, and ensuring

---

483 Hammergren 2003 p. 290 and 315-316.

484 Rittich 2004 pp. 4-5.

485 Legal and Judicial Reform: Strategic Directions 2003 pp. 33-34.

the greatest possible degree of local ownership and lead. There is similarly awareness of the need to improve co-ordination between state builders and development agencies with different approaches and timelines, and to ensure that they learn from each other. More troubling is that assistance providers are often locked in historical trajectories as to whom to work with, and remain confused as to how new change agents above, below and besides states should be identified and engaged. Similarly problematic is the failure to manage the disconnection between project cycles and the real timeframes required for institution and capacity building. Too often the time it takes to establish a sustainable rule of law culture is underestimated and local options by-passed because they are perceived to take to long time.

Translated into recommendations for future interventions, these observations suggest that a range of state and non-state institutions should preferably be engaged in the development of a single nationally owned reform plan that pays attention to the standards of politics and justice, the laws that authoritatively articulate them, the institutions that transform the rhetoric to reality, and the conditions for people to access them. The reform plan, in turn, should be based on a thorough and inclusive analysis of national needs and capacities, as well as current and contemplated international initiatives. Such assessments are important also to ensure ownership and to limit any negative side-effects of the contemplated reform strategies, particularly those with adverse impact on already vulnerable and victimized groups.[486]

[486] UNSG Report S/2004/616 p. 11.

7. REFERENCES

7.1 INTERNATIONAL AND UNITED NATIONS DOCUMENTS

7.1.1 STATUTORY DOCUMENTS

Charter of the United Nations, signed at San Francisco on 26 June 1945, entry into force 24 October 1945.

Statute of the International Court of Justice, based on the Statute of the Permanent Court of International Justice and adopted together with the UN Charter 1945.

Rome Statute of the International Criminal Court, adopted by the United Nations Diplomatic Conference of Plenipotentiaries on 17 July 1998, entry into force 1 July 2002.

7.1.2 CONVENTIONS

Convention (IV) respecting the Laws and Customs of War on Land and its annex: Regulations concerning the Laws and Customs of War on Land, Hague, 18 October 1907, entry into force 26 January 1910.

Convention (IV) Relative to the Protection of Civilian Persons in Time of War, Geneva, adopted 12 August 1949, entry into force 21 October 1950.

Convention on Recognition and Enforcement of International Arbitration Awards, New York, 10 June 1958, entry into force 7 June 1959.

International Covenant on Civil and Political Rights, adopted and opened for signature, ratification and accession by General Assembly resolution 2200A (XXI) of 16 december 1966, entry into force 23 March 1976.

International Covenant on Economic, Social and Cultural Rights, adopted and opened for signature, ratification and accession by General Assembly resolution 2200A (XXI) of 16 december 1966, entry into force 3 January 1976.

Vienna Convention on the Law of Treaties, signed at Vienna 23 May 1969, entry into force 27 January 1980.

Convention against Torture and Other Cruel, Inhuman or Degrading Treatment or Punishment, adopted and opened for signature, ratification and accession by General Assembly resolution 39/46 of 10 December 1984, entry into force 26 June 1987.

United Nations Convention against Corruption, adopted by the General Assembly by resolution 58/4 of 31 October 2003.

7.1.3 DECLARATIONS

Universal Declaration of Human Rights, adopted and proclaimed by General Assembly resolution 217 A (III) of 10 December 1948.

Declaration on the Right to Development, adopted by General Assembly resolution 41/128 of 4 December 1986.

United Nations Millennium Declaration, adopted by General Assembly resolution 55/2 of 8 September 2000.

7.1.4 RESOLUTIONS

Security Council Resolution 688 (1991) *on the situation in Iraq.*

Security Council Resolution 745 (1992) *on the situation in Cambodia.*

Security Council Resolution 770 (1992) *on the situation in Bosnia and Herzegovina.*

Security Council Resolution 814 (1993) *on the situation in Somalia.*

Security Council Resolution 827 (1993) *on the International Criminal Tribunal for the Former Yugoslavia (ICTY).*

Security Council Resolution 940 (1994) *on authorization to form a multinational force under unified command and control to restore the legitimately elected President and authorities of the Government of Haiti and extension of the mandate of the UN Mission in Haiti.*

Security Council Resolution 955 (1994) *on establishment of an International Tribunal and adoption of the Statute of the Tribunal.*

Security Council Resolution 1031 (1995) *on implementation of the Peace Agreement for Bosnia and Herzegovina and transfer of authority from the UN Protection Force to the multinational Implementation Force (IFOR).*

Security Council Resolution 1037 (1996) *on the situation in Croatia.*

Security Council Resolution 1076 (1996) *on the situation in Afghanistan.*

Security Council Resolution 1088 (1996) *on the situation in Bosnia and Herzegovina.*

Security Council Resolution 1103 (1997) *on the situation in Bosnia and Herzegovina.*

Security Council Resolution 1144 (1997) *on the situation in Bosnia and Herzegovina.*

Security Council Resolution 1160 (1998) *on the imposition of an arms embargo against Yugoslavia.*

Security Council Resolution 1184 (1998) *on the situation in Bosnia and Herzegovina.*

Security Council Resolution 1193 (1998) *on the situation in Afghanistan.*

Security Council Resolution 1199 (1998) *on the situation in Kosovo (FRY).*

Security Council Resolution 1214 (1998) *on the situation in Afghanistan.*

Security Council Resolution 1244 (1999) *on the situation relating Kosovo.*

Security Council Resolution 1246 (1999) *on the situation in Timor.*

Security Council Resolution 1256 (1999) *on the situation in Bosnia and Herzegovina.*

Security Council Resolution 1267 (1999) *on the situation in Afghanistan.*

Security Council Resolution 1272 (1999) *on the situation in East Timor.*

Security Council Resolution 1289 (2000) *on the situation in Sierra Leone.*

Security Council Resolution 1383 (2001) *on the situation in Afghanistan.*

Security Council Resolution 1386 (2001) *on the situation in Afghanistan.*

Security Council Resolution 1401 (2002) *on the situation in Afghanistan.*

Security Council Resolution 1410 (2002) *on the situation in East Timor.*

Security Council Resolution 1509 (2003) *on the situation in Liberia.*

7.1.5 CODES

United Nations Code of Conduct for Law Enforcement Officials, adopted by the General Assembly resolution 34/169 of 17 December 1979.

7.1.6 BASIC PRINCIPLES

United Nations Basic Principles on the Independence of the Judiciary, adopted by the Seventh United Nations Congress on the Prevention of Crime and the Treatment of Offenders held at Milan from 26 August to 6 September 1985 and endorsed by General Assembly resolutions 40/32 of 29 November 1985 and 40/146 of 13 December 1985.

United Nations Basic Principles on the Role of Lawyers, adopted by the Eighth United Nations Congress on the Prevention of Crime and the Treatment of Offenders, Havana, Cuba, 27 August to 7 September 1990.

7.1.7 GUIDELINES

United Nations Guidelines on the Role of Prosecutors, adopted by the Eighth United Nations Congress on the Prevention of Crime and the Treatment of Offenders, Havana, Cuba, 27 August to 7 September 1990.

7.2 REGIONAL DOCUMENTS

7.2.1 CONVENTIONS

European Convention for the Protection of Human Rights and Fundamental Freedoms, signed at Rome 4 November 1950.

Convention for Prevention of Torture and Inhuman or Degrading Treatment, Strasbourg, 26.XI.1987, entry into force 1 February 1989.

7.2.2 RECOMMENDATIONS

Council of Europe Committee of Ministers Recommendation No R (1981) 7 on measures facilitating access to justice.

Council of Europe Committee of Ministers Recommendation No R (1984) 5 on the principle of civil procedure designed to improve the functioning of justice.

Council of Europe Committee of Ministers Recommendation No R (1986) 12 concerning measures to prevent and reduce the excessive workload in the courts.

Council of Europe Committee of Ministers Recommendation No R (1987) 18 concerning the simplification of criminal justice.

Council of Europe Committee of Ministers Recommendation No R (1993) 1 on effective access to the law and to justice for the very poor.

Council of Europe Committee of Ministers Recommendation No R (1994) 12 to member states on the independence, efficiency and role of judges.

Council of Europe Committee of Ministers Recommendation No R (1995) 5 concerning the introduction and improvement of the functioning of appeal systems and procedures in civil and commercial cases.

Council of Europe Committee of Ministers Recommendation No R (1995) 12 on the management of criminal justice.

Council of Europe Committee of Ministers Recommendation No R (2000) 19 on the role of public prosecution in the criminal justice system.

Council of Europe Committee of Ministers Recommendation No R (2000) 21 on the freedom of exercise of the profession of lawyer.

Council of Europe Committee of Ministers Recommendation No R (2001) 2 concerning the design and re-design of court systems and legal information systems in a cost-effective manner.

Council of Europe Committee of Ministers Recommendation No R (2001) 3 on the delivery of court and other legal services to the citizen through the use of new technologies.

Council of Europe Committee of Ministers Recommendation No R (2001) 9 on alternatives to litigation between administrative authorities and private parties.

Council of Europe Committee of Ministers Recommendation No R (2003) 14 on the interoperability of information systems in the justice sector.

Council of Europe Committee of Ministers Recommendation No R (2003) 16 on the execution of administrative and judicial decisions in the field of administrative law.

Council of Europe Committee of Ministers Recommendation No R (2003) 17 on enforcement.

7.2.3 RESOLUTIONS

Resolution (76) 5, on Legal Aid in Civil, Commercial and Administrative Matters, adopted by the Council of Europe Committee of Ministers on 18 February 1976.

Resolution (78) 8, on Legal Aid and Advice, adopted by the Council of Europe Committee of Ministers on 2 March 1978.

7.2.4 GUIDELINES

Latimer House Guidelines for the Commonwealth on good practice governing relations between the Executive, Parliament and the Judiciary in the promotion of good governance, the rule of law and human rights to ensure the effective implementation of the Harare Principles, adopted 19 June 1998 by a Joint Colloquium held at Latimer House, the United Kingdom, 15-19 June 1998.

7.3 PEACE AGREEMENTS

Paris Agreement on a Comprehensive Political Settlement on the Cambodia Conflict of 1991, concluded in Paris on 23 October, 1991.

General Framework Agreement for Peace in Bosnia and Herzegovina, initialled in Dayton on 21 November 1995 and signed in Paris on 14 December 1995.

Interim Agreement for Peace and Self-Government in Kosovo, concluded in Rambouillet, France on 23 February 23, 1999.

Bonn Agreement on Provisional Arrangements in Afghanistan Pending the Re-establishment of Permanent Government Institutions, concluded on 5 December 2001.

7.4 NATIONAL CASES

Bosnia and Herzegovina Constitutional Court Decision No. U9/00 of 3 November 2000 on the Law on State Border Service.

7.5 PROFESSIONAL CODES OF ETHICS, ETC.

International Bar Association International Code of Ethics, first adopted 1956.

7.6 LITERATURE AND ANALYTICAL REPORTS

Adelman, J. & Centeno, M. A. (2002) "Between Liberalism and Neoliberalism: Law's Dilemma in Latin America", in: *Global Prescriptions: The Production, Exportation, and Importation of a New Legal Orthodoxy* (eds. Dezalay & Garth), Ann Arbor: University of Michigan Press.

Ajanant, J. (1996/1998) "The WTO and Developing Asian Economies: Emerging Issues and Challenges", in: *WTO & Asia-Pacific – The Asia-Pacific Region and the Expanding Borders of the WTO: Implications, Challenges and Opportunities* (ed. Buchanan), Victoria, Canada: UVic Centre for Asia-Pacific Initiatives.

Anger, J. (2004) "*Anti-corruption Strategies in Development Cooperation*", Sida Method Working Paper No. 3.

Assegaf, I. (2002) "Legends of the Fall: An Institutional Analysis of Indonesian Law Enforcement Agencies Combating Corruption", in: *Corruption in Asia: Rethinking the Governance Paradigm* (eds. Lindsey & Dick), Sydney: Federation Press.

"*Assistance to Justice and the Rule of Law in Afghanistan: A Strategic Analysis*" (2004), Centre for Humanitarian Dialogue, Hd Report 2004:4.

Bassiouni, M. C. (2002) "Introduction", in: *Post-Conflict Justice* (ed. Bassiouni), New York: Transnational Publishers.

Bergling, P. *et. al.* (1998) "*An Introduction to the Vietnamese Legal System*", Umeå: Department of Law, Umeå University.

Bergling, P. (1999) "*Legal Reform and Private Enterprise: The Vietnamese Experience*", Umeå Studies in Law, No. 1, Umeå: Department of Law, Umeå University.

Blair, H. & Hansen, G. (1994) "*Weighing in on the Scales of Justice: Strategic Approaches for Donor-Supported Rule of Law Programs*", USAID Program and Operations Assessment Report No. 7.

Bogdan, M. (1993) "*Komparativ rättskunskap*", Stockholm: Norstedts Juridik.

Bogdan, M. (1997) "Common law versus civil law in international development aid", in: *Festskrift til Ole Lando (Papers dedicated to Ole Lando)*, Copenhagen: GadJura.

Bourque, L. B. & Fielder E. P. (1995) "*How to Conduct Self-administered and Mail Surveys*", Thousand Oaks: Sage Publications.

Brahm, L. (1990) "Looking South: China hands see promise in Vietnam", *The China Business Review*, Vol. 17, No. 3, pp. 40-42.

Braithwaite, J. (1998) "Institutionalizing Distrust, Enculturating Trust" in: *Trust and Governance* (eds. Braithwite & Levi), New York: Sage Publications.

Brand, M. (2001) "Institution-Building and Human Rights Protection in Kosovo in the Light of UNMIK Legislation", *Nordic Journal of International Law*, Vol. 70, No. 4, pp. 461-488.

Brietzke, P. (2002) "Administrative Reforms in Indonesia", in: *Corruption in Asia: Rethinking the Governance Paradigm* (eds. Lindsey & Dick), Sydney: Federation Press.

Bring, O. (1997/1998) "The Legal Dimension of Multinational Peace Operations", *Juridisk Tidskrift*, Vol. 9, No. 4, pp. 944-951.

Brunetti, A. & Kisunko, G. & Weder, B. (1997a) "*Institutional Obstacles to Doing Business: Region-by-Region Results from a Worldwide Survey of the Private Sector*", Policy Research Working Paper 1759, Washington, D.C.: The World Bank.

Brunetti, A. & Kisunko, G. & Weder, B. (1997b) "*Credibility of Rules and Economic Growth: Evidence from a Worldwide Survey of the Private Sector*", Policy Research Working Paper 1760, Washington, D.C.: The World Bank.

Brunetti, A. & Kisunko, G. & Weder, B. (1997c) "*Institutions in Transition: Reliability of Rules and Economic Performance in Former Socialist Countries*", World Bank Policy Research Working Paper 1809.

Bulmer, M. (1983a) "General Introduction", in: *Social Research in Developing Countries: Surveys and Censuses in the Third World*, (eds. Bulmer & Warwick), Chichester: John Wiley & Sons Ltd.

Bulmer, M. (1983b) "Sampling", in: *Social Research in Developing Countries: Surveys and Censuses in the Third World*, (eds. Bulmer & Warwick), Chichester: John Wiley & Sons Ltd.

Bulmer, M. (1983c) "Interviewing and Field Organization", in: *Social Research in Developing Countries: Surveys and Censuses in the Third World*, (eds. Bulmer & Warwick), Chichester: John Wiley & Sons Ltd.

Bulmer, M. & Warwick, D. P. (1983) "Data Collection", in: *Social Research in Developing Countries: Surveys and Censuses in the Third World*, (eds. Bulmer & Warwick), Chichester: John Wiley & Sons Ltd.

Buscaglia, E. & Dakolias, M. (1999) "*An Analysis of the Causes of Corruption in the Judiciary*", Washington, D.C.: World Bank, Legal Department, Legal and Judicial Reform Unit Report.

Caplan, R. (2005) "*International Governance of War-Torn Territories: Rule and Reconstruction*", Oxford: Oxford University Press.

Carothers, T. (1998) "The Rule of Law Revival", *Foreign Affairs*, Vol. 77, No. 2, pp. 96-106.

Carty, A. (1992) "Introduction", in: *Law and Development*, (ed. Carty), Aldershot: Dartmouth.

Chanda, N. (1986) "*Brother Enemy: The War After the War*", New York: Coliver Books.

Chesterman, S. (2002) "*Justice Under International Administration: Kosovo, East Timor and Afghanistan*", New York: International Peace Academy Project on Transitional Administrations Reports.

Chesterman, S. (2003) "*You, the People: The United Nations, Transitional Administration, and State-Building*", New York: International Peace Academy Project on Transitional Administrations Reports.

Chesterman, S. & Ignatieff, M. & Thakur. R. (2004) "*Making States Work: From State Failure to State-Building*", New York: International Peace Academy/United Nations University Reports.

Chopra, J. (2000) "The UN's Kingdom of East Timor", *Survival*, Vol. 42, No. 3, pp. 27-39.

Clarke, D. (1999) "The Many Meanings of the Rule of Law", in: *Law, Capitalism and Power in Asia: The Rule of Law and Legal Institutions* (ed. Jayasuriya), London: Routledge.

Clarke, D. C. (1995) "The Execution of Civil Judgements in China", *The China Quarterly*, No. 141, pp. 65-81.

Clarke, D. C. (1996) "Methodologies for Research in Chinese Law", *U. B. C. Law Review*, Vol. 30, No. 1, pp. 201-209.

Clarke, D. C. (2004) "Empirical Research into the Chinese Legal System", in: *Beyond Common Knowledge: Empirical Approaches to the Rule of Law* (eds. Jensen & Heller), Stanford: Stanford University Press.

Cohen, J. A. (1990) "China's Influence on Vietnam's Foreign Business Laws", *The China Business Review*, Vol. 17, No. 3, pp. 43-45.

Coliver, S. (2000) "The Contribution of the International Criminal Tribunal for the Former Yugoslavia to Reconciliation in Bosnia and Herzegovina", in: *International Crimes, peace, and Human Rights: The Role of the International Criminal Court* (ed. Shelton), New York: Transnational Publishers.

"*Comprehensive Justice System Reform Program, Baseline Study Report*" (2005), Addis Ababa/Leiden: Ministry of Capacity Building, Justice System Reform Office/Center for International Legal Cooperation.

Corell, H. (2004) "FN, folkrätten och framtiden", *Svensk Juristtidning*, No. 4, pp. 333-350.

Corne, P. H. (1997) "*Foreign Investment in China: The Administrative Legal System*", Hong Kong: Hong Kong University Press.

Costea, P. (1990) "The Legal System and the Judiciary in the Marxist-Leninist Regimes of the Third World", *Review of Socialist Law*, Vol. 16, No. 3, pp. 225-277.

Cotterrell, R. (2001) "Is There a Logic of Legal Transplants?", in: *Adapting Legal Cultures* (eds. Nelken & Feest), Oxford and Portland: Hart Publishing.

"*Countries at the Crossroads: A Survey of Democratic Governance*" (2005), Lanham, MD.: Freedom House/Rowman & Littlefield Publishing.

Dakolias, M. & Thachuk, K. (2000) "Attacking Corruption in the Judiciary: A Critical Process in Judicial Reform", *Wisconsin International Law Journal*, Vol. 18, No. 2, pp. 353-402.

Dalberg-Larsen, J. (1984) "*Retsstaten Velfaerdsstaten og hvad så? Sammenhaenge mellem retsudvikling og samfundsudvikling set i et retssociologisk perspektiv*", Copenhagen: Akademisk Forlag.

David, R. & Brierley, J. E. C. (1985) "*Major Legal Systems in the World Today: An Introduction to the Comparative Study of Law*", London: Stevens & Sons.

de Soto, H. (1993) "The Missing Ingredient: What Poor Countries Will Need to Make Their Markets Work", *The Economist*, 11 Sept. 1993 pp. 10-12.

de Soto, H. (1989) "*The Other Path: The Invisible Revolution in the Third World*", New York: Harper & Row Publishers.

Deakin, S. & Lane, C. & Wilkinson, F. (1994) "'Trust' or Law? Towards an Integrated Theory of Contractual Relations Between Firms", *Journal of Law and Society*, Vol. 21, No. 3, pp. 329-349.

Dezalay, Y. & Garth, B. G. (1996) "*Dealing in Virtue: International Commercial Arbitration and the Construction of a Transnational Legal Order*", Chicago and London: University of Chicago Press.

Dezalay, Y. & Garth, B. G. (2001) "The Import and Export of Law and Legal Institutions: International Strategies in National Palace Wars" in: *Adapting Legal Cultures* (eds. Nelken & Feest), Oxford and Portland: Hart Publishing.

Dezalay, Y. & Garth, B. G. (2002a) "*The Internationalization of Palace Wars: Lawyers, Economists, and the Contest to Transform Latin American States*" Chicago: University of Chicago Press.

Dezalay, Y. & Garth, B. G. (2002b) "Legitimating the New Legal Orthodoxy" in: *Global Prescriptions: The Production, Exportation, and Importation of a New Legal Orthodoxy* (eds. Dezalay & Garth), Ann Arbor: University of Michigan Press.

Dicks, A. R. (1995) "Compartmentalized Law and Judicial Restraint: An Inductive View of Some Jurisdictional Barriers to Reform", *The China Quarterly*, No. 141, pp. 82-109.

Dietrich, M. K. (2000) "*Legal and Judicial Reform in Central Europe and the Former Soviet Union – Voices from Five Countries*", Washington D.C.: The World Bank, Legal Vice Presidency.

Doan Trong Truyen (1994) "Administrative Reform, Key Issues for the Reform of the State Apparatus", *Vietnam Law & Legal Forum*, Vol. 1, No. 2, pp. 30-31.

Doan Trong Truyen (1996) "Public Administration Reform in Vietnam", *Vietnam Law & Legal Forum*, Vol. 3, No. 28, pp. 3-7.

Donovan, D. (1993) "Cambodia: Building a Legal System from Scratch", *The International Lawyer*, Vol. 27, pp. 445-454.

Eggertsson, T. (1996) "A note on the economics of institutions", in: *Empirical Studies in Institutional Change*, (eds. Alston & Eggertsson & North), Cambridge, Mass.: Cambridge University Press.

Ehrenreich, R. (2003) "The New Imperialism: Violence, Norms and the "Rule of Law", *Michigan Law Review*, Vol. 101, No. 7, pp. 2275-2340.

Epstein, E. J. (1994) "Law and Legitimation in Post-Mao China", in: *Domestic Law Reforms in Post-Mao China*, (ed. Potter), New York: M. E. Sharpe.

Falk, P. (1997) "Legal Training: the Case of Vietnam – Some Reflections Concerning the Past, Present and Future", in: *Legal Assistance to Developing Countries: Swedish Perspectives on the Rule of Law*, (ed. Sevastik), Stockholm: Norstedts/Kluwer Law International.

Fforde, A. & de Vylder, S. (1996) "*From Plan to Market: the Economic Transition in Vietnam*", Boulder and Oxford: Westview Press.

"*Finding the Balance: The Scales of Justice in Kosovo*" (2002), International Crisis Group (ICG) Balkans Report No. 134.

Fogelklou, A. (1997a) "Ryssland", in: *På väg mot rättsstater i östeuropa*, (ed. Sterzel), 32 Rättsfondens skriftserie, Uppsala: Iustus Förlag.

Fogelklou, A. (1997b) "Principles of Rule of Law and Legal Development", in: *Legal Assistance to Developing Countries: Swedish Perspectives on the Rule of Law*, (ed. Sevastik), Stockholm: Norstedts/Kluwer Law International.

Fogelklou, A. (2000) "Legal Transition and Legal Thinking in Eastern and Central Europe", in: *Festskrift till Åke Frändberg*, Uppsala: Iustus Förlag.

Footer, M. E. (2003) "Technical Assistance and Trade Law Reform Post-Doha: Brave New World", in: *Law and Development: Facing Complexity in the 21st Century – Essays in Honour of Peter Slinn* (eds. Hatchard & Perry Kessaris), London and Portland: Cavendish Publishing.

Franck, T. M. (1972) "The New Development: Can American Law and Legal Institutions Help Developing Countries?", *Wisconsin Law Review*, Vol. 1972, No. 3, pp. 767-801.

Fraenkel, E. (1941) "*The Dual State: A Contribution to the Theory of Dictatorship*". London: Oxford University Press.

"*From Plan to Market: World Development Report 1996*", New York: The World Bank/Oxford University Press.

Fukuyama, F. (1992) "*The End of History and the Last Man*", New York: The Free Press/Avon Books.

Fukuyama, F. (2004) "*State Building, Governance and World Order in the Twenty-First Century*", London: Profile Books

Gelb, A. (1993) "Socialist Transformations: Some Lessons and Implications for Assistance", in: *Redefining the Role of the State and the Market in the Development Process*, Stockholm: Sida.

Ghai, Y. (1994) "*Human Rights and Governance: The Asia Debate*", The Asia Foundation Center for Asian Affairs, Occasional Paper No. 1.

Gillespie, J. (1995) "Recent Developments in the Commercial Legal System", in: *Dilemmas of Development: Vietnam Update 1994*, Political and Social Change Monograph 22, (ed. Tria Kerkvliet), Canberra: Australian National University.

Gillespie, J. (1996) "Bureaucratic Control of Business Regulation in Vietnam", in: *Asia Laws through Australian Eyes*, (ed. Taylor), Sydney: Law Book Company.

Gillespie, J. (1999) "Law and Development in 'The Market Place': An East Asian Perspective", in: *Law, Capitalism and Power in East Asia: The rule of law and legal institutions*, (ed. Jayasuriya), London and New York: Routledge.

Gillespie, J. (2002) "The Political-Legal Culture of Anti-Corruption in Vietnam" in: *Corruption in Asia: Rethinking the Governance Paradigm* (eds. Lindsey & Dick), Sydney: Federation Press.

Gillespie, J. (2004) "Concepts of Law in Vietnam: Transforming Statist Socialism", in: *Asian Discourses of Rule of Law: Theories and Implementation of Rule of Law in Twelve Asian Countries, France and the U.S.* (ed. Peerenboom), London and New York: Routledge.

Goodpaster, G. (2002) "Reflections on Corruption in Indonesia", in: *Corruption in Asia: Rethinking the Governance Paradigm* (eds. Lindsey & Dick), Sydney: Federation Press.

Gray, C. S. (1991) "*Reform of the Legal, Regulatory, and Judicial Environment: What Importance for Development Strategy?*", Harvard Institute for International Development Discussion Paper No. 403.

Gray, C. W. (1991) "Legal Process and Economic Development: A Case Study of Indonesia", *World Development*, Vol. 19, No. 7, pp. 763-777.

Gray, C. W. (1993) "*Evolving Legal Framework for Private Sector Development in Central and Eastern Europe*", World Bank Discussion Papers No. 209.

Gray, C. W. (1997) "Reforming Legal Systems in Developing and Transition Countries", *Finance & Development*, Vol. 34, No. 3, pp. 14-16.

Greenberg, D. F. (1980) "Law and Development in Light of Dependency Theory", *Research in Law and Sociology*, Vol. 3, pp. 129-159.

Hammergren, L. (2003) "International Assistance to Latin American Justice Programs: Toward an Agenda for Reforming the Reformers", in: *Beyond Common Knowledge: Empirical Approaches to the Rule of Law* (eds. Jensen & Heller), Stanford: Stanford University Press.

Harding, A. (2001) "Comparative Law and Legal Transplantation in South East Asia: Making Sense of the "Nomic Din", in: *Adapting Legal Cultures* (eds. Nelken & Feest), Oxford and Portland: Hart Publishing.

Hartmann. M. E. (2003) "*International Judges and Prosecutors in Kosovo*", United States Institute for Peace (USIP) Special Report 112.

Heger Boyle, E. & Meyer J. W. (2002) "Modern Law as a Secularized and Global Model: Implications for the Sociology of Law, in: *Global Prescriptions: The Production, Exportation, and Importation of a New Legal Orthodoxy* (eds. Dezalay & Garth), Ann Arbor: University of Michigan Press.

Heydebrand, W. (2001) "From Globalisation of Law to Law under Globalisation" in: *Adapting Legal Cultures* (eds. Nelken & Feest), Oxford and Portland: Hart Publishing.

Hoang The Lien, (1996) "Subject System in Vietnam's Civil Code", *Vietnam Law & Legal Forum*, Vol. 2, No. 18, pp. 22-25.

Holmes, L. (2002) "Functions and Dysfunctions of Corruption and its Reporting in Central and Eastern Europe", in: *Corruption in Asia: Rethinking the Governance Paradigm* (eds. Lindsey and Dick), Sydney: Federation Press.

Hurwitz, A. & Studdard, K. (2005) "*Rule of Law Programs in Peace Operations*", International Peace Academy, Security-Development Nexus Program Report.

"*In Larger Freedom: Towards Development, Security and Human Rights for All*", UN Secretary General Report A/59/2005.

Jayasuriya, K. (1999) "The Rule of Law and Governance in the East Asian State", *Australian Journal of Asian Law*, Vol. 1, No. 2, pp. 107-123.

Jayasuriya, K. (2002) "Governance, Post-Washington Consensus and the New Anti-Politics", in: *Corruption in Asia: Rethinking the Governance Paradigm* (eds. Lindsey & Dick), Sydney: Federation Press.

Jeong, J. (1997) "The Rise of State Corporatism in Vietnam", *Contemporary Southeast Asia*, Vol. 19, No. 2, pp. 152-171.

Johnsson, E. (1997) "Ungern", in: *På väg mot rättsstater i östeuropa*, (ed. Sterzel), 32 Rättsfondens skriftserie, Uppsala: Iustus Förlag AB.

Jones, E. L. (1983) "The Courtesy Bias in South-East Asian Surveys", in: *Social Research in Developing Countries: Surveys and Censuses in the Third World*, (eds. Bulmer & Warwick), Chichester: John Wiley & Sons Ltd.

"*Justice for All: A Comprehensive Needs Analysis for Justice in Afghanistan*" (2005) Government of the Islamic Republic of Afghanistan, Ministry of Justice, and the Justice Sector Consultative Group.

Karlström, B. (2003) "*Korruptionens anatomi: Orsaker, konsekvenser och botemedel*", Sida Method Working Paper No. 1.

Kennedy, D. (1999) "The International Anti-Corruption Campaign", Connecticut Journal of International Law, Vol. 14, pp. 455-465.

Kennedy, D. (2003) "Laws and Developments", in: *Law and Development: Facing Complexity in the 21st Century – Essays in Honour of Peter Slinn* (eds. Hatchard & Perry-Kessaris), London and Portland: Cavendish Publishing.

Kjaer, A. M. (2004) "*Governance*", Cambridge, U.K. and Malden, Mass.: Polity Press.

Klug, H. (2002) "Hybrid(ity) Rules: Creating Local Law in a Globalized World", in: *Global Prescriptions: The Production, Exportation, and Importation of a New Legal Orthodoxy* (eds. Dezalay & Garth), Ann Arbor: University of Michigan Press.

Kritz, N. J. (2002) "Progress and Humility: The Ongoing Search for Post-Conflict Justice", in: *Post-Conflict Justice* (ed. Bassiouni), New York: Transnational Publishers.

Larsson, K-A. (1994) "*Structural Adjustment, Aid & Development*", Stockholm: Sida.

Lateef, S. (1992) *Governance and Development*, Washington D.C.: The World Bank.

Le Minh Thong (1997) "Perfecting legislation in service of industrialization and modernization of the country", *Vietnam Law & Legal Forum*, Vol. 3, No. 30, pp. 18-23.

Le Thu Son (1996) "Vietnam one year after its integration into ASEAN – A view from the legal aspect" *Vietnam Law & Legal Forum*, Vol. 3, No. 27, pp. 24-26.

"*Legal and Judicial Reform: Strategic Directions*" (2003) World Bank Legal Vice Presidency Report.

Levy, E. (1950) "The Reception of Highly Developed Legal Systems by Peoples of Different Cultures", *Washington Law Review*, Vol. 25, pp. 233-245.

Libecap, G. D. (1996) "Economic variables and the development of the law: the case of western mineral rights", in: *Empirical Studies in Institutional Change*, (eds. Alston, Eggertsson & North), Cambridge, Mass.: Cambridge University Press.

Lindsey, T. (2002) "History Always Repeats? Corruption, Culture and 'Asian Values'" in: *Corruption in Asia: Rethinking the Governance Paradigm* (eds. Lindsey & Dick), Sydney: Federation Press.

Linton, S. (2001) "Rising From the Ashes: The Creation of a Viable Criminal Justice System in East Timor", *Melbourne University Law Review*, Vol. 25, pp. 122-180.

Ljunggren, B. (1993a) "Market Economies under Communist Regimes: Reform in Vietnam, Laos and Cambodia", in: *The Challenge of Reform in Indochina*, (ed. Ljunggren), Cambridge, Mass.: Harvard University Press.

Ljunggren, B. (1993b), "Toward a Deeper Understanding of the Role of the State and the Market", in: *Redefining the Role of the State and the Market in the Development Process*, Stockholm: Sida.

Mani, R (2002) "*Beyond Retribution: Seeking Justice in the Shadows of War*", Cambridge: Polity Press.

Marenin, O. (2005) "*Restoring Police Systems in Conflict Torn Nations: Process, Problems, Prospects*", DCAF Occasional Paper No. 7, Geneva Centre for the Democratic Control of Armed Forces.

Marr, D. G. (1981) "*Vietnamese Tradition on Trial, 1920-1945*", Berkeley and Los Angeles: University of California Press.

Mattei, U. (1997) "Three Patterns of Law: Taxonomy and Change in the World's Legal Systems", *American Journal of Comparative Law*, Vol. 45, pp. 5-44.

McGivern, B. P. (1996) "The WTO and Developing Asian Economies: Special Provisions for Dispute Resolution and Emerging Paradigms Within APEC", in: *WTO & ASIA-PACIFIC – The Asia-Pacific Region and the Expanding Borders of the WTO: Implications, Challenges and Opportunities* (ed. Buchanan), Victoria, Canada: UVic Centre for Asia-Pacific Initiatives.

McInerney, T. F. (2004) "Law and Development as Democratic Practice", *Voices of Development Jurists*, Vol. 1, No. 1.

Mikkelsen, B. (1995) "*Methods for Development Work and Research: A Guide for Practitioners*" New Delhi/Thousand Oaks/London: Sage Publications.

Mitchell, R. E. (1993) "Survey Materials Collected in the Developing Countries: Sampling, Measures, and Interviewing Obstacles to Intranational and International Comparisions", in: *Social Research in Developing Countries: Surveys and Censuses in the Third World*, (eds. Bulmer & Warwick), Chichester: John Wiley & Sons Ltd.

Nalin, C. E. (1994) "Bistånd, institutioner och ekonomisk politik", *Ekonomisk Debatt*, Vol. 22, No. 7, pp. 671-679.

Neilson, K. E. (1996) "*They Killed all the Lawyers: Rebuilding the Judicial System in Cambodia*", UVic Centre for Asia-Pacific Initiatives Occasional Papers, No. 13.

Neilson, W. A. W. (1993) "Regulation: An Introduction to Legal Sources, Administrative Models and Compliance Design", in: *Law and Economic Development: Cases and Materials from Southeast Asia*, (eds. Quah & Neilson), Singapore: Longman Singapore Publishers.

Neilson, W. A. W. (1998) "Vietnam's Economic Law Transformation within the ASEAN Community", in: Asia-Pacific Legal Development, (eds. Johnston & Ferguson), Vancouver: UBC Press.

Neilson, W. A. W. (1999) "The Rush to Law: The IMF Legal Conditionalities Meet Indonesia's Legal Culture Realities", in: *Indonesia after Soeharto: Reformasi and Reaction* (eds. Duncan & Lindsey), International Colloquium Proceedings.

Nelken, D. (2001) "Towards a Sociology of Legal Adaptation", in: *Adapting Legal Cultures* (eds. Nelken & Feest), Oxford and Portland: Hart Publishing.

Ngo Ba Thanh (1993) "The 1992 Constitution and the Rule of Law", in: *Vietnam and the Rule of Law*, (eds. Thayer & Marr), Political and Social Change Monograph 19, Canberra: Australian National University.

Ngo Ba Thanh (1994) "Vietnam's integration into a new humanist international legal order", *Vietnam Law & Legal Forum*, Vol. 1, No. 1, pp. 26-31.

Nguyen Dinh Loc (1996) "On the Settlement of Economic Disputes in Vietnam", *Vietnam Law & Legal Forum*, Vol. 2, No. 18, pp. 18-21.

Nguyen Duy Gia (1997) "Training and Developing the State Administrative Personnel", *Vietnam Law & Legal Forum*, Vol. 3, No. 36, pp. 18-22.

Nguyen Van Tam (1994) "On building an administrative jurisdiction system in Vietnam", *Vietnam Law & Legal Forum*, Vol. 1, No. 4, pp. 34-35.

Nicholson, P. (1999) "Vietnamese Legal Institutions in Comparative Perspective: Contemporary constitutions and courts considered", in: *Law, Capitalism and Power in East Asia: The Rule of Law and Legal Institutions,* (ed. Jayasuriya), London and New York: Routledge.

North, D. C. (1990) "*Institutions, Institutional Change and Economic Performance*", Cambridge and New York: Cambridge University Press.

North, D. C. (1981) "*Structure and Change in Economic History*", New York: W. W. Norton & Company.

Orth, J. V. (1998) "Exporting the Rule of Law", *North Carolina Journal of International Law and Commercial Regulation*, Vol. 24, pp. 71-82.

Österdahl, I. (1997) "By All Means, Intervene! The Security Council and the Use of Force under Chapter VII of the UN Charter in Iraq (to protect the Kurds), in Bosnia, Somalia, Rwanda and Haiti", *Nordic Journal of International Law*, Vol. 66, No. 2-3, pp. 241-271.

Österdahl, I. (2002) "FN-sanktioner och mänskliga rättigheter *eller* Hur kunde det bli på detta viset?", *Svensk Juristtidning*, Vol. 87, No. 10, pp. 894-916.

Peil, M. (1983) "Situational Variables", in: *Social Research in Developing Countries: Surveys and Censuses in the Third World*, (eds. Bulmer & Warwick), Chichester: John Wiley & Sons Ltd.

Peerenboom, R. (2004) "Varieties of Rule of Law: An Introduction and Provisional Conclusions", in: *Asian Discourses of Rule of Law: Theories and Implementation of Rule of Law in Twelve Asian Countries, France and the U.S.* (ed. Peerenboom), London and New York: Routledge.

Pham Hung (1995) "50 years of the People's Court", *Vietnam Law & Legal Forum*, Vol. 2, No. 13, pp. 19-21.

Pistor, K. & Wellons, P. A. (1998) "*The Role of Law and Legal Institutions in Asian Economic Development 1960–1995*", Final Comparative Report Prepared for the Asian Development Bank.

Porter, G. (1993) "*Vietnam: The Politics of Bureaucratic Socialism*", Ithaca and London: Cornell University Press.

Potter, P. B. (1996) "Cultural Aspects of Trade Dispute Resolution in China", in: *WTO & ASIA-PACIFIC – The Asia-Pacific Region and the Expanding Borders of the WTO: Implications, Challenges and Opportunities* (ed. Buchanan), Victoria, Canada: UVic Centre for Asia-Pacific Initiatives.

Potter, P. B. (1994) "Riding the Tiger: Legitimacy and Legal Culture in Post-Mao China", *The China Quarterly*, No. 138, pp. 325-358.

"*Report of the Panel on United Nations Peace Operations*" (2000), United Nations General Assembly/Security Council A/55/305 – S/2000/809. (Brahimi Report)

"*Report of the Secretary-General on the United Nations Transitional Administration in East Timor*" (2001), United Nations Security Council S/2001/983.

"*Report of the United Nations Secretary General on the Rule of Law and Transitional Justice in Conflict and Post-Conflict Societies*" (2004), United Nations Security Council S/2004/616.

Rittich, K. (2004) "*The Future of Law and Development: Second Generation Reforms and the Incorporation of the Social*", paper presented at the Cornell Law School "Practices of Law and Development Conference", April 18-20.

Rose, C. V. (1998) "The 'New' Law and Development Movement in the Post-Cold War Era: A Vietnam Case Study", *Law & Society Review*, Vol. 32, No. 1, pp. 93-140.

Rosenberg, N. & Birdzell, L. E. (1986) "*How the West Grew Rich: The Economic Transformation of the Industrial World*", New York: Basic Books.

Ruffert, M. (2001) "The Administration of Kosovo and East-Timor by the International Community", *International and Comparative Law Quarterly*, Vol. 50, No. 3, pp. 613-631.

Sandgren, C. (2005) "Korruption: Orsaker, effekter och strategier för bekämpning", *Tidsskrift for Rettsvitenskap*, No. 3, pp. 264-293.

Schwarz, A. (1996) "Enemy No. 1: Economic opening has unleashed corruption scourge", *Far Eastern Economic Review*, Vol. 159, No. 38, July 11, pp. 14-18.

Seidman, A. & Seidman, R. B. (1994) "*State and Law in the Development Process: Problem-Solving and Institutional Change in the Third World*", New York: St. Martin's Press.

Sellström, T. (2002) "*Sweden and National Liberation in Southern Africa – Volume II: Solidarity and Assistance 1970-1994*", Uppsala: Nordiska Afrikainstitutet.

Shihata, I. (1991) "*The World Bank in a Changing World: Selected Essays*", (eds. Tschofen & Parra), Dordrecht: Martinus Nijhoff Publishers.

Sidel, M. (1993) "Law Reform in Vietnam: The Complex Transition from Socialism and Soviet Models in Legal Scholarship and Training", *UCLA Pacific Basin Law Journal*, Vol. 11, pp. 221-259.

Sikkink, K. (2002) "Transnational Advocacy Networks and the Social Construction of Legal Rules", in: *Global Prescriptions: The Production, Exportation, and Importation of a New Legal Orthodoxy* (eds. Dezalay & Garth), Ann Arbor: University of Michigan Press.

Slaughter, A-M. (2002) "Breaking Out: The Proliferation of Actors in the International System", in: *Global Prescriptions: The Production, Exportation, and Importation of a New Legal Orthodoxy* (eds. Dezalay & Garth), Ann Arbor: University of Michigan Press.

Stahn, C. (2001) "International Territorial Administration in the former Yugoslavia: Origins, Developments and Challenges ahead", *Zeitschrift für Ausländisches öffentliches Recht und Völkerrecht*, Vol. 61, No 1, pp. 107-176.

Stein, P. (1984) "*Legal Institutions: The Development of Dispute Settlement*", London: Butterworths.

Stone, A. & Levy, B. & Paredes, R. (1996) "Public institutions and private transactions: a comparative analysis of the legal and regulatory environment for business transactions in Brazil and Chile", in: *Empirical Studies in Institutional Change*, (eds. Alston, Eggertsson & North). Cambridge, Mass.: Cambridge University Press.

"*Strengthening the Security-Development Nexus: Assessing International Policy and Practice Since the 1990s*" (2004) Conference Report, New York: International Peace Academy.

Strohmayer, H. (2001) "Collapse and Reconstruction of a Judicial System: The United Nations Missions in Kosovo and East Timor", *American Journal of International Law*, Vol. 95, pp. 46-63.

Sveaass, N. & Lavik, N. J. (2000) "Psychological Aspects of Human Rights Violations: The Importance of Justice and Reconciliation", *Nordic Journal of International Law*, Vol. 69, No. 1, pp. 35-52.

Tamanaha, B. Z. (1995) "The Lessons of Law-and-Development Studies", (Review article), *The American Journal of International Law*, Vol. 89, No. 2, pp. 470-486.

Tanner, M. S. (1995) "How a Bill Becomes a Law in China: Stages and Processes in Lawmaking", *The China Quarterly*, No. 141, pp. 39-64.

Taylor, V. (2002) "Anti-Corruption and Asian Legal Professions", in: *Corruption in Asia: Rethinking the Governance Paradigm* (eds. Lindsey & Dick), Sydney: Federation Press.

Teitel, R. G. (2000) "*Transitional Justice*", New York: Oxford University Press.

"*The Responsibility to Protect*" (2001) Report of the International Commission on Intervention and State Sovereignty (2001), Ottawa: International Development Research Centre.

"*The State in a Changing World*" (1997) World Development Report 1997, New York: The World Bank/Oxford University Press.

Tigar, M. E. & Levy, M. R. (1977) "*Law & the Rise of Capitalism*", New York: Monthly Review Press.

Tolonen, J. (1996) "Legal Aspects of Transformation: A General View", in: *Proceedings of the International Symposium on Law, Economics and Business in the Melting Pot: The Case of Regional Development and Cooperation in the Baltic States*, March 11-12, 1996, Tokai University European Center.

Tran Son (1994) "The Necessity of Setting Up Administrative Court", *Vietnam Law & Legal Forum* Vol. 1, No. 4. p. 36.

Trubek, D. M. (1972) "Toward a Social Theory of Law: An Essay on the Study of Law and Development", *The Yale Law Journal*, Vol. 82, No. 1, pp. 1-50.

Trubek, D. M. & Galanter, M. (1974) "Scholars in Self-Estrangement: Some Reflections on the Crisis in Development Studies in the United States", *Wisconsin Law Review*, Vol. 4, pp. 1062-1102.

Trubek, D. M. (2003) "*The "Rule of Law" in Development Assistance: Past, Present, and Future*", paper presented at the Cornell Law School "Practices of Law and Development Conference", April 18-20, 2004.

Trung Duc (1994) "Disadvantages Remain in Private Enterprise", *Vietnam Investment Review*, September 12, p. 20.

Tuori, K. (1997) "Towards a Multi-layered View of Modern Law", in: *Justice, Morality and Society – A Tribute to Aleksander Peczenik on the Occasion of his 60th Birthday 16 November 1997*, (eds. Aarnio & Alexy & Bergholtz), Lund: Juristförlaget.

van Hoecke, M. & Warrington, M. (1998) "Legal Cultures, Legal Paradigms and Legal Doctrine: Towards a New Model for Comparative Law", *International and Comparative Law Quarterly*, Vol. 47, No. 3, pp. 495-536.

van Rijckeghem, C. & Weder, B. (1997) "*Corruption and the Rate of Temptation: Do Low Wages in the Civil Service Cause Corruption?*" IMF Reserach Department Working Paper WP/97/73.

von Benda-Beckmann, F. (1989) "Scape-goat and Magic Charm: Law in Development Theory and Practice", *Journal of Legal Pluralism*, No. 28, pp. 129-148.

Vu Mao (1996) "The Civil Code - A Great Achievement in the 50-Year History of Legislation of the National Assembly of Vietnam", *Vietnam Law & Legal Forum*, Vol. 2, No. 17, pp. 17-22.

Waelde, T. W. & Gunderson, J. L. (1994) "Legislative Reform in Transition Economies: Western Transplants - A Short-cut to Social Market Economy Status?" *International and Comparative Law Quarterly*, Vol. 43, No. 2, pp. 347-378.

Ward, M. (1983) "Missing the Point: Sampling Methods and Types of Error in Third World Surveys in Identifying Poverty Issues", in: *Social Research in Developing Countries: Surveys and Censuses in the Third World*, (eds. Bulmer & Warwick), Chichester: John Wiley & Sons Ltd.

Watson, A. (1974) "*Legal Transplants: An Approach to Comparative Law*", Edinburgh: Scottish Academic Press.

Watson, A. (1977) "*Society and Legal Change*", Edinburgh: Scottish Academic Press.

Watson, A. (1985a) "*Sources of Law, Legal Change and Ambiguity*", Edinburgh: T. & T. Clark.

Watson, A. (1985b) "*The Evolution of Law*", Oxford: Blackwell.

Watson, A. (1988) "*Failures of Legal Imagination*", Edinburgh: Scottish Academic Press.

Watson, A. (1991) "Legal Origins and Legal Change", London: Hambledon Press.

Wilde, R. (2000) "The Ambivalent Mandates of International Organizations in Bosnia-Herzegovina, Kosovo and East Timor", in: *Proceedings of the Joint Meeting of the Australian & New Zealand Society of International Law and the American Society of International Law*, pp. 319–321.

Wilde, R. (2001) "Accountability and International Actors in Bosnia and Herzegovina, Kosovo and East Timor", *ILSA Journal of International & Comparative Law*, Vol. 7, pp. 455-460.

Wong, J. (1996) "China's WTO Membership", in: *WTO & Asia-Pacific – The Asia-Pacific Region and the Expanding Borders of the WTO: Implications, Challenges and Opportunities* (ed. Buchanan), Victoria, Canada: UVic Centre for Asia-Pacific Initiatives.

Wouters, J. & Naert, F. (2001) "How Effective is the European Security Architecture? Lessons from Bosnia and Kosovo", *International and Comparative Law Quarterly*, Vol. 50, No. 3, pp. 540-576.

Wuelker, G. (1983) "Questionnaires in Asia", in: *Social Research in Developing Countries: Surveys and Censuses in the Third World*, (eds. Bulmer & Warwick), Chichester: John Wiley & Sons Ltd.

Zimmermann, A. & Stahn, C. (2001) "Yugoslav Territory, United Nations Trusteeship or Sovereign State? Reflections on the Current and Future Legal Status of Kosovo", *Nordic Journal of International Law*, Vol. 70, No. 4, pp. 423-460.

APPENDICES

United Nations Basic Principles on the Independence of the Judiciary, adopted by the Seventh United Nations Congress on the Prevention of Crime and the Treatment of Offenders held at Milan from 26 August to 6 September 1985 and endorsed by General Assembly resolutions 40/32 of 29 November 1985 and 40/146 of 13 December 1985

Whereas in the Charter of the United Nations the peoples of the world affirm, inter alia, their determination to establish conditions under which justice can be maintained to achieve international co-operation in promoting and encouraging respect for human rights and fundamental freedoms without any discrimination,

Whereas the Universal Declaration of Human Rights enshrines in particular the principles of equality before the law, of the presumption of innocence and of the right to a fair and public hearing by a competent, independent and impartial tribunal established by law,

Whereas the International Covenants on Economic, Social and Cultural Rights and on Civil and Political Rights both guarantee the exercise of those rights, and in addition, the Covenant on Civil and Political Rights further guarantees the right to be tried without undue delay,

Whereas frequently there still exists a gap between the vision underlying those principles and the actual situation,

Whereas the organization and administration of justice in every country should be inspired by those principles, and efforts should be undertaken to translate them fully into reality,

Whereas rules concerning the exercise of judicial office should aim at enabling judges to act in accordance with those principles,

Whereas judges are charged with the ultimate decision over life, freedoms, rights, duties and property of citizens,

Whereas the Sixth United Nations Congress on the Prevention of Crime and the Treatment of Offenders, by its resolution 16, called upon the Committee on Crime Prevention and Control to include among its priorities the elaboration of guidelines relating to the independence of judges and the selection, professional training and status of judges and prosecutors,

Whereas it is, therefore, appropriate that consideration be first given to the role of judges in relation to the system of justice and to the importance of their selection, training and conduct,

The following basic principles, formulated to assist Member States in their task of securing and promoting the independence of the judiciary should be taken into account and respected by Governments within the framework of their national legislation and practice and be brought to the attention of judges, lawyers, members of the executive and the legislature and the public in general. The principles have been formulated principally with professional judges in mind, but they apply equally, as appropriate, to lay judges, where they exist.

Independence of the judiciary

1. The independence of the judiciary shall be guaranteed by the State and enshrined in the Constitution or the law of the country. It is the duty of all governmental and other institutions to respect and observe the independence of the judiciary.
2. The judiciary shall decide matters before them impartially, on the basis of facts and in accordance with the law, without any restrictions, improper influences, inducements, pressures, threats or interferences, direct or indirect, from any quarter or for any reason.
3. The judiciary shall have jurisdiction over all issues of a judicial nature and shall have exclusive authority to decide whether an issue submitted for its decision is within its competence as defined by law.
4. There shall not be any inappropriate or unwarranted interference with the judicial process, nor shall judicial decisions by the courts be subject to revision. This principle is without prejudice to judicial review or to mitigation or commutation by competent authorities of sentences imposed by the judiciary, in accordance with the law.
5. Everyone shall have the right to be tried by ordinary courts or tribunals using established legal procedures. Tribunals that do not use the duly established procedures of the legal process shall not be created to displace the jurisdiction belonging to the ordinary courts or judicial tribunals.
6. The principle of the independence of the judiciary entitles and requires the judiciary to ensure that judicial proceedings are conducted fairly and that the rights of the parties are respected.
7. It is the duty of each Member State to provide adequate resources to enable the judiciary to properly perform its functions.

Freedom of expression and association

8. In accordance with the Universal Declaration of Human Rights, members of the judiciary are like other citizens entitled to freedom of expression, belief, association and assembly; provided, however, that in exercising such rights, judges shall always conduct themselves in such a manner as to preserve the dignity of their office and the impartiality and independence of the judiciary.
9. Judges shall be free to form and join associations of judges or other organizations to represent their interests, to promote their professional training and to protect their judicial independence.

Qualifications, selection and training

10. Persons selected for judicial office shall be individuals of integrity and ability with appropriate training or qualifications in law. Any method of judicial selection shall safeguard against judicial appointments for improper motives. In the selection of judges, there shall be no discrimination against a person on the grounds of race, colour, sex, religion, political or other opinion, national or social origin, property, birth or status, except that a requirement, that a candidate for judicial office must be a national of the country concerned, shall not be considered discriminatory.

Conditions of service and tenure

11. The term of office of judges, their independence, security, adequate remuneration, conditions of service, pensions and the age of retirement shall be adequately secured by law.
12. Judges, whether appointed or elected, shall have guaranteed tenure until a mandatory retirement age or the expiry of their term of office, where such exists.
13. Promotion of judges, wherever such a system exists, should be based on objective factors, in particular ability, integrity and experience.
14. The assignment of cases to judges within the court to which they belong is an internal matter of judicial administration. Professional secrecy and immunity
15. The judiciary shall be bound by professional secrecy with regard to their deliberations and to confidential information acquired in the course of their duties other than in public proceedings, and shall not be compelled to testify on such matters.
16. Without prejudice to any disciplinary procedure or to any right of appeal or to compensation from the State, in accordance with national law, judges should enjoy personal immunity from civil suits for monetary damages for improper acts or omissions in the exercise of their judicial functions.

Discipline, suspension and removal

17. A charge or complaint made against a judge in his/her judicial and professional capacity shall be processed expeditiously and fairly under an appropriate procedure. The judge shall have the right to a fair hearing. The examination of the matter at its initial stage shall be kept confidential, unless otherwise requested by the judge.
18. Judges shall be subject to suspension or removal only for reasons of incapacity or behaviour that renders them unfit to discharge their duties.
19. All disciplinary, suspension or removal proceedings shall be determined in accordance with established standards of judicial conduct.
20. Decisions in disciplinary, suspension or removal proceedings should be subject to an independent review. This principle may not apply to the decisions of the highest court and those of the legislature in impeachment or similar proceedings.

United Nations Guidelines on the Role of Prosecutors, adopted by the Eighth United Nations Congress on the Prevention of Crime and the Treatment of Offenders, Havana, Cuba, 27 August to 7 September 1990

Whereas in the Charter of the United Nations the peoples of the world affirm, inter alia, their determination to establish conditions under which justice can be maintained, and proclaim as one of their purposes the achievement of international cooperation in promoting and encouraging respect for human rights and fundamental freedoms without distinction as to race, sex, language or religion,

Whereas the Universal Declaration of Human Rights enshrines the principles of equality before the law, the presumption of innocence and the right to a fair and public hearing by an independent and impartial tribunal,

Whereas frequently there still exists a gap between the vision underlying those principles and the actual situation,

Whereas the organization and administration of justice in every country should be inspired by those principles, and efforts undertaken to translate them fully into reality,

Whereas prosecutors play a crucial role in the administration of justice, and rules concerning the performance of their important responsibilities should promote their respect for and compliance with the above-mentioned principles, thus contributing to fair and equitable criminal justice and the effective protection of citizens against crime,

Whereas it is essential to ensure that prosecutors possess the professional qualifications required for the accomplishment of their functions, through improved methods of recruitment and legal and professional training, and through the provision of all necessary means for the proper performance of their role in combating criminality, particularly in its new forms and dimensions,

Whereas the General Assembly, by its resolution 34/169 of 17 december 1979, adopted the Code of Conduct for Law Enforcement Officials, on the recommendation of the Fifth United Nations Congress on the Prevention of Crime and the Treatment of Offenders,

Whereas in resolution 16 of the Sixth United Nations Congress on the Prevention of Crime and the Treatment of Offenders, the Committee on Crime Prevention and Control was called upon to include among its priorities the elaboration of guidelines relating to the independence of judges and the selection, professional training and status of judges and prosecutors,

Whereas the Seventh United Nations Congress on the Prevention of Crime and the Treatment of Offenders adopted the Basic Principles on the Independence of the Judiciary, subsequently endorsed by the General Assembly in its resolutions 40/32 of 29 november 1985 and 40/146 of 13 december 1985,

Whereas the Declaration of Basic Principles of Justice for Victims of Crime and Abuse of Power, recommends measures to be taken at the international and national levels to improve access to justice and fair treatment, restitution, compensation and assistance for victims of crime,

Whereas, in resolution 7 of the Seventh Congress the Committee was called upon to consider the need for guidelines relating, inter alia, to the selection, professional training and status of prosecutors, their expected tasks and conduct, means to enhance their contribution to the smooth functioning of the criminal justice system and their cooperation with the police, the scope of their discretionary powers, and their role in criminal proceedings, and to report thereon to future United Nations congresses,

The Guidelines set forth below, which have been formulated to assist Member States in their tasks of securing and promoting the effectiveness, impartiality and fairness of prosecutors in criminal proceedings, should be respected and taken into account by Governments within the framework of their national legislation and practice, and should be brought to the attention of prosecutors, as well as other persons, such as judges, lawyers, members of the executive and the legislature and the public in general. The present Guidelines have been formulated principally with public prosecutors in mind, but they apply equally, as appropriate, to prosecutors appointed on an ad hoc basis.

Qualifications, selection and training

1. Persons selected as prosecutors shall be individuals of integrity and ability, with appropriate training and qualifications.

2. States shall ensure that:

(a) Selection criteria for prosecutors embody safeguards against appointments based on partiality or prejudice, excluding any discrimination against a person on the grounds of race, colour, sex. Language, religion, political or other opinion, national, social or ethnic origin, property, birth, economic or other status, except that it shall not be considered discriminatory to require a candidate for prosecutorial office to be a national of the country concerned;

(b) Prosecutors have appropriate education and training and should be made aware of the ideals and ethical duties of their office, of the constitutional and statutory protections for the rights of the suspect and the victim, and of human rights and fundamental freedoms recognized by national and international law.

Status and conditions of service

3. Prosecutors, as essential agents of the administration of justice, shall at all times maintain the honour and dignity of their profession.

4. States shall ensure that prosecutors are able to perform their professional functions without intimidation, hindrance, harassment, improper interference or unjustified exposure to civil, penal or other liability.

5. Prosecutors and their families shall be physically protected by the authorities when their personal safety is threatened as a result of the discharge of prosecutorial functions.

6. Reasonable conditions of service of prosecutors, adequate remuneration and, where applicable, tenure, pension and age of retirement shall be set out by law or published rules or regulations.
7. Promotion of prosecutors, wherever such a system exists, shall be based on objective factors, in particular professional qualifications, ability, integrity and experience, and decided upon in accordance with fair and impartial procedures.

Freedom of expression and association
8. Prosecutors like other citizens are entitled to freedom of expression, belief, association and assembly. In particular, they shall have the right to take part in public discussion of matters concerning the law, the administration of justice and the promotion and protection of human rights and to join or form local, national or international organizations and attend their meetings, without suffering professional disadvantage by reason of their lawful action or their membership in a lawful organization. In exercising these rights, prosecutors shall always conduct themselves in accordance with the law and the recognized standards and ethics of their profession.
9. Prosecutors shall be free to form and join professional associations or other organizations to represent their interests, to promote their professional training and to protect their status.

Role in criminal proceedings
10. The office of prosecutors shall be strictly separated from judicial functions.
11. Prosecutors shall perform an active role in criminal proceedings, including institution of prosecution and, where authorized by law or consistent with local practice, in the investigation of crime, supervision over the legality of these investigations, supervision of the execution of court decisions and the exercise of other functions as representatives of the public interest.
12. Prosecutors shall, in accordance with the law, perform their duties fairly, consistently and expeditiously, and respect and protect human dignity and uphold human rights, thus contributing to ensuring due process and the smooth functioning of the criminal justice system.
13. In the performance of their duties, prosecutors shall:
(a) Carry out their functions impartially and avoid all political, social, religious, racial, cultural, sexual or any other kind of discrimination;
(b) Protect the public interest, act with objectivity, take proper account of the position of the suspect and the victim, and pay attention to all relevant circumstances, irrespective of whether they are to the advantage or disadvantage of the suspect;
(c) Keep matters in the* possession confidential, unless the performance of duty or the needs of justice require otherwise;
(d) Consider the views and concerns of victims when their personal interests are affected and ensure that victims are informed of their rights in accordance with the Declaration of Basic Principles of Justice for Victims of Crime and Abuse of Power.
14. Prosecutors shall not initiate or continue prosecution, or shall make every effort to stay proceedings, when an impartial investigation shows the charge to be unfounded.
15. Prosecutors shall give due attention to the prosecution of crimes committed by public officials, particularly corruption, abuse of power, grave violations of human rights and other

crimes recognized by international law and, where authorized by law or consistent with local practice, the investigation of such offences.
16. When prosecutors come into possession of evidence against suspects that they know or believe on reasonable grounds was obtained through recourse to unlawful methods, which constitute a grave violation of the suspect's human rights, especially involving torture or cruel, inhuman or degrading treatment or punishment, or other abuses of human rights, they shall refuse to use such evidence against anyone other than those who used such methods, or inform the Court accordingly, and shall take all necessary steps to ensure that those responsible for using such methods are brought to justice.

Discretionary functions
17. In countries where prosecutors are vested with discretionary functions, the law or published rules or regulations shall provide guidelines to enhance fairness and consistency of approach in taking decisions in the prosecution process, including institution or waiver of prosecution.

Alternatives to prosecution
18. In accordance with national law, prosecutors shall give due consideration to waiving prosecution, discontinuing proceedings conditionally or unconditionally, or diverting criminal cases from the formal justice system, with full respect for the rights of suspect(s) and the victim(s). For this purpose, States should fully explore the possibility of adopting diversion schemes not only to alleviate excessive court loads, but also to avoid the stigmatization of pre-trial detention, indictment and conviction, as well as the possible adverse effects of imprisonment.
19. In countries where prosecutors are vested with discretionary functions as to the decision whether or not to prosecute a juvenile, special considerations shall be given to the nature and gravity of the offence, protection of society and the personality and background of the juvenile. In making that decision, prosecutors shall particularly consider available alternatives to prosecution under the relevant juvenile justice laws and procedures. Prosecutors shall use their best efforts to take prosecutory action against juveniles only to the extent strictly necessary.

Relations with other government agencies or institutions
20. In order to ensure the fairness and effectiveness of prosecution, prosecutors shall strive to cooperate with the police, the courts, the legal profession, public defenders and other government agencies or institutions.

Disciplinary proceedings
21. Disciplinary offences of prosecutors shall be based on law or lawful regulations. Complaints against prosecutors which allege that they acted in a manner clearly out of the range of professional standards shall be processed expeditiously and fairly under appropriate procedures. Prosecutors shall have the right to a fair hearing. The decision shall be subject to independent review.
22. Disciplinary proceedings against prosecutors shall guarantee an objective evaluation and decision. They shall be determined in accordance with the law, the code of professional conduct

and other established standards and ethics and in the light of the present Guidelines. Observance of the Guidelines

23. Prosecutors shall respect the present Guidelines. They shall also, to the best of their capability, prevent and actively oppose any violations thereof.

24. Prosecutors who have reason to believe that a violation of the present Guidelines has occurred or is about to occur shall report the matter to their superior authorities and, where necessary, to other appropriate authorities or organs vested with reviewing or remedial power.

United Nations Basic Principles on the Role of Lawyers, adopted by the Eighth United Nations Congress on the Prevention of Crime and the Treatment of Offenders, Havana, Cuba, 27 August to 7 September 1990

Whereas in the Charter of the United Nations the peoples of the world affirm, inter alia, their determination to establish conditions under which justice can be maintained, and proclaim as one of their purposes the achievement of international cooperation in promoting and encouraging respect for human rights and fundamental freedoms without distinction as to race, sex, language or religion,

Whereas the Universal Declaration of Human Rights enshrines the principles of equality before the law, the presumption of innocence, the right to a fair and public hearing by an independent and impartial tribunal, and all the guarantees necessary for the defence of everyone charged with a penal offence,

Whereas the International Covenant on Civil and Political Rights proclaims, in addition, the right to be tried without undue delay and the right to a fair and public hearing by a competent, independent and impartial tribunal established by law,

Whereas the International Covenant on Economic, Social and Cultural Rights recalls the obligation of States under the Charter to promote universal respect for, and observance of, human rights and freedoms,

Whereas the Body of Principles for the Protection of All Persons under Any Form of Detention or Imprisonment provides that a detained person shall be entitled to have the assistance of, and to communicate and consult with, legal counsel,

Whereas the Standard Minimum Rules for the Treatment of Prisoners recommend, in particular, that legal assistance and confidential communication with counsel should be ensured to untried prisoners,

Whereas the Safe guards guaranteeing protection of those facing the death penalty reaffirm the right of everyone suspected or charged with a crime for which capital punishment may be imposed to adequate legal assistance at all stages of the proceedings, in accordance with article 14 of the International Covenant on Civil and Political Rights,

Whereas the Declaration of Basic Principles of Justice for Victims of Crime and Abuse of Power recommends measures to be taken at the international and national levels to improve access to justice and fair treatment, restitution, compensation and assistance for victims of crime,

Whereas adequate protection of the human rights and fundamental freedoms to which all persons are entitled, be they economic, social and cultural, or civil and political, requires that all persons have effective access to legal services provided by an independent legal profession,

Whereas professional associations of lawyers have a vital role to play in upholding professional standards and ethics, protecting their members from persecution and improper restrictions and infringements, providing legal services to all in need of them, and cooperating with governmental and other institutions in furthering the ends of justice and public interest,

The Basic Principles on the Role of Lawyers, set forth below, which have been formulated to assist Member States in their task of promoting and ensuring the proper role of lawyers, should be respected and taken into account by Governments within the framework of their national legislation and practice and should be brought to the attention of lawyers as well as other persons, such as judges, prosecutors, members of the executive and the legislature, and the public in general. These principles shall also apply, as appropriate, to persons who exercise the functions of lawyers without having the formal status of lawyers.

Access to lawyers and legal services

1. All persons are entitled to call upon the assistance of a lawyer of their choice to protect and establish their rights and to defend them in all stages of criminal proceedings.
2. Governments shall ensure that efficient procedures and responsive mechanisms for effective and equal access to lawyers are provided for all persons within their territory and subject to their jurisdiction, without distinction of any kind, such as discrimination based on race, colour, ethnic origin, sex, language, religion, political or other opinion, national or social origin, property, birth, economic or other status.
3. Governments shall ensure the provision of sufficient funding and other resources for legal services to the poor and, as necessary, to other disadvantaged persons. Professional associations of lawyers shall cooperate in the organization and provision of services, facilities and other resources.
4. Governments and professional associations of lawyers shall promote programmes to inform the public about their rights and duties under the law and the important role of lawyers in protecting their fundamental freedoms. Special attention should be given to assisting the poor and other disadvantaged persons so as to enable them to assert their rights and where necessary call upon the assistance of lawyers.

Special safeguards in criminal justice matters

5. Governments shall ensure that all persons are immediately informed by the competent authority of their right to be assisted by a lawyer of their own choice upon arrest or detention or when charged with a criminal offence.
6. Any such persons who do not have a lawyer shall, in all cases in which the interests of justice so require, be entitled to have a lawyer of experience and competence commensurate with the nature of the offence assigned to them in order to provide effective legal assistance, without payment by them if they lack sufficient means to pay for such services.
7. Governments shall further ensure that all persons arrested or detained, with or without criminal charge, shall have prompt access to a lawyer, and in any case not later than forty-eight hours from the time of arrest or detention.
8. All arrested, detained or imprisoned persons shall be provided with adequate opportunities, time and facilities to be visited by and to communicate and consult with a lawyer, without delay,

interception or censorship and in full confidentiality. Such consultations may be within sight, but not within the hearing, of law enforcement officials.

Qualifications and training

9. Governments, professional associations of lawyers and educational institutions shall ensure that lawyers have appropriate education and training and be made aware of the ideals and ethical duties of the lawyer and of human rights and fundamental freedoms recognized by national and international law.

10. Governments, professional associations of lawyers and educational institutions shall ensure that there is no discrimination against a person with respect to entry into or continued practice within the legal profession on the grounds of race, colour, sex, ethnic origin, religion, political or other opinion, national or social origin, property, birth, economic or other status, except that a requirement, that a lawyer must be a national of the country concerned, shall not be considered discriminatory.

11. In countries where there exist groups, communities or regions whose needs for legal services are not met, particularly where such groups have distinct cultures, traditions or languages or have been the victims of past discrimination, Governments, professional associations of lawyers and educational institutions should take special measures to provide opportunities for candidates from these groups to enter the legal profession and should ensure that they receive training appropriate to the needs of their groups.

Duties and responsibilities

12. Lawyers shall at all times maintain the honour and dignity of their profession as essential agents of the administration of justice.

13. The duties of lawyers towards their clients shall include:

(a) Advising clients as to their legal rights and obligations, and as to the working of the legal system in so far as it is relevant to the legal rights and obligations of the clients;

(b) Assisting clients in every appropriate way, and taking legal action to protect their interests;

(c) Assisting clients before courts, tribunals or administrative authorities, where appropriate.

14. Lawyers, in protecting the rights of their clients and in promoting the cause of justice, shall seek to uphold human rights and fundamental freedoms recognized by national and international law and shall at all times act freely and diligently in accordance with the law and recognized standards and ethics of the legal profession.

15. Lawyers shall always loyally respect the interests of their clients.

Guarantees for the functioning of lawyers

16. Governments shall ensure that lawyers (a) are able to perform all of their professional functions without intimidation, hindrance, harassment or improper interference; (b) are able to travel and to consult with their clients freely both within their own country and abroad; and (c) shall not suffer, or be threatened with, prosecution or administrative, economic or other sanctions for any action taken in accordance with recognized professional duties, standards and ethics.

17. Where the security of lawyers is threatened as a result of discharging their functions, they shall be adequately safeguarded by the authorities.

18. Lawyers shall not be identified with their clients or their clients' causes as a result of discharging their functions.
19. No court or administrative authority before whom the right to counsel is recognized shall refuse to recognize the right of a lawyer to appear before it for his or her client unless that lawyer has been disqualified in accordance with national law and practice and in conformity with these principles.
20. Lawyers shall enjoy civil and penal immunity for relevant statements made in good faith in written or oral pleadings or in their professional appearances before a court, tribunal or other legal or administrative authority.
21. It is the duty of the competent authorities to ensure lawyers access to appropriate information, files and documents in their possession or control in sufficient time to enable lawyers to provide effective legal assistance to their clients. Such access should be provided at the earliest appropriate time.
22. Governments shall recognize and respect that all communications and consultations between lawyers and their clients within their professional relationship are confidential.

Freedom of expression and association
23. Lawyers like other citizens are entitled to freedom of expression, belief, association and assembly. In particular, they shall have the right to take part in public discussion of matters concerning the law, the administration of justice and the promotion and protection of human rights and to join or form local, national or international organizations and attend their meetings, without suffering professional restrictions by reason of their lawful action or their membership in a lawful organization. In exercising these rights, lawyers shall always conduct themselves in accordance with the law and the recognized standards and ethics of the legal profession.

Professional associations of lawyers
24. Lawyers shall be entitled to form and join self-governing professional associations to represent their interests, promote their continuing education and training and protect their professional integrity. The executive body of the professional associations shall be elected by its members and shall exercise its functions without external interference.
25. Professional associations of lawyers shall cooperate with Governments to ensure that everyone has effective and equal access to legal services and that lawyers are able, without improper interference, to counsel and assist their clients in accordance with the law and recognized professional standards and ethics.

Disciplinary proceedings
26. Codes of professional conduct for lawyers shall be established by the legal profession through its appropriate organs, or by legislation, in accordance with national law and custom and recognized international standards and norms.
27. Charges or complaints made against lawyers in their professional capacity shall be processed expeditiously and fairly under appropriate procedures. Lawyers shall have the right to a fair hearing, including the right to be assisted by a lawyer of their choice.

28. Disciplinary proceedings against lawyers shall be brought before an impartial disciplinary committee established by the legal profession, before an independent statutory authority, or before a court, and shall be subject to an independent judicial review.
29. All disciplinary proceedings shall be determined in accordance with the code of professional conduct and other recognized standards and ethics of the legal profession and in the light of these principles.

United Nations Code of Conduct for Law Enforcement Officials, adopted by General Assembly Resolution 34/169 of 17 December 1979

Article 1

Law enforcement officials shall at all times fulfil the duty imposed upon them by law, by serving the community and by protecting all persons against illegal acts, consistent with the high degree of responsibility required by their profession.

Commentary:

(a) The term "law enforcement officials', includes all officers of the law, whether appointed or elected, who exercise police powers, especially the powers of arrest or detention.

(b) In countries where police powers are exercised by military authorities, whether uniformed or not, or by State security forces, the definition of law enforcement officials shall be regarded as including officers of such services.

(c) Service to the community is intended to include particularly the rendition of services of assistance to those members of the community who by reason of personal, economic, social or other emergencies are in need of immediate aid.

(d) This provision is intended to cover not only all violent, predatory and harmful acts, but extends to the full range of prohibitions under penal statutes. It extends to conduct by persons not capable of incurring criminal liability.

Article 2

In the performance of their duty, law enforcement officials shall respect and protect human dignity and maintain and uphold the human rights of all persons.

Commentary:

(a) The human rights in question are identified and protected by national and international law. Among the relevant international instruments are the Universal Declaration of Human Rights, the International Covenant on Civil and Political Rights, the Declaration on the Protection of All Persons from Being Subjected to Torture and Other Cruel, Inhuman or Degrading Treatment or Punishment, the United Nations Declaration on the Elimination of All Forms of Racial Discrimination, the International Convention on the Elimination of All Forms of Racial Discrimination, the International Convention on the Suppression and Punishment of the Crime of Apartheid, the Convention on the Prevention and Punishment of the Crime of Genocide, the Standard Minimum Rules for the Treatment of Prisoners and the Vienna Convention on Consular Relations.

(b) National commentaries to this provision should indicate regional or national provisions identifying and protecting these rights.

Article 3

Law enforcement officials may use force only when strictly necessary and to the extent required for the performance of their duty.

Commentary:

(a) This provision emphasizes that the use of force by law enforcement officials should be exceptional; while it implies that law enforcement officials may be authorized to use force as is reasonably necessary under the circumstances for the prevention of crime or in effecting or

assisting in the lawful arrest of offenders or suspected offenders, no force going beyond that may be used.
(b) National law ordinarily restricts the use of force by law enforcement officials in accordance with a principle of proportionality. It is to be understood that such national principles of proportionality are to be respected in the interpretation of this provision. In no case should this provision be interpreted to authorize the use of force which is disproportionate to the legitimate objective to be achieved.
(c) The use of firearms is considered an extreme measure. Every effort should be made to exclude the use of firearms, especially against children. In general, firearms should not be used except when a suspected offender offers armed resistance or otherwise jeopardizes the lives of others and less extreme measures are not sufficient to restrain or apprehend the suspected offender. In every instance in which a firearm is discharged, a report should be made promptly to the competent authorities.

Article 4
Matters of a confidential nature in the possession of law enforcement officials shall be kept confidential, unless the performance of duty or the needs of justice strictly require otherwise.
Commentary:
By the nature of their duties, law enforcement officials obtain information which may relate to private lives or be potentially harmful to the interests, and especially the reputation, of others. Great care should be exercised in safeguarding and using such information, which should be disclosed only in the performance of duty or to serve the needs of justice. Any disclosure of such information for other purposes is wholly improper.

Article 5
No law enforcement official may inflict, instigate or tolerate any act of torture or other cruel, inhuman or degrading treatment or punishment, nor may any law enforcement official invoke superior orders or exceptional circumstances such as a state of war or a threat of war, a threat to national security, internal political instability or any other public emergency as a justification of torture or other cruel, inhuman or degrading treatment or punishment.
Commentary:
(a) This prohibition derives from the Declaration on the Protection of All Persons from Being Subjected to Torture and Other Cruel, Inhuman or Degrading Treatment or Punishment, adopted by the General Assembly, according to which: "[Such an act is] an offence to human dignity and shall be condemned as a denial of the purposes of the Charter of the United Nations and as a violation of the human rights and fundamental freedoms proclaimed in the Universal Declaration of Human Rights [and other international human rights instruments]."
(b) The Declaration defines torture as follows:
"... torture means any act by which severe pain or suffering, whether physical or mental, is intentionally inflicted by or at the instigation of a public official on a person for such purposes as obtaining from him or a third person information or confession, punishing him for an act he has committed or is suspected of having committed, or intimidating him or other persons. It does not include pain or suffering arising only from, inherent in or incidental to, lawful

sanctions to the extent consistent with the Standard Minimum Rules for the Treatment of Prisoners."
(c) The term "cruel, inhuman or degrading treatment or punishment" has not been defined by the General Assembly but should be interpreted so as to extend the widest possible protection against abuses, whether physical or mental.

Article 6
Law enforcement officials shall ensure the full protection of the health of persons in their custody and, in particular, shall take immediate action to secure medical attention whenever required.
Commentary:
(a) "Medical attention", which refers to services rendered by any medical personnel, including certified medical practitioners and paramedics, shall be secured when needed or requested.
(b) While the medical personnel are likely to be attached to the law enforcement operation, law enforcement officials must take into account the judgement of such personnel when they recommend providing the person in custody with appropriate treatment through, or in consultation with, medical personnel from outside the law enforcement operation.
(c) It is understood that law enforcement officials shall also secure medical attention for victims of violations of law or of accidents occurring in the course of violations of law.

Article 7
Law enforcement officials shall not commit any act of corruption. They shall also rigorously oppose and combat all such acts.
Commentary:
(a) Any act of corruption, in the same way as any other abuse of authority, is incompatible with the profession of law enforcement officials. The law must be enforced fully with respect to any law enforcement official who commits an act of corruption, as Governments cannot expect to enforce the law among their citizens if they cannot, or will not, enforce the law against their own agents and within their agencies.
(b) While the definition of corruption must be subject to national law, it should be understood to encompass the commission or omission of an act in the performance of or in connection with one's duties, in response to gifts, promises or incentives demanded or accepted, or the wrongful receipt of these once the act has been committed or omitted.
(c) The expression "act of corruption" referred to above should be understood to encompass attempted corruption.

Article 8
Law enforcement officials shall respect the law and the present Code. They shall also, to the best of their capability, prevent and rigorously oppose any violations of them.
Law enforcement officials who have reason to believe that a violation of the present Code has occurred or is about to occur shall report the matter to their superior authorities and, where necessary, to other appropriate authorities or organs vested with reviewing or remedial power.

Commentary:
(a) This Code shall be observed whenever it has been incorporated into national legislation or practice. If legislation or practice contains stricter provisions than those of the present Code, those stricter provisions shall be observed.
(b) The article seeks to preserve the balance between the need for internal discipline of the agency on which public safety is largely dependent, on the one hand, and the need for dealing with violations of basic human rights, on the other. Law enforcement officials shall report violations within the chain of command and take other lawful action outside the chain of command only when no other remedies are available or effective. It is understood that law enforcement officials shall not suffer administrative or other penalties because they have reported that a violation of this Code has occurred or is about to occur.
(c) The term "appropriate authorities or organs vested with reviewing or remedial power" refers to any authority or organ existing under national law, whether internal to the law enforcement agency or independent thereof, with statutory, customary or other power to review grievances and complaints arising out of violations within the purview of this Code.
(d) In some countries, the mass media may be regarded as performing complaint review functions similar to those described in subparagraph (c) above. Law enforcement officials may, therefore, be justified if, as a last resort and in accordance with the laws and customs of their own countries and with the provisions of article 4 of the present Code, they bring violations to the attention of public opinion through the mass media.
(e) Law enforcement officials who comply with the provisions of this Code deserve the respect, the full support and the co-operation of the community and of the law enforcement agency in which they serve, as well as the law enforcement profession.

United Nations Convention against Corruption, Adopted by the General Assembly by Resolution 58/4 of 31 October 2003

PREAMBLE

The States Parties to this Convention,

Concerned about the seriousness of problems and threats posed by corruption to the stability and security of societies, undermining the institutions and values of democracy, ethical values and justice and jeopardizing sustainable development and the rule of law,

Concerned also about the links between corruption and other forms of crime, in particular organized crime and economic crime, including money-laundering,

Concerned further about cases of corruption that involve vast quantities of assets, which may constitute a substantial proportion of the resources of States, and that threaten the political stability and sustainable development of those States,

Convinced that corruption is no longer a local matter but a transnational phenomenon that affects all societies and economies, making international cooperation to prevent and control it essential,

Convinced also that a comprehensive and multidisciplinary approach is required to prevent and combat corruption effectively,

Convinced further that the availability of technical assistance can play an important role in enhancing the ability of States, including by strengthening capacity and by institution-building, to prevent and combat corruption effectively,

Convinced that the illicit acquisition of personal wealth can be particularly damaging to democratic institutions, national economies and the rule of law,

Determined to prevent, detect and deter in a more effective manner international transfers of illicitly acquired assets and to strengthen international cooperation in asset recovery,

Acknowledging the fundamental principles of due process of law in criminal proceedings and in civil or administrative proceedings to adjudicate property rights,

Bearing in mind that the prevention and eradication of corruption is a responsibility of all States and that they must cooperate with one another, with the support and involvement of individuals and groups outside the public sector, such as civil society, non-governmental organizations and community-based organizations, if their efforts in this area are to be effective,

Bearing also in mind the principles of proper management of public affairs and public property, fairness, responsibility and equality before the law and the need to safeguard integrity and to foster a culture of rejection of corruption,

Commending the work of the Commission on Crime Prevention and Criminal Justice and the United Nations Office on Drugs and Crime in preventing and combating corruption,

Recalling the work carried out by other international and regional organizations in this field, including the activities of the African Union, the Council of Europe, the Customs Cooperation Council (also known as the World Customs Organization), the European Union, the League of Arab States, the Organisation for Economic Cooperation and Development and the Organization of American States,

Taking note with appreciation of multilateral instruments to prevent and combat corruption, including, inter alia, the Inter-American Convention against Corruption, adopted by the Organization of American States on 29 March 1996, the Convention on the Fight against Corruption involving Officials of the European Communities or Officials of Member States of the European Union, adopted by the Council of the European Union on 26 May 1997, the Convention on Combating Bribery of Foreign Public Officials in International Business Transactions, adopted by the Organisation for Economic Cooperation and Development on 21 november 1997, the Criminal Law Convention on Corruption, adopted by the Committee of Ministers of the Council of Europe on 27 January 1999, the Civil Law Convention on Corruption, adopted by the Committee of Ministers of the Council of Europe on 4 november 1999, and the African Union Convention on Preventing and Combating Corruption, adopted by the Heads of State and Government of the African Union on 12 July 2003,

Welcoming the entry into force on 29 september 2003 of the United Nations Convention against Transnational Organized Crime,

Have agreed as follows:

CHAPTER I: GENERAL PROVISIONS

Article 1: statement of purpose
The purposes of this Convention are:
(a) To promote and strengthen measures to prevent and combat corruption more efficiently and effectively;
(b) To promote, facilitate and support international cooperation and technical assistance in the prevention of and fight against corruption, including in asset recovery;
(c) To promote integrity, accountability and proper management of public affairs and public property.

Article 2: use of terms
For the purposes of this Convention:

(a) "Public official" shall mean: (i) any person holding a legislative, executive, administrative or judicial office of a State Party, whether appointed or elected, whether permanent or temporary, whether paid or unpaid, irrespective of that person's seniority; (ii) any other person who performs a public function, including for a public agency or public enterprise, or provides a public service, as defined in the domestic law of the State Party and as applied in the pertinent area of law of that State Party; (iii) any other person defined as a "public official" in the domestic law of a State Party. However, for the purpose of some specific measures contained in chapter II of this Convention, "public official" may mean any person who performs a public function or provides a public service as defined in the domestic law of the State Party and as applied in the pertinent area of law of that State Party;
(b) "Foreign public official" shall mean any person holding a legislative, executive, administrative or judicial office of a foreign country, whether appointed or elected; and any person exercising a public function for a foreign country, including for a public agency or public enterprise;
(c) "Official of a public international organization" shall mean an international civil servant or any person who is authorized by such an organization to act on behalf of that organization;
(d) "Property" shall mean assets of every kind, whether corporeal or incorporeal, movable or immovable, tangible or intangible, and legal documents or instruments evidencing title to or interest in such assets;
(e) "Proceeds of crime" shall mean any property derived from or obtained, directly or indirectly, through the commission of an offence;
(f) "Freezing" or "seizure" shall mean temporarily prohibiting the transfer, conversion, disposition or movement of property or temporarily assuming custody or control of property on the basis of an order issued by a court or other competent authority;
(g) "Confiscation", which includes forfeiture where applicable, shall mean the permanent deprivation of property by order of a court or other competent authority;
(h) "Predicate offence" shall mean any offence as a result of which proceeds have been generated that may become the subject of an offence as defined in article 23 of this Convention;
(i) "Controlled delivery" shall mean the technique of allowing illicit or suspect consignments to pass out of, through or into the territory of one or more States, with the knowledge and under the supervision of their competent authorities, with a view to the investigation of an offence and the identification of persons involved in the commission of the offence.

Article 3: scope of application

1. This Convention shall apply, in accordance with its terms, to the prevention, investigation and prosecution of corruption and to the freezing, seizure, confiscation and return of the proceeds of offences established in accordance with this Convention.
2. For the purposes of implementing this Convention, it shall not be necessary, except as otherwise stated herein, for the offences set forth in it to result in damage or harm to state property.

Article 4: protection of sovereignty

1. States Parties shall carry out their obligations under this Convention in a manner consistent with the principles of sovereign equality and territorial integrity of States and that of non-intervention in the domestic affairs of other States.
2. Nothing in this Convention shall entitle a State Party to undertake in the territory of another State the exercise of jurisdiction and performance of functions that are reserved exclusively for the authorities of that other State by its domestic law.

CHAPTER II: PREVENTIVE MEASURES

Article 5: preventive anti-corruption policies and practices

1. Each State Party shall, in accordance with the fundamental principles of its legal system, develop and implement or maintain effective, coordinated anticorruption policies that promote the participation of society and reflect the principles of the rule of law, proper management of public affairs and public property, integrity, transparency and accountability.
2. Each State Party shall endeavour to establish and promote effective practices aimed at the prevention of corruption.
3. Each State Party shall endeavour to periodically evaluate relevant legal instruments and administrative measures with a view to determining their adequacy to prevent and fight corruption.
4. States Parties shall, as appropriate and in accordance with the fundamental principles of their legal system, collaborate with each other and with relevant international and regional organizations in promoting and developing the measures referred to in this article. That collaboration may include participation in international programmes and projects aimed at the prevention of corruption.

Article 6: preventive anti-corruption body or bodies

1. Each State Party shall, in accordance with the fundamental principles of its legal system, ensure the existence of a body or bodies, as appropriate, that prevent corruption by such means as:

(a) Implementing the policies referred to in article 5 of this Convention and, where appropriate, overseeing and coordinating the implementation of those policies;

(b) Increasing and disseminating knowledge about the prevention of corruption.

2. Each State Party shall grant the body or bodies referred to in paragraph 1 of this article the necessary independence, in accordance with the fundamental principles of its legal system, to enable the body or bodies to carry out its or their functions effectively and free from any undue influence. The necessary material resources and specialized staff, as well as the training that such staff may require to carry out their functions, should be provided.
3. Each State Party shall inform the Secretary-General of the United Nations of the name and address of the authority or authorities that may assist other States Parties in developing and implementing specific measures for the prevention of corruption.

Article 7: public sector

1. Each State Party shall, where appropriate and in accordance with the fundamental principles of its legal system, endeavour to adopt, maintain and strengthen systems for the recruitment, hiring, retention, promotion and retirement of civil servants and, where appropriate, other non-elected public officials:

(a) That are based on principles of efficiency, transparency and objective criteria such as merit, equity and aptitude;

(b) That include adequate procedures for the selection and training of individuals for public positions considered especially vulnerable to corruption and the rotation, where appropriate, of such individuals to other positions;

(c) That promote adequate remuneration and equitable pay scales, taking into account the level of economic development of the State Party;

(d) That promote education and training programmes to enable them to meet the requirements for the correct, honourable and proper performance of public functions and that provide them with specialized and appropriate training to enhance their awareness of the risks of corruption inherent in the performance of their functions. Such programmes may make reference to codes or standards of conduct in applicable areas.

2. Each State Party shall also consider adopting appropriate legislative and administrative measures, consistent with the objectives of this Convention and in accordance with the fundamental principles of its domestic law, to prescribe criteria concerning candidature for and election to public office.

3. Each State Party shall also consider taking appropriate legislative and administrative measures, consistent with the objectives of this Convention and in accordance with the fundamental principles of its domestic law, to enhance transparency in the funding of candidatures for elected public office and, where applicable, the funding of political parties.

4. Each State Party shall, in accordance with the fundamental principles of its domestic law, endeavour to adopt, maintain and strengthen systems that promote transparency and prevent conflicts of interest.

Article 8: codes of conduct for public officials

1. In order to fight corruption, each State Party shall promote, inter alia, integrity, honesty and responsibility among its public officials, in accordance with the fundamental principles of its legal system.

2. In particular, each State Party shall endeavour to apply, within its own institutional and legal systems, codes or standards of conduct for the correct, honourable and proper performance of public functions.

3. For the purposes of implementing the provisions of this article, each State Party shall, where appropriate and in accordance with the fundamental principles of its legal system, take note of the relevant initiatives of regional, interregional and multilateral organizations, such as the International Code of Conduct for Public Officials contained in the annex to General Assembly resolution 51/59 of 12 december 1996.

4. Each State Party shall also consider, in accordance with the fundamental principles of its domestic law, establishing measures and systems to facilitate the reporting by public officials

of acts of corruption to appropriate authorities, when such acts come to their notice in the performance of their functions.

5. Each State Party shall endeavour, where appropriate and in accordance with the fundamental principles of its domestic law, to establish measures and systems requiring public officials to make declarations to appropriate authorities regarding, inter alia, their outside activities, employment, investments, assets and substantial gifts or benefits from which a conflict of interest may result with respect to their functions as public officials.

6. Each State Party shall consider taking, in accordance with the fundamental principles of its domestic law, disciplinary or other measures against public officials who violate the codes or standards established in accordance with this article.

Article 9: public procurement and management of public finances

1. Each State Party shall, in accordance with the fundamental principles of its legal system, take the necessary steps to establish appropriate systems of procurement, based on transparency, competition and objective criteria in decision-making, that are effective, inter alia, in preventing corruption. Such systems, which may take into account appropriate threshold values in their application, shall address, inter alia:

(a) The public distribution of information relating to procurement procedures and contracts, including information on invitations to tender and relevant or pertinent information on the award of contracts, allowing potential tenderers sufficient time to prepare and submit their tenders;

(b) The establishment, in advance, of conditions for participation, including selection and award criteria and tendering rules, and their publication;

(c) The use of objective and predetermined criteria for public procurement decisions, in order to facilitate the subsequent verification of the correct application of the rules or procedures;

(d) An effective system of domestic review, including an effective system of appeal, to ensure legal recourse and remedies in the event that the rules or procedures established pursuant to this paragraph are not followed;

(e) Where appropriate, measures to regulate matters regarding personnel responsible for procurement, such as declaration of interest in particular public procurements, screening procedures and training requirements.

2. Each State Party shall, in accordance with the fundamental principles of its legal system, take appropriate measures to promote transparency and accountability in the management of public finances. Such measures shall encompass, inter alia:

(a) Procedures for the adoption of the national budget;

(b) Timely reporting on revenue and expenditure;

(c) A system of accounting and auditing standards and related oversight;

(d) Effective and efficient systems of risk management and internal control; and

(e) Where appropriate, corrective action in the case of failure to comply with the requirements established in this paragraph.

3. Each State Party shall take such civil and administrative measures as may be necessary, in accordance with the fundamental principles of its domestic law, to preserve the integrity of accounting books, records, financial statements or other documents related to public expenditure and revenue and to prevent the falsification of such documents.

Article 10: public reporting
Taking into account the need to combat corruption, each State Party shall, in accordance with the fundamental principles of its domestic law, take such measures as may be necessary to enhance transparency in its public administration, including with regard to its organization, functioning and decision-making processes, where appropriate. Such measures may include, inter alia:
(a) Adopting procedures or regulations allowing members of the general public to obtain, where appropriate, information on the organization, functioning and decision-making processes of its public administration and, with due regard for the protection of privacy and personal data, on decisions and legal acts that concern members of the public;
(b) Simplifying administrative procedures, where appropriate, in order to facilitate public access to the competent decision-making authorities; and
(c) Publishing information, which may include periodic reports on the risks of corruption in its public administration.

Article 11: measures relating to the judiciary and prosecution services
1. Bearing in mind the independence of the judiciary and its crucial role in combating corruption, each State Party shall, in accordance with the fundamental principles of its legal system and without prejudice to judicial independence, take measures to strengthen integrity and to prevent opportunities for corruption among members of the judiciary. Such measures may include rules with respect to the conduct of members of the judiciary.
2. Measures to the same effect as those taken pursuant to paragraph 1 of this article may be introduced and applied within the prosecution service in those States Parties where it does not form part of the judiciary but enjoys independence similar to that of the judicial service.

Article 12: private sector
1. Each State Party shall take measures, in accordance with the fundamental principles of its domestic law, to prevent corruption involving the private sector, enhance accounting and auditing standards in the private sector and, where appropriate, provide effective, proportionate and dissuasive civil, administrative or criminal penalties for failure to comply with such measures.
2. Measures to achieve these ends may include, inter alia:
(a) Promoting cooperation between law enforcement agencies and relevant private entities;
(b) Promoting the development of standards and procedures designed to safeguard the integrity of relevant private entities, including codes of conduct for the correct, honourable and proper performance of the activities of business and all relevant professions and the prevention of conflicts of interest, and for the promotion of the use of good commercial practices among businesses and in the contractual relations of businesses with the State;
(c) Promoting transparency among private entities, including, where appropriate, measures regarding the identity of legal and natural persons involved in the establishment and management of corporate entities;
(d) Preventing the misuse of procedures regulating private entities, including procedures regarding subsidies and licences granted by public authorities for commercial activities;

(e) Preventing conflicts of interest by imposing restrictions, as appropriate and for a reasonable period of time, on the professional activities of former public officials or on the employment of public officials by the private sector after their resignation or retirement, where such activities or employment relate directly to the functions held or supervised by those public officials during their tenure;
(f) Ensuring that private enterprises, taking into account their structure and size, have sufficient internal auditing controls to assist in preventing and detecting acts of corruption and that the accounts and required financial statements of such private enterprises are subject to appropriate auditing and certification procedures.
3. In order to prevent corruption, each State Party shall take such measures as may be necessary, in accordance with its domestic laws and regulations regarding the maintenance of books and records, financial statement disclosures and accounting and auditing standards, to prohibit the following acts carried out for the purpose of committing any of the offences established in accordance with this Convention:
(a) The establishment of off-the-books accounts;
(b) The making of off-the-books or inadequately identified transactions;
(c) The recording of non-existent expenditure;
(d) The entry of liabilities with incorrect identification of their objects;
(e) The use of false documents; and
(f) The intentional destruction of bookkeeping documents earlier than foreseen by the law.
4. Each State Party shall disallow the tax deductibility of expenses that constitute bribes, the latter being one of the constituent elements of the offences established in accordance with articles 15 and 16 of this Convention and, where appropriate, other expenses incurred in furtherance of corrupt conduct.

Article 13: participation of society
1. Each State Party shall take appropriate measures, within its means and in accordance with fundamental principles of its domestic law, to promote the active participation of individuals and groups outside the public sector, such as civil society, non-governmental organizations and community-based organizations, in the prevention of and the fight against corruption and to raise public awareness regarding the existence, causes and gravity of and the threat posed by corruption. This participation should be strengthened by such measures as:
(a) Enhancing the transparency of and promoting the contribution of the public to decision-making processes;
(b) Ensuring that the public has effective access to information;
(c) Undertaking public information activities that contribute to non-tolerance of corruption, as well as public education programmes, including school and university curricula;
(d) Respecting, promoting and protecting the freedom to seek, receive, publish and disseminate information concerning corruption. That freedom may be subject to certain restrictions, but these shall only be such as are provided for by law and are necessary:
(i) For respect of the rights or reputations of others;
(ii) For the protection of national security or ordre public or of public health or morals.
2. Each State Party shall take appropriate measures to ensure that the relevant anti-corruption bodies referred to in this Convention are known to the public and shall provide access to such

bodies, where appropriate, for the reporting, including anonymously, of any incidents that may be considered to constitute an offence established in accordance with this Convention.

Article 14: measures to prevent money-laundering
1. Each State Party shall:
(a) Institute a comprehensive domestic regulatory and supervisory regime for banks and non-bank financial institutions, including natural or legal persons that provide formal or informal services for the transmission of money or value and, where appropriate, other bodies particularly susceptible to money-laundering, within its competence, in order to deter and detect all forms of money-laundering, which regime shall emphasize requirements for customer and, where appropriate, beneficial owner identification, record-keeping and the reporting of suspicious transactions;
(b) Without prejudice to article 46 of this Convention, ensure that administrative, regulatory, law enforcement and other authorities dedicated to combating money-laundering (including, where appropriate under domestic law, judicial authorities) have the ability to cooperate and exchange information at the national and international levels within the conditions prescribed by its domestic law and, to that end, shall consider the establishment of a financial intelligence unit to serve as a national centre for the collection, analysis and dissemination of information regarding potential money-laundering.
2. States Parties shall consider implementing feasible measures to detect and monitor the movement of cash and appropriate negotiable instruments across their borders, subject to safeguards to ensure proper use of information and without impeding in any way the movement of legitimate capital. Such measures may include a requirement that individuals and businesses report the cross-border transfer of substantial quantities of cash and appropriate negotiable instruments.
3. States Parties shall consider implementing appropriate and feasible measures to require financial institutions, including money remitters:
(a) To include on forms for the electronic transfer of funds and related messages accurate and meaningful information on the originator;
(b) To maintain such information throughout the payment chain; and
(c) To apply enhanced scrutiny to transfers of funds that do not contain complete information on the originator.
4. In establishing a domestic regulatory and supervisory regime under the terms of this article, and without prejudice to any other article of this Convention, States Parties are called upon to use as a guideline the relevant initiatives of regional, interregional and multilateral organizations against money-laundering.
5. States Parties shall endeavour to develop and promote global, regional, subregional and bilateral cooperation among judicial, law enforcement and financial regulatory authorities in order to combat money-laundering.

CHAPTER III: CRIMINALIZATION AND LAW ENFORCEMENT

Article 15: bribery of national public officials

Each State Party shall adopt such legislative and other measures as may be necessary to establish as criminal offences, when committed intentionally:
(a) The promise, offering or giving, to a public official, directly or indirectly, of an undue advantage, for the official himself or herself or another person or entity, in order that the official act or refrain from acting in the exercise of his or her official duties;
(b) The solicitation or acceptance by a public official, directly or indirectly, of an undue advantage, for the official himself or herself or another person or entity, in order that the official act or refrain from acting in the exercise of his or her official duties.

Article 16: bribery of foreign public officials and officials of public international organizations

1. Each State Party shall adopt such legislative and other measures as may be necessary to establish as a criminal offence, when committed intentionally, the promise, offering or giving to a foreign public official or an official of a public international organization, directly or indirectly, of an undue advantage, for the official himself or herself or another person or entity, in order that the official act or refrain from acting in the exercise of his or her official duties, in order to obtain or retain business or other undue advantage in relation to the conduct of international business.
2. Each State Party shall consider adopting such legislative and other measures as may be necessary to establish as a criminal offence, when committed intentionally, the solicitation or acceptance by a foreign public official or an official of a public international organization, directly or indirectly, of an undue advantage, for the official himself or herself or another person or entity, in order that the official act or refrain from acting in the exercise of his or her official duties.

Article 17: embezzlement, misappropriation or other diversion of property by a public official

Each State Party shall adopt such legislative and other measures as may be necessary to establish as criminal offences, when committed intentionally, the embezzlement, misappropriation or other diversion by a public official for his or her benefit or for the benefit of another person or entity, of any property, public or private funds or securities or any other thing of value entrusted to the public official by virtue of his or her position.

Article 18: trading in influence

Each State Party shall consider adopting such legislative and other measures as may be necessary to establish as criminal offences, when committed intentionally:
(a) The promise, offering or giving to a public official or any other person, directly or indirectly, of an undue advantage in order that the public official or the person abuse his or her real or supposed influence with a view to obtaining from an administration or public authority of the State Party an undue advantage for the original instigator of the act or for any other person;
(b) The solicitation or acceptance by a public official or any other person, directly or indirectly, of an undue advantage for himself or herself or for another person in order that the public

official or the person abuse his or her real or supposed influence with a view to obtaining from an administration or public authority of the State Party an undue advantage.

Article 19: abuse of functions

Each State Party shall consider adopting such legislative and other measures as may be necessary to establish as a criminal offence, when committed intentionally, the abuse of functions or position, that is, the performance of or failure to perform an act, in violation of laws, by a public official in the discharge of his or her functions, for the purpose of obtaining an undue advantage for himself or herself or for another person or entity.

Article 20: illicit enrichment

Subject to its constitution and the fundamental principles of its legal system, each State Party shall consider adopting such legislative and other measures as may be necessary to establish as a criminal offence, when committed intentionally, illicit enrichment, that is, a significant increase in the assets of a public official that he or she cannot reasonably explain in relation to his or her lawful income.

Article 21: bribery in the private sector

Each State Party shall consider adopting such legislative and other measures as may be necessary to establish as criminal offences, when committed intentionally in the course of economic, financial or commercial activities:

(a) The promise, offering or giving, directly or indirectly, of an undue advantage to any person who directs or works, in any capacity, for a private sector entity, for the person himself or herself or for another person, in order that he or she, in breach of his or her duties, act or refrain from acting;

(b) The solicitation or acceptance, directly or indirectly, of an undue advantage by any person who directs or works, in any capacity, for a private sector entity, for the person himself or herself or for another person, in order that he or she, in breach of his or her duties, act or refrain from acting.

Article 22: embezzlement of property in the private sector

Each State Party shall consider adopting such legislative and other measures as may be necessary to establish as a criminal offence, when committed intentionally in the course of economic, financial or commercial activities, embezzlement by a person who directs or works, in any capacity, in a private sector entity of any property, private funds or securities or any other thing of value entrusted to him or her by virtue of his or her position.

Article 23: laundering of proceeds of crime

1. Each State Party shall adopt, in accordance with fundamental principles of its domestic law, such legislative and other measures as may be necessary to establish as criminal offences, when committed intentionally:

(a) (i) The conversion or transfer of property, knowing that such property is the proceeds of crime, for the purpose of concealing or disguising the illicit origin of the property or of helping any person who is involved in the commission of the predicate offence to evade the legal

consequences of his or her action; (ii) The concealment or disguise of the true nature, source, location, disposition, movement or ownership of or rights with respect to property, knowing that such property is the proceeds of crime;
(b) Subject to the basic concepts of its legal system:
(i) The acquisition, possession or use of property, knowing, at the time of receipt, that such property is the proceeds of crime;
(ii) Participation in, association with or conspiracy to commit, attempts to commit and aiding, abetting, facilitating and counselling the commission of any of the offences established in accordance with this article.
2. For purposes of implementing or applying paragraph 1 of this article:
(a) Each State Party shall seek to apply paragraph 1 of this article to the widest range of predicate offences;
(b) Each State Party shall include as predicate offences at a minimum a comprehensive range of criminal offences established in accordance with this Convention;
(c) For the purposes of subparagraph (b) above, predicate offences shall include offences committed both within and outside the jurisdiction of the State Party in question. However, offences committed outside the jurisdiction of a State Party shall constitute predicate offences only when the relevant conduct is a criminal offence under the domestic law of the State where it is committed and would be a criminal offence under the domestic law of the State Party implementing or applying this article had it been committed there;
(d) Each State Party shall furnish copies of its laws that give effect to this article and of any subsequent changes to such laws or a description thereof to the Secretary-General of the United Nations;
(e) If required by fundamental principles of the domestic law of a State Party, it may be provided that the offences set forth in paragraph 1 of this article do not apply to the persons who committed the predicate offence.

Article 24: concealment
Without prejudice to the provisions of article 23 of this Convention, each State Party shall consider adopting such legislative and other measures as may be necessary to establish as a criminal offence, when committed intentionally after the commission of any of the offences established in accordance with this Convention without having participated in such offences, the concealment or continued retention of property when the person involved knows that such property is the result of any of the offences established in accordance with this Convention.

Article 25: obstruction of justice
Each State Party shall adopt such legislative and other measures as may be necessary to establish as criminal offences, when committed intentionally:
(a) The use of physical force, threats or intimidation or the promise, offering or giving of an undue advantage to induce false testimony or to interfere in the giving of testimony or the production of evidence in a proceeding in relation to the commission of offences established in accordance with this Convention;
(b) The use of physical force, threats or intimidation to interfere with the exercise of official duties by a justice or law enforcement official in relation to the commission of offences

established in accordance with this Convention. Nothing in this subparagraph shall prejudice the right of States Parties to have legislation that protects other categories of public official.

Article 26: liability of legal persons

1. Each State Party shall adopt such measures as may be necessary, consistent with its legal principles, to establish the liability of legal persons for participation in the offences established in accordance with this Convention.
2. Subject to the legal principles of the State Party, the liability of legal persons may be criminal, civil or administrative.
3. Such liability shall be without prejudice to the criminal liability of the natural persons who have committed the offences.
4. Each State Party shall, in particular, ensure that legal persons held liable in accordance with this article are subject to effective, proportionate and dissuasive criminal or non-criminal sanctions, including monetary sanctions.

Article 27: participation and attempt

1. Each State Party shall adopt such legislative and other measures as may be necessary to establish as a criminal offence, in accordance with its domestic law, participation in any capacity such as an accomplice, assistant or instigator in an offence established in accordance with this Convention.
2. Each State Party may adopt such legislative and other measures as may be necessary to establish as a criminal offence, in accordance with its domestic law, any attempt to commit an offence established in accordance with this Convention.
3. Each State Party may adopt such legislative and other measures as may be necessary to establish as a criminal offence, in accordance with its domestic law, the preparation for an offence established in accordance with this Convention.

Article 28: knowledge, intent and purpose as elements of an offence

Knowledge, intent or purpose required as an element of an offence established in accordance with this Convention may be inferred from objective factual circumstances.

Article 29: statute of limitations

Each State Party shall, where appropriate, establish under its domestic law a long statute of limitations period in which to commence proceedings for any offence established in accordance with this Convention and establish a longer statute of limitations period or provide for the suspension of the statute of limitations where the alleged offender has evaded the administration of justice.

Article 30: prosecution, adjudication and sanctions

1. Each State Party shall make the commission of an offence established in accordance with this Convention liable to sanctions that take into account the gravity of that offence.
2. Each State Party shall take such measures as may be necessary to establish or maintain, in accordance with its legal system and constitutional principles, an appropriate balance between any immunities or jurisdictional privileges accorded to its public officials for the performance

of their functions and the possibility, when necessary, of effectively investigating, prosecuting and adjudicating offences established in accordance with this Convention.

3. Each State Party shall endeavour to ensure that any discretionary legal powers under its domestic law relating to the prosecution of persons for offences established in accordance with this Convention are exercised to maximize the effectiveness of law enforcement measures in respect of those offences and with due regard to the need to deter the commission of such offences.

4. In the case of offences established in accordance with this Convention, each State Party shall take appropriate measures, in accordance with its domestic law and with due regard to the rights of the defence, to seek to ensure that conditions imposed in connection with decisions on release pending trial or appeal take into consideration the need to ensure the presence of the defendant at subsequent criminal proceedings.

5. Each State Party shall take into account the gravity of the offences concerned when considering the eventuality of early release or parole of persons convicted of such offences.

6. Each State Party, to the extent consistent with the fundamental principles of its legal system, shall consider establishing procedures through which a public official accused of an offence established in accordance with this Convention may, where appropriate, be removed, suspended or reassigned by the appropriate authority, bearing in mind respect for the principle of the presumption of innocence.

7. Where warranted by the gravity of the offence, each State Party, to the extent consistent with the fundamental principles of its legal system, shall consider establishing procedures for the disqualification, by court order or any other appropriate means, for a period of time determined by its domestic law, of persons convicted of offences established in accordance with this Convention from:

(a) Holding public office; and

(b) Holding office in an enterprise owned in whole or in part by the State.

8. Paragraph 1 of this article shall be without prejudice to the exercise of disciplinary powers by the competent authorities against civil servants.

9. Nothing contained in this Convention shall affect the principle that the description of the offences established in accordance with this Convention and of the applicable legal defences or other legal principles controlling the lawfulness of conduct is reserved to the domestic law of a State Party and that such offences shall be prosecuted and punished in accordance with that law.

10. States Parties shall endeavour to promote the reintegration into society of persons convicted of offences established in accordance with this Convention.

Article 31: freezing, seizure and confiscation

1. Each State Party shall take, to the greatest extent possible within its domestic legal system, such measures as may be necessary to enable confiscation of:

(a) Proceeds of crime derived from offences established in accordance with this Convention or property the value of which corresponds to that of such proceeds;

(b) Property, equipment or other instrumentalities used in or destined for use in offences established in accordance with this Convention.

2. Each State Party shall take such measures as may be necessary to enable the identification, tracing, freezing or seizure of any item referred to in paragraph 1 of this article for the purpose of eventual confiscation.
3. Each State Party shall adopt, in accordance with its domestic law, such legislative and other measures as may be necessary to regulate the administration by the competent authorities of frozen, seized or confiscated property covered in paragraphs 1 and 2 of this article.
4. If such proceeds of crime have been transformed or converted, in part or in full, into other property, such property shall be liable to the measures referred to in this article instead of the proceeds.
5. If such proceeds of crime have been intermingled with property acquired from legitimate sources, such property shall, without prejudice to any powers relating to freezing or seizure, be liable to confiscation up to the assessed value of the intermingled proceeds.
6. Income or other benefits derived from such proceeds of crime, from property into which such proceeds of crime have been transformed or converted or from property with which such proceeds of crime have been intermingled shall also be liable to the measures referred to in this article, in the same manner and to the same extent as proceeds of crime.
7. For the purpose of this article and article 55 of this Convention, each State Party shall empower its courts or other competent authorities to order that bank, financial or commercial records be made available or seized. A State Party shall not decline to act under the provisions of this paragraph on the ground of bank secrecy.
8. States Parties may consider the possibility of requiring that an offender demonstrate the lawful origin of such alleged proceeds of crime or other property liable to confiscation, to the extent that such a requirement is consistent with the fundamental principles of their domestic law and with the nature of judicial and other proceedings.
9. The provisions of this article shall not be so construed as to prejudice the rights of bona fide third parties.
10. Nothing contained in this article shall affect the principle that the measures to which it refers shall be defined and implemented in accordance with and subject to the provisions of the domestic law of a State Party.

Article 32: protection of witnesses, experts and victims

1. Each State Party shall take appropriate measures in accordance with its domestic legal system and within its means to provide effective protection from potential retaliation or intimidation for witnesses and experts who give testimony concerning offences established in accordance with this Convention and, as appropriate, for their relatives and other persons close to them.
2. The measures envisaged in paragraph 1 of this article may include, inter alia, without prejudice to the rights of the defendant, including the right to due process:
(a) Establishing procedures for the physical protection of such persons, such as, to the extent necessary and feasible, relocating them and permitting, where appropriate, non-disclosure or limitations on the disclosure of information concerning the identity and whereabouts of such persons;

(b) Providing evidentiary rules to permit witnesses and experts to give testimony in a manner that ensures the safety of such persons, such as permitting testimony to be given through the use of communications technology such as video or other adequate means.
3. States Parties shall consider entering into agreements or arrangements with other States for the relocation of persons referred to in paragraph 1 of this article.
4. The provisions of this article shall also apply to victims insofar as they are witnesses.
5. Each State Party shall, subject to its domestic law, enable the views and concerns of victims to be presented and considered at appropriate stages of criminal proceedings against offenders in a manner not prejudicial to the rights of the defence.

Article 33: protection of reporting persons
Each State Party shall consider incorporating into its domestic legal system appropriate measures to provide protection against any unjustified treatment for any person who reports in good faith and on reasonable grounds to the competent authorities any facts concerning offences established in accordance with this Convention.

Article 34: consequences of acts of corruption
With due regard to the rights of third parties acquired in good faith, each State Party shall take measures, in accordance with the fundamental principles of its domestic law, to address consequences of corruption. In this context, States Parties may consider corruption a relevant factor in legal proceedings to annul or rescind a contract, withdraw a concession or other similar instrument or take any other remedial action.

Article 35: compensation for damage
Each State Party shall take such measures as may be necessary, in accordance with principles of its domestic law, to ensure that entities or persons who have suffered damage as a result of an act of corruption have the right to initiate legal proceedings against those responsible for that damage in order to obtain compensation.

Article 36: specialized authorities
Each State Party shall, in accordance with the fundamental principles of its legal system, ensure the existence of a body or bodies or persons specialized in combating corruption through law enforcement. Such body or bodies or persons shall be granted the necessary independence, in accordance with the fundamental principles of the legal system of the State Party, to be able to carry out their functions effectively and without any undue influence. Such persons or staff of such body or bodies should have the appropriate training and resources to carry out their tasks.

Article 37: cooperation with law enforcement authorities
1. Each State Party shall take appropriate measures to encourage persons who participate or who have participated in the commission of an offence established in accordance with this Convention to supply information useful to competent authorities for investigative and evidentiary purposes and to provide factual, specific help to competent authorities that may contribute to depriving offenders of the proceeds of crime and to recovering such proceeds.

2. Each State Party shall consider providing for the possibility, in appropriate cases, of mitigating punishment of an accused person who provides substantial cooperation in the investigation or prosecution of an offence established in accordance with this Convention.
3. Each State Party shall consider providing for the possibility, in accordance with fundamental principles of its domestic law, of granting immunity from prosecution to a person who provides substantial cooperation in the investigation or prosecution of an offence established in accordance with this Convention.
4. Protection of such persons shall be, mutatis mutandis, as provided for in article 32 of this Convention.
5. Where a person referred to in paragraph 1 of this article located in one State Party can provide substantial cooperation to the competent authorities of another State Party, the States Parties concerned may consider entering into agreements or arrangements, in accordance with their domestic law, concerning the potential provision by the other State Party of the treatment set forth in paragraphs 2 and 3 of this article.

Article 38: cooperation between national authorities
Each State Party shall take such measures as may be necessary to encourage, in accordance with its domestic law, cooperation between, on the one hand, its public authorities, as well as its public officials, and, on the other hand, its authorities responsible for investigating and prosecuting criminal offences. Such cooperation may include:
(a) Informing the latter authorities, on their own initiative, where there are reasonable grounds to believe that any of the offences established in accordance with articles 15, 21 and 23 of this Convention has been committed; or
(b) Providing, upon request, to the latter authorities all necessary information.

Article 39: cooperation between national authorities and the private sector
1. Each State Party shall take such measures as may be necessary to encourage, in accordance with its domestic law, cooperation between national investigating and prosecuting authorities and entities of the private sector, in particular financial institutions, relating to matters involving the commission of offences established in accordance with this Convention.
2. Each State Party shall consider encouraging its nationals and other persons with a habitual residence in its territory to report to the national investigating and prosecuting authorities the commission of an offence established in accordance with this Convention.

Article 40: bank secrecy
Each State Party shall ensure that, in the case of domestic criminal investigations of offences established in accordance with this Convention, there are appropriate mechanisms available within its domestic legal system to overcome obstacles that may arise out of the application of bank secrecy laws.

Article 41: criminal record
Each State Party may adopt such legislative or other measures as may be necessary to take into consideration, under such terms as and for the purpose that it deems appropriate, any previous

conviction in another State of an alleged offender for the purpose of using such information in criminal proceedings relating to an offence established in accordance with this Convention.

Article 42: jurisdiction

1. Each State Party shall adopt such measures as may be necessary to establish its jurisdiction over the offences established in accordance with this Convention when:
(a) The offence is committed in the territory of that State Party; or
(b) The offence is committed on board a vessel that is flying the flag of that State Party or an aircraft that is registered under the laws of that State Party at the time that the offence is committed.
2. Subject to article 4 of this Convention, a State Party may also establish its jurisdiction over any such offence when:
(a) The offence is committed against a national of that State Party; or
(b) The offence is committed by a national of that State Party or a stateless person who has his or her habitual residence in its territory; or
(c) The offence is one of those established in accordance with article 23, paragraph 1 (b) (ii), of this Convention and is committed outside its territory with a
view to the commission of an offence established in accordance with article 23, paragraph 1 (a) (i) or (ii) or (b) (i), of this Convention within its territory; or
(d) The offence is committed against the State Party.
3. For the purposes of article 44 of this Convention, each State Party shall take such measures as may be necessary to establish its jurisdiction over the offences established in accordance with this Convention when the alleged offender is present in its territory and it does not extradite such person solely on the ground that he or she is one of its nationals.
4. Each State Party may also take such measures as may be necessary to establish its jurisdiction over the offences established in accordance with this Convention when the alleged offender is present in its territory and it does not extradite him or her.
5. If a State Party exercising its jurisdiction under paragraph 1 or 2 of this article has been notified, or has otherwise learned, that any other States Parties are conducting an investigation, prosecution or judicial proceeding in respect of the same conduct, the competent authorities of those States Parties shall, as appropriate, consult one another with a view to coordinating their actions.
6. Without prejudice to norms of general international law, this Convention shall not exclude the exercise of any criminal jurisdiction established by a State Party in accordance with its domestic law.

CHAPTER IV: INTERNATIONAL COOPERATION

Article 43: international cooperation

1. States Parties shall cooperate in criminal matters in accordance with articles 44 to 50 of this Convention. Where appropriate and consistent with their domestic legal system, States Parties shall consider assisting each other in investigations of and proceedings in civil and administrative matters relating to corruption.

2. In matters of international cooperation, whenever dual criminality is considered a requirement, it shall be deemed fulfilled irrespective of whether the laws of the requested State Party place the offence within the same category of offence or denominate the offence by the same terminology as the requesting State Party, if the conduct underlying the offence for which assistance is sought is a criminal offence under the laws of both States Parties.

Article 44: extradition

1. This article shall apply to the offences established in accordance with this Convention where the person who is the subject of the request for extradition is present in the territory of the requested State Party, provided that the offence for which extradition is sought is punishable under the domestic law of both the requesting State Party and the requested State Party.
2. Notwithstanding the provisions of paragraph 1 of this article, a State Party whose law so permits may grant the extradition of a person for any of the offences covered by this Convention that are not punishable under its own domestic law.
3. If the request for extradition includes several separate offences, at least one of which is extraditable under this article and some of which are not extraditable by reason of their period of imprisonment but are related to offences established in accordance with this Convention, the requested State Party may apply this article also in respect of those offences.
4. Each of the offences to which this article applies shall be deemed to be included as an extraditable offence in any extradition treaty existing between States Parties. States Parties undertake to include such offences as extraditable offences in every extradition treaty to be concluded between them. A State Party whose law so permits, in case it uses this Convention as the basis for extradition, shall not consider any of the offences established in accordance with this Convention to be a political offence.
5. If a State Party that makes extradition conditional on the existence of a treaty receives a request for extradition from another State Party with which it has no extradition treaty, it may consider this Convention the legal basis for extradition in respect of any offence to which this article applies.
6. A State Party that makes extradition conditional on the existence of a treaty shall:
(a) At the time of deposit of its instrument of ratification, acceptance or approval of or accession to this Convention, inform the Secretary-General of the United Nations whether it will take this Convention as the legal basis for cooperation on extradition with other States Parties to this Convention; and
(b) If it does not take this Convention as the legal basis for cooperation on extradition, seek, where appropriate, to conclude treaties on extradition with other States Parties to this Convention in order to implement this article.
7. States Parties that do not make extradition conditional on the existence of a treaty shall recognize offences to which this article applies as extraditable offences between themselves.
8. Extradition shall be subject to the conditions provided for by the domestic law of the requested State Party or by applicable extradition treaties, including, inter alia, conditions in relation to the minimum penalty requirement for extradition and the grounds upon which the requested State Party may refuse extradition.

9. States Parties shall, subject to their domestic law, endeavour to expedite extradition procedures and to simplify evidentiary requirements relating thereto in respect of any offence to which this article applies.
10. Subject to the provisions of its domestic law and its extradition treaties, the requested State Party may, upon being satisfied that the circumstances so warrant and are urgent and at the request of the requesting State Party, take a person whose extradition is sought and who is present in its territory into custody or take other appropriate measures to ensure his or her presence at extradition proceedings.
11. A State Party in whose territory an alleged offender is found, if it does not extradite such person in respect of an offence to which this article applies solely on the ground that he or she is one of its nationals, shall, at the request of the State Party seeking extradition, be obliged to submit the case without undue delay to its competent authorities for the purpose of prosecution. Those authorities shall take their decision and conduct their proceedings in the same manner as in the case of any other offence of a grave nature under the domestic law of that State Party. The States Parties concerned shall cooperate with each other, in particular on procedural and evidentiary aspects, to ensure the efficiency of such prosecution.
12. Whenever a State Party is permitted under its domestic law to extradite or otherwise surrender one of its nationals only upon the condition that the person will be returned to that State Party to serve the sentence imposed as a result of the trial or proceedings for which the extradition or surrender of the person was sought and that State Party and the State Party seeking the extradition of the person agree with this option and other terms that they may deem appropriate, such conditional extradition or surrender shall be sufficient to discharge the obligation set forth in paragraph 11 of this article.
13. If extradition, sought for purposes of enforcing a sentence, is refused because the person sought is a national of the requested State Party, the requested State Party shall, if its domestic law so permits and in conformity with the requirements of such law, upon application of the requesting State Party, consider the enforcement of the sentence imposed under the domestic law of the requesting State Party or the remainder thereof.
14. Any person regarding whom proceedings are being carried out in connection with any of the offences to which this article applies shall be guaranteed fair treatment at all stages of the proceedings, including enjoyment of all the rights and guarantees provided by the domestic law of the State Party in the territory of which that person is present.
15. Nothing in this Convention shall be interpreted as imposing an obligation to extradite if the requested State Party has substantial grounds for believing that the request has been made for the purpose of prosecuting or punishing a person on account of that person's sex, race, religion, nationality, ethnic origin or political opinions or that compliance with the request would cause prejudice to that person's position for any one of these reasons.
16. States Parties may not refuse a request for extradition on the sole ground that the offence is also considered to involve fiscal matters.
17. Before refusing extradition, the requested State Party shall, where appropriate, consult with the requesting State Party to provide it with ample opportunity to present its opinions and to provide information relevant to its allegation.
18. States Parties shall seek to conclude bilateral and multilateral agreements or arrangements to carry out or to enhance the effectiveness of extradition.

Article 45: transfer of sentenced persons

States Parties may consider entering into bilateral or multilateral agreements or arrangements on the transfer to their territory of persons sentenced to imprisonment or other forms of deprivation of liberty for offences established in accordance with this Convention in order that they may complete their sentences there.

Article 46: mutual legal assistance

1. States Parties shall afford one another the widest measure of mutual legal assistance in investigations, prosecutions and judicial proceedings in relation to the offences covered by this Convention.
2. Mutual legal assistance shall be afforded to the fullest extent possible under relevant laws, treaties, agreements and arrangements of the requested State Party with respect to investigations, prosecutions and judicial proceedings in relation to the offences for which a legal person may be held liable in accordance with article 26 of this Convention in the requesting State Party.
3. Mutual legal assistance to be afforded in accordance with this article may be requested for any of the following purposes:
(a) Taking evidence or statements from persons;
(b) Effecting service of judicial documents;
(c) Executing searches and seizures, and freezing;
(d) Examining objects and sites;
(e) Providing information, evidentiary items and expert evaluations;
(f) Providing originals or certified copies of relevant documents and records, including government, bank, financial, corporate or business records;
(g) Identifying or tracing proceeds of crime, property, instrumentalities or other things for evidentiary purposes;
(h) Facilitating the voluntary appearance of persons in the requesting State Party;
(i) Any other type of assistance that is not contrary to the domestic law of the requested State Party;
(j) Identifying, freezing and tracing proceeds of crime in accordance with the provisions of chapter V of this Convention;
(k) The recovery of assets, in accordance with the provisions of chapter V of this Convention.
4. Without prejudice to domestic law, the competent authorities of a State Party may, without prior request, transmit information relating to criminal matters to a competent authority in another State Party where they believe that such information could assist the authority in undertaking or successfully concluding inquiries and criminal proceedings or could result in a request formulated by the latter State Party pursuant to this Convention.
5. The transmission of information pursuant to paragraph 4 of this article shall be without prejudice to inquiries and criminal proceedings in the State of the competent authorities providing the information. The competent authorities receiving the information shall comply with a request that said information remain confidential, even temporarily, or with restrictions on its use. However, this shall not prevent the receiving State Party from disclosing in its proceedings information that is exculpatory to an accused person. In such a case, the receiving State Party shall notify the transmitting State Party prior to the disclosure and, if so requested, consult with the transmitting State Party. If, in an exceptional case, advance notice is not

possible, the receiving State Party shall inform the transmitting State Party of the disclosure without delay.
6. The provisions of this article shall not affect the obligations under any other treaty, bilateral or multilateral, that governs or will govern, in whole or in part, mutual legal assistance.
7. Paragraphs 9 to 29 of this article shall apply to requests made pursuant to this article if the States Parties in question are not bound by a treaty of mutual legal assistance. If those States Parties are bound by such a treaty, the corresponding provisions of that treaty shall apply unless the States Parties agree to apply paragraphs 9 to 29 of this article in lieu thereof. States Parties are strongly encouraged to apply those paragraphs if they facilitate cooperation.
8. States Parties shall not decline to render mutual legal assistance pursuant to this article on the ground of bank secrecy.
9. (a) A requested State Party, in responding to a request for assistance pursuant to this article in the absence of dual criminality, shall take into account the purposes of this Convention, as set forth in article 1;
(b) States Parties may decline to render assistance pursuant to this article on the ground of absence of dual criminality. However, a requested State Party shall, where consistent with the basic concepts of its legal system, render assistance that does not involve coercive action. Such assistance may be refused when requests involve matters of a de minimis nature or matters for which the cooperation or assistance sought is available under other provisions of this Convention;
(c) Each State Party may consider adopting such measures as may be necessary to enable it to provide a wider scope of assistance pursuant to this article in the absence of dual criminality.
10. A person who is being detained or is serving a sentence in the territory of one State Party whose presence in another State Party is requested for purposes of identification, testimony or otherwise providing assistance in obtaining evidence for investigations, prosecutions or judicial proceedings in relation to offences covered by this Convention may be transferred if the following conditions are met:
(a) The person freely gives his or her informed consent;
(b) The competent authorities of both States Parties agree, subject to such conditions as those States Parties may deem appropriate.
11. For the purposes of paragraph 10 of this article:
(a) The State Party to which the person is transferred shall have the authority and obligation to keep the person transferred in custody, unless otherwise requested or authorized by the State Party from which the person was transferred;
(b) The State Party to which the person is transferred shall without delay implement its obligation to return the person to the custody of the State Party from which the person was transferred as agreed beforehand, or as otherwise agreed, by the competent authorities of both States Parties;
(c) The State Party to which the person is transferred shall not require the State Party from which the person was transferred to initiate extradition proceedings for the return of the person;
(d) The person transferred shall receive credit for service of the sentence being served in the State from which he or she was transferred for time spent in the custody of the State Party to which he or she was transferred.

12. Unless the State Party from which a person is to be transferred in accordance with paragraphs 10 and 11 of this article so agrees, that person, whatever his or her nationality, shall not be prosecuted, detained, punished or subjected to any other restriction of his or her personal liberty in the territory of the State to which that person is transferred in respect of acts, omissions or convictions prior to his or her departure from the territory of the State from which he or she was transferred.
13. Each State Party shall designate a central authority that shall have the responsibility and power to receive requests for mutual legal assistance and either to execute them or to transmit them to the competent authorities for execution. Where a State Party has a special region or territory with a separate system of mutual legal assistance, it may designate a distinct central authority that shall have the same function for that region or territory. Central authorities shall ensure the speedy and proper execution or transmission of the requests received. Where the central authority transmits the request to a competent authority for execution, it shall encourage the speedy and proper execution of the request by the competent authority. The Secretary-General of the United Nations shall be notified of the central authority designated for this purpose at the time each State Party deposits its instrument of ratification, acceptance or approval of or accession to this Convention. Requests for mutual legal assistance and any communication related thereto shall be transmitted to the central authorities designated by the States Parties. This requirement shall be without prejudice to the right of a State Party to require that such requests and communications be addressed to it through diplomatic channels and, in urgent circumstances, where the States Parties agree, through the International Criminal Police Organization, if possible.
14. Requests shall be made in writing or, where possible, by any means capable of producing a written record, in a language acceptable to the requested State Party, under conditions allowing that State Party to establish authenticity. The Secretary-General of the United Nations shall be notified of the language or languages acceptable to each State Party at the time it deposits its instrument of ratification, acceptance or approval of or accession to this Convention. In urgent circumstances and where agreed by the States Parties, requests may be made orally but shall be confirmed in writing forthwith.
15. A request for mutual legal assistance shall contain:
(a) The identity of the authority making the request;
(b) The subject matter and nature of the investigation, prosecution or judicial proceeding to which the request relates and the name and functions of the authority conducting the investigation, prosecution or judicial proceeding;
(c) A summary of the relevant facts, except in relation to requests for the purpose of service of judicial documents;
(d) A description of the assistance sought and details of any particular procedure that the requesting State Party wishes to be followed;
(e) Where possible, the identity, location and nationality of any person concerned; and
(f) The purpose for which the evidence, information or action is sought.
16. The requested State Party may request additional information when it appears necessary for the execution of the request in accordance with its domestic law or when it can facilitate such execution.

17. A request shall be executed in accordance with the domestic law of the requested State Party and, to the extent not contrary to the domestic law of the requested State Party and where possible, in accordance with the procedures specified in the request.
18. Wherever possible and consistent with fundamental principles of domestic law, when an individual is in the territory of a State Party and has to be heard as a witness or expert by the judicial authorities of another State Party, the first State Party may, at the request of the other, permit the hearing to take place by video conference if it is not possible or desirable for the individual in question to appear in person in the territory of the requesting State Party. States Parties may agree that the hearing shall be conducted by a judicial authority of the requesting State Party and attended by a judicial authority of the requested State Party.
19. The requesting State Party shall not transmit or use information or evidence furnished by the requested State Party for investigations, prosecutions or judicial proceedings other than those stated in the request without the prior consent of the requested State Party. Nothing in this paragraph shall prevent the requesting State Party from disclosing in its proceedings information or evidence that is exculpatory to an accused person. In the latter case, the requesting State Party shall notify the requested State Party prior to the disclosure and, if so requested, consult with the requested State Party. If, in an exceptional case, advance notice is not possible, the requesting State Party shall inform the requested State Party of the disclosure without delay.
20. The requesting State Party may require that the requested State Party keep confidential the fact and substance of the request, except to the extent necessary to execute the request. If the requested State Party cannot comply with the requirement of confidentiality, it shall promptly inform the requesting State Party.
21. Mutual legal assistance may be refused:
(a) If the request is not made in conformity with the provisions of this article;
(b) If the requested State Party considers that execution of the request is likely to prejudice its sovereignty, security, ordre public or other essential interests;
(c) If the authorities of the requested State Party would be prohibited by its domestic law from carrying out the action requested with regard to any similar offence, had it been subject to investigation, prosecution or judicial proceedings under their own jurisdiction;
(d) If it would be contrary to the legal system of the requested State Party relating to mutual legal assistance for the request to be granted.
22. States Parties may not refuse a request for mutual legal assistance on the sole ground that the offence is also considered to involve fiscal matters.
23. Reasons shall be given for any refusal of mutual legal assistance.
24. The requested State Party shall execute the request for mutual legal assistance as soon as possible and shall take as full account as possible of any deadlines suggested by the requesting State Party and for which reasons are given, preferably in the request. The requesting State Party may make reasonable requests for information on the status and progress of measures taken by the requested State Party to satisfy its request. The requested State Party shall respond to reasonable requests by the requesting State Party on the status, and progress in its handling, of the request. The requesting State Party shall promptly inform the requested State Party when the assistance sought is no longer required.

25. Mutual legal assistance may be postponed by the requested State Party on the ground that it interferes with an ongoing investigation, prosecution or judicial proceeding.
26. Before refusing a request pursuant to paragraph 21 of this article or postponing its execution pursuant to paragraph 25 of this article, the requested State Party shall consult with the requesting State Party to consider whether assistance may be granted subject to such terms and conditions as it deems necessary. If the requesting State Party accepts assistance subject to those conditions, it shall comply with the conditions.
27. Without prejudice to the application of paragraph 12 of this article, a witness, expert or other person who, at the request of the requesting State Party, consents to give evidence in a proceeding or to assist in an investigation, prosecution or judicial proceeding in the territory of the requesting State Party shall not be prosecuted, detained, punished or subjected to any other restriction of his or her personal liberty in that territory in respect of acts, omissions or convictions prior to his or her departure from the territory of the requested State Party. Such safe conduct shall cease when the witness, expert or other person having had, for a period of fifteen consecutive days or for any period agreed upon by the States Parties from the date on which he or she has been officially informed that his or her presence is no longer required by the judicial authorities, an opportunity of leaving, has nevertheless remained voluntarily in the territory of the requesting State Party or, having left it, has returned of his or her own free will.
28. The ordinary costs of executing a request shall be borne by the requested State Party, unless otherwise agreed by the States Parties concerned. If expenses of a substantial or extraordinary nature are or will be required to fulfil the request, the States Parties shall consult to determine the terms and conditions under which the request will be executed, as well as the manner in which the costs shall be borne.
29. The requested State Party:
(a) Shall provide to the requesting State Party copies of government records, documents or information in its possession that under its domestic law are available to the general public;
(b) May, at its discretion, provide to the requesting State Party in whole, in part or subject to such conditions as it deems appropriate, copies of any government records, documents or information in its possession that under its domestic law are not available to the general public.
30. States Parties shall consider, as may be necessary, the possibility of concluding bilateral or multilateral agreements or arrangements that would serve the purposes of, give practical effect to or enhance the provisions of this article.

Article 47: transfer of criminal proceedings
States Parties shall consider the possibility of transferring to one another proceedings for the prosecution of an offence established in accordance with this Convention in cases where such transfer is considered to be in the interests of the proper administration of justice, in particular in cases where several jurisdictions are involved, with a view to concentrating the prosecution.

Article 48: law enforcement cooperation
1. States Parties shall cooperate closely with one another, consistent with their respective domestic legal and administrative systems, to enhance the effectiveness of law enforcement action to combat the offences covered by this Convention. States Parties shall, in particular, take effective measures:

(a) To enhance and, where necessary, to establish channels of communication between their competent authorities, agencies and services in order to facilitate the secure and rapid exchange of information concerning all aspects of the offences covered by this Convention, including, if the States Parties concerned deem it appropriate, links with other criminal activities;
(b) To cooperate with other States Parties in conducting inquiries with respect to offences covered by this Convention concerning:
(i) The identity, whereabouts and activities of persons suspected of involvement in such offences or the location of other persons concerned;
(ii) The movement of proceeds of crime or property derived from the commission of such offences;
(iii) The movement of property, equipment or other instrumentalities used or intended for use in the commission of such offences;
(c) To provide, where appropriate, necessary items or quantities of substances for analytical or investigative purposes;
(d) To exchange, where appropriate, information with other States Parties concerning specific means and methods used to commit offences covered by this Convention, including the use of false identities, forged, altered or false documents and other means of concealing activities;
(e) To facilitate effective coordination between their competent authorities, agencies and services and to promote the exchange of personnel and other experts, including, subject to bilateral agreements or arrangements between the States Parties concerned, the posting of liaison officers;
(f) To exchange information and coordinate administrative and other measures taken as appropriate for the purpose of early identification of the offences covered by this Convention.
2. With a view to giving effect to this Convention, States Parties shall consider entering into bilateral or multilateral agreements or arrangements on direct cooperation between their law enforcement agencies and, where such agreements or arrangements already exist, amending them. In the absence of such agreements or arrangements between the States Parties concerned, the States Parties may consider this Convention to be the basis for mutual law enforcement cooperation in respect of the offences covered by this Convention. Whenever appropriate, States Parties shall make full use of agreements or arrangements, including international or regional organizations, to enhance the cooperation between their law enforcement agencies.
3. States Parties shall endeavour to cooperate within their means to respond to offences covered by this Convention committed through the use of modern technology.

Article 49: joint investigations
States Parties shall consider concluding bilateral or multilateral agreements or arrangements whereby, in relation to matters that are the subject of investigations, prosecutions or judicial proceedings in one or more States, the competent authorities concerned may establish joint investigative bodies. In the absence of such agreements or arrangements, joint investigations may be undertaken by agreement on a case-by-case basis. The States Parties involved shall ensure that the sovereignty of the State Party in whose territory such investigation is to take place is fully respected.

Article 50: special investigative techniques

1. In order to combat corruption effectively, each State Party shall, to the extent permitted by the basic principles of its domestic legal system and in accordance with the conditions prescribed by its domestic law, take such measures as may be necessary, within its means, to allow for the appropriate use by its competent authorities of controlled delivery and, where it deems appropriate, other special investigative techniques, such as electronic or other forms of surveillance and undercover operations, within its territory, and to allow for the admissibility in court of evidence derived there from.
2. For the purpose of investigating the offences covered by this Convention, States Parties are encouraged to conclude, when necessary, appropriate bilateral or multilateral agreements or arrangements for using such special investigative techniques in the context of cooperation at the international level. Such agreements or arrangements shall be concluded and implemented in full compliance with the principle of sovereign equality of States and shall be carried out strictly in accordance with the terms of those agreements or arrangements.
3. In the absence of an agreement or arrangement as set forth in paragraph 2 of this article, decisions to use such special investigative techniques at the international level shall be made on a case-by-case basis and may, when necessary, take into consideration financial arrangements and understandings with respect to the exercise of jurisdiction by the States Parties concerned.
4. Decisions to use controlled delivery at the international level may, with the consent of the States Parties concerned, include methods such as intercepting and allowing the goods or funds to continue intact or be removed or replaced in whole or in part.

CHAPTER V: ASSET RECOVERY

Article 51: general provision

The return of assets pursuant to this chapter is a fundamental principle of this Convention, and States Parties shall afford one another the widest measure of cooperation and assistance in this regard.

Article 52: prevention and detection of transfers of proceeds of crime

1. Without prejudice to article 14 of this Convention, each State Party shall take such measures as may be necessary, in accordance with its domestic law, to require financial institutions within its jurisdiction to verify the identity of customers, to take reasonable steps to determine the identity of beneficial owners of funds deposited into high-value accounts and to conduct enhanced scrutiny of accounts sought or maintained by or on behalf of individuals who are, or have been, entrusted with prominent public functions and their family members and close associates. Such enhanced scrutiny shall be reasonably designed to detect suspicious transactions for the purpose of reporting to competent authorities and should not be so construed as to discourage or prohibit financial institutions from doing business with any legitimate customer.
2. In order to facilitate implementation of the measures provided for in paragraph 1 of this article, each State Party, in accordance with its domestic law and inspired by relevant initiatives of regional, interregional and multilateral organizations against money-laundering, shall:

(a) Issue advisories regarding the types of natural or legal person to whose accounts financial institutions within its jurisdiction will be expected to apply enhanced scrutiny, the types of

accounts and transactions to which to pay particular attention and appropriate account-opening, maintenance and record-keeping measures to take concerning such accounts; and
(b) Where appropriate, notify financial institutions within its jurisdiction, at the request of another State Party or on its own initiative, of the identity of particular natural or legal persons to whose accounts such institutions will be expected to apply enhanced scrutiny, in addition to those whom the financial institutions may otherwise identify.
3. In the context of paragraph 2 (a) of this article, each State Party shall implement measures to ensure that its financial institutions maintain adequate records, over an appropriate period of time, of accounts and transactions involving the persons mentioned in paragraph 1 of this article, which should, as a minimum, contain information relating to the identity of the customer as well as, as far as possible, of the beneficial owner.
4. With the aim of preventing and detecting transfers of proceeds of offences established in accordance with this Convention, each State Party shall implement appropriate and effective measures to prevent, with the help of its regulatory and oversight bodies, the establishment of banks that have no physical presence and that are not affiliated with a regulated financial group. Moreover, States Parties may consider requiring their financial institutions to refuse to enter into or continue a correspondent banking relationship with such institutions and to guard against establishing relations with foreign financial institutions that permit their accounts to be used by banks that have no physical presence and that are not affiliated with a regulated financial group.
5. Each State Party shall consider establishing, in accordance with its domestic law, effective financial disclosure systems for appropriate public officials and shall provide for appropriate sanctions for non-compliance. Each State Party shall also consider taking such measures as may be necessary to permit its competent authorities to share that information with the competent authorities in other States Parties when necessary to investigate, claim and recover proceeds of offences established in accordance with this Convention.
6. Each State Party shall consider taking such measures as may be necessary, in accordance with its domestic law, to require appropriate public officials having an interest in or signature or other authority over a financial account in a foreign country to report that relationship to appropriate authorities and to maintain appropriate records related to such accounts. Such measures shall also provide for appropriate sanctions for non-compliance.

Article 53: measures for direct recovery of property

Each State Party shall, in accordance with its domestic law:
(a) Take such measures as may be necessary to permit another State Party to initiate civil action in its courts to establish title to or ownership of property
acquired through the commission of an offence established in accordance with this Convention;
(b) Take such measures as may be necessary to permit its courts to order those who have committed offences established in accordance with this Convention to pay compensation or damages to another State Party that has been harmed by such offences; and
(c) Take such measures as may be necessary to permit its courts or competent authorities, when having to decide on confiscation, to recognize another State Party's claim as a legitimate owner of property acquired through the commission of an offence established in accordance with this Convention.

Article 54: mechanisms for recovery of property through international cooperation in confiscation

1. Each State Party, in order to provide mutual legal assistance pursuant to article 55 of this Convention with respect to property acquired through or involved in the commission of an offence established in accordance with this Convention, shall, in accordance with its domestic law:

(a) Take such measures as may be necessary to permit its competent authorities to give effect to an order of confiscation issued by a court of another State Party;

(b) Take such measures as may be necessary to permit its competent authorities, where they have jurisdiction, to order the confiscation of such property of foreign origin by adjudication of an offence of money-laundering or such other offence as may be within its jurisdiction or by other procedures authorized under its domestic law; and

(c) Consider taking such measures as may be necessary to allow confiscation of such property without a criminal conviction in cases in which the offender cannot be prosecuted by reason of death, flight or absence or in other appropriate cases.

2. Each State Party, in order to provide mutual legal assistance upon a request made pursuant to paragraph 2 of article 55 of this Convention, shall, in accordance with its domestic law:

(a) Take such measures as may be necessary to permit its competent authorities to freeze or seize property upon a freezing or seizure order issued by a court or competent authority of a requesting State Party that provides a reasonable basis for the requested State Party to believe that there are sufficient grounds for taking such actions and that the property would eventually be subject to an order of confiscation for purposes of paragraph 1 (a) of this article;

(b) Take such measures as may be necessary to permit its competent authorities to freeze or seize property upon a request that provides a reasonable basis for the requested State Party to believe that there are sufficient grounds for taking such actions and that the property would eventually be subject to an order of confiscation for purposes of paragraph 1 (a) of this article; and

(c) Consider taking additional measures to permit its competent authorities to preserve property for confiscation, such as on the basis of a foreign arrest or criminal charge related to the acquisition of such property.

Article 55: international cooperation for purposes of confiscation

1. A State Party that has received a request from another State Party having jurisdiction over an offence established in accordance with this Convention for confiscation of proceeds of crime, property, equipment or other instrumentalities referred to in article 31, paragraph 1, of this Convention situated in its territory shall, to the greatest extent possible within its domestic legal system:

(a) Submit the request to its competent authorities for the purpose of obtaining an order of confiscation and, if such an order is granted, give effect to it; or

(b) Submit to its competent authorities, with a view to giving effect to it to the extent requested, an order of confiscation issued by a court in the territory of the requesting State Party in accordance with articles 31, paragraph 1, and 54, paragraph 1 (a), of this Convention insofar as it relates to proceeds of crime, property, equipment or other instrumentalities referred to in article 31, paragraph 1, situated in the territory of the requested State Party.

2. Following a request made by another State Party having jurisdiction over an offence established in accordance with this Convention, the requested State Party shall take measures to identify, trace and freeze or seize proceeds of crime, property, equipment or other instrumentalities referred to in article 31, paragraph 1, of this Convention for the purpose of eventual confiscation to be ordered either by the requesting State Party or, pursuant to a request under paragraph 1 of this article, by the requested State Party.

3. The provisions of article 46 of this Convention are applicable, mutatis mutandis, to this article. In addition to the information specified in article 46, paragraph 15, requests made pursuant to this article shall contain:

(a) In the case of a request pertaining to paragraph 1 (a) of this article, a description of the property to be confiscated, including, to the extent possible, the location and, where relevant, the estimated value of the property and a statement of the facts relied upon by the requesting State Party sufficient to enable the requested State Party to seek the order under its domestic law;

(b) In the case of a request pertaining to paragraph 1 (b) of this article, a legally admissible copy of an order of confiscation upon which the request is based issued by the requesting State Party, a statement of the facts and information as to the extent to which execution of the order is requested, a statement specifying the measures taken by the requesting State Party to provide adequate notification to bona fide third parties and to ensure due process and a statement that the confiscation order is final;

(c) In the case of a request pertaining to paragraph 2 of this article, a statement of the facts relied upon by the requesting State Party and a description of the actions requested and, where available, a legally admissible copy of an order on which the request is based.

4. The decisions or actions provided for in paragraphs 1 and 2 of this article shall be taken by the requested State Party in accordance with and subject to the provisions of its domestic law and its procedural rules or any bilateral or multilateral agreement or arrangement to which it may be bound in relation to the requesting State Party.

5. Each State Party shall furnish copies of its laws and regulations that give effect to this article and of any subsequent changes to such laws and regulations or a description thereof to the Secretary-General of the United Nations.

6. If a State Party elects to make the taking of the measures referred to in paragraphs 1 and 2 of this article conditional on the existence of a relevant treaty, that State Party shall consider this Convention the necessary and sufficient treaty basis.

7. Cooperation under this article may also be refused or provisional measures lifted if the requested State Party does not receive sufficient and timely evidence or if the property is of a de minimis value.

8. Before lifting any provisional measure taken pursuant to this article, the requested State Party shall, wherever possible, give the requesting State Party an opportunity to present its reasons in favour of continuing the measure.

9. The provisions of this article shall not be construed as prejudicing the rights of bona fide third parties.

Article 56: special cooperation

Without prejudice to its domestic law, each State Party shall endeavour to take measures to permit it to forward, without prejudice to its own investigations, prosecutions or judicial proceedings, information on proceeds of offences established in accordance with this Convention to another State Party without prior request, when it considers that the disclosure of such information might assist the receiving State Party in initiating or carrying out investigations, prosecutions or judicial proceedings or might lead to a request by that State Party under this chapter of the Convention.

Article 57: return and disposal of assets

1. Property confiscated by a State Party pursuant to article 31 or 55 of this Convention shall be disposed of, including by return to its prior legitimate owners, pursuant to paragraph 3 of this article, by that State Party in accordance with the provisions of this Convention and its domestic law.

2. Each State Party shall adopt such legislative and other measures, in accordance with the fundamental principles of its domestic law, as may be necessary to enable its competent authorities to return confiscated property, when acting on the request made by another State Party, in accordance with this Convention, taking into account the rights of bona fide third parties.

3. In accordance with articles 46 and 55 of this Convention and paragraphs 1 and 2 of this article, the requested State Party shall:

(a) In the case of embezzlement of public funds or of laundering of embezzled public funds as referred to in articles 17 and 23 of this Convention, when confiscation was executed in accordance with article 55 and on the basis of a final judgement in the requesting State Party, a requirement that can be waived by the requested State Party, return the confiscated property to the requesting State Party;

(b) In the case of proceeds of any other offence covered by this Convention, when the confiscation was executed in accordance with article 55 of this Convention and on the basis of a final judgement in the requesting State Party, a requirement that can be waived by the requested State Party, return the confiscated property to the requesting State Party, when the requesting State Party reasonably establishes its prior ownership of such confiscated property to the requested State Party or when the requested State Party recognizes damage to the requesting State Party as a basis for returning the confiscated property;

(c) In all other cases, give priority consideration to returning confiscated property to the requesting State Party, returning such property to its prior legitimate owners or compensating the victims of the crime.

4. Where appropriate, unless States Parties decide otherwise, the requested State Party may deduct reasonable expenses incurred in investigations, prosecutions or judicial proceedings leading to the return or disposition of confiscated property pursuant to this article.

5. Where appropriate, States Parties may also give special consideration to concluding agreements or mutually acceptable arrangements, on a case-by-case basis, for the final disposal of confiscated property.

Article 58: financial intelligence unit
States Parties shall cooperate with one another for the purpose of preventing and combating the transfer of proceeds of offences established in accordance with this Convention and of promoting ways and means of recovering such proceeds and, to that end, shall consider establishing a financial intelligence unit to be responsible for receiving, analysing and disseminating to the competent authorities reports of suspicious financial transactions.

Article 59: bilateral and multilateral agreements and arrangements
States Parties shall consider concluding bilateral or multilateral agreements or arrangements to enhance the effectiveness of international cooperation undertaken pursuant to this chapter of the Convention.

CHAPTER VI: TECHNICAL ASSISTANCE AND INFORMATION EXCHANGE

Article 60: training and technical assistance
1. Each State Party shall, to the extent necessary, initiate, develop or improve specific training programmes for its personnel responsible for preventing and combating corruption. Such training programmes could deal, inter alia, with the following areas:
(a) Effective measures to prevent, detect, investigate, punish and control corruption, including the use of evidence-gathering and investigative methods;
(b) Building capacity in the development and planning of strategic anticorruption policy;
(c) Training competent authorities in the preparation of requests for mutual legal assistance that meet the requirements of this Convention;
(d) Evaluation and strengthening of institutions, public service management and the management of public finances, including public procurement, and the private sector;
(e) Preventing and combating the transfer of proceeds of offences established in accordance with this Convention and recovering such proceeds;
(f) Detecting and freezing of the transfer of proceeds of offences established in accordance with this Convention;
(g) Surveillance of the movement of proceeds of offences established in accordance with this Convention and of the methods used to transfer, conceal or disguise such proceeds;
(h) Appropriate and efficient legal and administrative mechanisms and methods for facilitating the return of proceeds of offences established in accordance with this Convention;
(i) Methods used in protecting victims and witnesses who cooperate with judicial authorities; and
(j) Training in national and international regulations and in languages.
2. States Parties shall, according to their capacity, consider affording one another the widest measure of technical assistance, especially for the benefit of developing countries, in their respective plans and programmes to combat corruption, including material support and training in the areas referred to in paragraph 1 of this article, and training and assistance and the mutual exchange of relevant experience and specialized knowledge, which will facilitate international cooperation between States Parties in the areas of extradition and mutual legal assistance.

3. States Parties shall strengthen, to the extent necessary, efforts to maximize operational and training activities in international and regional organizations and in the framework of relevant bilateral and multilateral agreements or arrangements.
4. States Parties shall consider assisting one another, upon request, in conducting evaluations, studies and research relating to the types, causes, effects and costs of corruption in their respective countries, with a view to developing, with the participation of competent authorities and society, strategies and action plans to combat corruption.
5. In order to facilitate the recovery of proceeds of offences established in accordance with this Convention, States Parties may cooperate in providing each other with the names of experts who could assist in achieving that objective.
6. States Parties shall consider using subregional, regional and international conferences and seminars to promote cooperation and technical assistance and to stimulate discussion on problems of mutual concern, including the special problems and needs of developing countries and countries with economies in transition.
7. States Parties shall consider establishing voluntary mechanisms with a view to contributing financially to the efforts of developing countries and countries with economies in transition to apply this Convention through technical assistance programmes and projects.
8. Each State Party shall consider making voluntary contributions to the United Nations Office on Drugs and Crime for the purpose of fostering, through the Office, programmes and projects in developing countries with a view to implementing this Convention.

Article 61: collection, exchange and analysis of information on corruption

1. Each State Party shall consider analysing, in consultation with experts, trends in corruption in its territory, as well as the circumstances in which corruption offences are committed.
2. States Parties shall consider developing and sharing with each other and through international and regional organizations statistics, analytical expertise concerning corruption and information with a view to developing, insofar as possible, common definitions, standards and methodologies, as well as information on best practices to prevent and combat corruption.
3. Each State Party shall consider monitoring its policies and actual measures to combat corruption and making assessments of their effectiveness and efficiency.

Article 62: other measures: implementation of the Convention through economic development and technical assistance

1. States Parties shall take measures conducive to the optimal implementation of this Convention to the extent possible, through international cooperation, taking into account the negative effects of corruption on society in general, in particular on sustainable development.
2. States Parties shall make concrete efforts to the extent possible and in coordination with each other, as well as with international and regional organizations:
(a) To enhance their cooperation at various levels with developing countries, with a view to strengthening the capacity of the latter to prevent and combat corruption;
(b) To enhance financial and material assistance to support the efforts of developing countries to prevent and fight corruption effectively and to help them implement this Convention successfully;

(c) To provide technical assistance to developing countries and countries with economies in transition to assist them in meeting their needs for the implementation of this Convention. To that end, States Parties shall endeavour to make adequate and regular voluntary contributions to an account specifically designated for that purpose in a United Nations funding mechanism. States Parties may also give special consideration, in accordance with their domestic law and the provisions of this Convention, to contributing to that account a percentage of the money or of the corresponding value of proceeds of crime or property confiscated in accordance with the provisions of this Convention;
(d) To encourage and persuade other States and financial institutions as appropriate to join them in efforts in accordance with this article, in particular by providing more training programmes and modern equipment to developing countries in order to assist them in achieving the objectives of this Convention.
3. To the extent possible, these measures shall be without prejudice to existing foreign assistance commitments or to other financial cooperation arrangements at the bilateral, regional or international level.
4. States Parties may conclude bilateral or multilateral agreements or arrangements on material and logistical assistance, taking into consideration the financial arrangements necessary for the means of international cooperation provided for by this Convention to be effective and for the prevention, detection and control of corruption.

CHAPTER VII: MECHANISMS FOR IMPLEMENTATION

Article 63: conference of the States Parties to the Convention

1. A Conference of the States Parties to the Convention is hereby established to improve the capacity of and cooperation between States Parties to achieve the objectives set forth in this Convention and to promote and review its implementation.
2. The Secretary-General of the United Nations shall convene the Conference of the States Parties not later than one year following the entry into force of this Convention. Thereafter, regular meetings of the Conference of the States Parties shall be held in accordance with the rules of procedure adopted by the Conference.
3. The Conference of the States Parties shall adopt rules of procedure and rules governing the functioning of the activities set forth in this article, including rules concerning the admission and participation of observers, and the payment of expenses incurred in carrying out those activities.
4. The Conference of the States Parties shall agree upon activities, procedures and methods of work to achieve the objectives set forth in paragraph 1 of this article, including:
(a) Facilitating activities by States Parties under articles 60 and 62 and chapters II to V of this Convention, including by encouraging the mobilization of voluntary contributions;
(b) Facilitating the exchange of information among States Parties on patterns and trends in corruption and on successful practices for preventing and combating it and for the return of proceeds of crime, through, inter alia, the publication of relevant information as mentioned in this article;
(c) Cooperating with relevant international and regional organizations and mechanisms and non-governmental organizations;

(d) Making appropriate use of relevant information produced by other international and regional mechanisms for combating and preventing corruption in order to avoid unnecessary duplication of work;
(e) Reviewing periodically the implementation of this Convention by its States Parties;
(f) Making recommendations to improve this Convention and its implementation;
(g) Taking note of the technical assistance requirements of States Parties with regard to the implementation of this Convention and recommending any action it may deem necessary in that respect.
5. For the purpose of paragraph 4 of this article, the Conference of the States Parties shall acquire the necessary knowledge of the measures taken by States Parties in implementing this Convention and the difficulties encountered by them in doing so through information provided by them and through such supplemental review mechanisms as may be established by the Conference of the States Parties.
6. Each State Party shall provide the Conference of the States Parties with information on its programmes, plans and practices, as well as on legislative and administrative measures to implement this Convention, as required by the Conference of the States Parties. The Conference of the States Parties shall examine the most effective way of receiving and acting upon information, including, inter alia, information received from States Parties and from competent international organizations. Inputs received from relevant non-governmental organizations duly accredited in accordance with procedures to be decided upon by the Conference of the States Parties may also be considered.
7. Pursuant to paragraphs 4 to 6 of this article, the Conference of the States Parties shall establish, if it deems it necessary, any appropriate mechanism or body to assist in the effective implementation of the Convention.

Article 64: secretariat

1. The Secretary-General of the United Nations shall provide the necessary secretariat services to the Conference of the States Parties to the Convention.
2. The secretariat shall:
(a) Assist the Conference of the States Parties in carrying out the activities set forth in article 63 of this Convention and make arrangements and provide the necessary services for the sessions of the Conference of the States Parties;
(b) Upon request, assist States Parties in providing information to the Conference of the States Parties as envisaged in article 63, paragraphs 5 and 6, of this Convention; and
(c) Ensure the necessary coordination with the secretariats of relevant international and regional organizations.

CHAPTER VIII: FINAL PROVISIONS

Article 65: implementation of the Convention

1. Each State Party shall take the necessary measures, including legislative and administrative measures, in accordance with fundamental principles of its domestic law, to ensure the implementation of its obligations under this Convention.

2. Each State Party may adopt more strict or severe measures than those provided for by this Convention for preventing and combating corruption.

Article 66: settlement of disputes

1. States Parties shall endeavour to settle disputes concerning the interpretation or application of this Convention through negotiation.
2. Any dispute between two or more States Parties concerning the interpretation or application of this Convention that cannot be settled through negotiation within a reasonable time shall, at the request of one of those States Parties, be submitted to arbitration. If, six months after the date of the request for arbitration, those States Parties are unable to agree on the organization of the arbitration, any one of those States Parties may refer the dispute to the International Court of Justice by request in accordance with the Statute of the Court.
3. Each State Party may, at the time of signature, ratification, acceptance or approval of or accession to this Convention, declare that it does not consider itself bound by paragraph 2 of this article. The other States Parties shall not be bound by paragraph 2 of this article with respect to any State Party that has made such a reservation.
4. Any State Party that has made a reservation in accordance with paragraph 3 of this article may at any time withdraw that reservation by notification to the Secretary-General of the United Nations.

Article 67: signature, ratification, acceptance, approval and accession

1. This Convention shall be open to all States for signature from 9 to 11 december 2003 in Merida, Mexico, and thereafter at United Nations Headquarters in New York until 9 december 2005.
2. This Convention shall also be open for signature by regional economic integration organizations provided that at least one member State of such organization has signed this Convention in accordance with paragraph 1 of this article.
3. This Convention is subject to ratification, acceptance or approval.
Instruments of ratification, acceptance or approval shall be deposited with the Secretary-General of the United Nations. A regional economic integration organization may deposit its instrument of ratification, acceptance or approval if at least one of its member States has done likewise. In that instrument of ratification, acceptance or approval, such organization shall declare the extent of its competence with respect to the matters governed by this Convention. Such organization shall also inform the depositary of any relevant modification in the extent of its competence.
4. This Convention is open for accession by any State or any regional economic integration organization of which at least one member State is a Party to this Convention. Instruments of accession shall be deposited with the Secretary General of the United Nations. At the time of its accession, a regional economic integration organization shall declare the extent of its competence with respect to matters governed by this Convention. Such organization shall also inform the depositary of any relevant modification in the extent of its competence.

Article 68: entry into force
1. This Convention shall enter into force on the ninetieth day after the date of deposit of the thirtieth instrument of ratification, acceptance, approval or accession. For the purpose of this paragraph, any instrument deposited by a regional economic integration organization shall not be counted as additional to those deposited by member States of such organization.
2. For each State or regional economic integration organization ratifying, accepting, approving or acceding to this Convention after the deposit of the thirtieth instrument of such action, this Convention shall enter into force on the thirtieth day after the date of deposit by such State or organization of the relevant instrument or on the date this Convention enters into force pursuant to paragraph 1 of this article, whichever is later.

Article 69: amendment
1. After the expiry of five years from the entry into force of this Convention, a State Party may propose an amendment and transmit it to the Secretary-General of the United Nations, who shall thereupon communicate the proposed amendment to the States Parties and to the Conference of the States Parties to the Convention for the purpose of considering and deciding on the proposal. The Conference of the States Parties shall make every effort to achieve consensus on each amendment. If all efforts at consensus have been exhausted and no agreement has been reached, the amendment shall, as a last resort, require for its adoption a two-thirds majority vote of the States Parties present and voting at the meeting of the Conference of the States Parties.
2. Regional economic integration organizations, in matters within their competence, shall exercise their right to vote under this article with a number of votes equal to the number of their member States that are Parties to this Convention. Such organizations shall not exercise their right to vote if their member States exercise theirs and vice versa.
3. An amendment adopted in accordance with paragraph 1 of this article is subject to ratification, acceptance or approval by States Parties.
4. An amendment adopted in accordance with paragraph 1 of this article shall enter into force in respect of a State Party ninety days after the date of the deposit with the Secretary-General of the United Nations of an instrument of ratification, acceptance or approval of such amendment.
5. When an amendment enters into force, it shall be binding on those States Parties which have expressed their consent to be bound by it. Other States Parties shall still be bound by the provisions of this Convention and any earlier amendments that they have ratified, accepted or approved.

Article 70: denunciation
1. A State Party may denounce this Convention by written notification to the Secretary-General of the United Nations. Such denunciation shall become effective one year after the date of receipt of the notification by the Secretary General.
2. A regional economic integration organization shall cease to be a Party to this Convention when all of its member States have denounced it.

Article 71: depositary and languages

1. The Secretary-General of the United Nations is designated depositary of this Convention.

2. The original of this Convention, of which the Arabic, Chinese, English, French, Russian and Spanish texts are equally authentic, shall be deposited with the Secretary-General of the United Nations.

IN WITNESS WHEREOF, the undersigned plenipotentiaries, being duly authorized thereto by their respective Governments, have signed this Convention.

European Convention for the Protection of Human Rights and Fundamental Freedoms (Rome, 4 Nov. 1950), Arts. 1 – 7, 13, and 17 – 18, as amended by Protocol No. 11

Article 1 – Obligation to respect human rights
The High Contracting Parties shall secure to everyone within their jurisdiction the rights and freedoms defined in Section I of this Convention.

SECTION I – RIGHTS AND FREEDOMS

Article 2 – Right to life
1 Everyone's right to life shall be protected by law. No one shall be deprived of his life intentionally save in the execution of a sentence of a court following his conviction of a crime for which this penalty is provided by law.
2 Deprivation of life shall not be regarded as inflicted in contravention of this article when it results from the use of force which is no more than absolutely necessary:
   a in defence of any person from unlawful violence;
   b in order to effect a lawful arrest or to prevent the escape of a person lawfully detained;
   c in action lawfully taken for the purpose of quelling a riot or insurrection.

Article 3 – Prohibition of torture
No one shall be subjected to torture or to inhuman or degrading treatment or punishment.

Article 4 – Prohibition of slavery and forced labour
1 No one shall be held in slavery or servitude.
2 No one shall be required to perform forced or compulsory labour.
3 For the purpose of this article the term "forced or compulsory labour" shall not include:
   a any work required to be done in the ordinary course of detention imposed according to the provisions of Article 5 of this Convention or during conditional release from such detention;
   b any service of a military character or, in case of conscientious objectors in countries where they are recognised, service exacted instead of compulsory military service;
   c any service exacted in case of an emergency or calamity threatening the life or well-being of the community;
   d any work or service which forms part of normal civic obligations.

Article 5 – Right to liberty and security
1 Everyone has the right to liberty and security of person. No one shall be deprived of his liberty save in the following cases and in accordance with a procedure prescribed by law:
   a the lawful detention of a person after conviction by a competent court;
   b the lawful arrest or detention of a person for non- compliance with the lawful order of a court or in order to secure the fulfilment of any obligation prescribed by law;

- c the lawful arrest or detention of a person effected for the purpose of bringing him before the competent legal authority on reasonable suspicion of having committed an offence or when it is reasonably considered necessary to prevent his committing an offence or fleeing after having done so;
- d the detention of a minor by lawful order for the purpose of educational supervision or his lawful detention for the purpose of bringing him before the competent legal authority;
- e the lawful detention of persons for the prevention of the spreading of infectious diseases, of persons of unsound mind, alcoholics or drug addicts or vagrants;
- f the lawful arrest or detention of a person to prevent his effecting an unauthorised entry into the country or of a person against whom action is being taken with a view to deportation or extradition.

2 Everyone who is arrested shall be informed promptly, in a language which he understands, of the reasons for his arrest and of any charge against him.

3 Everyone arrested or detained in accordance with the provisions of paragraph 1.c of this article shall be brought promptly before a judge or other officer authorised by law to exercise judicial power and shall be entitled to trial within a reasonable time or to release pending trial. Release may be conditioned by guarantees to appear for trial.

4 Everyone who is deprived of his liberty by arrest or detention shall be entitled to take proceedings by which the lawfulness of his detention shall be decided speedily by a court and his release ordered if the detention is not lawful.

5 Everyone who has been the victim of arrest or detention in contravention of the provisions of this article shall have an enforceable right to compensation.

Article 6 – Right to a fair trial

1 In the determination of his civil rights and obligations or of any criminal charge against him, everyone is entitled to a fair and public hearing within a reasonable time by an independent and impartial tribunal established by law. Judgment shall be pronounced publicly but the press and public may be excluded from all or part of the trial in the interests of morals, public order or national security in a democratic society, where the interests of juveniles or the protection of the private life of the parties so require, or to the extent strictly necessary in the opinion of the court in special circumstances where publicity would prejudice the interests of justice.

2 Everyone charged with a criminal offence shall be presumed innocent until proved guilty according to law.

3 Everyone charged with a criminal offence has the following minimum rights:

- a to be informed promptly, in a language which he understands and in detail, of the nature and cause of the accusation against him;
- b to have adequate time and facilities for the preparation of his defence;
- c to defend himself in person or through legal assistance of his own choosing or, if he has not sufficient means to pay for legal assistance, to be given it free when the interests of justice so require;
- d to examine or have examined witnesses against him and to obtain the attendance and examination of witnesses on his behalf under the same conditions as witnesses against him;

e to have the free assistance of an interpreter if he cannot understand or speak the language used in court.

Article 7 – No punishment without law

1 No one shall be held guilty of any criminal offence on account of any act or omission which did not constitute a criminal offence under national or international law at the time when it was committed. Nor shall a heavier penalty be imposed than the one that was applicable at the time the criminal offence was committed.

2 This article shall not prejudice the trial and punishment of any person for any act or omission which, at the time when it was committed, was criminal according to the general principles of law recognised by civilised nations.

Article 13 – Right to an effective remedy

Everyone whose rights and freedoms as set forth in this Convention are violated shall have an effective remedy before a national authority notwithstanding that the violation has been committed by persons acting in an official capacity.

Article 17 – Prohibition of abuse of rights

Nothing in this Convention may be interpreted as implying for any State, group or person any right to engage in any activity or perform any act aimed at the destruction of any of the rights and freedoms set forth herein or at their limitation to a greater extent than is provided for in the Convention.

Article 18 – Limitation on use of restrictions on rights

The restrictions permitted under this Convention to the said rights and freedoms shall not be applied for any purpose other than those for which they have been prescribed.

Council of Europe Committee of Ministers Recommendation (1994)12 to Member States on the Independence, Efficiency and Role of Judges

(Adopted by the Committee of Ministers on 13 October 1994 at the 518th meeting of the Ministers' Deputies)

The Committee of Ministers, under the terms of Article 15.*b* of the Statute of the Council of Europe,

Having regard to Article 6 of the Convention for the Protection of Human Rights and Fundamental Freedoms (hereinafter referred to as "the Convention") which provides that "everyone is entitled to a fair and public hearing within a reasonable time by an independent and impartial tribunal established by law";

Having regard to the United Nations Basic Principles on the Independence of the Judiciary, endorsed by the United Nations General Assembly in november 1985;

Noting the essential role of judges and other persons exercising judicial functions in ensuring the protection of human rights and fundamental freedoms;

Desiring to promote the independence of judges in order to strengthen the Rule of Law in democratic states;

Aware of the need to reinforce the position and powers of judges in order to achieve an efficient and fair legal system;

Conscious of the desirability of ensuring the proper exercise of judicial responsibilities which are a collection of judicial duties and powers aimed at protecting the interests of all persons,

Recommends that governments of member states adopt or reinforce all measures necessary to promote the role of individual judges and the judiciary as a whole and strengthen their independence and efficiency, by implementing, in particular, the following principles:

Scope of the recommendation

1. This recommendation is applicable to all persons exercising judicial functions, including those dealing with constitutional, criminal, civil, commercial and administrative law matters.
2. With respect to lay judges and other persons exercising judicial functions, the principles laid down in this recommendation apply except where it is clear from the context that they only apply to professional judges, such as regarding the principles concerning the remuneration and career of judges.

Principle I – General principles on the independence of judges

1. All necessary measures should be taken to respect, protect and promote the independence of judges.
2. In particular, the following measures should be taken:

a. The independence of judges should be guaranteed pursuant to the provisions of the Convention and constitutional principles, for example by inserting specific provisions in the constitutions or other legislation or incorporating the provisions of this recommendation in internal law. Subject to the legal traditions of each state, such rules may provide, for instance, the following:

i. decisions of judges should not be the subject of any revision outside any appeals procedures as provided for by law;

ii. the terms of office of judges and their remuneration should be guaranteed by law;

iii. no organ other than the courts themselves should decide on its own competence, as defined by law;

iv. with the exception of decisions on amnesty, pardon or similar, the government or the administration should not be able to take any decision which invalidates judicial decisions retroactively.

b. The executive and legislative powers should ensure that judges are independent and that steps are not taken which could endanger the independence of judges.

c. All decisions concerning the professional career of judges should be based on objective criteria, and the selection and career of judges should be based on merit, having regard to qualifications, integrity, ability and efficiency. The authority taking the decision on the selection and career of judges should be independent of the government and the administration. In order to safeguard its independence, rules should ensure that, for instance, its members are selected by the judiciary and that the authority decides itself on its procedural rules.

However, where the constitutional or legal provisions and traditions allow judges to be appointed by the government, there should be guarantees to ensure that the procedures to appoint judges are transparent and independent in practice and that the decisions will not be influenced by any reasons other than those related to the objective criteria mentioned above. These guarantees could be, for example, one or more of the following:

i. a special independent and competent body to give the government advice which it follows in practice; or

ii. the right for an individual to appeal against a decision to an independent authority; or

iii. the authority which makes the decision safeguards against undue or improper influences.

d. In the decision-making process, judges should be independent and be able to act without any restriction, improper influence, inducements, pressures, threats or interferences, direct or indirect, from any quarter or for any reason. The law should provide for sanctions against persons seeking to influence judges in any such manner. Judges should have unfettered freedom to decide cases impartially, in accordance with their conscience and their interpretation of the facts, and in pursuance of the prevailing rules of the law. Judges should not be obliged to report on the merits of their cases to anyone outside the judiciary.

e. The distribution of cases should not be influenced by the wishes of any party to a case or any person concerned with the results of the case. Such distribution may, for instance, be made by drawing of lots or a system for automatic distribution according to alphabetic order or some similar system.

f. A case should not be withdrawn from a particular judge without valid reasons, such as cases of serious illness or conflict of interest. Any such reasons and the procedures for such withdrawal should be provided for by law and may not be influenced by any interest of the government or administration. A decision to withdraw a case from a judge should be taken by an authority which enjoys the same judicial independence as judges.

3. Judges, whether appointed or elected, shall have guaranteed tenure until a mandatory retirement age or the expiry of their term of office, where such exists.

Principle II – The authority of judges

1. All persons connected with a case, including state bodies or their representatives, should be subject to the authority of the judge.
2. Judges should have sufficient powers and be able to exercise them in order to carry out their duties and maintain their authority and the dignity of the court.

Principle III – Proper working conditions

1. Proper conditions should be provided to enable judges to work efficiently and, in particular, by:

a. recruiting a sufficient number of judges and providing for appropriate training such as practical training in the courts and, where possible, with other authorities and bodies, before appointment and during their career. Such training should be free of charge to the judge and should in particular concern recent legislation and case-law. Where appropriate, the training should include study visits to European and foreign authorities as well as courts;

b. ensuring that the status and remuneration of judges is commensurate with the dignity of their profession and burden of responsibilities;

c. providing a clear career structure in order to recruit and retain able judges;

d. providing adequate support staff and equipment, in particular office automation and data processing facilities, to ensure that judges can act efficiently and without undue delay;

e. taking appropriate measures to assign non-judicial tasks to other persons, in conformity with Recommendation No. R (86) 12 concerning measures to prevent and reduce the excessive workload in the courts.

2. All necessary measures should be taken to ensure the safety of judges, such as ensuring the presence of security guards on court premises or providing police protection for judges who may become or are victims of serious threats.

Principle IV – Associations

Judges should be free to form associations which, either alone or with another body, have the task of safeguarding their independence and protect their interests.

Principle V – Judicial responsibilities

1. In proceedings, judges have the duty to protect the rights and freedoms of all persons.
2. Judges have the duty and should be given the power to exercise their judicial responsibilities to ensure that the law is properly applied and cases are dealt with fairly, efficiently and speedily.
3. Judges should in particular have the following responsibilities:

a. to act independently in all cases and free from any outside influence;

b. to conduct cases in an impartial manner in accordance with their assessment of the facts and their understanding of the law, to ensure that a fair hearing is given to all parties and that the procedural rights of the parties are respected pursuant to the provisions of the Convention;

c. to withdraw from a case or decline to act where there are valid reasons, and not otherwise. Such reasons should be defined by law and may, for instance, relate to serious health problems, conflicts of interest or the interests of justice;

d. where necessary, to explain in an impartial manner procedural matters to parties;

e. where appropriate, to encourage the parties to reach a friendly settlement;

f. except where the law or established practice otherwise provides, to give clear and complete reasons for their judgments, using language which is readily understandable;

g. to undergo any necessary training in order to carry out their duties in an efficient and proper manner.

Principle VI – Failure to carry out responsibilities and disciplinary offences

1. Where judges fail to carry out their duties in an efficient and proper manner or in the event of disciplinary offences, all necessary measures which do not prejudice judicial independence should be taken. Depending on the constitutional principles and the legal provisions and traditions of each state, such measures may include, for instance:

a. withdrawal of cases from the judge;

b. moving the judge to other judicial tasks within the court;

c. economic sanctions such as a reduction in salary for a temporary period;

d. suspension.

2. Appointed judges may not be permanently removed from office without valid reasons until mandatory retirement. Such reasons, which should be defined in precise terms by the law, could apply in countries where the judge is elected for a certain period, or may relate to incapacity to perform judicial functions, commission of criminal offences or serious infringements of disciplinary rules.

3. Where measures under paragraphs 1 and 2 of this article need to be taken, states should consider setting up, by law, a special competent body which has as its task to apply any disciplinary sanctions and measures, where they are not dealt with by a court, and whose decisions shall be controlled by a superior judicial organ, or which is a superior judicial organ itself. The law should provide for appropriate procedures to ensure that judges in question are given at least all the due process requirements of the Convention, for instance that the case should be heard within a reasonable time and that they should have a right to answer any charges.

Council of Europe Committee of Ministers Recommendation (2000)19 to Member States on the Role of Public Prosecution in the Criminal Justice System

(Adopted by the Committee of Ministers on 6 October 2000 at the 724th meeting of the Ministers' Deputies)

The Committee of Ministers, under the terms of Article 15.*b* of the Statute of the Council of Europe,

Recalling that the aim of the Council of Europe is to achieve a greater unity between its members;

Bearing in mind that it is also the Council of Europe's purpose to promote the rule of law; which constitutes the basis of all genuine democracies;

Considering that the criminal justice system plays a key role in safeguarding the rule of law;

Aware of the common need of all member states to step up the fight against crime both at national and international level;

Considering that, to that end, the efficiency of not only national criminal justice systems but also international co-operation on criminal matters should be enhanced, whilst safeguarding the principles enshrined in the Convention for the Protection of Human Rights and Fundamental Freedoms;

Aware that the public prosecution also plays a key role in the criminal justice system as well as in international co-operation in criminal matters;

Convinced that, to that end, the definition of common principles for public prosecutors in member states should be encouraged;

Taking into account all the principles and rules laid down in texts on criminal matters adopted by the Committee of Ministers,

Recommends that governments of member states base their legislation and practices concerning the role of public prosecution in the criminal justice system on the following principles:

Functions of the public prosecutor

1. "Public prosecutors" are public authorities who, on behalf of society and in the public interest, ensure the application of the law where the breach of the law carries a criminal sanction, taking into account both the rights of the individual and the necessary effectiveness of the criminal justice system.
2. In all criminal justice systems, public prosecutors:

- decide whether to initiate or continue prosecutions;

- conduct prosecutions before the courts;
- may appeal or conduct appeals concerning all or some court decisions.

3. In certain criminal justice systems, public prosecutors also:

- implement national crime policy while adapting it, where appropriate, to regional and local circumstances;
- conduct, direct or supervise investigations;
- ensure that victims are effectively assisted;
- decide on alternatives to prosecution;
- supervise the execution of court decisions;
- etc.

Safeguards provided to public prosecutors for carrying out their functions

4. States should take effective measures to guarantee that public prosecutors are able to fulfil their professional duties and responsibilities under adequate legal and organisational conditions as well as adequate conditions as to the means, in particular budgetary means, at their disposal. Such conditions should be established in close co-operation with the representatives of public prosecutors.
5. States should take measures to ensure that:
   a. the recruitment, the promotion and the transfer of public prosecutors are carried out according to fair and impartial procedures embodying safeguards against any approach which favours the interests of specific groups, and excluding discrimination on any ground such as sex, race, colour, language, religion, political or other opinion, national or social origin, association with a national minority, property, birth, or other status;
   b. the careers of public prosecutors, their promotions and their mobility are governed by known and objective criteria, such as competence and experience;
   c. the mobility of public prosecutors is governed also by the needs of the service;
   d. public prosecutors have reasonable conditions of service such as remuneration, tenure and pension commensurate with their crucial role as well as an appropriate age of retirement and that these conditions are governed by law;
   e. disciplinary proceedings against public prosecutors are governed by law and should guarantee a fair and objective evaluation and decision which should be subject to independent and impartial review;
   f. public prosecutors have access to a satisfactory grievance procedure, including where appropriate access to a tribunal, if their legal status is affected;
   g. public prosecutors, together with their families, are physically protected by the authorities when their personal safety is threatened as a result of the proper discharge of their functions.
6. States should also take measures to ensure that public prosecutors have an effective right to freedom of expression, belief, association and assembly. In particular they should have the right to take part in public discussion of matters concerning the law, the administration of justice and the promotion and protection of human rights and to join or form local, national or international organisations and attend their meetings in a private capacity, without suffering professional disadvantage by reason of their lawful action or their membership in a lawful organisation. The rights mentioned above can only be limited in so far as this is prescribed by law and is necessary to preserve the constitutional[3] position

of the public prosecutors. In cases where the rights mentioned above are violated, an effective remedy should be available.

7. Training is both a duty and a right for all public prosecutors, before their appointment as well as on a permanent basis. States should therefore take effective measures to ensure that public prosecutors have appropriate education and training, both before and after their appointment. In particular, public prosecutors should be made aware of:
   a. the principles and ethical duties of their office;
   b. the constitutional and legal protection of suspects, victims and witnesses;
   c. human rights and freedoms as laid down by the Convention for the Protection of Human Rights and Fundamental Freedoms, especially the rights as established by Articles 5 and 6 of this Convention;
   d. principles and practices of organisation of work, management and human resources in a judicial context;
   e. mechanisms and materials which contribute to consistency in their activities.
   Furthermore, states should take effective measures to provide for additional training on specific issues or in specific sectors, in the light of present-day conditions, taking into account in particular the types and the development of criminality, as well as international co-operation on criminal matters.
8. In order to respond better to developing forms of criminality, in particular organised crime, specialisation should be seen as a priority, in terms of the organisation of public prosecutors, as well as in terms of training and in terms of careers. Recourse to teams of specialists, including multi-disciplinary teams, designed to assist public prosecutors in carrying out their functions should also be developed.
9. With respect to the organisation and the internal operation of the Public Prosecution, in particular the assignment and re-assignment of cases, this should meet requirements of impartiality and independence and maximise the proper operation of the criminal justice system, in particular the level of legal qualification and specialisation devoted to each matter.
10. All public prosecutors enjoy the right to request that instructions addressed to him or her be put in writing. Where he or she believes that an instruction is either illegal or runs counter to his or her conscience, an adequate internal procedure should be available which may lead to his or her eventual replacement.

Relationship between public prosecutors and the executive and legislative powers

11. States should take appropriate measures to ensure that public prosecutors are able to perform their professional duties and responsibilities without unjustified interference or unjustified exposure to civil, penal or other liability. However, the public prosecution should account periodically and publicly for its activities as a whole and, in particular, the way in which its priorities were carried out.
12. Public prosecutors should not interfere with the competence of the legislative and the executive powers.
13. Where the public prosecution is part of or subordinate to the government, states should take effective measures to guarantee that:

a. the nature and the scope of the powers of the government with respect to the public prosecution are established by law;
b. government exercises its powers in a transparent way and in accordance with international treaties, national legislation and general principles of law;
c. where government gives instructions of a general nature, such instructions must be in writing and published in an adequate way;
d. where the government has the power to give instructions to prosecute a specific case, such instructions must carry with them adequate guarantees that transparency and equity are respected in accordance with national law, the government being under a duty, for example:
- to seek prior written advice from either the competent public prosecutor or the body that is carrying out the public prosecution;
- duly to explain its written instructions, especially when they deviate from the public prosecutor's advices and to transmit them through the hierarchical channels;
- to see to it that, before the trial, the advice and the instructions become part of the file so that the other parties may take cognisance of it and make comments;

e. public prosecutors remain free to submit to the court any legal arguments of their choice, even where they are under a duty to reflect in writing the instructions received;
f. instructions not to prosecute in a specific case should, in principle, be prohibited. Should that not be the case, such instructions must remain exceptional and be subjected not only to the requirements indicated in paragraphs *d.* and *e.* above but also to an appropriate specific control with a view in particular to guaranteeing transparency.

14. In countries where the public prosecution is independent of the government, the state should take effective measures to guarantee that the nature and the scope of the independence of the public prosecution is established by law.
15. In order to promote the fairness and effectiveness of crime policy, public prosecutors should co-operate with government agencies and institutions in so far as this is in accordance with the law.
16. Public prosecutors should, in any case, be in a position to prosecute without obstruction public officials for offences committed by them, particularly corruption, unlawful use of power, grave violations of human rights and other crimes recognised by international law.

Relationship between public prosecutors and court judges

17. States should take appropriate measures to ensure that the legal status, the competencies and the procedural role of public prosecutors are established by law in a way that there can be no legitimate doubt about the independence and impartiality of the court judges. In particular states should guarantee that a person cannot at the same time perform duties as a public prosecutor and as a court judge.
18. However, if the legal system so permits, states should take measures in order to make it possible for the same person to perform successively the functions of public prosecutor and those of judge or vice versa. Such changes in functions are only possible at the explicit request of the person concerned and respecting the safeguards.

19. Public prosecutors must strictly respect the independence and the impartiality of judges; in particular they shall neither cast doubts on judicial decisions nor hinder their execution, save where exercising their rights of appeal or invoking some other declaratory procedure.
20. Public prosecutors must be objective and fair during court proceedings. In particular, they should ensure that the court is provided with all relevant facts and legal arguments necessary for the fair administration of justice.

Relationship between public prosecutors and the police

21. In general, public prosecutors should scrutinise the lawfulness of police investigations at the latest when deciding whether a prosecution should commence or continue. In this respect, public prosecutors will also monitor the observance of human rights by the police.
22. In countries where the police is placed under the authority of the public prosecution or where police investigations are either conducted or supervised by the public prosecutor, that state should take effective measures to guarantee that the public prosecutor may:
    a. give instructions as appropriate to the police with a view to an effective implementation of crime policy priorities, notably with respect to deciding which categories of cases should be dealt with first, the means used to search for evidence, the staff used, the duration of investigations, information to be given to the public prosecutor, etc.;
    b. where different police agencies are available, allocate individual cases to the agency that it deems best suited to deal with it;
    c. carry out evaluations and controls in so far as these are necessary in order to monitor compliance with its instructions and the law;
    d. sanction or promote sanctioning, if appropriate, of eventual violations.
23. States where the police is independent of the public prosecution should take effective measures to guarantee that there is appropriate and functional co-operation between the Public Prosecution and the police.

Duties of the public prosecutor towards individuals

24. In the performance of their duties, public prosecutors should in particular:
    a. carry out their functions fairly, impartially and objectively;
    b. respect and seek to protect human rights, as laid down in the Convention for the Protection of Human Rights and Fundamental Freedoms;
    c. seek to ensure that the criminal justice system operates as expeditiously as possible.
25. Public prosecutors should abstain from discrimination on any ground such as sex, race, colour, language, religion, political or other opinion, national or social origin, association with a national minority, property, birth, health, handicaps or other status.
26. Public prosecutors should ensure equality before the law, and make themselves aware of all relevant circumstances including those affecting the suspect, irrespective of whether they are to the latter's advantage or disadvantage.
27. Public prosecutors should not initiate or continue prosecution when an impartial investigation shows the charge to be unfounded.
28. Public prosecutors should not present evidence against suspects that they know or believe on reasonable grounds was obtained through recourse to methods which are contrary to

the law. In cases of any doubt, public prosecutors should ask the court to rule on the admissibility of such evidence.

29. Public prosecutors should seek to safeguard the principle of equality of arms, in particular by disclosing to the other parties – save where otherwise provided in the law – any information which they possess which may affect the justice of the proceedings.
30. Public prosecutors should keep confidential information obtained from third parties, in particular where the presumption of innocence is at stake, unless disclosure is required in the interest of justice or by law.
31. Where public prosecutors are entitled to take measures which cause an interference in the fundamental rights and freedoms of the suspect, judicial control over such measures must be possible.
32. Public prosecutors should take proper account of the interests of the witnesses, especially take or promote measures to protect their life, safety and privacy, or see to it that such measures have been taken.
33. Public prosecutors should take proper account of the views and concerns of victims when their personal interests are affected and take or promote actions to ensure that victims are informed of both their rights and developments in the procedure.
34. Interested parties of recognised or identifiable status, in particular victims, should be able to challenge decisions of public prosecutors not to prosecute; such a challenge may be made, where appropriate after an hierarchical review, either by way of judicial review, or by authorising parties to engage private prosecution.
35. States should ensure that in carrying out their duties, public prosecutors are bound by "codes of conduct". Breaches of such codes may lead to appropriate sanctions in accordance with paragraph 5 above. The performance of public prosecutors should be subject to regular internal review.
36. *a.* With a view to promoting fair, consistent and efficient activity of public prosecutors, states should seek to:
    - give prime consideration to hierarchical methods of organisation, without however letting such organisational methods lead to ineffective or obstructive bureaucratic structures;
    - define general guidelines for the implementation of criminal policy;
    - define general principles and criteria to be used by way of references against which decisions in individual cases should be taken, in order to guard against arbitrary decision-making.

    b. The above-mentioned methods of organisation, guidelines, principles and criteria should be decided by parliament or by government or, if national law enshrines the independence of the public prosecutor, by representatives of the public prosecution.

    c. The public must be informed of the above-mentioned organisation, guidelines, principles and criteria; they shall be communicated to any person on request.

International co-operation

37. Despite the role that might belong to other organs in matters pertaining to international judicial co-operation, direct contacts between public prosecutors of different countries

should be furthered, within the framework of international agreements where they exist or otherwise on the basis of practical arrangements.

38. Steps should be taken in a number of areas to further direct contacts between public prosecutors in the context of international judicial co-operation. Such steps should in particular consist in:
a. disseminating documentation;
b. compiling a list of contacts and addresses giving the names of the relevant contact persons in the different prosecuting authorities, as well as their specialist fields, their areas of responsibility, etc;
c. establishing regular personal contacts between public prosecutors from different countries, in particular by organising regular meetings between Prosecutors General;
d. organising training and awareness-enhancing sessions;
e. introducing and developing the function of liaison law officers based in a foreign country;
f. training in foreign languages;
g. developing the use of electronic data transmission;
h. organising working seminars with other states, on questions regarding mutual aid and shared crime issues.

39. In order to improve rationalisation and achieve co-ordination of mutual assistance procedures, efforts should be taken to promote:
a. among public prosecutors in general, awareness of the need for active participation in international co-operation, and
b. the specialisation of some public prosecutors in the field of international co-operation,
To this effect, states should take steps to ensure that the public prosecutor of the requesting state, where he or she is in charge of international co-operation, may address requests for mutual assistance directly to the authority of the requested state that is competent to carry out the requested action, and that the latter authority may return directly to him or her the evidence obtained.

Council of Europe Committee of Ministers Recommendation (2000)21 to Member States on the Freedom of Exercise of the Profession of Lawyer

(Adopted by the Committee of Ministers on 25 October 2000 at the 727th meeting of the Ministers' Deputies)

The Committee of Ministers, under the terms of Article 15.*b* of the Statute of the Council of Europe,

Having regard to the provisions of the European Convention on Human Rights;

Having regard to the United Nations Basic Principles on the Role of Lawyers, endorsed by the General Assembly of the United Nations in december 1990;

Having regard to Recommendation No. R (94) 12 on the independence, efficiency and role of judges, adopted by the Committee of Ministers of the Council of Europe on 13 October 1994;

Underlining the fundamental role that lawyers and professional associations of lawyers also play in ensuring the protection of human rights and fundamental freedoms;

Desiring to promote the freedom of exercise of the profession of lawyer in order to strengthen the rule of law, in which lawyers take part, in particular in the role of defending individual freedoms;

Conscious of the need for a fair system of administration of justice which guarantees the independence of lawyers in the discharge of their professional duties without any improper restriction, influence, inducement, pressure, threats or interference, direct or indirect, from any quarter or for any reason;

Aware of the desirability of ensuring a proper exercise of lawyers' responsibilities and, in particular, of the need for lawyers to receive sufficient training and to find a proper balance between their duties towards the courts and those towards their clients;

Considering that access to justice may require persons in an economically weak position to obtain the services of lawyers,

Recommends the governments of member states to take or reinforce, as the case may be, all measures they consider necessary with a view to the implementation of the principles contained in this recommendation.

For the purpose of this recommendation, "lawyer" means a person qualified and authorised according to the national law to plead and act on behalf of his or her clients, to engage in the practice of law, to appear before the courts or advise and represent his or her clients in legal matters.

Principle I – General principles on the freedom of exercise of the profession of lawyer

1. All necessary measures should be taken to respect, protect and promote the freedom of exercise of the profession of lawyer without discrimination and without improper interference from the authorities or the public, in particular in the light of the relevant provisions of the European Convention on Human Rights.
2. Decisions concerning the authorisation to practice as a lawyer or to accede to this profession, should be taken by an independent body. Such decisions, whether or not they are taken by an independent body, should be subject to a review by an independent and impartial judicial authority.
3. Lawyers should enjoy freedom of belief, expression, movement, association and assembly, and, in particular, should have the right to take part in public discussions on matters concerning the law and the administration of justice and to suggest legislative reforms.
4. Lawyers should not suffer or be threatened with any sanctions or pressure when acting in accordance with their professional standards.
5. Lawyers should have access to their clients, including in particular to persons deprived of their liberty, to enable them to counsel in private and to represent their clients according to established professional standards.
6. All necessary measures should be taken to ensure the respect of the confidentiality of the lawyer-client relationship. Exceptions to this principle should be allowed only if compatible with the rule of law.
7. Lawyers should not be refused access to a court before which they are qualified to appear and should have access to all relevant files when defending the rights and interests of their clients in accordance with their professional standards.
8. All lawyers acting in the same case should be accorded equal respect by the court.

Principle II – Legal education, training and entry into the legal profession

1. Legal education, entry into and continued exercise of the legal profession should not be denied in particular by reason of sex or sexual preference, race, colour, religion, political or other opinion, ethnic or social origin, membership of a national minority, property, birth or physical disability.
2. All necessary measures should be taken in order to ensure a high standard of legal training and morality as a prerequisite for entry into the profession and to provide for the continuing education of lawyers.
3. Legal education, including programmes of continuing education, should seek to strengthen legal skills, increase awareness of ethical and human rights issues, and train lawyers to respect, protect and promote the rights and interests of their clients and support the proper administration of justice.

Principle III – Role and duty of lawyers

1. Bar associations or other lawyers' professional associations should draw up professional standards and codes of conduct and should ensure that, in defending the legitimate rights and interests of their clients, lawyers have a duty to act independently, diligently and fairly.

2. Professional secrecy should be respected by lawyers in accordance with internal laws, regulations and professional standards. Any violation of this secrecy, without the consent of the client, should be subject to appropriate sanctions.

3. The duties of lawyers towards their clients should include:

a. advising them on their legal rights and obligations, as well as the likely outcome and consequences of the case, including financial costs;

b. endeavouring first and foremost to resolve a case amicably;

c. taking legal action to protect, respect and enforce the rights and interests of their clients;

d. avoiding conflicts of interest;

e. not taking up more work than they can reasonably manage.

4. Lawyers should respect the judiciary and carry out their duties towards the court in a manner consistent with domestic legal and other rules and professional standards. Any abstention by lawyers from their professional activities should avoid damage to the interests of clients or others who require their services.

Principle IV – Access for all persons to lawyers

1. All necessary measures should be taken to ensure that all persons have effective access to legal services provided by independent lawyers.

2. Lawyers should be encouraged to provide legal services to persons in an economically weak position.

3. Governments of member states should, where appropriate to ensure effective access to justice, ensure that effective legal services are available to persons in an economically weak position, in particular to persons deprived of their liberty.

4. Lawyers' duties towards their clients should not be affected by the fact that fees are paid wholly or in part from public funds.

Principle V – Associations

1. Lawyers should be allowed and encouraged to form and join professional local, national and international associations which, either alone or with other bodies, have the task of strengthening professional standards and safeguarding the independence and interests of lawyers.

2. Bar associations or other professional lawyers' associations should be self-governing bodies, independent of the authorities and the public.

3. The role of Bar associations or other professional lawyers' associations in protecting their members and in defending their independence against any improper restrictions or infringements should be respected.

4. Bar associations or other professional lawyers' associations should be encouraged to ensure the independence of lawyers and, *inter alia*, to:

a. promote and uphold the cause of justice, without fear;

b. defend the role of lawyers in society and, in particular, to maintain their honour, dignity and integrity;

c. promote the participation by lawyers in schemes to ensure the access to justice of persons in an economically weak position, in particular the provision of legal aid and advice;

d. promote and support law reform and discussion on existing and proposed legislation;

e. promote the welfare of members of the profession and assist them or their families if circumstances so require;

f. co-operate with lawyers of other countries in order to promote the role of lawyers, in particular by considering the work of international organisations of lawyers and international intergovernmental and non-governmental organisations;

g. promote the highest possible standards of competence of lawyers and maintain respect by lawyers for the standards of conduct and discipline.

5. Bar associations or other professional lawyers' associations should take any necessary action, including defending lawyers' interests with the appropriate body, in case of:

a. arrest or detention of a lawyer;

b. any decision to take proceedings calling into question the integrity of a lawyer;

c. any search of lawyers themselves or their property;

d. any seizure of documents or materials in a lawyers' possession;

e. publication of press reports which require action on behalf of lawyers.

Principle VI – Disciplinary proceedings

1. Where lawyers do not act in accordance with their professional standards, set out in codes of conduct drawn up by Bar associations or other associations of lawyers or by legislation, appropriate measures should be taken, including disciplinary proceedings.

2. Bar associations or other lawyers' professional associations should be responsible for or, where appropriate, be entitled to participate in the conduct of disciplinary proceedings concerning lawyers.

3. Disciplinary proceedings should be conducted with full respect of the principles and rules laid down in the European Convention on Human Rights, including the right of the lawyer concerned to participate in the proceedings and to apply for judicial review of the decision.

4. The principle of proportionality should be respected in determining sanctions for disciplinary offences committed by lawyers.

International Bar Association International Code of Ethics, First adopted 1956; this edition 1988

Rules

1 A lawyer who undertakes professional work in a jurisdiction where he is not a full member of the local profession shall adhere to the standards of professional ethics in the jurisdiction in which he has been admitted. He shall also observe all ethical standards which apply to lawyers of the country where he is working.

2 Lawyers shall at all times maintain the honour and dignity of their profession. They shall, in practice as well as in private life, abstain from any behaviour which may tend to discredit the profession of which they are members.

3 Lawyers shall preserve independence in the discharge of their professional duty. Lawyers practising on their own account or in partnership where permissible, shall not engage in any other business or occupation if by doing so they may cease to be independent.

4 Lawyers shall treat their professional colleagues with the utmost courtesy and fairness. Lawyers who undertake to render assistance to a foreign colleague shall always keep in mind that the foreign colleague has to depend on them to a much larger extent than in the case of another lawyer of the same country. Therefore their responsibility is much greater, both when giving advice and when handling a case. For this reason it is improper for lawyers to accept a case unless they can handle it promptly and with due competence, without undue interference by the pressure of other work. To the fees in these cases Rule 19 applies.

5 Except where the law or custom of the country concerned otherwise requires, any oral or written communication between lawyers shall in principle be accorded a confidential character as far as the Court is concerned, unless certain promises or acknowledgements are made therein on behalf of a client.

6 Lawyers shall always maintain due respect towards the Court. Lawyers shall without fear defend the interests of their clients and without regard to any unpleasant consequences to themselves or to any other person. Lawyers shall never knowingly give to the Court incorrect information or advice which is to their knowledge contrary to the law.

7 It shall be considered improper for lawyers to communicate about a particular case directly with any person whom they know to be represented in that case by another lawyer without the latter's consent.

8 A lawyer should not advertise or solicit business except to the extent and in the manner permitted by the rules of the jurisdiction to which that lawyer is subject. A lawyer should not advertise or solicit business in any country in which such advertising or soliciting is prohibited.

9 A lawyer should never consent to handle a case unless: (a) the client gives direct instructions, or, (b) the case is assigned by a competent body or forwarded by another lawyer, or (c) instructions are given in any other manner permissible under the relevant local rules or regulations.

10 Lawyers shall at all times give clients a candid opinion on any case.
They shall render assistance with scrupulous care and diligence. This applies also if they are assigned as counsel for an indigent person. Lawyers shall at any time be free to refuse to handle a case, unless it is assigned by a competent body. Lawyers should only withdraw from a case during its course for good cause, and if possible in such a manner that the client's interests are not adversely affected. The loyal defence of a client's case may never cause advocates to be other than perfectly candid, subject to any right or privilege to the contrary which clients choose them to exercise, or knowingly to go against the law.

11 Lawyers shall, when in the client's interest, endeavour to reach a solution by settlement out of court rather than start legal proceedings. Lawyers should never stir up litigation.

12 Lawyers should not acquire a financial interest in the subject matter of a case which they are conducting. Neither should they, directly or indirectly, acquire property about which litigation is pending before the Court in which they practice.

13 Lawyers should never represent conflicting interests in litigation. In non-litigation matters, lawyers should do so only after having disclosed all conflicts or possible conflicts of interest to all parties concerned and only with their consent. This Rule also applies to all lawyers in a firm.

14 Lawyers should never disclose, unless lawfully ordered to do so by the Court or as required by Statute, what has been communicated to them in their capacity as lawyers even after they have ceased to be the client's counsel. This duty extends to their partners, to junior lawyers assisting them and to their employees.

15 In pecuniary matters lawyers shall be most punctual and diligent.
They should never mingle funds of others with their own and they should at all times be able to refund money they hold for others. They shall not retain money they receive for their clients for longer than is absolutely necessary.

16 Lawyers may require that a deposit is made to cover their expenses, but the deposit should be in accordance with the estimated amount of their charges and the probable expenses and labour.

17 Lawyers shall never forget that they should put first not their right to compensation for their services, but the interests of their clients and the exigencies of the administration of justice. The Lawyer's right to ask for a deposit or to demand payment of out of-pocket expenses and commitments, failing payment of which they may withdraw from the case

or refuse to handle it, should never be exercised at a moment at which the client may be unable to find other assistance in time to prevent irreparable damage being done. Lawyers' fees should, in the absence or non-applicability of official scales, be fixed on a consideration of the amount involved in the controversy and the interest of it to the client, the time and labour involved and all other personal and factual circumstances of the case.

18 A contract for a contingent fee, where sanctioned by the law or by professional rules and practice, should be reasonable under all circumstances of the case, including the risk and uncertainty or the compensation and subject to supervision of a court as to its reasonableness.

19 Lawyers who engage a foreign colleague to advise on a case or to cooperate in handling it, are responsible for the payment of the latter's charges except where there has been express agreement to the contrary. When lawyers direct a client to a foreign colleague they are not responsible for the payment of the latter's charges, but neither are they entitled to a share of the fee of this foreign colleague.

20 Lawyers should not permit their professional services or their names to be used in any way which would make it possible for persons to practise law who are not legally authorised to do so. Lawyers shall not delegate to a legally unqualified person not in their employ and control any functions which are by the law or custom of the country in which they practise only to be performed by a qualified lawyer.

21 It is not unethical for lawyers to limit or exclude professional liability subject to the rules of their local Bar Association and to there being no statutory or constitutional prohibitions.

Latimer House Guidelines for the Commonwealth, 19 June 1998 on good practice governing relations between the executive, parliament and the judiciary in the promotion of good governance, the rule of law and human rights to ensure the effective implementation of the Harare Principles

PREAMBLE

RECALLING the renewed commitment at the 1997 Commonwealth Heads of Government Meeting at Edinburgh to the Harare Principles and the Millbrook Commonwealth Action Programme and, in particular, the pledge in paragraph 9 of the Harare Declaration to work for the protection and promotion of the fundamental political values of the Commonwealth:

- democracy;
- democratic processes and institutions which reflect national circumstances, the rule of law and the independence of the judiciary;
- just and honest government;
- fundamental human rights, including equal rights and opportunities for all citizens regardless of race, colour, creed or political belief;
- equality for women, so that they may exercise their full and equal rights.

Representatives of the Commonwealth Parliamentary Association, the Commonwealth Magistrates' and Judges' Association, the Commonwealth Lawyers' Association and the Commonwealth Legal Education Association at Latimer House in the United Kingdom from 15 to 19 June 1998:

HAVE RESOLVED to adopt the following **Principles and Guidelines** and propose them for consideration by the Commonwealth Heads of Government Meeting and for effective implementation by member countries of the Commonwealth.

PRINCIPLES

The successful implementation of these Guidelines calls for a commitment, made in the utmost good faith, of the relevant national institutions, in particular, the executive, parliament and the judiciary, to the essential principles of good governance, fundamental human rights and the rule of law, including the independence of the judiciary, so that the legitimate aspirations of all the peoples of the Commonwealth should be met.

Each institution must exercise responsibility and restraint in the exercise of power within its own constitutional sphere so as not to encroach on the legitimate discharge of constitutional functions by the other institutions.

It is recognised that the special circumstances of small and/or under resourced jurisdictions may require adaptation of these Guidelines.

It is recognised that redress of gender imbalance is essential to accomplish full and equal rights in society and to achieve true human rights. Merit and the capacity to perform public office regardless of disability should be the criteria of eligibility for appointment or election.

GUIDELINES

I Parliament and the judiciary

1 The legislative function is the primary responsibility of parliament as the elected body representing the people. Judges may be constructive and purposive in the interpretation of legislation, but must not usurp parliament's legislative function. Courts should have the power to declare legislation to be unconstitutional and of no legal effect. However, there may be circumstances where the appropriate remedy would be for the court to declare the incompatibility of a statute with the Constitution, leaving it to the legislature to take remedial legislative measures.

2 Commonwealth parliaments should take speedy and effective steps to implement their countries' international human rights obligations by enacting appropriate human rights legislation. Special legislation (such as equal opportunity laws) is required to extend the protection of fundamental rights to the private sphere. Where domestic incorporation has not occurred, international instruments should be applied to aid interpretation.

3 Judges should adopt a generous and purposive approach in interpreting a Bill of Rights. This is particularly important in countries which are in the process of building democratic traditions. Judges have a vital part to play in developing and maintaining a vibrant human rights environment throughout the Commonwealth.

4 International law and, in particular, human rights jurisprudence can greatly assist domestic courts in interpreting a Bill of Rights. It also can help expand the scope of a Bill of Rights making it more meaningful and effective.

5 While dialogue between the judiciary and the government may be desirable or appropriate, in no circumstances should such dialogue compromise judicial independence.

6 People should have easy and unhindered access to courts, particularly to enforce their fundamental rights. Any existing procedural obstacles to access to justice should be removed.

7 People should also be made aware of, and have access to, other important fora for human rights dispute resolution, particularly Human Rights Commissions, Offices of the Ombudsman and mechanisms for alternative dispute resolution.

8 Everyone, especially judges, parliamentarians and lawyers, should have access to human rights education.

II Preserving judicial independence

1 Judicial autonomy

In jurisdictions that do not already have an appropriate independent process in place, judicial appointments should be made on merit by a judicial services commission or by an appropriate officer of state acting on the advice of such a commission.

Judicial appointments should normally be permanent; whilst in some jurisdictions, contract appointments may be inevitable, such appointments should be subject to appropriate security of tenure.

The judicial services commission should be established by the Constitution or by statute, with a majority of members drawn from the senior judiciary.

Appointments to all levels of the judiciary should have, as an objective, the achievement of equality between women and men.

Judicial vacancies should be advertised. Recommendations for appointment should come from the commission.

2 Funding

Sufficient funding to enable the judiciary to perform its functions to the highest standards should be provided.

Appropriate salaries, supporting staff, resources and equipment are essential to the proper functioning of the judiciary.

As a matter of principle, judicial salaries and benefits should be set by an independent commission and should be maintained.

The administration of monies allocated to the judiciary should be under the control of the judiciary.

3 Training

A culture of judicial education should be developed.

Training should be organised, systematic and ongoing and under the control of an adequately funded judicial body.

Judicial training should include the teaching of the law, judicial skills and the social context, including ethnic and gender issues.

The curriculum should be controlled by judicial officers who should have the assistance of lay specialists.

For jurisdictions without adequate training facilities, access to facilities in other jurisdictions should be provided.

Courses in judicial education should be offered to practising lawyers as part of their ongoing professional development training.

III Preserving the independence of parliamentarians

1 Article 9 of the Bill of Rights 1688 is re-affirmed. This article provides:

> *That the Freedome of Speech and Debates or Proceedings in Parlyement ought not to be impeached or questioned in any court or place out of Parlyement.*

2 Security of members during their parliamentary term is fundamental to parliamentary independence and therefore:

(a) the expulsion of members from parliament as a penalty for leaving their parties (floor-crossing) should be viewed as a possible infringement of members independence; anti-defection measures may be necessary in some jurisdictions to deal with corrupt practices;

(b) laws allowing for the recall of members during their elected term should be viewed with caution, as a potential threat to the independence of members;

(c) the cessation of membership of a political party of itself should not lead to the loss of a member's seat.

3 In the discharge of their functions, members should be free from improper pressures and accordingly:

(a) the criminal law and the use of defamation proceedings are not appropriate mechanisms for restricting legitimate criticism of the government or the parliament;

(b) the defence of qualified privilege with respect to reports of parliamentary proceedings should be drawn as broadly as possible to permit full public reporting and discussion of public affairs;

(c) the offence of contempt of parliament should be drawn as narrowly as possible.

IV Women in parliament

1 To improve the numbers of women members in Commonwealth parliaments, the role of women within political parties should be enhanced including the appointment of more women to executive roles within political parties.

2 Pro-active searches for potential candidates should be undertaken by political parties.

3 Political parties in nations with proportional representation should be required to ensure an adequate gender balance on their respective lists of candidates for election. Women, where relevant, should be included in the top part of the candidates lists of political parties. Parties should be called upon publicly to declare the degree of representation of women on their lists and to defend any failure to maintain adequate representation.

4 Where there is no proportional representation, candidate search and/or selection committees of political parties should be gender balanced as should representation at political conventions and this should be facilitated by political parties by way of amendment to party constitutions; women should be put forward for safe seats.

5 Women should be elected to parliament through regular electoral processes. The provision of reservations for women in national constitutions, whilst useful, tends to be insufficient for securing adequate and long term representation by women.

6 Men should work in partnership with women to redress constraints on women entering parliament. True gender balance requires the appositional element of the inclusion of men in the process of dialogue and remedial action to address the necessary inclusion of both genders in all aspects of public life.

1 **Judicial ethics**

(a) A Code of Ethics and Conduct should be developed and adopted by each judiciary as a means of ensuring the accountability of judges;
(b) the Commonwealth Magistrates' and Judges' Association should be encouraged to complete its Model Code of Judicial Conduct now in development;
(c) the Association should also serve as a repository of codes of judicial conduct developed by Commonwealth judiciaries, which will serve as a resource for other jurisdictions.

2 **Parliamentary ethics**

(a) Conflict of interest guidelines and Codes of Conduct should require full disclosure by ministers and members of their financial and business interests;
(b) members of parliament should have privileged access to advice from statutorily established Ethics Advisors;
(c) whilst responsive to the needs of society and recognising minority views in society, members of parliament should avoid excessive influence of lobbyists and special interest groups.

VI Accountability mechanisms

1 judicial accountability

(a) Discipline:

(i) in cases where a judge is at risk of removal, the judge must have the right to be fully informed of the charges, to be represented at a hearing, to make a full defence, and to be judged by an independent and impartial tribunal. Grounds for removal of a judge should be limited to:
  (A) inability to perform judicial duties; and
  (B) serious misconduct;
(ii) in all other matters, the process should be conducted by the chief judge of the courts;
(iii) disciplinary procedures should not include the public admonition of judges. Any admonitions should be delivered in private, by the chief judge.

(b) Public criticism:

(i) legitimate public criticism of judicial performance is a means of ensuring accountability;
(ii) the criminal law and contempt proceedings are not appropriate mechanisms for restricting legitimate criticism of the courts.

2 Executive accountability

(a) Accountability of the executive to parliament:

Parliamentary procedures should provide adequate mechanisms to enforce the accountability of the executive to parliament. These should include:
(i) a committee structure appropriate to the size of parliament, adequately resourced and with the power to summon witnesses, including ministers. Governments should be required to announce publicly, within a defined time period, their responses to committee reports;
(ii) standing orders should provide appropriate opportunities for members to question ministers and full debate on legislative proposals;
(iii) the Public Accounts should be independently audited by the Auditor General who is responsible to and must report directly to parliament;
(iv) the chair of the Public Accounts Committee should normally be an opposition member;
(v) offices of the Ombudsman, Human Rights Commissions and Access to Information Commissioners should report regularly to parliament.

(b) Judicial review

Commonwealth governments should endorse and implement the principles of judicial review enshrined in the Lusaka Statement on Government under the Law.

VII The law-making process

I Women should be involved in the work of national law commissions in the law-making process. Ongoing assessment of legislation is essential so as to create a more gender balanced society. Gender-neutral language should be used in the drafting and use of legislation.

2 Procedures for the preliminary examination of issues in proposed legislation should be adopted and published so that:

(a) there is public exposure of issues, papers and consultation on major reforms including, where possible, a draft bill;

(b) standing orders provide a delay of some days between introduction and debate to enable public comment unless suspended by consent or a significantly high percentage vote of the chamber; and

(c) major legislation can be referred to a select committee allowing for the detailed examination of such legislation and the taking of evidence from members of the public.

3 Model standing orders protecting members' rights and privileges and permitting the incorporation of variations, to take local circumstances into account, should be drafted and published.

4 Parliament should be serviced by a professional staff independent of the regular public service.

5 Adequate resources to government and non government back benchers should be provided to improve parliamentary input and should include provision for:

(a) training of new members;

(b) secretarial, office, library and research facilities;

(c) drafting assistance including private members bills.

6 An all-party committee of members of parliament should review and administer parliament's budget which should not be subject to amendment by the executive.

7 Appropriate legislation should incorporate international human rights instruments to assist in interpretation and to ensure that ministers certify compliance with such instruments, on introduction of the legislation.

8 It is recommended that 'sunset' legislation (for the expiry of all subordinate legislation not renewed) should be enacted subject to power to extend the life of such legislation.

VIII The role of non-judicial and non-parliamentary institutions

1 The Commonwealth Statement on Freedom of Expression (set out in Appendix 2) provides essential guarantees to which all Commonwealth countries should subscribe.

2 The executive must refrain from all measures directed at inhibiting the freedom of the press, including indirect methods such as the misuse of official advertising.

3 An independent, organised legal profession is an essential component in the protection of the rule of law.

4 Adequate legal aid schemes should be provided for poor and disadvantaged litigants, including public interest advocates.

5 Legal professional organisations should assist in the provision, through pro bono schemes, of access to justice for the impecunious.

6 The executive must refrain from obstructing the functioning of an independent legal profession by such means as withholding licensing of professional bodies.

7 Human Rights Commissions, Offices of the Ombudsman and Access to Information Commissioners can play a key role in enhancing public awareness of good governance and rule of law issues and adequate funding and resources should be made available to enable them to discharge these functions. Parliament should accept responsibility in this regard.
Such institutions should be empowered to provide access to alternative dispute resolution mechanisms.

IX Measures for implementation and monitoring compliance

These guidelines should be forwarded to the Commonwealth Secretariat for consideration by Law Ministers and Heads of Government.

If these Guidelines are adopted, an effective monitoring procedure, which might include a Standing Committee, should be devised under which all Commonwealth jurisdictions accept an obligation to report on their compliance with these Guidelines.
Consideration of these reports should form a regular part of the Meetings of Law Ministers and of Heads of Government.

Lightning Source UK Ltd.
Milton Keynes UK
UKHW051512280223
417795UK00029B/441

9 789050 955812